WAKEFIELD PRESS

ALICE SPRINGS

Long-time Alice Springs resident Stuart Traynor left the cultural melting pot of Wollongong for the Northern Territory on the eve of Cyclone Tracy seeking adventure, and finding it in abundance. After a spell in secondary schools and Aboriginal education, he 'won the lottery' in the 1980s, joining the Conservation Commission of the Northern Territory, a vibrant and well-funded organisation that encouraged initiative. As the senior officer in charge of community education, his work involved training programs across the Territory, writing for a range of audiences and organising community events. For many years he was a weekly voice on ABC Territory Radio, raising awareness of NT flora and fauna, local history and conservation issues. He was honoured with life membership of the Australian Association for Environmental Education and recognition from the Alice Springs Town Council for his community service work.

Stuart Traynor spent eight years researching the history of central Australia for this book.

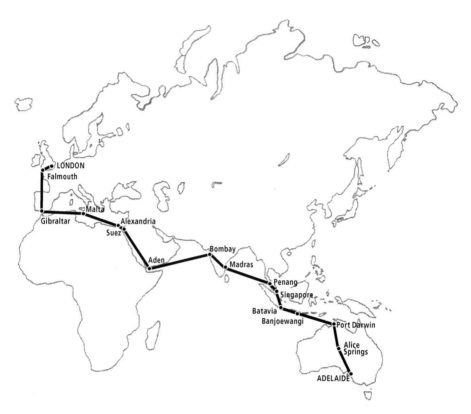

The final section of a submarine cable from England to Port Darwin was laid in November 1871.
The overland telegraph line was completed in August 1872.

ALICE SPRINGS

From singing wire to iconic outback town

Stuart Traynor

**Wakefield
Press**

Wakefield Press
16 Rose Street
Mile End
South Australia 5031
www.wakefieldpress.com.au

First published 2016

Edited by Julia Beaven, Wakefield Press
Designed and typeset by Wakefield Press

National Library of Australia Cataloguing-in-Publication entry

Creator:	Traynor, Stuart, author.
Title:	Alice Springs: from singing wire to iconic outback town / Stuart Traynor.
ISBN:	978 1 74305 449 9 (paperback).
Notes:	Includes bibliographical references and index.
Subjects:	Overland Telegraph Line (N.T. and S.A.) – History.
	Cities and towns – Growth.
	Alice Springs (N.T.) – Social life and customs.
	Alice Springs (N.T.) – Economic conditions.
	Alice Springs (N.T.) – History.
Dewey Number:	994.291

CORIOLE

McLAREN VALE

This book is dedicated to Kas, Ellie and Carrie –
celebrating the rich life we shared in the heart of Australia;
and it's a tribute to Jessie White, Nora Meyers
and all the other Bungalow children.

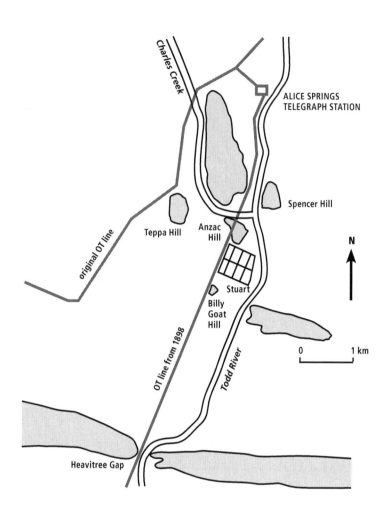

Alice Springs region and the town of Stuart before World War 1

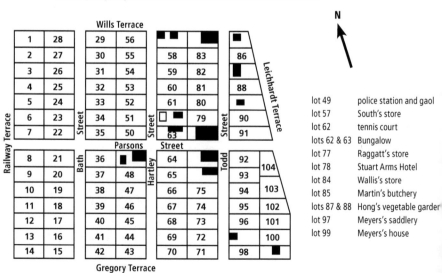

lot 49   police station and gaol
lot 57   South's store
lot 62   tennis court
lots 62 & 63   Bungalow
lot 77   Raggatt's store
lot 78   Stuart Arms Hotel
lot 84   Wallis's store
lot 85   Martin's butchery
lots 87 & 88   Hong's vegetable garden
lot 97   Meyers's saddlery
lot 99   Meyers's house

Contents

Prologue

The voyage of the *Atalanta*

There was mist about and not much wind this Sunday morning 8 April 1866 as the *Atalanta* approached Port Adelaide.[1] Edward Allchurch had been on deck from an early hour. The 37-year-old policeman from Brighton in Sussex opened a hatch to get air into his family's stuffy and cramped living quarters, then rang the bell to advise passengers of the morning church service. Hopefully this would be their last day on board. Ten weeks had passed since the three-masted sailing ship left England with 394 immigrants on board. Five days earlier, off the coast of Western Australia, seaman Thomas Moore had fallen overboard while working on the forecastle. The loss had cast gloom over the ship.

It had not been an easy trip for Edward Allchurch. His wife Anne was seven months pregnant when they set sail from Plymouth on 23 January and was sick for much of the journey. Edward had his hands full keeping an eye on their three young children Harry, Emily and Annie. He was also one of the ship's constables and frequently on duty checking the passengers kept the ship clean, and young single men were away from the young single women. Many were seasick and the ship's doctor had his hands full.

The Suez Canal was not yet open so their route to Australia took them around the bottom of Africa and across the Indian Ocean. Excavation work began in April 1859 but wasn't completed until November 1869. Anne gave birth to a daughter in the early hours of Saturday 10 March with the ship near the Cape of Good Hope. Edward told Captain John Ballingall, 'It's a great fat girl with dark hair,' and asked for the latitude and longitude. The child was named Atalanta Hope Allchurch, later shortened to Attie.[2]

As she was taking her first breath, her sisters Emily and little Annie were beginning to wheeze. Whooping cough had broken out on the ship. Edward wrote in his diary three days later: 'A poor little child died last night ... I thought they would be sure to read over [it] but not so they opened the cabin windows and threw it out.' It was the seventh to die during the voyage. A couple of weeks before the ship finally berthed at Port Adelaide, everyone started to itch. Edward penned: 'This morning the subject is all about lice, to use plain language we are all getting lousy, try all we can to prevent it.'

Among his fellow emigrants was William Whitfield Mills, a 21-year-old from Devon, who'd set off for South Australia seeking opportunity and adventure. Edward and Anne Allchurch didn't know it then but this young man and their newborn daughter would achieve fame in the heart of Australia. Mills would discover a large waterhole in 1871 and call it the Alice Spring, after the wife of his boss, Postmaster-General Charles Todd. Alice Todd never visited the place and her husband only saw it once. Attie Allchurch was destined to live there in the early 1900s with children of her own.

Edward, Anne and young William Mills had no idea what the future held when they finally walked down the gangplank at Port Adelaide docks. They could write to their relatives on the other side of the globe, telling them of their new life, but would have to wait six months for a reply. There was talk of laying a communication cable, across the seafloor from England to Australia, but there were technical hitches and the British Government wasn't willing to cough up the cash to make it happen.

The colony of South Australia had been established in 1836, founded on ideas proposed by Edward Gibbon Wakefield. He suggested the British Government sell land at a reasonable price to encourage free settlers. The government could then use the money generated to bring more settlers. There was no need to employ convicts. Colonel William Light was appointed the colony's first surveyor-general and came up with a bold and imaginative plan for the colony's capital. He chose a site by the River Torrens, some distance inland of its port, and laid out a grid of streets encircled by parks and greenery. It was named after Queen Adelaide, the wife of King William IV. The population had grown to 30,000 by the time the *Atalanta* tied up at the wharf in 1866 and plans were in place to illuminate Light's city with gas streetlights.

Edward Allchurch was offered work as a policeman and served in the city for 18 months. In 1868 he took charge of the police station at Glenelg and three more sons and another daughter were born there. He remained by the sea for the rest of his life, becoming one of the area's best known and respected residents. He died at the age of 88 in April 1917.

In October 1871, when his daughter Attie was five years old, three British ships sailed into Port Darwin on the other side of the continent, and dropped their anchors into the warm waters lapping Australia's north coast. They'd come to lay the last leg of the long-awaited submarine communication cable from England. The South Australian Government was stringing a wire across the continent to connect Adelaide to it. This wire became known as the overland telegraph line, or simply the OT.

Attie Allchurch married telegraph operator Thomas Andrew Bradshaw in April 1890. Nine years later, she bravely followed him into the great Australian nothingness with her young children after her husband had been appointed post and stationmaster at the Alice Springs telegraph station.

In the 1960s their eldest daughter Doris worked with journalist Douglas Lockwood on *Alice on the Line*, a bestselling book about the family's life on the OT line between 1899 and 1908. Cattleman Bryan Bowman went to central Australia in 1921 and wrote a few books of his own. He said:

> The theme song of the old North Road and the OT line was the hum of the wires. You were seldom out of earshot of it whether riding along the road, staying at a bush pub or just camping somewhere along the road. It was at its peak on a still night when it could be heard half a mile from the Line. Some people didn't like it but to me it was romantic music and gave me a feeling of not being entirely isolated from the outside world and one could speculate on what messages of hope or tragedy the wires were carrying between Europe and Australia.[3]

Most of the singing wire has now gone, pulled down in the 1980s, although travellers to the outback can still find stretches of sagging wire and iron poles. Building that line was one of the most significant events in the nation's history. However, the Australian Government saw no need to preserve it once it was superseded by new technology.

1

Connecting Australia to the world

Adelaide's survey yard was a hive of activity on Monday morning 5 September 1870 when William Mills turned up at 7.30 with more than 40 others. He was now an experienced surveyor, having joined the South Australian colonial service two months after arriving. He and the other men assembled near the River Torrens that morning were heading north to build the central section of the government's overland telegraph line. A larger party of 65 men had left the previous Monday. Charles Todd, the cheerful Postmaster-General and Superintendent of Telegraphs, took the 9 am rollcall and farewelled the second contingent. He urged them to keep clear of pubs on their way to Port Augusta. Governor Sir James Fergusson said they all looked like men of business and their success would be heard from one end of the world to the other if they completed the work within the time allotted.[1]

William Mills had worked with the survey party that finally established a settlement on Australia's north coast. The local Aboriginal people had lived in harmony with the uncompromising tropical environment for thousands of years but white settlers who went there with high hopes in 1824, 1827, 1838 and 1864 found the top end of Australia a land of failure. It exhausted and overwhelmed them. This didn't deter South Australia's energetic Surveyor-General George Woodroffe Goyder. Mills was one of the men who landed at Port Darwin with him on 5 February 1869 to carve civilisation from the termite-ridden woodland.

Adelaide politician Henry Bull Templar Strangways was the driving force behind this latest attempt at colonisation. Three months earlier, on 3 November 1868, he'd assumed the position of chief secretary and with it leadership of South Australia's colonial government. His predecessor John Hart tried introducing the term premier in 1866, but it was a controversial issue.[2] Strangways proved a forceful and influential figure, though his term in office was brief.

South Australia had pushed hard to gain control of the big chunk of the continent north of the 26th parallel of latitude and the Colonial Office in London eventually agreed. It transferred administration from Sydney to Adelaide in 1863, having rejected the idea in 1861 when it granted another strip of land to South Australia. The Western Territory lay between South Australia's western boundary, then set as longitude 132°, and Western Australia's border at longitude 129°. It belonged to New South Wales but the politicians in Sydney were happy to onload it.[3] The South Australians had high hopes their new Northern Territory would reap rich rewards but little happened in the years between 1863 and 1868.

Strangways was determined to finally make progress and figured his surveyor-general was the man for the job. Goyder left Port Adelaide on 23 December 1868 aboard the chartered barque *Moonta* with a survey party of 134 men and an impressive entourage of horses, working bullocks, sheep and goats. They toiled for seven months in the oppressive heat and humidity, plagued night after night by mosquitoes and sandflies. All told, they surveyed more than 2700 square kilometres of land, including a main town located inside the large natural harbour that John Lort Stokes of the British survey ship HMS *Beagle* named Port Darwin on 9 September 1839.[4] Goyder's town plan featured half-acre blocks and wide streets named after the surveyors and workmen themselves, rather than English royalty or politicians. His surveyors also planned three smaller townships. Two of them were sited on rivers running into Port Darwin and the third was cut out of the bush 150 kilometres inland, near Freds Pass in the Daly Range. Goyder envisaged the road to Freds Pass as the main highway to the interior of the continent.[5] His job done, he returned to Adelaide at the end of September 1869 on the government's schooner *Gulnare*, along with 29 of his party. The majority of the men, including William Mills, remained until early in the New Year.[6]

Many of the other men assembling in the survey yard in September 1870 had been in the north with George Goyder. Like Mills, they'd jumped at the opportunity to head off on another adventure, this time to the heart of the continent. The South Australian Government had given Charles Todd the daunting task of stringing a galvanised-iron wire across the continent from Port Augusta to Port Darwin. He only had 16 months to plant 36,000 telegraph poles and build a dozen repeater stations at approximately 250-kilometre intervals. His political masters had cut a bold and risky deal with the British–Australian Telegraph Company, which was laying the last leg of a submarine cable from England to Australia's north coast. There were those in the east who doubted the plucky South Australians could pull it off. Queenslanders were more savage in their criticism. They were miffed because the company had reneged on an understanding to connect the cable to their fledgling telegraph network.

Todd's overland telegraph line was the country's first big development project – but not a national effort. Australia was an assortment of self-governing colonies in 1870, rather than one nation. South Australia and Queensland, the two youngest colonies, had competed for the right to risk a fortune of their citizens' money on new but vulnerable technology. The South Australians prevailed, but only at the very last minute, with a move that enraged their rivals.

It would be possible to exchange messages between England and Australia's colonial capitals in just a couple of hours if Todd could succeed despite the considerable odds stacked against him. Telegraph wires already linked Adelaide with Melbourne, Sydney and Brisbane, and a submarine cable had been laid on the bed of Bass Strait from Melbourne to Launceston where it joined the telegraph line to Hobart.

The new marvel of telegraphy
The telegraph and railways were to the 19th century what internet and air travel are to the 21st century, providing unprecedented rapid communication

and transport. The American Samuel Morse had revolutionised communication across the globe. Short messages akin to modern mobile phone text could be transmitted along a wire using electricity, and the code he developed in the 1830s with his often forgotten collaborator Alfred Vail. These messages were expensive and required highly skilled telegraph operators but were being embraced by governments and businesses.

Telegraph lines were a common sight in England, Europe and America by the 1850s and it wasn't long before Australia's colonial governments started building their own. These lines were generally trouble-free but it was a while before cables laid on the sea floor proved as reliable. One was successfully laid across the English Channel in 1851 and another across the Irish Sea in 1853 but spanning the broad oceans was a tougher proposition. Nonetheless, in 1854 the Mediterranean Submarine Cable Company proposed to link England, India and Australia via a series of submarine cables and overland lines. It was an audacious project by a company only formed the previous year.

The company's promoters Brett and Carmichael wrote to the Australian colonial governments outlining their plan to land a cable on the west coast of Australia. They wanted a contribution towards the cost of building a telegraph line from Exmouth Gulf to Adelaide and on to Melbourne and Sydney.[7] It was audacious because submarine cables were still in their infancy and there was only a solitary short telegraph line in Australia at the time, running from Melbourne to Williamstown and completed in February 1854.[8] The company managed to lay a cable across the Mediterranean Sea but it promptly failed and their proposed extension to India and Australia was abandoned.

The Atlantic Telegraph Company laid a cable from Ireland to Newfoundland in 1858 but it stopped working after a short time and its shareholders lost their money. Despite this, cable entrepreneurs continued to seek private investment and government support for schemes to link the continents. The most persistent promoters of an Anglo–Australian cable were British businessmen Lionel and Frank Gisborne.[9] Frank Gisborne came to Australia in 1859 to talk to its various colonial governments on behalf of the Red Sea and India Telegraph Company.[10] He called on the South Australian governor, Sir Richard MacDonnell, in Adelaide in July 1859. His company had laid a cable down the Red Sea from Suez to Aden by that time and manufactured another, which it intended laying across the Arabian Sea to Karachi in December. There were telegraph lines running across India to Rangoon, in neighbouring Burma, and an extension to Singapore was planned.

Frank Gisborne had an agreement with the Netherlands Government willing to pay for a cable from Singapore to Batavia (now Jakarta), capital of their Dutch East Indies (now Indonesia). Gisborne wanted the Australian governments to contribute an estimated £800,000 to the cost of connecting Australia to Java. The first submarine cable would go from Banjoewangi in Java to Port Essington on the north coast of Australia, via Timor. A second would be laid through the Torres Strait to Cape York. A third cable would run down the east coast from Cape York to Cleveland Bay, with a fourth from there to the new settlement at Moreton Bay, now Brisbane.[11] It would then just be a matter of building a telegraph line from Brisbane to Sydney.[12] The cable companies wanted to maximise the length of submarine cables, rather than use overland lines, because the longer the cable, the more money in it for them. However, Gisborne had overlooked the fact that his proposed route around the north and east coasts involved laying cable on a sea floor with lots of coral. In subsequent years he modified his scheme to include a telegraph line from the Gulf of Carpentaria to Brisbane.

Why not an overland route?
The Gisborne scheme came to nothing because the Englishman was unable to convince all the Australian colonies to back it financially.[13] South Australia had other ideas. Its governor MacDonnell was advocating an alternative route in1859. Why not bring the cable ashore at the mouth of the Victoria River in the Northern Territory, or further west at Cambridge Gulf in Western Australia, and then build a telegraph line south to Adelaide?[14]

Adelaide was the first port of call in Australia for most of the ships sailing from Europe and so the first to receive news from overseas. In addition, the colony had played a leading role in the development of telegraphy in Australia in the preceding couple of years, under the direction of its superintendent of telegraphs Charles Todd. Governor MacDonnell wanted Adelaide to become the telegraph capital of Australia but Gisborne's scheme would have the opposite effect, putting it at the wrong end of an intercolonial telegraph network.[15] Gisborne's scheme would hand the advantage to Queensland, allowing it to charge the other colonies a transit fee for all messages it relayed in and out of Australia.[16]

However, MacDonnell could see beyond this simple revenue issue. Constructing an overland telegraph line through the heart of Australia to Adelaide, rather than laying cable around the north coast to Brisbane, would be an enormous boost for the economy of South Australia and stimulate development of the huge expanse of unsettled country lying between its existing outposts in the Flinders Ranges and the north coast.

Sir Richard MacDonnell came to South Australia in June 1855. He was a well-educated man, fond of both outdoor and intellectual activities, which he duly fostered in the colony. He'd graduated in law from Trinity College Dublin where he'd excelled in both the sciences and the classics. Before he came to Adelaide he served as the chief justice of Gambia and then as its governor, followed by brief spells administering St Lucia and St Vincent in the Caribbean. He was a strong energetic leader but not always diplomatic and so clashed with other strong-willed figures in Adelaide politics at the time. His years as governor were characterised by his clear commitment to advancing the colony's future, encouraging exploration and settling outback areas. He was well aware of South Australia's economic limitations and realised its future depended upon the discovery of minerals and new grazing land in the north.

MacDonnell asked Charles Todd to prepare a detailed report on the practicability and likely cost of an overland telegraph line.[17] Todd was not an imposing man but he had proven a very able administrator and was as energetic as the governor. He was recruited from the Royal Observatory at Greenwich and arrived in the colony five months after MacDonnell. He too had thoughts of global telecommunication in his head. His speech at his wedding before he left England in 1855 included a quip that he would like to see a telegraphic string stretching around the world like the pearl necklace adorning the neck of his young wife Alice. At his farewell from Greenwich a month later he reputedly said he hoped 'he would be instrumental in bringing England and Australia into telegraphic communication'.[18]

Todd discussed the proposal with Frank Gisborne when the cable entrepreneur visited Adelaide in 1859. Gisborne could see that the South Australians lacked enthusiasm for his company's scheme but he was equally unimpressed with theirs. No white man had been to the heart of the continent and the Top End of Australia had defied three attempts at white settlement. In the end it didn't matter because his company's cable across the Arabian Sea to Karachi failed a couple of weeks after it was laid later that year. It was going to be a while before anything happened in Australia.

2

Arguably Australia's greatest explorer

Three-and-a-half years elapsed before John McDouall Stuart, arguably Australia's greatest explorer, proved the feasibility of an overland telegraph route. His epic crossing of the continent from south to north in 1862 was an achievement touted well beyond Australia's shores. It was the culmination of four-and-a-half years of relentless endeavour by a remarkably persistent and driven man. Stuart was constantly in the saddle between May 1858 and December 1862, exploring South Australia and the Northern Territory. Unlike his tragic and less competent contemporaries Burke and Wills, he lived to tell the tale because he knew when it was time to stop, retreat and try again.

Stuart got close to the Northern Territory border in 1859. He reached Attack Creek, 1000 kilometres further north, in 1860 before being forced to turn around and head all the way back to Adelaide. He tried again in 1861, getting as far as Newcastle Waters before having to call it quits. He finally succeeded in 1862. Today there is a highway, which bears this indomitable explorer's name, stretching across the continent from Port Augusta to Darwin. It diverges from the tracks of his equally indomitable little mare Polly but is a fitting memorial to an amazing quest to reach the geographical centre of Australia and then go beyond it to the north coast.

A small giant with two dubious friends

John McDouall Stuart was a small, wiry man born at Dysart in Scotland where his father was an army captain. He studied civil engineering at the Scottish Naval and Military Academy before sailing to South Australia in September 1838, a few days after his 23rd birthday. There was plenty of survey work available in the new colony and he quickly found a job as a draftsman. Five years after he landed in the colony, he joined Charles Sturt's quest to be the first white man to reach the geographical centre of Australia.

Like many others, Captain Sturt was convinced there was a sea in the heart of the continent and took a boat to sail on it. His expedition stirred up interest in Adelaide. The day he departed, 10 August 1844, was declared a public holiday. Sturt led his men east to the Murray River and then followed the Darling upstream. They went beyond present-day Broken Hill to the Coopers Creek and ended up in the Simpson Desert north-west of Birdsville. To his great disappointment, there was no inland sea on which to launch the boat and access to the centre was blocked by a seemingly endless expanse of red sand dunes. John McDouall Stuart learned a valuable lesson from this lumbering expedition with wagons and stock. He realised the key to success in the parched heart of Australia was to travel light and keep on the move. He chewed this over many times in the years after he returned to Adelaide, contemplating a foray of his own to the centre.

After a short, unsuccessful business venture in the city, Stuart worked in the Port Lincoln area for several years. In 1854 he accompanied William Finke as surveyor on a trip to the North Flinders Ranges in search of copper and gold. Finke was born into a wealthy family in Hanover and was on board one of the first ships to sail to South Australia after the colony was established at the end of 1836. He soon made money from land speculation and acquired a reputation for being a sharp businessman, though some of his enterprises had a dubious odour to them. The shy German and the quiet Scot spent a lot of time in the Flinders Ranges and sussed out a number of potential mining claims. Finke had a good knowledge of rocks and geology. As they picked over the region's natural resources, the two men wondered what might lie in the flat land beyond the ranges. South Australians called this the Far

North Country and Edward John Eyre was the only explorer to have really penetrated it.

William Finke's main interest was mining but his equally shrewd friend James Chambers had broader business interests. Chambers hungered for land and the prospect of a stock route across the continent to the north-west coast, from where horses and other stock might be shipped to India and China.[1] Like Finke, he was an early South Australian settler. He quickly set himself up as a carrier when he arrived from England with his wife Catherine in 1837. He sold his business before a trip back to England in 1853 to visit family but returned with horses, sheep and cattle of the best breeds.[2] He then devoted his energy to building up a pastoral and mining empire, which he directed from his mansion Montefiore House in North Adelaide. He loved a drink, and reputedly started the day with a whisky, but it did not distract him from the business of making money.

Chambers and Finke lodged claims for a number of localities Stuart surveyed in the Flinders Ranges. In 1857 they started mining copper from a deposit near the southern boundary of Oratunga, a pastoral run that James Chambers' brother John had stocked five years earlier. It was the first mine in the North Flinders Ranges.[3]

The following year Finke employed Stuart to explore the country on the western side of Lake Torrens and he set off from Oratunga in May with two other men. They came across a significant watercourse running into another large expanse of salt, later named Lake Eyre. From there they rode west to the largely treeless moonscape, now known as the Coober Pedy opal fields. Then they worked their way south, through present-day Tarcoola, to Smoky and Streaky bays, and finished up at Port Augusta. Stuart called the watercourse Chambers Creek but it was later renamed Stuart Creek. It had long stretches of water that he assumed were permanent and he said it was 'as fine a creek of water I have seen in the Colony'.[4] He asked the government for land there, as a reward for his exploration, and was eventually given a 14-year lease on 1000 square miles, rent free for four years.

William Finke engaged Stuart again in 1859, with James Chambers also chipping in money. They wanted him to go further north, to the Davenport

Range to check it out for gold. This range, west of Lake Eyre, was discovered the previous year by Peter Warburton, the colony's police commissioner, who named its highest point Mount Margaret.[5] Stuart left in April, accompanied by David Herrgott and Louis Muller, both of whom had spent time on the Victorian goldfields. One of John Chambers' stockmen rode with them part of the way.[6] They headed first to Chambers Creek so Stuart could survey the land he wanted there. David Herrgott discovered an impressive cluster of mound springs on the way, releasing an abundance of hot water. Stuart named them Herrgott Springs. In the following two months, they explored the western side of Lake Eyre and went north to latitude 27°S, beyond present-day Oodnadatta. They were only 100 kilometres from South Australia's border with the Northern Territory but had to turn back because they'd run out of horseshoes. They got back to Chambers Creek at the end of June 1859.

Stuart had opened the door to the centre of the continent. On 18 July, he met with Sir Richard MacDonnell in Adelaide.[7] The governor was impressed. MacDonnell had encouraged exploration since coming to Adelaide in 1855 and urged the government to support a transcontinental expedition led by Stuart. The response was miserly. All the politicians would offer was a reward of £2000 to the first person to cross the continent through the centre. James Chambers was not satisfied with this and petitioned officials to commit three times this figure to a Stuart expedition: £1000 at the start and a further £5000 on its successful completion.[8] He did not get a favourable response.[9] Concern in some circles about Chambers' business dealings, and those of his partner Finke, was undoubtedly a factor in this.

While Stuart was exploring South Australia's Far North, his two patrons had gotten into hot water over a scheme to sell their copper mining interests in the North Flinders to English speculators. Finke boarded a ship for England on 18 June 1859 to float an entity called the Great Northern Copper Mining Company on the London market. James Chambers had persuaded a prominent South Australian, the former sea captain John Hart, to go with Finke as guide and adviser. Just four days before the ship was due to leave, Chambers and Finke asked their friend Commissioner for Lands John Neales to issue leases for a couple more claims they had in the Flinders. A new Act had come into force governing the terms of mineral leases in the colony but no regulations had yet been issued under it. Despite this, Neales obligingly did what he was asked but instead of sending the leases to the chief secretary's office for endorsement, he sent them directly to the governor Sir Richard MacDonnell for a quick signature. MacDonnell was concerned that this was not the normal procedure but assumed all was in order and promptly complied with the request. However, questions were soon asked about their validity and new leases had to be prepared and mailed to England.[10] This was embarrassing for the governor, but worse was to come.

In October 1859, four months after Finke and Hart sailed for England, MacDonnell set off on horseback to inspect land Stuart had recently explored in the Far North. His party included George Goyder and Chief Inspector of Police George Hamilton. The governor was away from Adelaide three months during which time he named several geographical features.[11] Most notable among these was Lake Eyre, honouring the man who had explored to the shore of this lake's southern extension in 1840. Eyre had thought it was part of Lake Torrens, which he assumed formed a giant horseshoe of salt around the top of the Flinders Ranges.

MacDonnell checked out the Chambers and Finke copper mines on his way north. He was unhappy when he saw that no big lode of copper had been found, and in fact it looked like the richest deposits had already been worked out. He was even more upset when he later learnt that a statement he had made to parliament was used out of context in the Great Northern Copper Mining Company's prospectus: 'for the purpose of giving ... a fictitious value to the mines ...'[12] The investors Finke found in London had no idea they were buying shares in a company of dubious value and doubtful prospects. There was a parliamentary inquiry into the affair in June the following year but Finke and Chambers managed to survive the episode. A subsequent inquiry in October 1862 cleared John Hart of any wrongdoing.[13] But the affair tarnished MacDonnell's reputation with the Colonial Office in London, despite his attempts to explain the unauthorised use of his name.[14] Relations between the governor and Stuart's two dubious patrons were permanently soured, though he retained his admiration for the little explorer.

On to the heart of the continent

Stuart was keen to attempt a transcontinental crossing and Chambers and Finke were just as keen to reap the benefits that might come from his exploits. They were willing to pay the costs of another venture north even though the government had declined. However, before he did this they wanted him to go to the Mount Margaret area and survey proposed grazing leases for their Adelaide friends, the Levi brothers.

Chambers and Finke felt Stuart needed a reliable lieutenant and employed William Kekwick to accompany him. They saddled up and rode north from the Flinders Ranges in early October, with Louis Muller and two stockmen, Strong and Smith. Surveying the Mount Margaret leases in the extreme summer heat was hard going. Muller, Strong and Smith weren't happy with the conditions under which they were expected to work and the inadequate food. This was no-frills travel at its most extreme. Smith had had enough by mid November and left one night when the others were asleep.

The men spent the days before and after Christmas looking for gold in the Davenport Range but found nothing. Their supplies were running low by this time and so they headed back to Chambers Creek, reaching it in late January 1860. Stuart was suffering badly from sandy blight but keen to go north again as soon as possible. However, Muller and Strong made it clear they didn't want to be a part of it. The dogged little Scot decided to rest in a lonely shepherd's hut at Chambers Creek while his eyesight recovered and loyal Kekwick rode south to Oratunga, for new men and supplies.

Kekwick was away for a month and Stuart was very unhappy when he returned near the end of February with just an overweight 18-year-old boy named Benjamin Head. The embarrassed Kekwick explained that he couldn't find anyone else willing to go with them. Stuart's attempt to reach the geographical centre of the continent would be nothing like the grand enterprise Captain Sturt had mounted in 1844. He'd said over the years the key to success was to travel light but even he hadn't imagined it would be quite like this. Still, he was going to have a crack at it and the motley trio rode off from Chambers Creek with 13 horses on 2 March 1860. In Stuart's saddlebags was a Union Jack, made by Esther Knowles, wife of the station manager. She had given it to Kekwick for Stuart to plant in the centre of the continent and it was a sign that at least one other person at the station, apart from young Ben Head, had faith in him. A month later they crossed the 26th parallel of latitude, the invisible line between South Australia and the Northern Territory. They were the first white men to enter the southern half of the territory whose northern coast had defied three attempts at white settlement. There's a possibility Ludwig Leichhardt may have made it to Australia's heartland on his ill-fated 1848 expedition, but what happened to him is an enduring mystery.

The southern part of the Northern Territory is quite different to the flat, stony plains of the Lake Eyre region of South Australia. Stuart, Kekwick and Head encountered red sandhills and sand plains covered with spinifex and majestic desert oaks. The drooping foliage of these distinctive trees sang to the men as the warm breezes blew through them. On 4 April 1860 Stuart looked down from the saddle of his faithful mare Polly at a major watercourse. He named it the Finke River after his German patron. It is the longest river in central Australia and said to be the oldest in the world, having followed the same general course for 100 million years, from a time when central Australia was much wetter. These days the Finke is mostly a long ribbon of sand, lined with river red gums, but it's never completely dry. Substantial stretches of water survive the toughest droughts, supporting over a dozen species of fish and countless waterbirds. Two days later they came to an amazing column of rock extending up out of the sandhills. Stuart called it Chambers Pillar. His two patrons live on in the Northern Territory, long after their business dealings raised eyebrows in Adelaide.

The three men followed a tributary of the Finke, the Hugh River, through the James and Waterhouse ranges. Ahead of them lay a significantly larger range, running parallel to the other two and extending east–west for over 250 kilometres. Stuart wrote in his diary on 12 April:

> I have named it the MacDonnell Range, after His Excellency the Governor-in-Chief of South Australia, as a token of my gratitude for his kindness to me on many occasions.

Ten days later he figured they had finally reached the centre of Australia. They camped by a mountain, which he calculated, from his astronomical observations, was close to latitude 22° S and longitude 133° 30'. This put them half way between the north coast and the top of the Great Australian Bight, and midway between the western and eastern extremities of the continent. Stuart decided to name it Mount Sturt to honour the man whose 1844–1845 attempt to reach this point ended unsuccessfully in the Simpson Desert. However, the published version of his journal, edited in England by William Hardman, says: 'I will name it Central Mount Stuart.' Sir Richard MacDonnell was responsible for the change. When the Scotsman showed him his map on his return to Adelaide late in 1860, the governor said, 'Not so, it shall be named Mount Stuart.'[15]

Stuart and Kekwick climbed to the summit on 23 April 1860, leaving Ben Head behind to tend the horses. They built a cairn into which they jammed a pole with Esther Knowles' Union Jack nailed to it, along with a message in a bottle. They gave three hearty cheers for the British flag, which Stuart described in his journal as 'the emblem of civil and religious liberty'. He added 'may it be a sign to the natives that the dawn of liberty, civilisation and Christianity is about to break upon them'. Pity the poor, unsuspecting natives!

From Central Mount Stuart the three intrepid explorers made a couple of attempts to reach the mouth of the Victoria River by going north-west into the Tanami Desert. Lack of water forced them back and they went north instead. Warramunga warriors confronted them on 26 June 1860 at a place now called Attack Creek. Running low on supplies and with scurvy taking its toll on them all, Stuart decided to abandon the expedition and return to Adelaide. In the meantime the ill-fated Burke and Wills expedition had left Melbourne on 10 August, bound for the Gulf of Carpentaria. The Victorians were lavishly funded and carried loads of supplies and equipment, in stark contrast to the way Stuart was travelling.

South Australia's great explorer finds a way to the north coast
James Chambers and William Finke were happy to fund another expedition at the beginning of 1861, in return for first crack at any new pastoral country

and minerals Stuart might discover. Once again MacDonnell pressed the South Australian Government for funds; this time the politicians sanctioned expenditure of up to £2500. Stuart's party would be larger and hopes were high they could go all the way across the continent. William Kekwick was again second in charge and Benjamin Head also put up his hand but had to pull out at the last minute. His health had not recovered from the deprivations of the previous expedition when he'd lost a huge amount of weight. Eight new men rode across the Northern Territory border with Stuart and Kekwick in the February heat. They got to Newcastle Waters in May but were unable to progress, despite two months of trying. The waterless Tanami Desert blocked their way north-west to the Victoria River and a seemingly impenetrable forest of tall lancewood scrub and prickly bulwaddy prevented them going north. It tore the horses' flesh, the men's clothing and their saddlebags when they tried to force their way through it. An attempt to find a way north-east to the Gulf of Carpentaria also proved fruitless. Frustrated and running low on supplies, Stuart realised that yet again he had no alternative but to go all the way back to Adelaide. He arrived on 23 September 1861 but had no intention of giving up on his great quest.

He met with Governor MacDonnell the day after his return and another expedition was soon organised. By the end of November 1861 the indomitable Scot was ready to head off again, in the heat of summer. He clung to the strategy of finding a way to the mouth of the Victoria River but he would try for the Adelaide River on the north coast if that wasn't possible. His party included Kekwick and Frank Thring, from the last expedition, and nine new men, though two pulled out within the first few weeks.

A route through to the Victoria River again proved elusive but the explorers miraculously stumbled on a narrow corridor through the lancewood and bulwaddy scrub of Newcastle Waters and into more open and better watered country. Stuart finally reached the north coast on 24 July 1862 after pushing through mangrove trees 100 kilometres east of present-day Darwin. Journey's end was no sandy beach with waves gently breaking on the shore. He trudged across an expanse of sticky mud exposed by the low tide, dipped his feet in the warm water of the Arafura Sea, and washed his face and hands as he had promised Governor MacDonnell he would do. They had followed the Mary River to the coast but, unlike the Adelaide River further west, it doesn't run proudly into the sea. The Mary peters out, 15 kilometres from the shore, emptying into a broad coastal wetland of swamps, mudflats and mangroves.

Having literally been through hell and high water in the past two years, you'd expect Stuart might have rested awhile, savouring his triumph and enjoying the glorious weather that Australia's Top End turns on in July. But they lingered only one more day before he signalled it was time to begin the long journey back to Adelaide. He feared they would have trouble finding water on the way and many of the horses were growing weak from the effects of worms and poor feed. There was plenty of grass in the tropics but its nutritional value was low so the men jettisoned equipment to ease the burden of the tired horses struggling to carry their loads.

The five-month trip back to Adelaide was a terrible ordeal for the exhausted explorer with deteriorating eyesight. He could no longer observe the stars with his sextant and determine their latitude. He was also suffering from the advanced effects of scurvy, his painful teeth and gums preventing him chewing food. He found it increasingly difficult to talk and had great trouble sleeping at night because of the pains in his limbs. Nearing the MacDonnell Ranges at the end of October 1862, he found it difficult to ride with his swollen and painful feet and legs. His ankles were black. The men had to lift him in and out of the saddle. With the situation becoming critical, they rigged up a stretcher between two horses to carry him through the mountainous country. His breath smelt of death and he was reduced to a shadow of his former self. Wherever they could, the men went looking for native cucumber and other bush vegetables to relieve the symptoms of his scurvy. As a result his condition gradually improved but he remained very weak.

Despite oppressively hot weather and shrinking waterholes in northern South Australia, the men made it safely back to settled country and the news that James Chambers, patron and friend, had died in August, unaware Stuart had finally achieved his goal. Stuart's supporter Richard MacDonnell was also absent from the wellwishers who greeted him at the Adelaide railway station on 17 December 1862.[16] The governor's term in office had ended and he'd left for England in March.

The deprivations Stuart suffered during his expeditions took a heavy toll on his health. He died in 1866 in his native Scotland, barely four years later. There were only seven people at this loner's funeral, ironic considering his place in Australian history. He had been a man of few words and a tough taskmaster but he inspired lifelong loyalty and affection from the men who travelled with him. His courage and dogged determination were pivotal to his success but they were tempered by an unfailing regard for the welfare of his companions and horses. Unlike his tragic contemporaries Burke and Wills, he knew when to admit defeat and withdraw. Each time he faced an insurmountable barrier in 1860 and 1861, he was wise enough to turned around, ride back to Adelaide, regroup and try again. He had an amazing capacity to cope with the hardship of dry country, intense summer heat and poor food, day after day, month after month. Scurvy, deteriorating eyesight and a troublesome duodenal ulcer, with severe bouts of vomiting blood, added to his trials but did not deter him. His weakness for alcohol was well known in Adelaide but he never drank on his expeditions. Some in high places looked down their noses at him and he was never rewarded with imperial honours. However, most South Australians could see beyond his bouts of drunkenness to hail him as a hero.

His success in 1862 led to renewed moves by South Australia to gain control of the Northern Territory.[17] On 6 July 1863, just six months after his successful crossing, the Colonial Office issued Letters Patent, transferring it to Adelaide's jurisdiction.

3

Queenslanders get the rough end of the pineapple

English entrepreneur Frank Gisborne was a persistent man, a quality he shared with the indomitable explorer John McDouall Stuart. Unable to sell the Australian colonies a communication link with the rest of the world in 1859 he persevered throughout the 1860s to raise the money needed for a submarine cable to Australia.

On 15 July 1862 he wrote to the Australian colonies on behalf of a new company, the Anglo–Australian and China Telegraph Company. Their prospectus outlined a system of cables that would extend telegraphic communication to Singapore, Saigon, Manila, Hong Kong and Brisbane.[1] For the Australians, this scheme was no different to the one he'd had trouble selling three years earlier. In London he met with Richard MacDonnell. The former governor pressed him on the practicability of an overland telegraph line but Gisborne remained sceptical. However, he was willing to consider bringing a cable ashore at Cambridge Gulf, rather than Brisbane, if the Australian colonies would pay his company a subsidy of £50,000 per annum for 30 years and if South Australia would build a line through the centre of the continent by the end of 1864.[2]

This scheme had the same fate as his 1859 one. The unreliability of the early cables and the reluctance of some Australian colonies to contribute money continued to put Gisborne's goal out of reach. In 1866 he modified his original plan to lay a cable through the Torres Strait and the coral seas of north Queensland to Brisbane. In November of that year he sought financial support from the British Government to bring a cable ashore in the Gulf of Carpentaria and connect there with the Queensland telegraph system. He was confident he could raise money from private enterprise if the government was seen to be a significant investor. He put this to them but their response was unequivocally negative.[3] The Australian colonies also declined to contribute to the cost, though the fledgling Queensland Government was sticking its neck out and making some positive moves.

An Intercolonial Postal Conference was held in Melbourne from 4–20 March 1867. This is best remembered for Henry Parkes' famous speech advocating federation. The Queenslanders also did something significant.[4] They gave the other Australian colonies formal notice of their intention to extend their existing telegraph line to the Gulf of Carpentaria, in readiness for a cable connection in the near future.[5]

The indefatigable Frank Gisborne responded the following year with another cable proposal and asked the British, Dutch and Australian governments to contribute to the cost.[6] By this time, there were other players in the wings. His persistence over ten years would not pay off. It was ultimately someone else who ended Australia's isolation – and the enterprising Queenslanders were also in for a rude shock.

A former Manchester textile magnate arrives on the scene

Improvements in cable technology and the success of a new Atlantic cable in 1866 gave private investors confidence. A significant breakthrough was the invention of the reflecting (or mirror) galvanometer by British scientist William Thomson, a consultant to the Atlantic Telegraph Company. He patented it in 1858. The instrument could detect very weak electrical impulses and enabled submarine cables to work with a low current. The early long-distance cables failed because they used a higher current, which destroyed the gutta-percha insulation.

In January 1865, the Turkish Government had completed a landline from Baghdad to Fao (now Al-Faw) at the top of the Persian Gulf in Iraq. It joined a submarine cable laid from Fao to Karachi six months earlier, making it possible to send messages from England to India, via Turkey and Iraq, along a mostly overland route. However, the service was expensive and not very good. Messages could take a week or more to travel along the line and often became garbled as they were relayed through countries where the operators did not speak English.[7]

British interests wanted something better and work began in 1868 on a new, mostly submarine link from England to India, with an extension to Singapore in the offing. The principal figure behind this was financier John Pender, a former Manchester textile magnate. He had invested in the Atlantic Telegraph Company and was a director. He was also chairman of the Telegraph Construction and Maintenance Company formed in 1864, the world's major manufacturer of submarine cable.[8] Pender's plan was to lay cables from the south coast of England to Gibraltar, across the bed of the Mediterranean to Malta and then to Alexandria in Egypt. A landline would carry the messages the short distance south to Suez, alongside the new canal. Then they would travel by another submarine cable to Aden, and across the Arabian Sea to Bombay. The work would be carried out by three new companies he was setting up. Once India was linked to England, John Pender's next move would be to bring Singapore on line, with cables across the Bay of Bengal from Madras to Penang and from Penang to Singapore. A landline already linked Bombay and Madras. Pender then intended connecting Australia to Singapore.

His company wasn't the only one offering to link Australia to the rest of the world by this time. In May 1869, W.B. Towler of the Great Anglo–Australian Telegraph Company proposed a cable from Singapore to the North West Cape on Australia's west coast. A telegraph line would need to be built via Perth to Adelaide and the existing Australian telegraph network. Meanwhile, Alex Fraser of the Eastern Asia Telegraph Company was promoting a cable from Singapore to Burketown in the Gulf of Carpentaria. However, he told the South Australian Government he was amenable to landing it in the Northern Territory, at their new settlement of Port Darwin. If that happened, a line would need to be built across northern Australia to connect it to the Queensland telegraph system.[9]

Most South Australians held little hope of an overland telegraph line from their northern shores to Adelaide. Most talk was of a connection to the Queensland telegraph system and the Queenslanders had little reason to doubt this would eventually happen. By 1869 they had strung a wire up their east coast as far as Cardwell, north of Townsville.[10] A submarine cable would most likely be brought ashore in the Gulf of Carpentaria, 700 kilometres from Cardwell – a long way but only a quarter the distance between Port Darwin and Port Augusta, South Australia's northern-most telegraph station.

The Queenslanders were confident everything was in their favour but they were destined to suffer bitter disappointment within a year. To their great surprise, they were bowled over by an audacious, last-minute deal between a faltering South Australian Government and the biggest company in the cable business. All their efforts to link up with an overseas cable, and all the money they spent, would prove to be in vain. They were destined to end up with the rough end of the proverbial pineapple.

South Australia's dream becomes reality

Sherard Osborn, a former Royal Navy captain, was the managing director of the Telegraph Construction and Maintenance Company in 1869. His company's agent in Australia forwarded a memorandum to the South Australian Government in August that year, outlining their plans to link Australia to England via Singapore.[11] Their preference was to lay submarine cable from Singapore to Sumatra and Java and then more across the Timor Sea to the Northern Territory. The cable could be brought ashore either at Melville Island or the nearby Cobourg Peninsula. They envisaged the Australian colonies cooperating to build a line from there to the Queensland telegraph system. If the prosperous colony of Victoria preferred a connection via the west and south, then the company was willing to lay a cable from the western tip of Java to North West Cape on the Western Australian coast. It would then be up to the Australian colonies to build a line south to Perth, across to Albany and then east to Adelaide. However, this wasn't the company's preferred option.

In March 1870, the South Australians received more correspondence from Sherard Osborn, dated 22 January. It included a prospectus for a new company, the British–Australian Telegraph (BAT) Company, and a significant change to the August 1869 proposal. The BAT was actually a subsidiary of the Telegraph Construction and Maintenance Company, though that wasn't immediately obvious.[12] South Australia's new settlement at Port Darwin was established by this time and the prospectus said the BAT would land a cable there and build a telegraph line, at its own expense, across the north to the Queensland telegraph system at Burketown. They were sending Sherard Osborn's brother Noel to Australia to discuss this plan with the Australian colonial governments. The company needed South Australia's permission to build a line through their new territory to the Roper River and on from there to the Queensland border.[13] Their willingness to build a telegraph line across northern Australia at their own expense, rather than laying more cable around the north coast, was a surprising development. The South Australians replied quickly, advising of their willingness to facilitate the company's plans, but they re-affirmed their preference for a telegraph line from Port Darwin to Adelaide instead of Burketown.[14]

Adelaide was the first port of call in Australia for the ship on which Noel Osborn was travelling and so the South Australians were in a position to influence him before he talked to Queensland. They quickly went to work when he arrived at the beginning of April 1870. Charles Todd met with him to clarify the company's intentions. Noel Osborn made it clear that, unlike the earlier plans by Frank Gisborne, his company was not seeking a subsidy from the Australian colonies. It would recover its costs from the charges it would levy for telegraph traffic. All it was asking of South Australia was the necessary facilities to land a cable at Port Darwin and a corridor of land for a telegraph line and repeater stations.[15]

Osborn organised a meeting with the chief secretary, Henry Strangways, after he talked to Todd. He told Strangways that Todd had been non-committal but found the colony's leading politician much more forthcoming. Strangways was a doer, not a ditherer. His second name Bull was very apt. So keen was he to see a telegraph line to Adelaide that he not only argued persuasively for it but also offered to pay the full cost of building it. However, he asked Osborn not to mention this to anyone for the moment.

He needed time to persuade his colleagues. He had led a shaky government for the past 18 months and it was on the brink of collapse. It was only destined to last another month but his tenuous grip on power did not prevent him from making this bold decision.

It was fortuitous for South Australia that such a decisive man was holding the reins of power at that crucial hour. Strangways subsequently talked to Todd and asked him to write a report on the proposed line, with the knowledge that the government would go ahead and build it.[16] He needed to know how much it would cost but Todd was tardy in getting back to him. He eventually replied on 18 April: 'It would not be safe to estimate the cost at less than £80 per mile, or say £120,000, which is the sum I would recommend should be provided by loan.'[17]

Noel Osborn contacted his company directors once he had the go-ahead from Strangways' government. His message was posted on a mail ship about to leave Adelaide for Colombo and telegraphed to England from there. Not surprisingly, the Queenslanders were outraged at the change of plans when they eventually heard about them from Charles Todd. Their agent-general in London contacted the BAT company and they did all they could to stop the deal.[18] They reiterated that their own line was already on its way from Cardwell to Normanton, at the bottom of the Gulf of Carpentaria.[19] They questioned South Australia's ability to plant poles and string wire across 3000 kilometres of country that was mostly unsettled. Noel Osborn also expressed doubts that South Australia could do it when he initially talked to Henry Strangways, but his company could hardly turn down an offer that represented a considerable saving to them.

On 4 June, Noel Osborn got word from London confirming that the company would bring the cable ashore at Port Darwin, provided the South Australian Government guaranteed to have an overland telegraph line to Adelaide built and open for traffic by 1 January 1872. Needless to say, he did not get a good reception when he eventually reached Brisbane in July.

Sir James Anderson, a director of the cable company, spoke 16 years later of their relief in avoiding the responsibility of building a line across the tropical north of Australia.[20] He said:

Besides looking up all information obtainable as to exports and imports of those Colonies, we also read up all about the travels in the interior of Australia, in order that we might be able to judge as to the feasibility of approaching the south coast by land. As a rule, the travelling expeditions ended disastrously. Some of the enterprising pioneers lost their lives, some never being heard of again. As to the route from Port Darwin to the Roper River, we read of want of water sometimes, and at other times of too much water, in the shape of floods. We read also of alligators and cannibals, and the whole description was simply appalling to those interested in carrying a line of telegraph through Australia on commercial principles. The contractors naturally sent out an experienced traveller to advise them of the best course to adopt, and I am sure you will understand how rejoiced we were when South Australia took this job off our hands. Although something like £70,000 was provided for making that land line, it seemed very obvious then – and I am persuaded now – it would have gone far to ruin us both financially and in reputation, if we had been compelled to erect that line from Port Darwin to the Roper at our own cost. The money subscribed would have done little towards it.[21]

On 9 June 1870 a bill drafted by Strangways was presented to the South Australian House of Assembly authorising a loan of £120,000 to build the line. It was debated and passed next day. It passed through the Legislative Council on 14 June.[22] Adelaide's squabbling politicians had momentarily put aside their differences, thrown caution to the wind and dug deep into their taxpayers' coffers. They would run a wire to the middle of nowhere and beyond. If it was not completed on time, the government would have to pay the cable company penalties of £70 for each day it was delayed.[23] This was a momentous event in the colony's and the country's history but they were taking an enormous risk. What was in it for them?

South Australia lacked the population and natural resources of Victoria and New South Wales. Its politicians gambled their future on a tenuous iron wire because they desperately wanted the economic development likely to happen along the route of the overland telegraph line. South Australia's newly acquired Northern Territory and the vast plains of north-western

Queensland held the promise of productive land and undiscovered mineral wealth. If, as originally planned, the BAT Company had built a line from Port Darwin to Queensland, then Brisbane would have reaped the economic benfits as Adelaide continued to struggle.

4

A positive and popular man

Charles Todd faced a truly daunting list of tasks. It's a wonder he slept in the weeks of June and July 1870, with the unrelenting pressure. After the parliamentary debate, and a firm commitment made to the British cable company, the responsibility for making things happen was dumped on the shoulders of the diminutive public servant. He stood only 165 centimetres tall but is a giant of Australian history. His son-in-law, the Nobel Prize winning physicist Sir William Bragg, later said Todd 'had no commanding personality' and yet he inspired scores of men to achieve what many thought impossible.[1] The people who worked for him liked and respected their positive boss with a good sense of humour, and a fondness for puns. He was kindly and tolerant, but at the same time a leader of exceptional drive. It was due to his great skills as an organiser that he was able to get things moving so quickly.

The metal wire upon which South Australia's fortunes were suspended had to cross 3000 kilometres of largely unsettled country in just 18 months. It would be relatively straightforward getting through the Flinders Ranges but then they faced the parched, sparsely timbered stony plains and salt lakes further north, followed by the red sand dunes of the southern Northern Territory. A pass had to be found through the rugged MacDonnell Ranges in the heart of the continent. Thick mulga scrub covered the plains north of the ranges. While construction teams worked their way north, workers sent to Port Darwin by ship would start poling southwards in the build-up to the oppressive wet season. Once they crossed the tropical rivers and swamps of the Top End they would have to cut a path through the dense lancewood and tangled bullwaddy scrub that had troubled John McDouall Stuart. It was a daunting task, requiring 36,000 poles, pins and insulators, plus tonnes of galvanised-iron wire.

The logistics were unprecedented with precious little time to get the necessary supplies of wire, insulators, batteries and telegraph instruments from England and Germany. South Australia's agent-general in London, Frank Dutton, worked overtime to ensure it was delivered on the first available ships. Large quantities of other supplies were assembled locally at breakneck speed: tools, ladders, rope and pulleys, water tanks, tents and bedding, medical supplies and cooking facilities. There were no towns along the way and so large stocks of food had to be procured. Dozens of drays and wagons were needed to carry all this equipment and strong, healthy livestock selected to haul them. The best horses available in the colony were tested for their strength, along with bullock teams to pull the heaviest loads. Todd also hired a hundred camels from Thomas Elder's stud at Beltana in the Flinders Ranges.[2] Local suppliers, tradesmen and manufacturers were put under tremendous pressure but a buzz of excitement permeated Adelaide. People wanted to be involved. Selecting the right men to go north and build the line was itself a huge task. Hundreds of applications were received for a diverse range of jobs: surveyors, linemen, labourers, axemen, sawyers, saddlers, stockmen, teamsters and bullock drivers, blacksmiths and wheelwrights, storemen and cooks.

Wooden poles for the line would be cut along the way but Todd ordered a quantity of iron ones from England for the treeless gibber plains of South Australia's Far North. He pored over John McDouall Stuart's journal and realised there would be other places where the men would have trouble finding healthy timber five metres long and 30 centimetres in diameter at the base. So wooden poles would need to be stockpiled whenever possible and carted up the line with the other equipment. He had a number of the German-style wagons, in common use in the colony at that time, modified to handle the poles. Their undercarriage was altered so their trays could be extended when carrying poles and shortened when empty.[3]

The telegraph signals would not be powerful enough to travel unaided all the way along the line, requiring construction of 11 repeater stations between the existing one at Port Augusta and the new cable station at Port Darwin. Thus men with carpentry and stonemasonry skills were needed. Corrugated roofing iron would also have to be transported long distances, along with guttering and water tanks to collect the run-off from the roofs.

Divvying up the work

One of Todd's first tasks was to get specifications written and call for tenders to construct the line. He managed to do this by 25 June 1870, less than a fortnight after the bill to build the line passed through parliament.[4] Local entrepreneurs were keen to do the work and the government decided to split it between two contractors. Todd accepted the tender of Joseph Darwent and William Dalwood to construct 800 kilometres of line from Port Darwin down to latitude 18°S. John Rounsevell would build the remainder.[5]

Dalwood was familiar with the Top End of Australia having been a member of George Goyder's 1869 survey party. He and Darwent signed a contract on 20 July 1870 but negotiations with Rounsevell dragged on and eventually broke down.[6] So Todd opted for three sections instead of two. Darwent and Dalwood agreed to build an extra 160 kilometres, down to latitude 19½°S, near Tennant Creek.[7] There would be a central section extending south from Tennant Creek, as far as latitude 26½°S. It was just an arbitrary spot on the map, south of the Northern Territory border, near the point where the Stevenson and Hamilton rivers merge and become the Macumba. Government workers would build this central section. In August, Todd called for new tenders to build the southern section, down to Port Augusta. Businessman Edward (Ned) Meade Bagot got the nod.[8] John Rounsevell ended up getting a contract to cart goods and equipment up the track from Port Augusta, using horses and bullock teams.[9]

Todd appointed William McMinn as the government's overseer for the northern section but this decision would come back to haunt him. Richard Burton and James Stapleton were appointed sub-overseers. Stapleton was an experienced telegraph operator from Canada who would supervise the technical aspects of the line in the north.[10] Todd chose W.H. Abbott and Benjamin Herschel Babbage to supervise Ned Bagot's southern section.[11] Darwent and Dalwood only had a few weeks, once they signed their contract, to organise supplies and get their men on a ship to Port Darwin.[12] Their contract specified commencing work on 15 November – and they did.[13]

Bagot's section was mostly settled country. It included South Australia's northernmost pastoral run, established on the western side of Lake Eyre in 1862, with the station homestead near Mount Margaret in the Davenport Range. John McDouall Stuart surveyed this lease in late 1859, before his first venture into the Northern Territory. Mount Margaret was three quarters of the way from Port Augusta to the Macumba River. Todd rightly thought it would be fairly straightforward work, despite the lack of timber in the Lake Eyre region. He was not overly concerned about the task facing the men employed by Darwent and Dalwood in the north. They would have access to shipping at Port Darwin and plentiful timber. He thought the central section would pose the greatest challenges because of supply issues, the arid nature of the inland, and getting across the rugged MacDonnell Ranges. They had to find a suitable route through the MacDonnell Ranges because Stuart's pass was unsuitable for heavy drays and wagons.

Todd split the government's central section into five sub-sections of roughly 1½ degrees of latitude, designated A to E, and put a surveyor in charge of each work party: Richard Knuckey, Gilbert McMinn, James Beckwith, Alfred Woods and William Harvey. Beckwith became seriously ill not long after starting and Todd persuaded him to return to Adelaide in late November.[14] Gilbert McMinn assumed responsibility for sub-section C, as well as his own sub-section B. However, he and Todd were confident that young William Mills, Beckwith's sub-overseer, could lead the men with minimal direction from McMinn.[15]

The five parties comprised a total of 108 men.[16] Todd equipped them with 15 horse wagons, 17 bullock drays, a bullock wagon and five lighter express wagons. He provided 165 horses and 210 bullocks to haul them, plus additional packhorses and riding horses.[17] He planned to establish two depots in the southern half of the continent. The first would be at the Peake

Creek, 80 kilometres north-west of Mount Margaret. It was just a solitary stockman's hut and a few cattle when the men started north in 1870. Some mound springs on the southern side of the creek produced a steady supply of water. Todd decided William Blood would be the storekeeper there. He chose Harley Bacon to take charge of the second depot, established a few months later on the Finke River over 200 kilometres north of the Peake.

Andrew Hart had overall charge of the camels hired from Thomas Elder, determining how and where they would be deployed.[18] Faiz and Tagh Mahomet acted as jemaders, or foremen, overseeing the Afghan cameleers who came with the animals.[19] Elder later helped the brothers set up their own business and they became big operators in camel haulage in the 1890s. Hadji Mullah Merban was another who played a leading role during the construction. He eventually settled in Adelaide, married a white woman and became a spiritual leader of the Afghan community in South Australia. Hadji means holy man.

Thomas Elder had built a pastoral empire larger than his native Scotland and could see that camels were the answer to transportation in the dry interior of Australia. He provided capital for the first large-scale importation of these hardy animals for commercial purposes and formed a partnership with Samuel Stuckey who shipped 124 camels and 31 handlers from the port of Karachi in 1865. Three of the camels died en route; the remainder were safely unloaded at Port Augusta at the end of that year. Their Afghan handlers then walked them to Umberatana station in the northern Flinders Ranges in the blazing heat of January 1866. Articles appeared in the Adelaide newspapers about the camel experiment but only Elder's name was mentioned and he alone credited with the idea. As time went on, Stuckey's role in the camel program was largely forgotten, which irked him considerably.[20] A number of the animals died from mange but Elder was able to establish a successful camel stud at Beltana, south-west of Umberatana, with Faiz Mahomet in charge of the breeding program. The Mahomet brothers, from Kandehar in Afghanistan, were working in Karachi when Stuckey recruited them in 1865.

Todd purchased 1933 sheep so his men would have fresh meat. Stephen Jarvis and Thomas Smith collected them from Beltana station early in

September and took the sheep north, with seven other stockmen, through South Australia's salt lakes, to the Peake.[21] Jarvis had been the manager of the Mount Margaret run until signing on for Todd's great enterprise as sub-overseer of Alfred Woods' sub-section D, and had established the outstation at the Peake back in 1863. Once there, they consigned the sheep to storekeeper Harley Bacon and prepared the place for the arrival of the main party.[22]

Todd's sheep weren't the only ones about to head into the heart of the continent. As the construction parties were leaving Adelaide, some enterprising drovers were preparing to take 4300 sheep, 150 goats and 300 horses across Australia.[23] Ralph and John Milner heard the South Australian Government was offering a reward for the first thousand sheep or hundred cattle to be taken overland to the Top End.[24] They left Port Augusta in September accompanied by a former ship's pilot Edward Kirk, teamster John (Yorkey) Thompson, bullockies Jack Brown and Bill Lamb, and stockmen Arthur Ashwin, Harry Pybus and Jack Wooding. A young Aboriginal man called Charlie and his wife Fanny went too. Charlie later accompanied Colonel Peter Warburton on his 1874 expedition from the OT line to the West Australian coast. Despite a lot of trouble along the way, the Milner brothers' livestock eventually made it to their destination in time for Christmas 1871.

John Ross's expedition to the centre of the continent

Charles Todd faced logistical problems and had no precise knowledge of much of the land through which the line was to be built. He said in 1886 'we knew nothing except what we could glean from Stuart's journals' and noted 'Stuart was dead and could not help us'.[25] Ideally, an exploration party should have been given a couple of months to peg out a route, find water and suitable timber for the poles, and choose locations for the repeater stations. A lot of animals would be travelling with the construction workers and so a route suitable for heavy wagons had to be chosen with adequate feed for the livestock.

However, time was against Todd. He hired John Ross to explore the country north of the Peake, as far as the MacDonnell Ranges, and then return south to report what he found. Ross was a Scotsman, like John McDouall Stuart, but tall and convivial whereas his deceased countryman was short and intensely private. He was one of the few men with knowledge of the northern part of South Australia after moving sheep from drought-stricken Umberatana station in the Flinders Ranges beyond the Peake to the Macumba River in 1869.[26] Todd's written instructions to Ross in Adelaide in July stipulated:

> As it is probable the advanced construction parties will arrive at Mount Margaret by the end of September or middle of October, you are not to extend this exploration further than will permit of your returning to Mount Margaret by the latter date so as to avoid delays in deciding the route to be followed by the telegraph.

Once in the Northern Territory, Todd hoped his construction parties could stick close to the 134° meridian of longitude as far as Mount Gwynne in the heart of the continent. This peak, named by John McDouall Stuart, is 55 kilometres north-east of Central Mount Stuart. Todd didn't want them to deviate west along the Hugh River to Owen Springs as Stuart had done 10 years earlier.[27] Stuart crossed the rugged MacDonnell Ranges at Brinkley Bluff, 60 kilometres west of longitude 134°. Eliminating his westward deviation would save significant wire and poles. However, financial considerations weren't the only reason Todd wanted Ross to stay east of Stuart's tracks. He had carefully studied the great explorer's journal and realised they would be unable to get heavily laden vehicles through the mountain pass Stuart used.

Ross set out from Mount Margaret on 14 August 1870, with the surveyor William Harvey, who Todd appointed to map their route, plus Alfred Giles, Thomas Crispe and William Hearne.[28] They crossed the 26th parallel of latitude into the Northern Territory at the end of August. Here the stony gibber plains of northern South Australia gave way to sandhills and spiky spinifex country devoid of water, feed for livestock, and timber suitable for telegraph poles.

In September they found a dry creek bed, which Ross thought was the river Stuart had named the Hugh. Harvey disagreed and was correct. It was actually the eastern end of an entirely different watercourse later named the Todd River. The tall Scotsman didn't have much idea where they were. They managed to find water next day, their horses having gone 72 hours without a drink. Aboriginal people camped there ran off at the sight of the white men. Water was clearly a scarce commodity but Ross didn't think twice about taking over the Aboriginal people's precious supply.

Following the riverbed upstream would have taken them north-west to Alice Springs. Instead they continued north and ended up in rugged ranges 90 kilometres east of Alice Springs. They were close to the Arltunga area where gold was discovered in 1887.[29]

Ross decided to head back south to Mount Margaret and report what they had found. They took a more westerly path through country no better than that encountered on their way north. They discovered a significant stretch of water, in sand dune country, at the beginning of October. It was at the junction of a creek Ross called the Alice, after Mrs Todd, and the Hugh River, named by John McDouall Stuart in 1860. Keen to locate Chambers Pillar, Stuart's prominent landmark, they headed further west and camped that night in sight of it. Next day they carved their names in the sandstone. Ross's craftsman-like engraving survives to this day. He was better at graffiti than he was at exploring. This side trip to the pillar cleared all doubts about where they'd been in the previous three weeks.

Ross and his party were back at the Peake in South Australia by 19 October. They found Stephen Jarvis and Thomas Smith camped at the outstation with Charles Todd's flock of sheep. They'd arrived a fortnight earlier.[30] In the meantime, the government's construction parties were making good progress towards the Peake, having left Port Augusta at the end of September. Giles, Crispe and Hearne stayed at the outstation to repair their gear, shoe the horses, and jerk some of the local beef. Ross and surveyor Harvey rode further south to confer with the superintendent of telegraphs, who'd left Adelaide at the start of October.

Todd sends John Ross north a second time

Ross and Harvey ran into Charles Todd on 22 October 1870 at Strangways Springs, an impressive set of hot springs south of Mount Margaret.[31] He was disappointed when he heard their report. Ross outlined a route for the telegraph line from the Peake to the Hugh but was unable to tell Todd where it should go from there.

Todd instructed them to return to where the Alice ran into the Hugh.[32] He wanted them to have a close look at the country due north of it as far as Mount Gwynne. Having done that, they were to report to surveyor Alfred Woods, who Todd placed in overall charge of his five construction parties. Woods should be near the Hugh River by the end of January 1871.

Meanwhile the Milner brothers and their intrepid sheep were making steady progress from Port Augusta. They reached Strangways Springs at the end of November where they ran into Todd, on his way back to Adelaide. He had ventured to the Peake after conferring with Ross and Harvey and enjoyed a fortnight with the men before heading south again.[33] Despite the steadily increasing temperatures, there was a frenzy of activity never before seen at that lonely outpost.

There were a few storms and sprinklings of rain but the weather was oppressively hot as Ross, Harvey, Giles, Crispe and Hearne rode north once more, and they were plagued by hordes of flies and small ants.[34] Thankfully the cool nights brought relief for both men and animals. Aboriginal people visited their camps on a couple of occasions and, in Ross's words, 'made themselves quite at home'.[35] The men examined the country north of the Alice Creek, as Todd had directed, but found more sandhills and spinifex. The further they went in the summer heat, the harder it became to find water for their struggling horses. It was clear the construction parties would have trouble bringing their teams and other livestock through this country.

Rather than persevering, they headed north-east and by mid December were back in the rocky ranges they'd reached in September having achieved nothing. A watercourse later named the Ross River took them to picturesque Trephina Gorge, now a popular tourist spot. They could see more mountains to the north-east. Ross named them the Harts Range after John Hart, who had taken the reins of government from Henry Strangways. It was splendid scenery but no place for heavily laden drays and wagons. He described the area in his diary as 'the most extraordinary jumble of mountain country I have ever seen'.[36] Nonetheless, they continued north, reaching Mount Gwynne on New Year's Day 1871. Central Mount Stuart was visible in the distance. Harvey surprised the others by going to his swag and bringing back a bottle of rum wrapped in a flannel shirt. None of them had any idea he had carried it securely for hundreds of kilometres. They celebrated with a drink each, then corked the bottle and put it back in the swag. This was the first alcohol consumed in central Australia.[37]

The next day they headed to Central Mount Stuart where they could see tracks made in 1862 by John McDouall Stuart's horses. Ross, Harvey and Hearne climbed to the top of the mountain and found a message the great explorer had left in a bottle in April 1860. Ross didn't open it, deciding instead to give it to Todd.

He then led his men south, following Stuart's tracks through the western MacDonnells to report to Alfred Woods. Woods later criticised Ross for not using his initiative to try for another more suitable route for the telegraph line. Returning via Stuart's pass achieved nothing. At one point Harvey left the party to take a bearing on their position and was missing for two nights.[38] Alfred Giles later described him as being 'rather of an excitable nature, not an experienced bushman, and not one who could withstand unusual hardship'.[39] Ross considered him 'constitutionally weak and likely to get confused'.[40] The men, concerned for his safety, searched for him but eventually, exhausted, he made his own way back to camp. His lame horse had cast every shoe.

The five men camped near the junction of the Hugh and the Finke on 24 January. Their horses could go no further, being mostly shoeless and tender-footed because Ross had not taken sufficient horseshoe nails to meet their needs. Giles later wrote that they'd 'limped along like cats on hot bricks'. All their provisions were gone by this stage and they resorted to shooting ducks and fishing to get a feed. They had welcome visitors two days later. Surveyors Alfred Woods, Gilbert McMinn and William Mills rode into their camp, with storekeeper Harley Bacon and three others. The men were delighted to see they had two packhorses laden with fresh supplies.[41]

Richard Knuckey had now surveyed all of his sub-section A, from the Stevenson River to Crown Point on the lower Finke. McMinn and Mills needed to know where the next sections would go. The surveyors were not pleased when Ross reported. He had led his small party on two epic journeys in six months but had failed both times to find a suitable route through the heart of the continent. Woods was unhappy that Ross had not pursued other possibilities when Todd's suggestions proved unsuitable. He wrote in his diary that day: 'Mr Ross's exploration has not been, nor is it now, when most needed, of the slightest use to us.' Four days later he added, 'Mr Ross does not appear to keep the object in view'.[42]

Soon the junction of the Hugh and the Finke was a hive of activity. Men steadily arrived to establish the government's second depot there. The place quickly turned into another tent city, like the one that had popped up at the Peake in November. The men built a substantial store for Harley Bacon, with bush timber uprights and a canvas roof.[43] On 4 February 1871, a hundred camels arrived with wire and other supplies, dropping to their knees when their Afghan handlers called *hooshta*.[44] There was plenty of water at the junction but all around was an expanse of red dunes, which became known as the Depot Sandhills. They were cursed by many a traveller heading north by wagon or buggy in subsequent years. It truly was camel country.

A big plus was the abundance of young trees along the riverbanks, the right size for telegraph poles. The big question was where to plant those poles? Finding a suitable route to the foot of the MacDonnell Ranges was now a matter of urgency. The line could go no further until the issue was resolved.[45] Alfred Woods had lost faith in John Ross. In his view, the tall Scotsman had failed miserably. He decided to give his fellow surveyors Gilbert McMinn and William Mills a crack at finding a way through the MacDonnell Ranges. Ross could go north and explore the country between Mount Gwynne and the Roper River, in the Top End of the Territory.

5

The singing wire to Alice

Surveyors Gilbert McMinn and William Mills were keen to prove their mettle and succeed where John Ross had failed. They left the depot on 8 February 1871 and headed up the Hugh River to its junction with Alice Creek. The plan was for Mills and three men to continue along the Hugh as it deviated westwards but to look for an alternative to John McDouall Stuart's tracks. Meanwhile McMinn and five others would explore further to the east.

With the summer sun beating down, McMinn's party initially rode through the same dry sandhill country north of Alice Creek where Ross had been. However, they didn't veer north-east towards the Phillipson Creek and the Fergusson Range, as Ross had done. Instead, they headed north-west to the end of the Waterhouse Range where they found a watercourse with small fruit that resembled oranges. McMinn named it Orange Creek. The men could see the MacDonnell Ranges in the distance and the possibility of a clear path to them.[1] They rode on, through the Pine Gap area where the American and Australian governments would build a secret base for electronic evesdropping in the late 1960s. On 17 February they camped a short distance south of a large gap in the main range, which McMinn named Temple Bar but is now Honeymoon Gap.

They were forced to leave the horses at the gap next morning because the ground was wet and boggy from recent rains and they walked a couple of kilometres north to a gap in a parallel range. McMinn named it Simsons Gap.

His diary sheds no light on who Simson was and it's not clear why the letter p was later added to the spelling. That gap was full of water and clearly not suitable for the telegraph line. However, McMinn could see a long break in the ranges further east when he climbed a nearby hill.[2] He was convinced this might be a suitable route but, running low on supplies, they packed up and rode west towards the Hugh River to find Mills. The two parties met up at the end of February and then returned south to the depot.

Gilbert McMinn was confident they could now cross the MacDonnells, albeit with an unwanted deviation west from longitude 134°. They would follow the Hugh River to the Waterhouse Range and Owen Springs, as Stuart had done, but then turn east again towards Temple Bar. He got to work straightaway, surveying this route, so his men of sub-section B could start planting poles and stringing wire. In the meantime, Mills would go to confirm the break in the range McMinn had seen in the distance was indeed suitable for sub-section C.

It's unclear why Gilbert McMinn chose the unusual name Temple Bar, just as the identity of Simpson remains a mystery. McMinn was born in Ireland in 1841 but came to South Australia as a child in 1850 with his mother and seven siblings, following the death of her husband. Was the gap reminiscent of the well-known landmark in London's Fleet Street? It was originally the gateway to the old city, established in the Roman days.[3] Was McMinn thinking he had found the gateway that would enable the telegraph line to pass through the rugged ranges to the mulga plains of the north?[4] Intriguingly, there's another gap a short distance west of Temple Bar the construction workers called the Toll Gate.[5]

Mills and two others headed off to Temple Bar on 7 March.[6] They got there four days later and continued east another 15 kilometres to a much bigger gap in the range. Mills called this one Heavitree Gap after his school in Devon. He was unaware of its spiritual significance to the local Arrernte (a-ren-ta) people who call it Ntaripe (n-tuh-rip-a). Women and children were not permitted to walk through it. It is an extraordinary scenic feature with an equally extraordinary geological history. The ancestral Todd River began cutting this huge gap in the tough, quartzite range 20 million years ago, when the climate was wetter and the river more powerful. These days it's usually just a ribbon of sand but there is more than enough water trickling beneath its surface to sustain the large river red gums that line its banks. Occasionally it runs a banker if a desert storm dumps enough rain over its catchment in the rocky hills to the north.

Mills and his companions followed the dry riverbed upstream for several kilometres. They found a string of waterholes, the largest of which he named the Alice Spring in honour of Charles Todd's wife. The three men watered their horses there and then pushed on, towards the Strangways Range, a further 75 kilometres north. Mills had no doubt his workers could bring the telegraph line through Temple Bar to the Alice Spring and then string the wire over the rocky hills to the mulga plains beyond the MacDonnells. The country surrounding his Alice Spring was much better than the sandhills and parched plains Ross had encountered further to the east.

Arrernte people tell a story about an important man named Unchalka (or Ntyarlke), later tagged King Charlie. He was a custodian of the caterpillar dreaming, the sacred site Heavitree Gap (Ntaripe), and another even more significant gap further east. That one is Anthwerrke (n-turk-a), named Emily Gap after Emily Burt, the wife of Mills's deputy Adam Burt. According to Arrernte folklore, Unchalka was at Temple Bar when the first white men came through there and he approached them in a spirit of friendship.[7] It's an intriguing story because William Mills made no mention of meeting Aboriginal people when he wrote his September 1872 report to Charles Todd. Perhaps Unchalka greeted some of the construction workers who arrived later?

Ross continues north, as do the Milner brothers' sheep

John Ross remained at the depot for seven weeks before he set off on his new assignment to try and redeem his reputation. Neither William Harvey nor Tom Crispe was prepared to go with him. Relations between Ross and Harvey had been quite strained on their two previous ventures.[8] Harvey had questioned Ross's assumptions about their location. The disagreement about the amount of food Ross intended taking to the Roper River was the last straw for Harvey. They'd run short on both the previous trips and he thought it would be the same this time. He decided to join his men, who were also camped near the depot, on their way north to construct the line between Barrow Creek and Attack Creek.[9]

Ross recruited two new men, Robert Abrahams and William Gregory. Alfred Giles and William Hearne had no problems with Ross and were willing to accompany him a third time. They left the depot with 11 weeks rations on 7 March and followed the roundabout route McMinn was surveying for the line. Mills and his two companions set off for Temple Bar that same day but took a shortcut and travelled with a greater sense of urgency. Somehow Ross missed the idyllic waterhole Mills had named the Alice Spring on 11 March but ran into him a kilometre or so north. Mills had explored to the Strangways Range and was on his way south again. The two groups chatted briefly before going their separate ways.[10]

The drenching rain that bogged Gilbert McMinn's horses at Temple Bar in February slowed the Milner brothers' sheep further south at the Finke River. They had spent Christmas at Bulldog Creek, a few kilometres north of Mount Margaret, and got to the Neales River on 2 January. The construction parties' heavily laden wagons left a clear track for the sheep to follow and they made good progress. They were also fortunate to be travelling in a wetter than average season but, even so, the last stretch to the Finke River was 130 kilometres of waterless country. The river was dry when they got there in early February, apart from a salty waterhole, but it came down a banker that night due to steady rain upstream. They camped there for five weeks and had to swim the sheep across the river to get them moving north again. The water was a couple of hundred metres wide and up to the men's armpits in places.[11]

Ross and his men had no holdups on their way to the Roper River, arriving on 19 May, 10 weeks after leaving the depot.[12] The Milner brothers were camped near Owen Springs by then with a new crop of lambs, making up for losses they had suffered crossing the Finke.[13] However, disaster struck at the Devils Marbles in the middle of the year. They bedded down one night and awoke to find 3000 of their sheep dying after eating a poisonous pea, *Gastrolobium grandiflorum*, a low shrub with red and yellow flowers. The leaves contain sodium fluoracetate, the chemical manufactured and sold as a poison under the trade name 1080. Native animals that have evolved alongside the plants have a natural resistance to the chemical but it is deadly for stock and dogs.[14]

More trouble was to strike further north at Attack Creek in August.[15] They set up a camp there, after nearly a year on the track, and Ralph Milner went ahead to explore the route to Newcastle Waters. His brother stayed behind with the sheep and was resting under a tree when a tall Aboriginal man approached him, armed with a club and a boomerang. John Milner had allowed him into the camp the previous day, despite the protests of the others, saying, 'Let him stop. There's no harm in the blackfellow.' Arthur Ashwin was about to mount his horse to check on the sheep when he heard a dull thud. He turned around and saw the Aboriginal man had clubbed Milner on the forehead, fatally smashing his skull. He drew his gun and shot the man twice. Attack Creek was clearly no less hostile now than when John McDouall Stuart had named it in 1860.

That wasn't the end of the trouble. They were camped just past Powell Creek one night when the dogs started growling. Armed men were sneaking up on them and so they let six of the dogs loose. They heard people taking off through the bush, and one man yelling for about five minutes. The dogs returned to camp with blood on their jaws 10 minutes later. Next morning they found an Aboriginal man lying dead with his throat torn out. From the number of footprints, there must have been 200 of his countrymen surrounding the camp.[16] Ahead of the flock lay dense stands of lancewood and bullwaddy. It was tough country to negotiate but they eventually got through it to Daly Waters and reached the Roper River in December 1871.[17] The teams constructing the northern section of the line had set up a depot there and some of the Milner sheep became their Christmas dinner.

Completing the line

The workers employed by contractor Ned Bagot started building the southern section of the telegraph line in October 1870. It proved a slow, drawn-out process with poles being the problem. There was plenty of timber in the

Flinders Ranges for the Port Augusta end of the line but the men's progress was hampered by a shortage of trees on the vast, saltbush plains further north. They had to scrounge for whatever timber they could find and wait for iron poles to arrive from Europe. Todd allowed Bagot to install poles at a spacing of 10 to the mile instead of 20 in order to get the wire strung up and operational by the start of January 1872.[18] Iron poles were planted in between as they became available and the contract was satisfactorily completed by the end of March 1872.[19]

Finding suitable timber was less of a problem for Richard Knuckey between the Stevenson River and Crown Point on the Finke. His sub-section was completed with three months to spare on 30 September 1871. Gilbert McMinn was responsible for the line from Crown Point to the northern end of Lawrence Gorge in the Waterhouse Range. His teams began erecting poles on 15 February 1871 and finished the job on 15 November, with six weeks up their sleeve.[20] William Mills's workers commenced the next section on 22 March 1871. It stretched to the Reynolds Range, 100 kilometres north of Alice Springs. The wire was up by 29 December, two days before Todd's deadline for completing the line.[21] Alfred Woods finished the leg to Barrow Creek in mid October.[22] The local Aboriginal people must have got a shock when they saw the Woodforde Creek stripped of all its serviceable trees for a distance of 25 kilometres.

William Harvey's men were the last to begin work. After parting company with John Ross, Harvey moved his team 400 kilometres north to their starting point near Barrow Creek. They got there on 24 May 1871 and planted their first poles a week later. The vegetation was mostly low scrub and spinifex grass, devoid of suitable timber. They had to cart poles long distances but managed to get the wire strung up to Tennant Creek by 1 November. Like Ned Bagot in the south, they took a few liberties with Todd's specifications, planting poles 160 metres apart in some places, instead of 80, as a temporary measure. The occasional pole was small and crooked and so plans were made to cart iron poles up the line and install them where needed as soon as it was possible to do so.[23]

Matters did not go so well in the north, despite a promising start. Todd thought it would be easier work than the central section but this assumption proved way off the mark. The men employed by contractors Darwent and Dalwood planted their first pole at Port Darwin with great ceremony on 15 September 1870 as the dry season was drawing to an end. They toiled hard in the build-up to the wet and had erected poles to Pine Creek, 225 kilometres south-east of Port Darwin, by Christmas. Anyone who has lived in northern Australia during the build-up will know this was quite an achievement. The heat and humidity increase markedly between September and December; truly debilitating months for anyone engaged in manual labour, as the equatorial belt of low pressure steadily moves down into the southern hemisphere. The monsoon trough, as it is known, is usually lying across the north of Australia by New Year. Then the skies open up, flooding the country.

The men continued working in January 1871 as the rains tumbled down. Their heavy vehicles were frequently bogged but they reached the Katherine River by the end of the month. A long line of poles stretched behind them but the flooded river blocked progress south. The men had no real understanding of the north's seasonal cycle and decided to camp there and wait, thinking the rain might soon stop. It was still pouring three weeks later when they decided to cross on rafts and resume the poling. Supplies were dwindling rapidly and mould grew on food that remained. It was impossible to get new supplies to them from Port Darwin. Large stretches of country now resembled swamps and their canvas offered limited protection from the drenching rain. Work continued through March but many of the men were very disgruntled by then, and rightly so. Poling came to a standstill at the King River, 325 kilometres from Port Darwin, in April 1871. They were beaten for the moment and retreated to the Katherine. Some went further back to the Adelaide River.

At this point the government's overseer William McMinn, the younger brother of Gilbert McMinn, made a disastrous decision. At the Katherine on 3 May 1871, he took the drastic step of declaring the contract for the northern section null and void. He said the contractors' arrangements for transporting supplies were inadequate and he accused them of mismanagement. A month later he sailed for Adelaide on the government schooner *Gulnare* to confer with officials about the situation. A significant number of the men from the northern construction party were on board with him.[24]

Todd was away from Adelaide when William McMinn arrived but the shocked politicians moved quickly. The government dispatched the railways engineer Robert Patterson north with six ships loaded with new men and supplies, but they didn't get to Port Darwin until late August. McMinn had unwisely terminated the contract as the wet season was finally drawing to an end. Most of the following dry season was squandered by the time things got rolling again. It's likely Darwent and Dalwood could have satisfactorily completed their contract by the deadline of 31 December 1871 if McMinn had not made his rash decision. Instead, the line wasn't completed until 22 August 1872, eight months after the due date.

On 26 October 1871, three British ships sailed into Port Darwin: cargo ships *Hibernia* and *Edinburgh* loaded with big reels of copper cable insulated with gutta-percha, and the passenger ship *Investigator* carrying engineers and electricians. The men retrieved a prefabricated hut from the hold of the *Edinburgh*, erected it onshore and dug a trench down to the low water mark. On the morning of Tuesday 7 November, they hauled a cable from the hold of the *Hibernia*, dragged it ashore and connected it to instruments inside the hut. They promptly climbed back on board their ships and sailed north-west towards Java. When the cable ran out, its end was spliced to the one on board the *Edinburgh* and the ships resumed their journey. The cable was soon connected to a telegraph line running across the island of Java to Banjoewangi at its eastern end. On 20 November the commander of the three ships Captain Robert Halpin sent a message to William Bloomfield Douglas, the government resident in Port Darwin. It declared he was now connected to the rest of the world and finished with the words 'Advance Australia'.[25] The cable functioned well, albeit to no avail, until 24 June 1872 when it abruptly went dead and the company couldn't get it back into service for four months, a fortuitous reprieve for the struggling South Australians![26] The cable's failure relieved Charles Todd of considerable stress and put a stop to the stiff penalties the government had to pay for failing to meet its contractual obligation.

Todd's triumph

In 1954, men from the Postmaster-General (PMG) Line Training School in Adelaide erected a marble column on the Stuart Highway between Dunmarra and Newcastle Waters, 650 kilometres south of Darwin.[27] They had transported the column from South Australia in pieces and assembled it by the roadside, with a plaque saying:

> The north and south parts of this epic overland telegraph line were finally joined about one mile west of this spot by R.C. Patterson, engineer, at 3.15 pm on Thursday, August 22, 1872, thus making possible for the first time instantaneous telegraph communications between Australia and Great Britain.

The PMG men realised the travelling public would never see the monument if they erected it where the wires were actually joined, in dense lancewood scrub and prickly bullwaddy. Robert Patterson told Charles Todd the join was 'two miles to the east of Frew's Ironstone Pond' and added: 'The clearing over this length was exceedingly heavy; I believe by far the heaviest on the continent.'[28] The time on the plaque is incorrect. Patterson pulled the ends together earlier in the day, around 12.15 pm, and the line was declared officially open at 1 pm. His first attempt was quite comical. He got a sharp electric shock and let go of the wire with a loud yell. Prudent use of a handkerchief prevented a repeat.[29] John Lewis was one of the men who witnessed the event. He later wrote:

> Twenty-one shots were fired from our revolvers, and a bottle of supposed brandy was broken over the last post. (I think it was tea.) Among those present were Messrs. Patterson, Rutt, Mitchell, Howley, Ricks, Hands, Bayfield, Hack and myself.[30]

Charles Todd was 500 kilometres south at Central Mount Stuart. He'd reached the foot of the mountain at 4 pm and set himself up for the night among the tea-trees in the bed of the Hanson River. At 6.30 pm he used his portable morse set to contact operators John Mueller and Ted Harris at Alice Springs. They told him Patterson made the final join six hours earlier. He then 'talked' to Adelaide. It was a bitterly cold night but he sat until nearly midnight receiving messages of congratulations from various dignitaries including the chief secretary Henry Ayers, the mayor of Adelaide, and foreign consuls. Ayers told him, 'We opened the line at 1.00 pm this day,' and Todd replied:

> Many thanks for your kind congratulations on the completion of the Adelaide and Port Darwin telegraph, which, as an important link in the electric chain of communication connecting the Australian Colonies with the mother country and the whole of the civilised world, will, I trust, rebound to the credit of South Australia, and amply repay her for the great outlay she has incurred in its construction by advancing her material interests and prosperity, notwithstanding the delays and mishaps which have occurred on the northern portion of the work. We have this day, within two years from the date it was commended, completed a line of 2,000 miles long through the very centre of Australia, until a few years ago a terra incognita and supposed to be a desert, and I have the satisfaction of seeing the successful completion of a scheme I officially advanced 14 years ago.[31]

The total cost of building the line blew out to three times the original estimate of £120,000.[32] However, the cost overrun didn't dampen the euphoria of South Australians. The OT line ranks as one of the great construction feats of the 19th century. Those who know the outback and its challenges know what Todd's men achieved. Australia would no longer be cut off from the rest of the world once the British–Australian Telegraph Company got its cable back into service. That was restored on 21 October 1872 and 1843 international messages were sent by the end of the year. It took more than two months for a letter to travel to England on a ship in 1855, the year Charles Todd arrived in Adelaide. Sending a telegraph message to London in 1872 wasn't instantaneous like emailing or texting today. It still took a couple of hours and was very expensive but an enormous breakthrough for the Australian colonies.[33] For the Aboriginal people of central Australia, the joining of the wires on 22 August 1872 brought an end to thousands of years of relatively unchanged existence. Their lives would never be the same again.

A man of vision

History has heaped praise on Charles Todd and rightly so. He did not put up a single pole or length of wire but his place in Australian history is richly deserved. He provided the meticulous planning, organisation and attention to detail needed to get the line built. However, it is regrettable the pivotal contribution of another man was forgotten as Todd basked in the glory. Even more regrettable is that Todd played a role in diminishing that man's part in the story.

Richard MacDonnell has been largely forgotten, even though he has a major mountain range named after him. Historian Mervyn Hartwig grasped his decisive contribution and said so in his 1965 doctoral thesis: 'Governor MacDonnell was the first to suggest that an overland telegraph should be carried from Port Augusta to the northern coast.' Writer Ann Moyal concurred in her 1984 book *Clear Across Australia*: 'But what of Todd? Historians and popular writers have traditionally cast the quiet and competent Englishman as the visionary who first conceived Australia's epic overland route. Todd indeed claimed the priority for himself. The moving force, however, was not the able public servant who would carry the line, but South Australia's exploration-minded Governor.'[34]

Frank Clune was one of those popular writers extolling Todd and calling him 'a Man of Vision'. His wonderful 1955 book *Overland Telegraph* reads like an adventure novel and gets most of the facts right – but not this one. John Bailey followed suit in his excellent 2006 read *Mr Stuart's Track*. He wrote: 'As early as 1857, Todd had begun pestering Governor MacDonnell with the idea that the telegraph could be brought overland to South Australia.'[35] This is not so. Archival records make it clear that the idea was MacDonnell's.

Charles Sturt had tried lifting the veil covering the heart of Australia but it was still an unknown region when the governor began making the case for an overland telegraph line. John McDouall Stuart had not yet begun his epic quest for the Centre. MacDonnell sent a despatch to the Colonial Office in London on 8 December 1858 stating:

It is therefore very possible that further exploration may prove the route across this continent from the North coast to Adelaide to be eventually the easiest and cheapest mode of reaching one of the existing commercial capitals of these Colonies.[36]

He attached a report he'd asked Todd to write, evaluating three proposals the Colonial Office had forwarded to Adelaide earlier in the year. Todd was as interested as the governor in the schemes cable entrepreneurs were proposing but he was not advocating any particular route at this stage. Of the two most likely, he favoured a cable around the north coast to Queensland rather than one to Western Australia. MacDonnell noted this in his despatch. Todd reiterated his view in his half-yearly report to the Commissioner of Public Works:

> It will be seen, by my report, that I consider, so far at least as I am able to judge from the information given, the terms offered by Mr. Gisborne as the most favourable for these Colonies.[37]

Todd harboured a few doubts about a telegraph line through the Centre but MacDonnell was unwavering in his pursuit of it. He sent another despatch to London six weeks later saying his Executive Council felt it inadvisable to support any of the current schemes to connect Australia with Europe:

> until steps shall have been taken to ascertain by exploration the practicability of connecting this Province by Electric Telegraph with the mouth of the Victoria River or some point on the North Coast of Australia near Cambridge Gulf, or even westward of there.[38]

MacDonnell sent a third despatch on the matter after Stuart returned to Adelaide in July 1859, having got to within 100 kilometres of the Northern Territory border. He said further exploration should be undertaken before a commitment was made to the Gisborne proposal.[39] Todd was supporting the governor's scheme by this time but he still had reservations. He wrote to the Commissioner of Public Works in July 1859:

The third route has naturally enough obtained advocates in South Australia, where our hopes have been raised by the discovery of valuable country by Messrs. Stuart, Babbage, and Warburton; and the confident tone assumed by those explorers as to its extension northwards; but nowhere else am I aware of its being regarded with similar favour – perhaps owing to the generally-prevailing belief of the desert character of the whole interior. Having had occasional conversations with the three gentlemen I have just named, I do think it probable that an overland route will ultimately be found practical.

However, he added the proviso:

I do not wish it to be understood that I am advocating a line across a desert; it is only on its being shown to traverse country available for settlement that I recommend its adoption.[40]

A month later MacDonnell advised the Colonial Office that he'd read Stuart's journal and examined the map of this latest expedition.

I believe the general interests of all these colonies are more than ever concerned in finding a direct route across the Continent for the Telegraphic wires which are eventually to connect them with India and Europe – a route which, if practicable, is infinitely preferable in my opinion, to that proposed by Mr Gisborne.[41]

MacDonnell also wrote to Treasurer William Younghusband urging the South Australian Government to give Stuart financial assistance to mount an expedition across Australia. He said it 'would settle forever the practicality of carrying the wire'.[42] Stuart subsequently named the MacDonnell Ranges in central Australia after the governor in April 1860 'as a token of my gratitude for his kindness to me on many occasions'. A further despatch from MacDonnell to London on 10 October 1859 is significant. It contains the statement:

I am not aware that anyone previous to myself had called attention to the latter route, and though at first it had few advocates, yet every new exploration towards the Interior naturally raises the reflection whether it be not premature to support a circular route along uninhabited shores, whether East or West, when it may perhaps be quite practicable to adopt a nearly direct and cheaper one across the Continent, and, at the same time secure thereby many collateral advantages.[43]

Todd rewrites the history

Richard MacDonnell left Australia after his term as governor ended in March 1862. Charles Todd subsequently exaggerated the role he played and the former governor's visionary advocacy was steadily obscured as the years passed. As early as 1869, Todd began positioning himself as the prime mover behind the great enterprise. On 30 August that year, he sent a letter marked 'unofficial' to Sir James Fergusson who had just taken over as governor. It included the intriguing lines:

> I have the honour to enclose for your Excellency's information a copy of my report (just printed for Parliament) on the Anglo–Australian Telegraph. You will observe that I have confined myself to the consideration of the two principal routes that have been suggested – although on the map appended to the report I have marked the line originally recommended by me & warmly supported at the time by Sir Richard MacDonnell. ie line directly across the interior from Pt. Augusta to Pt. Darwin.[44]

MacDonnell was governor of Hong Kong by this time and not on hand to set the record straight. It's unlikely he knew Todd was now subscribing him a secondary, supporting role. Todd continued to imply he was the main player in correspondence he sent to the treasurer seven months later, though admittedly the wording was more ambiguous this time. On 18 April 1870 he wrote:

> It is some eleven or twelve years since I first drew the attention of the Government to the practicability of erecting a land line from Port Augusta to the Northern Coast, and every addition of our knowledge of the interior since acquired, has confirmed the views I then advanced.[45]

Eight years later he attended a conference in Melbourne convened to consider laying a second cable to Australia. He was asked during his presentation on behalf of South Australia:

You also mentioned that the overland route from Adelaide to Port Darwin was undertaken by your Government at your suggestion?

Todd replied:

Yes; I advocated it as long ago as 1858; and you will see a despatch from Sir Richard MacDonnell to the Secretary of State, dated August 1859, in the Parliamentary Papers of South Australia for 1861, in which I advocated a line being taken right across the continent; and from 1858 to the time it was erected I was continually bringing the matter before my Government.[46]

Todd was in London in February 1886 as the special guest at the 4th Ordinary General Meeting of the Royal Colonial Institute of Great Britain. His address, entitled 'Telegraphic Enterprise in Australasia', referred to British businessman Frank Gisborne visiting Australia in July 1859. Todd said:

English capitalists did not believe in long land lines through unsettled country, and their plans involved therefore a maximum of submarine cable and a minimum length of overland telegraphs ... whilst in the colonies, others as well as myself made light of difficulties which frightened English promoters, and advocated land lines which we knew would facilitate the settlement of the country ... About that time or early in 1859, having read an account of A.C. Gregory's exploration from the Victoria River to Moreton Bay, I first conceived the feasibility of a line across the interior from Port Augusta to Cambridge Gulf and in July of that year (or some months prior to Gisborne's visit) submitted my views in a letter to the late Sir R.G. MacDonnell, KCMG, CB, then Governor of the Colony, and roughly estimated the cost at about £178,000.[47]

MacDonnell was also in London when Todd spoke but lying in the Kensal Green Cemetery, where the explorer John McDouall Stuart was also buried. The former governor died in France in 1881. Had he been alive, he no doubt would have disputed Todd's recollection of events. It is clear Todd had long dreamed of playing a role in connecting Australia to the rest of the world. However, the records suggest he was a cautious and quiet supporter rather than the forthright and persistent advocate he was now claiming to be.

By the late 1860s, Todd thought it unlikely that a line would be built to Adelaide. The odds were in favour of a cable being connected to the rapidly expanding Queensland telegraph system rather than the South Australian one. He was not boldly promoting an overland telegraph line as MacDonnell had done in the late 1850s. Indeed, in October 1869, he expressed the opinion that South Australia's best interests would be served by a new proposal from W.B. Towler, of the Great Anglo–Australian Telegraph Co. Ltd, to lay a cable from Java to the west coast of Australia, with a telegraph line down to Perth and another one following the south coast to Adelaide.[48]

In the end it was Henry Strangways who turned things decisively in favour of South Australia at the last minute, when Noel Osborn turned up in Adelaide in April 1870.[49] Annoyed by Todd's dithering, he committed South Australia to building a line through the Centre and had the crucial legislation drawn up. The former chief secretary took exception to public statements Todd made when he retired in February 1905. Adelaide's papers the *Observer* and the *Chronicle* reported an interview with Todd in which he declared:

> With regard to the line to Port Darwin as early as the beginning of 1858 I submitted a scheme to the then Governor, Sir Richard MacDonnell, which was embodied in a despatch to the Secretary of State for the Colonies. Other proposals were afterwards submitted for connecting Australia with England. Mr Gisborne's proposition was to lay a cable from East Java to Moreton Bay. I steadily kept my own pet project in view, and our brave explorer – Stuart – having succeeded in crossing the continent, greatly assisted me ... The thing, however, slumbered until 1870 when Commander Osborne, a brother of Admiral Sherard Osborne, visited Australia, called at Adelaide, and proposed on behalf of an English Company (afterwards the Eastern Extension Company) to lay a cable from Singapore via Java to Port Darwin, and to erect a landline around the Gulf of Carpentaria to join the telegraph line in Queensland. I recommended my old scheme, and that we should carry the line direct from the head of Spencer's Gulf to Port Darwin and the north coast to meet the cable. This

was strongly supported by Mr. Strangways who was in office at the time, and the Governor (Sir James Fergusson).[50]

Strangways was living in England by this time but wrote to the mayor of Glenelg:

I have always understood that the overland telegraph line to Melbourne was initiated by Sir Richard Macdonnell and that Mr Todd merely carried out the orders given to him ... Sir Charles has no claim to speak of the Central Australian line as his pet project, and his account of the negotiations for the construction are altogether wrong, and in some respects the reverse of the facts ... Sir Charles Todd's statement that he recommended the scheme, and that I and my colleagues supported it is exactly the reverse of the actual facts. If the construction of that Central line had depended on Mr Todd, it would not have been made. Those who knew the Mr Todd of those days will remember that Mr Todd, though he always discharged his official duties efficiently, never took any unnecessary responsibility on himself.[51]

There's no doubt Todd wanted a telegraph line to Adelaide but the history is a little different to what he would have us believe. With MacDonnell off the scene, he must have thought it safe to promote himself. He didn't need to. He has an honoured place in Australian history and diminishing MacDonnell's role was unfair and unnecessary. MacDonnell had written glowingly about Todd to the Colonial Office way back on 10 October 1859, saying:

I cannot conclude this part of my subject without expressing the obligations of this Government to the energetic and highly competent superintendence of Mr. Charles Todd over the Telegraphic Department, which is mainly indebted to him for its present extremely efficient state.[52]

It's a pity Todd wasn't so generous in return. There was more than enough glory for them to share.

6

Atherreyurre, the Alice spring

The singing wire to the Alice wasn't pretty but it worked. William Mills's section took a crooked route through the MacDonnell Ranges but that could be straightened out later. The young surveyor had repaid the confidence Charles Todd and Gilbert McMinn had shown in him.

McMinn's men actually strung up the last stretches of Mills's wire so he and his crew could work on the unfinished northern section.[1] Gilbert McMinn also took on the job of building a repeater station at the waterhole Mills had found on 11 March 1871. Daytime temperatures were climbing steadily by the time he got there on 18 November and there was no time to waste. His first priority was to get temporary shelter erected to protect the telegraph instruments and batteries. They were on their way from South Australia with the men Charles Todd had chosen to operate the stations at the Alice, Barrow Creek and Tennant Creek. He wanted them to establish communication with Adelaide as soon as possible.

Mills named the waterhole in honour of Todd's wife Alice but it was Atherreyurre (a-tuh-ree-oo-ra) to the local Arrernte people. Of all the locations where Todd's men built telegraph stations, this was undoubtedly the most picturesque. It's nestled amid distinctive, rocky hills strewn with large boulders, and the majestic main range of the MacDonnells forming a stunning backdrop. The hills around the waterhole are remnants of molten granite that came from deep below the earth's surface over 1.6 billion years ago. Gilbert McMinn's men began stockpiling suitable pieces of this rock to construct the walls of a substantial stone building designed by Todd. It was U-shaped, with a galvanised-iron roof to collect rainwater. Similar-looking telegraph stations were built at Charlotte Waters and Barrow Creek.

The men had to go further afield to collect limestone to burn and make lime for their mortar. There was an extensive formation of this rock on the southern side of Heavitree Gap, eight kilometres away. They dug a limekiln in early December and laid the foundations for the building in the week before Christmas. The work proceeded slowly due to the absence of skilled stonemasons but they eventually produced an impressive structure that has stood the test of time.[2]

It was built like a fortress with gun ports in its external walls through which the men could fire on any would-be attackers. This was never necessary because the local Arrernte people were remarkably tolerant of the intruders squatting on one of their prime pieces of real estate. The building's southern wing is now one long open room containing a display telling the history of the place. It was originally divided into four rooms, with the telegraph office in the south-west corner. The eastern wing housed the batteries of Meidinger cells powering the line.

A special place, criss-crossed by dreaming tracks

The waterhole Mills named after Mrs Alice Todd isn't actually a spring. It's simply a depression where water pools on top of an impervious layer of granite beneath the riverbed. Rivers in central Australia run upside down! They may look completely dry but water continues to trickle through the sand a few metres down in all but the driest seasons. The telegraph men used a hand-operated whip to draw water for their thirsty stock. This was an ancient device widely used in Middle Eastern countries where it's called a *shaduf*. It consisted of a long pole, mounted like a seesaw, with a rope and bucket tied to one end and a counterweight attached to the other. You pulled on the rope to lower the bucket into the water and the counterweight pulled it back up again. It was 42 years before the telegraph station got a windmill in 1914.

Edwin (Ted) Harris was the young man Charles Todd chose to be the assistant operator at Alice Springs. Nearly 70 years after he arrived at the end of December 1871, Adelaide's paper the *Advertiser* published his memories of the waterhole:

> there was a beautiful swimming pool just below McMinn's camp where the telegraph station was being built. It was about five chains long, two chains wide, ten feet deep and as clear as crystal. On the far side was a belt of green reeds and rushes, which made the place resemble a spring. Needless to say, the pool was much appreciated. We got our water supply from a well made with two big packing cases let down in the sand and covered with a lid. We were getting very thundery weather at the time, but no rain. One night the lightning was so bad that we could not work and had to cut out the instruments. We were having a quiet game of nap and at 10 pm something seemed to be on the move outside. We went out and saw the Todd coming down bank high. It lasted about two days and gradually subsided, but alas our lovely pool had gone with its bank of green rushes, and nothing remained but a bed of white sand. We were very sad about it. Early in 1875 the soakage was not too good, and we put down a well on the bank. At 25 feet we struck a good supply of water. We did not use it much as some rain came and the soakage was replenished.[3]

About 200 Arrernte people lived in the surrounding area when the telegraph station was built. The white men chose a spot where the Aboriginal people traditionally gathered to exchange goods and prepare for ceremonies.[4] They didn't ask permission to settle there, next to one of the Arrernte's people's most reliable sources of water, but relations between black and white were generally good in the 60 years the station operated, from 1872 until 1932. Todd had made it clear to the men building the OT line:

> Should any natives be met with, they are to be treated kindly but firmly ... No one is to be allowed to visit the natives' camp without special permission ... If a native camp or burial ground is met with, the property of the natives is to be left untouched ... It is most strictly forbidden to fire upon the natives except in the last extremity, when it may become necessary for the safety of the party.[5]

It's remarkable that the Arrernte people were so accommodating towards their uninvited guests who had no appreciation of their spiritual beliefs and sacred places. People and land are intimately linked in the spiritual life of Aboriginal people and the site William Mills chose is criss-crossed by several dreaming tracks. Arenge (a-rung-a), an old hill-kangaroo spirit-ancestor, dug out the waterhole during the creation era. The long, rocky hill running north-south between the Charles Creek and the Todd River is associated with the travels of a caterpillar spirit-ancestor Utnerrengatye (oot-na-run-gat-ya) who came from Mount Zeil, west of Alice Springs. About a kilometre north of the waterhole is Werlatye-Terre (will-utch ta-ra), a women's business site associated with two sisters who travelled through the area during the creation era, followed by some uninitiated boys. Two kilometres south is Tyuretye (chur-it-ja), a wedgetail eagle ceremonial site, as well as a place where the caterpillar spirit-ancestor and the uninitiated boys stopped on their journeys. It includes the junction of the Todd River and Charles Creek, plus the prominent feature named Spencer Hill, after the Melbourne academic Baldwin Spencer who spent years documenting the people's beliefs.

The first stationmaster doesn't make it

It was cloudy, hot and humid at Alice Springs on the afternoon of 28 December 1871 when Ray Boucaut arrived with a party of telegraph operators. Gilbert McMinn had been expecting them but not the sombre news they delivered. One of the operators, Carl Wilhelm Immanuel Kraegen, had got lost on the way and died of thirst in sandhill country a hundred kilometres to the south.[6] The experienced 40-year-old, chosen by Todd to take charge of the Alice Springs station, had perished while travelling with John Mueller and Richard Watson, the men Todd chose to run the stations at Barrow Creek and Tennant Creek.

Kraegen had been at the government's depot at the Peake in South Australia for some time assisting with the transport of materials and rations.[7] Mueller and Watson joined him there on 7 November after a month on the track from Port Augusta. With them were three other telegraph operators destined for the central section of the OT line: Joe Johnston, Ebenezer Flint and Ted Harris. Charles Todd had asked Ray Boucaut to escort them all up the line and deliver them safely to their postings. Boucaut was a surveyor who had pegged the first 400 kilometres of the southern section for contractor Ned Bagot. Benjamin Clarke was also travelling with them. He was responsible for ensuring all the telegraph equipment and batteries were correctly installed between Port Augusta and Tennant Creek and that the telegraph operators were able to work the line properly.

They reached Charlotte Waters safely at the end of November and Joe Johnston remained there to take charge of its new telegraph station. The party was split at this point. The wagons carrying the batteries for Alice Springs, Barrow Creek and Tennant Creek were still some distance down the track and Clarke decided he should wait for them to catch up. Even though Kraegen, Mueller and Watson were unfamiliar with the country to the north, Clarke agreed to let them go ahead to prepare for the installation of their telegraph equipment. He would follow with the slow-moving wagons, Boucaut and the two young operators Flint and Harris. This fateful decision cost Kraegen his life.[8]

The three men left Charlotte Waters on horseback in oppressive heat on 4 December with two extra horses to carry their gear. They had a rough map showing where they could find water but struggled to locate it. By 6 December one of their two packhorses was knocked up and they left him, piling all their things on to the other. They pushed on through taxing sand-dune country and reached the point where the Alice Creek runs into the Hugh River late the next day. There was more than enough water there to meet their needs but none as they went further up the Hugh towards the Waterhouse Range and Owen Springs. Mueller and Watson tried digging a soak in the blazing heat with a tomahawk and knife, while Kraegen held back the thirsty horses. Without a shovel they couldn't go deep enough to reach water.

Kraegen had expended less energy than the other two and volunteered to go on ahead to a spot where their map indicated water. He'd bring some back for the others. He took Mueller's horse as well as his own, in case it knocked up, but failed to return that night. There was no sign of him the next day either. Mueller and Watson wandered in all directions, under a burning sun, for two days, vainly looking for water. Finally, in desperation, on 10 December they shot Watson's mount, cut its throat and drank the blood. That gruesome measure proved unnecessary because later that day they stumbled on a small waterhole that saved their lives. They decided the best thing would be to turn around and head back south to the main party.

They made it to the Alice Creek with their one remaining horse and camped by the waterhole for five nights recovering from their ordeal. On the morning of 16 December they headed a little further south, to the junction of the Hugh and the Finke River where Harley Bacon's depot had been located in the first half of the year. They were within sight of it around 2 pm when they spotted Benjamin Clarke and a telegraph line inspector named Thomas Young approaching from the south.[9] Boucaut and the two young operators Flint and Harris joined them that night. Next day three more men made an appearance: John Loudon and two others with mail for the construction workers up the line.

Kraegen had been missing for over a week by this stage. Thomas Young found his body on 20 December. He was lying on his stomach by a telegraph pole, about ten kilometres from where he'd left Watson and Mueller. Not far away was a waterhole on the Hugh River that would have saved his life if he'd known of its existence.[10] Ironically, a couple of days later the skies opened and rain fell, drenching the sandy ground in which they buried him. The telegraph men built a railing around his grave and engraved a piece of tin, which they nailed to a board for a headstone.

Boucaut, Clarke and the telegraph operators pushed on and spent Christmas Day 1871 sheltering from the rain under a tarpaulin at McClures Springs, a long, narrow waterhole on the Hugh River, south of the Waterhouse Range. It had started raining in the afternoon and fell heavily all night. 'Only thing which reminded us of Christmas' Mueller wrote in his diary, 'was a good plum pudding'. Three days later they rode into Gilbert McMinn's camp with their sombre news.

Carl Kraegen had a wife and three small children in New South Wales. Tragically, Mrs Kraegen died shortly after her husband, unaware of his fate.

Their two daughters and son were brought up in an orphanage. The boy Edward became a telegraph operator like his dad. He went in search of his father's grave in 1926, catching a train to the end of the line at Oodnadatta and then riding a camel north. He wasn't able to find it but he met a travelling missionary who later did and sent him a photo. Carl Kraegen's grandson Frank and his own son John travelled by four-wheel drive from Alice Springs to Maryvale station in 1962 and found the headstone, fallen over but still legible. Nearby were bits of old pole, a broken insulator and tangled wire.[11]

Young Mueller steps up

Benjamin Clarke decided John Mueller should stay at Alice Springs with Ted Harris, rather than going on to Barrow Creek. Richard Watson would work Barrow Creek with Ebenezer Flint instead of going up to Tennant Creek. Clarke himself would take charge of that third station until Todd could send a replacement.[12]

Alice Springs was a much more idyllic place to be posted than further up the line but Mueller was yet to appreciate this the day he arrived. He wrote in his diary: 'Was not very favourably impressed with appearance – sheep had eaten all the grass – nice hole near camp for bathing – only foundation of house finished.' He wasted no time settling in. He built a chook house the next day, 29 December, and had a swim in the waterhole. Then he worked with Clarke setting up the batteries to establish contact with Charlotte Waters. Kraegen's death had cast a shadow over the camp but the men at Alice Springs felt good about completing their part of the line on time. Mueller celebrated by firing off rockets in the evening of 30 December. We can only speculate what the local Arrernte people thought of this pyrotechnic display. Clarke was having trouble with the line but managed to get a message through to Charlotte Waters on New Year's Eve, advising Joe Johnston of Kraegen's death. A thunderstorm that night brought the old year to an end.[13]

Like so many of the interesting characters appointed to the OT line in its early days, John Mueller was young, adventurous and undaunted by the prospect of working in the middle of nowhere. Charles Todd backed Benjamin Clarke's judgement that the 21-year-old could do the job at Alice Springs. He wasn't lacking self-confidence and came from enterprising stock. His father, Ferdinand Muller (who used a different spelling), was one of a congregation of Lutherans who left Prussia, now eastern Germany, with their pastor G.D. Fritzsche, to escape religious persecution from the Kaiser. They sailed from Hamburg on the *Skjold* in 1841 and initially camped in the hills south-east of Adelaide. Ferdinand located land north of Hahndorf suitable for a settlement and 18 families moved there. They called it Lobethal, which means Valley of Praise. He ran the school they established for the next 41 years.[14]

His son was born on 23 March 1850 and used John, the Australian form of his name, in preference to the German Johannes Ferdinand on his birth certificate. He joined the telegraph service as a 15-year-old messenger at Mount Barker in 1865, was a quick learner, and was promoted to junior operator 14 months later. Time in the Adelaide telegraph office and at Mount Gambier followed before Todd sent him up the OT line.

The diary he kept on the trip north reveals a young bloke who liked to drink and party. After being closeted with his sober boss Todd on the afternoon of 27 September 1871, he rushed to the Adelaide railway station where he was farewelled by mates. He managed a few drinks with another group of friends at the docks at Port Adelaide, where he boarded the steamship *Lubra* for Port Augusta with other men bound for the OT line, including Benjamin Clarke. Surveyor Ray Boucaut was waiting for them at Port Augusta with two more young telegraph operators, Ted Harris and Ebenezer Flint. The pubs of Port Augusta got a workout before they hit the road north.[15] John Mueller was a cheery, popular young bloke but his drinking was to become a problem.

Todd visits his wife's spring

New Year's Day 1872 was memorable for the men at Alice Springs. Australia's isolation did not end that day as stipulated in the contract with the British cable company; another eight months elapsed before the northern section of the OT line was completed. However, nature turned on a sight that raised the men's spirits. They saw the Todd River run as rain tumbled out of the skies over its catchment in the hills to the north. The sunburnt country soaked up the water, softening the soil on the riverbank and enabling them to establish a vegetable garden. On the afternoon of 3 January, the line came alive with a message back from Joe Johnston at Charlotte Waters advising that they now had communication all the way to Adelaide. He had passed on the news about Kraegen's death.

That same day Charles Todd boarded the SS *Omeo* and headed north, via Newcastle on the east coast. The government had decided he should go to the Top End and help Robert Patterson move things along.[16] He spent most of 1872 in the Northern Territory, based at the Roper River in the first half of the year. It was near impossible to transport supplies down the track from Port Darwin to Patterson's men, with another wet season in full swing. The country was awash and so they were shipped inland from the Gulf of Carpentaria via the flooded Roper.

Todd took a boat to Port Darwin in April, sailing into the harbour in early May as the dry season was finally dawning. He spent a fortnight there and was able to inspect parts of the line built by contractors Darwent and Dalwood before William McMinn had made the disastrous decision to declare their contract null and void a year earlier. The country had begun to dry out by the time he got back to the Roper. On 13 June he started south towards Adelaide with cadet surveyor Christopher Bagot.[17] They were at Daly Waters on 24 June when Port Darwin transmitted the astounding news that the submarine cable from Java had gone dead.[18] They were camped at Central Mount Stuart when the line was finally completed with a ceremonial joining of the wires near Frew's Ironstone Pond, over 500 kilometres to his north.

Glowing with pride in what they had achieved, Todd continued south, carefully inspecting his new telegraph line as he went. A few days later he emerged from the mulga and made his way across the grassy Burt Plain towards Alice Springs with the magnificent MacDonnell Ranges looming in the distance. Todd reached the waterhole named in honour of his wife Alice before noon on Wednesday 28 August 1872 and inspected the telegraph equipment set up in the south-west corner room of the new stone building that Gilbert McMinn's men had constructed. The submarine cable was still dead so there was no international traffic being transmitted along the wire.

However, his two young operators John Mueller and Ted Harris were ready and waiting.

He had decided that each of the telegraph stations on the central section of the line would have a staff of six men: two telegraph operators, three linemen and a cook.[19] John Loudon, Tom Hanley and and a man named Coles were the first linemen appointed to Alice Springs.[20] Their cook, Robinson, had been a member of Gilbert McMinn's sub-section B team.[21] The linemen's duties were quite diverse and each of the men appointed to these positions over the years was a jack-of-all-trades rather than a trained technician. They repaired damage to the line, did general maintenance around the station, and looked after the station's livestock.

John Loudon was one of the men who had buried Kraegen's body the previous December.[22] Not much is recorded of his fellow lineman Coles but Tom Hanley went on to become one of the longest serving OT workers. He was employed on the line for 40 years until his retirement in 1911 at the age of 65. By that time he was line inspector for No. 8 Line Party, a team of three men travelling constantly on the long track between Oodnadatta and Attack Creek in a light buggy, accompanied by a heavily laden wagon drawn by 10 horses.[23] It took them the best part of a year to complete the round trip. On their way they carried out routine maintenance: replacing cracked insulators; ensuring the lightning rods were in good condition; getting rid of hornet nests that might interfere with the current; and clearing overhanging vegetation, grass and undergrowth to reduce the risk of bushfires damaging the wooden poles.

Todd enjoyed the hospitality of the men at Alice Springs for over a week before continuing on to the Charlotte Waters telegraph station where he received another warm welcome. The station named after his wife quickly assumed a greater prominence than any other, except the terminus at Port Darwin. Strategically located in the heart of the continent, it became the supply depot for the lonely outposts north of it.

7

The line in John Mueller's day

The energetic and thorough superintendent of telegraphs was making plans to improve his OT line even before it was completed in August 1872. To get the wire up and open for traffic as soon as possible, Charles Todd allowed some sections to be built with poles spaced 160 metres apart, rather than the 80 he'd originally specified. Those missing poles had to be added as soon as possible. He was also concerned about the impact termites and bushfires might have in the north and so he telegraphed the chief secretary Henry Ayers when he got to Tennant Creek in July 1872 requesting another 6000 iron poles be ordered from England and delivered to the Roper River depot. His priority was the section from the Elsey Crossing south to Tennant Creek.[1] He was confident the wooden poles would last for some years but thought it most economical to begin replacing them while they still had bullock and horse teams in the north to do the haulage.

The chief secretary agreed and Todd arranged for a number of vehicles, horses and bullocks to be left at the Roper when the northern construction parties left for Adelaide on the *Omeo*. A small group of mechanics and stockmen agreed to stay behind with storekeeper Fred Davies. He had been among the reinforcements who went north on the *Omeo* with Todd in January 1872 and was happy to stay longer.[2] They would service all the wagons and drays and mend the harnesses ready for the new poles arriving the following year.

Surveyor Richard Knuckey sailed from Adelaide on 9 April 1873 with 60 men to carry out the repoling. They worked steadily from June until December 1873 when the wet season forced a break. They completed the work the following dry season and headed back up the line to Port Darwin at the end of September 1874. The bulk of the men, horses and bullocks then caught the steamer *Gothenburg* back to Adelaide, leaving a rebuilt 600-kilometre section of line, much of it continuous iron poles, with the remainder alternate wood and iron.[3] Other parts of the line were steadily improved in the years that followed, either by contractors or the linemen based at the various telegraph stations.[4] The entire line between Southport and Alice Springs was upgraded by 1878, a distance of nearly 1300 kilometres.[5]

Despite the haste in getting it constructed, the OT line worked well from the start but there were doubts about the submarine cable. It was out of action from 22 June until 20 October 1872 and went dead a further 20 times in the first five years, albeit for shorter periods.[6] Consequently, in 1878, South Australia and the colonies of New South Wales, Victoria and Western Australia agreed to pay the British cable company £32,400 a year for 20 years for a duplicate cable. The Queenslanders declined to contribute, along with Tasmania and New Zealand. The new cable was in place by January 1880, with two sections: one from Singapore to Banjoewangi and the second from Banjoewangi to Port Darwin. This eliminated the need to use the Dutch telegraph line across Java. A message could get to London in two to three hours once this second cable was laid to Singapore.[7]

Working on the line

A pair of wires was used when telegraphy was first invented but it wasn't long before people realised they only needed one. The earth could be used to complete the electric circuit, instead of a second wire, and the current is actually stronger when this is done.[8] This discovery substantially reduced the cost of erecting long telegraph lines.

The electric current came from batteries. The ones that Benjamin Clarke carefully escorted up the line to Alice Springs in 1871 were made of glass and called Meidinger cells. They were a variation on the wet cell invented by

British chemist John Daniell in 1836 where zinc metal reacted with a copper sulphate solution. Each one stood approximately 25 centimetres high when fully assembled. Despite their size, they only produced about 1.08 volts, little more than the small AA batteries we use today. So a large bank of them was required to provide the 16 milliamps of current that ran along the OT line. Between 120 and 150 were connected in series at Alice Springs to maintain an electromotive force of 120 V. The actual number depended on how much current leakage there was from the wire with variations in the weather.[9] Maintaining the batteries in good order was a never-ending task for the telegraph station's operators and linemen. They had to keep them clean and regularly replace the copper sulphate crystals.

A morse key is basically a switch that turns the electric current off and on. Learning to send morse code is relatively straightforward but it took special training and a lot of time to learn to receive it, using the equipment installed on the OT line. There was an instrument called a sounder at the receiving end of the line, with a metal armature that clicked rapidly when a message was being sent. It sat inside a wooden box, called a resonator, to amplify the clicks. An electromagnet was the sounder's main component. With each pulse of electricity sent along the line, the iron core of this electromagnet attracted a metal armature until it hit a metal stop. When the current ceased momentarily, a spring pulled the armature back again until it hit another stop. The result was two clicking sounds. The operator interpreted the time interval between the two clicks as either a dot or a dash. A dot was a short time interval, a dash a longer one. As well as sounders, the telegraph stations on the OT line were equipped with a device called a register. It also featured an electromagnet attracting and then releasing a metal armature. However, the electromagnet was connected to a device that made ink marks on a long roll of paper tape. The operator could interpret the space between the marks as either dots or dashes. Todd's men preferred to use a sounder and write the messages down as they heard them, rather than rely on the register. Messages could be lost if the register malfunctioned. However, it was a very handy device in case the office had to be left unattended for a while or if the operator was new to the business and lacking in confidence.

A top operator could transmit at a rate of 35 words a minute but few could 'read' at this speed. The norm was 20 to 25 words a minute. Each operator had his own style of transmitting, which others on the line occasionally learned to recognise, like different styles of handwriting. Almost from the beginning, morse telegraph operators began taking shortcuts to speed up their transmissions, as people do these days when texting on a mobile phone. For example, m x h n y was commonly used in place of merry Christmas and a happy new year.

In 1879, American Walter Phillips published a standardised set of abbreviations, which became known as the Phillips Code. He was primarily interested in speeding the transmission of newspaper reports. Many of his abbreviations were straightforward, such as fri for Friday, mtg for meeting and xps for expense. Others were less obvious such as kaq for king and queen. The Phillips Code established rules for abbreviations. For example, words ending in ous had those letters replaced by the letter x and so famous became fmx.

Benjamin Clarke installed an automatic repeater when he set up the Alice Springs station's instruments at the end of 1871, the only inland station equipped with one when the OT line opened in August 1872; they were installed at other stations before long.[10]

The telegraph operators soon realised the inland weather conditions were generally so favourable that there was no need to repeat every message at each of the stations between the Central Telegraph Office in Adelaide and Port Darwin. Leakage of current was rarely an issue because of infrequent rain or heavy dew. Signals could travel a lot further than the 250 kilometres separating each station and so three of them assumed more importance than the others as time went on: Powell Creek, Alice Springs and Hergott Springs (now Marree), which opened in 1884.[11] Beltana, Strangways Springs, Charlotte Waters and Barrow Creek gradually declined in importance on the southern half of the line.

Telegraph operators in the 19th century were seen as members of an elite and glamorous service but everyday life on the line could be monotonous, especially once automatic repeaters were installed. Dudley Kelsey, who served at various locations in the north from 1880 and 1901, wrote in his memoirs:

Day after day, and night after night, duties and occupations were practically the same. While the staff realised that certain isolation had been overcome, little or no outside news came their way. A single wire crossed Australia, and the line circuit was usually busy night and day, transmitting and receiving cipher messages, which were unintelligible to the staff.[12]

Cipher was used with confidential information but also to reduce the high cost of using the submarine cable. Paying nearly £10 to send 20 words was a considerable impost. The British–Australian Telegraph Company levied a heavy charge of £8 9s for 20 words between London and Port Darwin in 1872; South Australia charged an extra 17s 6d for the use of its line taking the cost to £9 6s 6d. Then there were charges tacked on by the other colonies. A 20-word international message ended up costing £9 8s 6d if it was going to Victoria, £9 12s 6d to New South Wales, and £9 16s 6d to Queensland or Tasmania.[13]

Businesses responded by using codes to reduce the number of words they had to pay for. A number of books were published pertaining to a variety of business situations. A popular one was *Bloomer's Commercial Cryptograph: A Telegraph Code and Double Index-Holocryptic Cypher*, first published in 1874 by the New York firm of D. Appleton & Co. A sentence might be reduced to a single code word. For example, 'camp' meant 'What amount of stock have you on hand?' while 'forehead' meant 'Will a few days delay in shipping make any difference to you?' These messages would be readily understood by the businesses receiving them but meaningless to a telegraph operator listening to the clicking of his instruments.

Charles Todd was a fastidious man who set high standards for the operators at his telegraph stations and established a number of daily routines. Much of the international traffic on the OT line was transmitted at night, given the time difference between England and Australia. However, if there was international traffic during the daytime, it always took precedence over other use of the line, except in cases of emergency.

Each station was expected to ensure their equipment was clean and in perfect adjustment at the start of each day and exchange GM (good morning) with the Central Telegraph Office in Adelaide at 8.30 am. This was done in geographical order, commencing with the southernmost station. At 9.40 am stations sent their daily weather reports to Adelaide, again in geographical order. Another daily function was a time check so clocks could be reset to keep them accurate. This was done at 1 pm each day.[14]

Todd had realised the OT line provided an opportunity, not previously available, to gather weather information from across the continent. In 1873 he made it a duty of all his telegraph operators to take a range of weather readings, several times a day, and transmit them to Adelaide next morning.[15] The data was collated by clerks working under Todd's watchful eye. As a result, from 1877 national weather maps began appearing in Australian newspapers and Australians gained an understanding of national weather conditions for the first time. As well as being acknowledged a leading figure in telegraphy, Charles Todd has been called the father of meteorology in Australia and a pioneering figure in the uncertain science of weather prediction.

The men at Alice Springs acquired an additional responsibility towards the end of John Mueller's seven years in charge. Alice Springs became a post office from 1 January 1878 when a six-weekly packhorse mail service was introduced. Previously people's letters, newspapers, magazines and small parcels were simply entrusted to teamsters or any other reliable person travelling the track. This system worked because the white population of central Australia was still very small. Dissatisfaction soon surfaced because people had to wait three months or more for a reply to a letter dropped at the telegraph station.[16] In contrast, a fortnightly mail service operated between the Peake telegraph station and Adelaide. Alice Springs's handful of hardy residents asked why they couldn't have one of the same frequency. They reckoned they were better off under the old system. Their agitating paid off to a degree and they had monthly deliveries by packhorse by the end of 1879, but waited until 1898 for a fortnightly service.[17]

Mueller's men
The telegraph operators Charles Todd appointed to Alice Springs in the early days were mostly young blokes barely into their 20s. He had faith in these rising stars and it's clear they saw their isolated posting as a great

opportunity, not a hardship, and they repaid his confidence, putting his enterprise onto a sound footing. There was a romance about working on the OT line that captured the imagination of South Australians from the moment the colony secured the contract to build it.

Ted Harris worked with John Mueller at Alice Springs from 1872 until 1875. Nine thousand messages were transmitted along the line during 1873 so Todd sent them a third telegraph operator in August that year: Bill Pounsett, a 21-year-old with a telegraph pedigree.[18] His father was postmaster at Willunga in South Australia. Bill was as proficient with pen and ink as he was with a morse key. A sketch he made in 1876, before he left to marry his Willunga sweetheart Sarah Whitefield, is one of the earliest images of the telegraph station.

Enthusiastic, 19-year-old Frank Gillen replaced Ted Harris in June 1875 and stayed three years, followed by 11 down the line at Charlotte Waters. He came back to Alice Springs early in 1891 as stationmaster and served another eight years. Gillen was one of the great characters of the OT line, developing a genuine affection for the Aboriginal people. He learned enough of the Arrernte language to be able to communicate with them on cultural matters and was renowned around the world by the turn of the century for his pioneering anthropological work.

Another 19-year-old took Bill Pounsett's place in 1876. Ted Johns transferred from the Peake, two stations down the line. The highest point on the main MacDonnell range east of Heavitree Gap is named after him, albeit mispelt Mount John. He left at Christmas 1879 but opted for five years in the Top End, after some recreation leave and a short spell working in Adelaide. He clearly enjoyed his time in the Northern Territory.

Another operator from Mueller's time a long time on the line was Frank Scott. He was just 18 when appointed to Alice Springs in September 1878 following Frank Gillen's transfer to Charlotte Waters. He too thrived on the outback way of life, spending 10 years at Alice Springs and then moving up to Tennant Creek for 12. He finished up working at Barrow Creek, remaining in that area after the repeater station was closed during World War I. He bought the nearby Stirling cattle station and ran it until his death in 1923.

The place soon grows

The OT line was just a narrow corridor through the heart of the Australia in 1872 and the Alice Springs telegraph station a tiny island in Aboriginal land. Stationmaster John Mueller and his five companions lived and worked in their fortress-like barracks. They had an outside dunny but there's no evidence of a bathroom where they could spruce up in comfort and privacy. Being an all male domain, they shaved and washed in the building's courtyard in warm weather and by the stove in the kitchen when it was cold. The only other structures in 1872 were stockyards, Mueller's chook house, and a small store for the linemen located north-east of the main building.

Surveyor Gilbert McMinn left a letter for Charles Todd when he eventually departed Alice Springs for Adelaide in July 1872, after eight months at the new station.[19] Todd, at Tennant Creek, read it when he got to Alice Springs at the end of August.[20] With McMinn's letter were plans for two more stone buildings: a large store, for the station's bulk supplies, equipment and buggy, plus a blacksmith shop for the linemen. The store was completed in 1873 but the linemen had to wait a couple of years for their blacksmith shop.[21] Frank Gillen was given the honour of laying its foundation stone on 6 May 1876. It was built near the well sunk on the western side of the river early in 1875.

The growing white population and the introduction of a regular postal service in January 1878 necessitated better facilities for receiving and distributing mail. A new post and telegraph office was constructed on the southern side of the original building.[22] Moving the telegraphic equipment out of the main building provided extra living space for the staff. The new post and telegraph office was spacious but apparently not a wonderful place to work. South Australian politician Simpson Newland was critical after a visit in 1887.[23] He reported:

> it is cold in winter and hot and ill-ventilated in summer. For a room continually occupied it is about as comfortless as it could well be constructed. In the long cold winter nights it must be miserable work attending to the duties of the office in that poor place. Perhaps when funds are available the Postmaster-General will, with that consideration

for those beneath his rule which actuates him, have some improvement made.

All the buildings constructed at the Alice Springs telegraph station in the 1870s and 1880s were simple and uncluttered. Their proportions – length to height, roof height to wall height, and windows to walls – are in the Georgian style of architecture, the prevailing style in South Australia in the early 1800s. The use of internal space and lack of airflow is in stark contrast to contemporary design. The rooms are a series of boxes joined end to end. There were no open spaces, with one area flowing into another, and no L-shaped rooms. Bathrooms, toilets and laundries were simple structures located away from the buildings. These traditional box-shaped, stone buildings with no eaves had worked well in the English climate but absorbed heat and held it in central Australia. Early sketches and photos reveal there were no verandahs on the original telegraph station building, except on the southern side, until the 1890s. It was a stifling hot box for several months of the year, with no relief at night. The telegraph station staff had better living conditions than most other people in central Australia of their era but life must have been a struggle for much of the year, battling the heat, dust and flies.

Popular and respected, despite a lifelong battle with the bottle

Todd's little outpost at Alice Springs became the focal point of a growing community during the years John Mueller was in charge. Telegraph operators were allowed extended leave after three years on the line and he went to Adelaide for a break in May 1875. One of Adelaide's newspapers reported:

> On the eve of his departure a handsome testimonial was presented to Mr. Mueller by his fellow officers and the employees at the station as a mark of the cordial feeling existing between them.[24]

The paper also reported his return to work at the end of the year:

> Mr J.F. Mueller, stationmaster at Alice Springs, returned to that place on the 9th instant after his six months leave of absence and was welcomed

with rejoicing, in fact the occasion was completely a gala one, and evidently showed the favourable estimation with which Mr Mueller was held by those connected with him on the line. I understand that in addition to his former position he has received the rank of Inspector of the stations as far north as Powell's Creek, besides which he has matured, to a full blown JP.[25]

Official records say John Mueller was in charge of the station until 31 August 1879, but he actually left towards the end of 1878.[26] Todd transferred him to Bordertown in South Australia and he was postmaster there nearly four years. Then he had a spell working as an operator at the Central Telegraph Office in Adelaide. It was a world away from the life he lived at Alice Springs. He resigned from the telegraph service on 31 August 1884 but it's not clear why or what he did next. Maybe it had something to do with his lifelong problem with alcohol. Whatever the reason, he was back in central Australia within a couple of years. Gold was discovered at Arltunga in the East MacDonnells in April 1887 and John Mueller was one of the first men there, taking out a claim late in the year.[27]

A monthly mail service was established between Alice Springs and Arltunga in January 1891. Joseph Harding, who opened the store there, was nominally postmaster but Mueller performed the actual duties.[28] Then, in April 1895, he was appointed mining warden for the goldfields, a position previously held by Mounted Constable William Garnet South. South was posted to Adelaide and recommended Mueller replace him.

> Mr Mueller was once Senior Inspecting Officer on the OTL and afterwards went to Adelaide, where, I regret to say, I hear he became partial to intoxicants but I have known him for the last 8 years on the Algibuckina and Arltunga Fields during which time he has been sober, hardworking and honest and has gained the esteem and respect of all classes.[29]

Mueller did the job for 11 years but on 15 September 1906, Mounted Constable Fred McLeod escorted him south to Port Augusta to face charges of embezzlement. He was convicted of embezzling £49 9s 1d during the

Winnecke goldrush days, 1902–1903. The jury recommended mercy 'owing to extenuating circumstances' but he was dismissed from his position and sent to prison.[30] He served six months in Port Augusta Gaol but then returned to the goldfields in June 1907 as a prospector.

He later became the bookkeeper at Bond Springs station.[31] Cattleman Jim Turner got to know him well in his later years and described him as 'an educated man … and a wonderful conversationalist'. He said Mueller 'enjoyed his liquor, often to excess, a habit which hindered the execution of his duty at times but not his popularity'.[32] He died at Wigley Waterhole, north of the telegraph station, on 1 January 1922 from shock following a fall from a sulky, on his way home from town. He was buried in the Stuart Cemetery in George Crescent, Alice Springs, with kindred spirits from the town's pioneering days. He had never married.

8

The dawn of civilisation
and Christianity

The Alice Springs region is not a desert. It is an area of ruggedly beautiful mountain country whose origins lie in an extended period of earth movement and upheaval 340 million years ago – resulting in the ancestral MacDonnell Ranges with peaks that were once around 3000 metres high. That's twice the height of Mount Zeil, today's tallest point.

Winter days are mild with glorious blue skies though nights can be chilly because of the elevation and dry air. In contrast, summer days are very hot, with temperatures over 40°C from November to March. Even so, the weather is not as debilitating as the tropical north. The rainfall is erratic but there is sufficient to sustain a diverse range of plant and animal life. It's misleading to talk about the average annual rainfall but if you crunch some figures, over a decent length of time, you get 270 mm per year. This is significantly higher than the desert areas either side of Alice Springs: the Simpson to the east and the Great Sandy, Tanami, Gibson and Great Victoria deserts to the west. Even in the driest of seasons there are permanent waterholes in sheltered gorges among the MacDonnell Ranges. Alice Springs is an oasis compared to Uluru (Ayers Rock), 470 kilometres to the south-west. The OT construction parties found plenty of good water if they dug down into central Australia's sunbaked ground. There was grass for stock and gardens could be established, provided they were protected from the extremes of summer heat and winter frost. Company soon arrived.

The Mueller years from 1872 until 1878 were a significant period of change in central Australia. The desert country west of the telegraph line was explored in the hope of finding a stock route to the west coast. Seven cattle stations were established. A large area around the Alice Springs telegraph station was declared a grazing reserve and stocked with 3000 sheep.[1] Work began on a network of trig points so the country could be accurately surveyed and mapped. Scant regard was given to the needs of the Aboriginal people as their traditional lands were usurped. An exception to this was the arrival of a couple of Lutheran missionaries from Germany in June 1877. They set themselves up on the banks of the Finke River, 130 kilometres west of the telegraph station, with the aim of converting the Arrernte to Christianity. Seventeen years earlier John McDouall Stuart had stood on top of Central Mount Stuart, raised the British flag and said 'may it be a sign to the natives that the dawn of liberty, civilisation and Christianity is about to break upon them'. By the Mueller era, their date with destiny had well and truly arrived.

More exploring

Gilbert McMinn undertook a short exploring trip before he headed home to Adelaide in July 1872. He wanted to follow the river running through the Alice and see where it ended up. It soon peters out in the flat, sandy country south-east of Heavitree Gap but then reforms again. Four days riding took him to the dry country John Ross had crossed in his fruitless attempts to find a route for the telegraph line through the East MacDonnells.[2] McMinn realised the dry riverbed Ross named the Todd in December 1870 is the same one that forms in the hills north of the telegraph station he'd just built.

He returned to Alice Springs and packed up his things. Government storeman Harley Bacon was joining him for the trip down the line, having also spent the past few months at Alice Springs.[3] McMinn had work to do on the way to Charlotte Waters. Floodwaters in February had washed away a section of the line where it crossed the Finke River east of Marchant Springs.[4] It was out of action for a fortnight but that was of little consequence because there was still a big gap in the line up north. He organised a work party to erect a tall mast on each side of the river so the telegraph wire could be hoisted higher above the riverbed, out of the reach of future floods. Several tonnes of rock were packed around the base of the masts to hold them firmly in place.[5]

Gilbert McMinn and Harley Bacon had company on the Finke on 12 August 1872. Explorers Ernest Giles and Samuel Carmichael from Victoria arrived that evening after a long day's ride from Charlotte Waters telegraph station and a week enjoying the hospitality of stationmaster Joe Johnston. With them was a young man named Alec Robinson who'd joined them at the Peake, plus a small Scottish terrier dog called Monkey.[6] They intended riding all the way to the west coast. 'For several years previous to my taking the field', Giles wrote in his journal, 'I had desired to be the first to penetrate into this unknown region, where for a thousand miles in a straight line, no white man's foot had ever wandered'. He had hopes of 'finding an overland route for stock through central Australia' to the settled districts of Western Australia.[7]

The early 1870s was a remarkable period of desert exploration and Giles' small party was the first to venture into the heart of the continent since the completion of the telegraph line. The well-educated, 37-year-old Englishman was something of a romantic and his writing is rich in descriptive detail, colourful phrases, and literary quotations. However, he was no slouch in the bush. He had the resilience, tenacity and dogged determination of Scotsman John McDouall Stuart. The Victorian Government botanist Baron Ferdinand von Mueller raised a considerable amount of money for the Burke and Wills expedition of 1862 and launched another public appeal for Giles.[8] It failed dismally but he was happy to contribute cash from his own coffers, if Giles would collect specimens of new plants found along the way. The rest of the money for the expedition was provided by Giles and Carmichael themselves, along with Giles's Melbourne businessman brother-in-law George Gill.[9] After camping a while with McMinn and Bacon, the three explorers and Monkey headed north through the sand dunes towards Chambers Pillar. They then followed the Finke River to its source in the West MacDonnell Ranges. When he was at Charlotte Waters, Giles learned that Aboriginal people called it Larapinta, meaning snake.[10]

Giles, Carmichael and Robinson were the first white people to visit many of the places that are now major tourist attractions in central Australia. They saw the tall palm trees that have grown in the Finke Gorge and nearby Palm Valley since the days when dinosaurs roamed the area. They reached the striking mountain ranges immortalised in the watercolours of Hermannsburg painter Albert Namatjira. They didn't get to the stunning Ormiston Gorge area because the high water level in the picturesque Glen Helen Gorge prevented them from going further north. Instead, they ventured west and Giles mapped the two high peaks which Baron von Mueller later named Mount Sonder and Mount Zeil. Mount Zeil is the highest point in Australia west of the Great Divide.

Early in September they reached Gosse Bluff, the spectacular circular feature where a comet crashed to earth 140 million years ago. By the end of that month they were only 100 kilometres from the border of the Northern Territory and Western Australia. It had been tough going through areas of thick waterless scrub, constantly annoyed by biting ants and persistent flies, their horses with tender feet from the constant brushing against prickly spinifex grass. It had rained on a couple of occasions but the sandy ground quickly soaked up the water. Faced with the prospect of more of this dry and difficult country further west, Giles retreated. 'I was only too thankful to get out of this horrible region', he wrote. They headed south where the country was more open 'though the spinifex was as lively as ever'. While it was clear the region wasn't going to provide the stock route they were hoping for, there were many signs of Aboriginal people living there and being sustained by the country. Giles wrote: 'They do not seem to care much for our company; for ever since we left the Glen of Palms, these cave-dwelling, reptile-eating Troglodytes have left us severely alone.' Later he remarked 'the natives were about, burning, burning, ever burning; one would think they were of the fabled salamander race, and lived on fire instead of water'.[11]

Two weeks more riding took them to an extensive area of good grassland that Giles named the Vale of Tempe. Thirteen years later, in 1885, geologist Dr Charles Chewings would establish a cattle station a little east called Tempe Downs. As they progressed south, Giles noticed the continued fall of the country and wondered if the lay of the land might eventually lead them to a considerable watercourse or freshwater basin. Instead they came to an enormous expanse of salt, preventing further travel to either the south or west. Giles decided to name it Lake Mueller after his patron, the Baron. In the distance, beyond the great salt lake, they could see a high peak that he wanted to name Mount Ferdinand. However, Ferdinand von Mueller declined both these honourable mentions and insisted they be Lake Amadeus and Mount Olga 'in honour of two enlightened royal patrons of science' – Philip Amadeus, the King of Spain from 1870 until 1873, and Queen Olga, the wife of the German King Karl I of Württemberg (who had raised Ferdinand von Mueller to a peerage in 1871).[12]

With the days now very hot, the horses in poor condition and no signs of freshwater, Giles realised he wasn't going to reach the west coast. He would need to try a different course if he was to make it. It was time to retreat east to the safety of the telegraph line. At the beginning of November, they found abundant supplies of water in a range, which Giles named after his brother-in-law George Gill. The spectacular tourist attraction Kings Canyon is located at the edge of this range but the Aboriginal people living in the area made it clear to these first white visitors they were not welcome. Heading further east they came across a considerable number of Aboriginal people who were familiar with white people and approached them in a friendly manner. They reached the junction of the Finke and the Hugh rivers on 21 November 1872. The place was a hive of activity early in the previous year with Harley Bacon's depot and store located there. Now there was just the screeching of pink and grey galahs and the far-carrying *creee-creee* of the black cockatoos.

Company for Christmas

Giles was surprised to meet Colonel Peter Egerton Warburton, his son Richard and five other men at Charlotte Waters at the end of November. They were on their way up the OT line with the same objective as him: finding a route from the heart of the continent to the west coast. He also learnt that South Australian surveyors William Christie Gosse and Edwin Berry were up the track in advance of Warburton, Gosse's brother Henry plus six others. They also planned to head west. Intercolonial jealousy was strong and the

Victorian was concerned that the South Australians might beat him. Both expeditions had camels, which Giles now realised gave them a good chance of success.

The Gosse expedition was government-funded. The South Australians had decided to explore the country west of the telegraph line and offered Alfred Woods leadership of it. He'd been in charge of the five parties building the central section of the telegraph line but declined the offer to lead this new expedition. Gilbert McMinn's name was then suggested. Knowing he was on his way down the line to Adelaide, the Commissioner of Crown Lands telegraphed a message to Charlotte Waters on 13 September.[13] The government wanted the expedition to start at once but McMinn, like Woods, wasn't keen on the idea of heading off into the unknown in the extreme heat of summer. Both men were also uncomfortable with the decision to hire some of Thomas Elder's camels. Neither of the men liked working with the animals or their Afghan handlers.[14] So, 30-year-old Gosse got the nod instead.

He was a native of Hertfordshire, in England, who migrated to South Australia as a young boy in 1850 with his father, a doctor. In 1859, at 17, he became a cadet in the surveyor-general's department and was an experienced surveyor when given command of this new venture. Colonel Warburton had wanted the job, just as he'd been keen to lead the ill-fated Burke and Wills expedition of 1861–1862, and he wasn't happy when the Victorians had snubbed him.[15] The influential Thomas Elder had promoted his cause in Melbourne and he had some local support but there were others who doubted his ticker and his competency. Events in 1873 would lend weight to this view.

Peter Egerton Warburton was a man with a colourful history. Born in England in 1813, he'd served as an officer of the British Army in India for two decades, rising to the rank of major. In 1853 he sailed to South Australia and took up the position of commissioner of police. However, he was dismissed in 1867 after a secret police inquiry found 'that other employment more congenial to his habit and tastes should be found'.[16] He was given command of the South Australian volunteer military force with the rank of colonel.

Warburton was miffed when the South Australian Government chose Gosse over him but, undeterred, he convinced Thomas Elder to sponsor a private expedition and Walter Watson Hughes also chipped in some cash. Hughes was another prominent South Australian property owner and, like Elder, saw the prospect of acquiring more pastoral land.[17] Warburton's would be the first Australian expedition to depend solely on camels. While Gosse had camels, he was also taking horses, a wagon and dray. Warburton and his son Richard left Adelaide on 21 September 1872 and their party reached Alice Springs four days before Christmas. The Gosse group had arrived a few days earlier. The lonely telegraph station was all of a sudden not so lonely.

From that point the situation became somewhat farcical as the two rival expeditions hung around Alice Springs for a couple of months, sitting out a wet season that never came, while trying to avoid each other. Neither Warburton nor Gosse had any real understanding of the climate in the centre of the continent. They wrongly assumed the tropical wet season always extended as far south as the MacDonnell Ranges. They were misled by the exceptional rains that had fallen the previous summer when Todd's men were completing the telegraph line.[18]

Neither party headed towards Western Australia until April 1873. While they sat biding their time, five other adventurous outfits were heading up the line towards Alice Springs. There were two mobs of horses bound for the Top End, two herds of cattle destined for central Australia, plus a very large mob of sheep.[19] Life at the frontier was about to dramatically change.

Cattle and sheep invade the Arrernte lands

Leases were granted for the Northern Territory's first cattle stations, Undoolya and Owen Springs, on 1 April 1872, nearly five months before the final joining of the telegraph wires. OT line contractor Ned Bagot was given the right to graze cattle across a huge area of the MacDonnell Ranges from Temple Bar east, almost to the Ross River. His wealthy South Australian friend Joseph Gilbert was granted land south and west of Bagot's lease. In neither case was the slightest consideration given to how this might affect the Arrernte people.

They initially sent 450 cattle north but had over 3000 head on the two leases by October 1874.[20] Bagot's son Ted and stepson Jim Churchill Smith drove the first lot of cattle north while Bill Gilbert was on the track behind them with a herd for his father's lease. They set off from South Australia in June 1872 and were in close contact all the way. The above average rainfall made it an ideal time for overlanding stock.

They ran into the congenial Charles Todd west of Lake Eyre in October and spent an evening camped with him. The superintendent of telegraphs was heading towards Beltana telegraph station in the Flinders Ranges after his months in the north.[21] The cattle were grazing on the Stevenson River in November when Gosse's party passed them on the way to Alice Springs. The young stockmen moved over the border to Charlotte Waters in time for Christmas and stayed there until mid January 1873.

There they were overtaken by two mobs of horses bound for the Top End. Tom Hamilton, with William Hassel and four others, brought 120 from Bringalbert station in western Victoria. Travelling behind were 230 horses belonging to Thomas Elder, with boss drover Fred Campbell and eight other men.[22] Ted Bagot, Jim Churchill Smith and Bill Gilbert saw a fair bit of Campbell as they headed north at more or less the same pace, up the Finke River and then along the Hugh towards Owen Springs.

Bagot and Smith reached the MacDonnell Ranges in March 1873 and camped at Emily Gap with their cattle, not knowing how sacred the place is for the local Arrernte people. Fred Campbell and his horses were further east at Jessie Gap, another significant place.[23] The men had no concept of Aboriginal spirituality or any inkling that what they had done was akin to taking livestock inside a cathedral.

The stepbrothers looked around for a site suitable for a homestead and chose one, north-east of Emily Gap, near Mount Undoolya.[24] Bill Gilbert camped near the telegraph station when he arrived in April but moved his cattle west to Owen Springs once he'd selected a site for his homestead. He couldn't stick around the telegraph station because a large flock of sheep was heading that way.

As part of the provisioning of his repeater stations, Charles Todd had contracted Alfred Giles in November 1872 to take 5000 sheep north. He knew the Northern Territory as well as any white man, having travelled with John Ross in 1870 and 1871. He was an enterprising man and decided to supplement his income by taking 100 horses north as well to sell in the Top End where gold had been discovered.[25] The sheep were from Thomas Elder's Beltana station in the Flinders Ranges, like the camels Warburton and Gosse were using. The bulk of them would be located at Alice Springs, with smaller numbers distributed to the other telegraph stations between Charlotte Waters and Yam Creek. The sheep made it safely to Alice Springs in the second half of May 1873 but there were no fences to contain them.[26] The telegraph men had their work cut out keeping an eye on them all and ensuring they didn't fall prey to the local dingo population.

Spare a thought for the Arrernte people. They had shown great forbearance in the months since the telegraph men arrived and commandeered some of their choice real estate. The horses, bullocks, camels and sheep that came with the construction parties drank their precious water and stripped the vegetation from their land. The arrival of more livestock was tough enough for the Arrernte without the added shock of seeing them overrun the sacred Emily and Jessie gaps. Now Alfred Giles had brought thousands more sheep. The Arrernte watched these hard-hooved animals trample the banks of their creeks and foul the water in a way the soft-footed native wildlife had never done. These strange animals, with their voracious appetite, were also having a profound impact on the food and medicinal plants they relied on. It is no wonder skirmishes occurred in the years that followed as the Arrernte tried to assert their rights to land and protect their sacred places.

Gosse climbs Ayers Rock but Warburton nearly perishes

Gosse and his men finally left Alice Springs on 23 April 1873, heading 150 kilometres up the telegraph line and then west to avoid the MacDonnell Ranges. Gosse hoped this might be a suitable route to Perth but it was waterless country and the horses suffered badly. The good pastoral land around Alice Springs quickly gave way to sand plains covered in prickly spinifex. The last week of May brought good falls of rain but it disappeared into the sandy ground.

The men were on half rations by the middle of June and so Gosse was pleasantly surprised when he came across the tracks of three bullocks near Mount Liebig, halfway between the telegraph line and the Western Australian border. He and his brother managed to track down the runaways but it was a while before the beef made it onto the barbecue. The three determined animals had walked 250 kilometres and Gosse wrote in his journal:

> we came upon the bullocks in splendid condition. They are three that were lost from Alice Springs just before we arrived there, and were always supposed to have made down the country. This has evidently been their head quarters, and they might remain here for years before anybody found them. I think it would be a pity to disappoint them after they had shown such a decided taste for exploring.[27]

Gosse didn't like his chances of getting to the west on their current latitude, so decided to head down to the well-watered George Gill Range that Ernest Giles had found the previous year. Pushing further south, they managed to find a way across the eastern tip of Giles's great expanse of salt, Lake Amadeus. On 19 July they reached a remarkable monolith, which Gosse named Ayers Rock, after Sir Henry Ayers. 'This rock', he wrote, 'is certainly the most wonderful natural feature I have ever seen'.[28] Riding around it, he found a deep, permanent waterhole he named Maggie Springs. From there, he and cameleer Kamran became the first white men to climb the rock.

Looking east from the summit, they could see Mount Connor, named after another South Australian politician M.L. Connor; to the west was Mount Olga, which Giles had spotted from Lake Amadeus the previous year. Some mountains were visible to the south and Gosse named them the Musgrave Ranges after Sir Anthony Musgrave, who had succeeded Sir James Fergusson as governor of South Australia in March. His men became the first tourist group to visit Mount Olga on 8 August.

Gosse was now ready to have another crack at pushing through to the west coast. They headed towards the Mann and the Tomkinson ranges, located near the point where the borders of the Northern Territory, South Australia and Western Australia meet. They travelled into Western Australia roughly 50 kilometres south-east of where the Aboriginal community of Warburton is located today.[29] Ahead of them was a waterless expanse of sandhills and spinifex. It was September, temperatures were rising and Gosse realised he had no prospect of getting his animals and vehicles through this inhospitable country. It was time to head back east to the safety of the telegraph line. They set off towards the Musgrave Ranges and followed the Alberga River from there as it flowed east out of the Musgraves to join the Macumba River. They reached the telegraph line in mid December 1873 at a point north of present-day Oodnadatta. Gosse had not achieved the government's objective but he and Edwin Berry had mapped a huge area of central Australia.

Warburton's expedition was a debacle even though he made it to the coast and got a couple of awards for his trouble. The Colonel left the telegraph station on 15 April 1873, eight days before Gosse.[30] He'd decided to skirt along the northern side of the MacDonnell Ranges to Haast Bluff but this route was as dry and challenging as the one Gosse had selected 100 kilometres further north. He quickly abandoned the idea of going south-west to Perth and surprisingly opted for Sturt Creek in the north-west of the continent. It was the desolate point Augustus Gregory reached in 1856 when he'd landed on the north coast and followed the Victoria River inland.[31]

The camels plodded through arid country and by early June they were east of Lake Mackay, one of a number of dry salt lakes straddling the border of Western Australia and the Northern Territory. Things were not looking good. Warburton employed a novel strategy for finding water in the desert: kidnapping Aboriginal people. His men spotted a woman with a small boy and an infant on 18 June. They grabbed the boy and put him on one of the camels but he showed no fear, chattering away in his own language. They made signs to indicate they needed water and he pointed west. They headed in that direction and soon found native wells, staying there for over a month.

They continued west, through the heart of the Great Sandy Desert, at a ponderously slow pace, which seriously depleted their provisions. Warburton remarked in his journal on 9 August: 'Truly this is a desert!' The Aboriginal people in the region had the good sense to avoid contact with the white men.

At the end of August they captured a young Aboriginal woman and tried to get her to reveal the location of her people's waterholes; she gnawed through the rope they used to tie her to a tree and escaped. They followed her tracks and luckily came upon a depression with fresh water and ducks.

Proceeding further west, they captured another Aboriginal woman on 4 September. Warburton described her as 'a howling, hideous old hag'. They tied her thumbs behind her back and put a rope around her neck and attached it to a tree. In response, she wailed all night and in the next two days led them backwards and forwards over many sandhills. This exhausted the long-suffering camels and Warburton's patience. He let her go though he admitted he 'was savage enough to have hung her up to the first tree'. The Colonel had little respect for the Aboriginal people but they showed considerably more generosity of spirit. On 8 October he and his son Richard ran into nine armed men while looking for water. After an initial period of tension, they lowered their spears and took the two white men to their camp and gave them water and a wallaby.

As the daytime temperatures rose in the latter part of the year, Warburton resorted to travelling at night, but the men were tormented by ants when they tried sleeping during the day. The Great Sandy Desert took its toll on both men and animals. Unlike John McDouall Stuart who always looked after his horses, Warburton pushed his camels very hard. Only two of 17 survived the journey. His scant regard for these creatures was on a par with his disrespect for the Aboriginal people.

They finally managed to crawl out of the desert in early December 1873 at the Oakover River, east of present-day Port Hedland. Warburton was so weak by this time he had to be tied to a camel; his son was also pretty crook. They got to Roebourne, the oldest town on the north-west coast, on 26 January 1874. While they could rightly claim to be the first to travel from central Australia to the west coast, they were lucky they lived to tell the tale. The Colonel was awarded the Gold Medal of the Royal Geographical Society and made a Companion of Saint Michael and Saint George. However, his expedition achieved little and his backers Thomas Elder and Walter Hughes didn't get much for their money.

His Victorian rival Ernest Giles forged a better reputation in the annals of Australian exploration. He teamed up with an old London schoolfriend William Tietkens and eventually found a way to Perth. He was not deterred after failing a second time in 1873–1874. That expedition cost the life of a member of his party, Alfred Gibson, who perished in an area of desert now bearing his name. Giles tried again in 1875, showing the persistence of the dogged Scotsman John McDouall Stuart. It was a case of third time lucky but on a route well to the south of Alice Springs. He set off early in May 1875, with camels courtesy of Thomas Elder, and rode through the Woomera region and the picturesque salt lakes north-west of Port Augusta to the Nullarbor Plain. He reached Perth on 10 November 1875. These days the transcontinental railway more or less follows the route he took. His seven-man party included Alec Ross, the son of Charles Todd's OT line explorer John Ross. Giles didn't rest on his laurels. Remarkably, he set off again on 13 January 1876, travelling up the Murchison River and then heading back east through the Gibson Desert where he'd failed before, reaching the Peake telegraph station on 23 August 1876.

German missionaries set out to save Aboriginal souls

In early August 1876, the telegraph station staff had a visit from Georg Heidenreich, a Lutheran pastor from Bethany in South Australia's Barossa Valley. His church had decided to establish a mission on the Finke River 130 kilometres west of Alice Springs and Heidenreich was charged with getting it established. Waiting down the track at Dalhousie Springs were two young Germans, Hermann Kempe and Wilhelm Schwarz, who'd sailed from Hamburg on 21 July 1875 to minister to the unsuspecting Arrernte people. Both the men had a trade in addition to being ordained ministers. Kempe was a blacksmith and Schwarz a baker.[32] They'd set off from Hahndorf in the Adelaide Hills on 22 October 1875 unaware it would be June 1877 before they reached their destination.

They'd made their way north through the Flinders Ranges and across the stark gibber plains on the western side of the dry Lake Eyre in the fierce heat of summer. This country was unlike anything they had experienced in their native land. They had some respite in May 1876 at the stark spot called Angle Pole, near South Australia's Neales River. To their great relief rain fell on the night of 9 May and kept falling steadily for the next two days. It was a godsend for them and their support crew of drovers and teamsters. Their entourage included 2420 sheep, 33 horses, 24 head of cattle, five dogs, four hens and a young rooster. They'd lost 900 sheep, down the track near William Creek, from lack of water and the burning heat.

They reached Dalhousie Springs, 70 kilometres south-east of Charlotte Waters telegraph station, on 29 May 1876 to find several groups of stockmen and cattle taking refuge near the mound springs. Despite the recent rain, drought gripped the north of South Australia and it was clear they would have to camp here too, until more rain fell. It was while they were stuck at Dalhousie that the intrepid Heidenreich decided to ride north and check out the mission site. He left on 28 June with missionary Kempe and one of the drovers, Gottlieb Haemmerling.

With a dray to carry their provisions and only a couple of horses, they made it safely to the Owen Springs cattle station three weeks later, on 19 July. There they met Archie Conway who'd managed the station since its founder Bill Gilbert returned to Adelaide in September 1873. They spent a fortnight exploring the land the government had allotted them to the west and were delighted with the quality of it. They got back to Owen Springs on 5 August. Heidenreich left Kempe and Haemmerling there for a couple of days while he rode east to the Alice Springs telegraph station. He wanted the operators to send a message down the line for him, enquiring when supplies they'd ordered would arrive at Dalhousie. In the meantime, missionary Kempe did some blacksmithing work for Archie Conway.

It wasn't until January 1877 that drought-breaking rains fell over the northern parts of South Australa. On 9 April the missionaries and their stock left Dalhousie, where they'd been stuck for more than 10 months, and reached their destination two months later. On Friday 8 June 1877, they began digging a well on the site, on the northern side of the Finke River, where they had chosen to live. Hermannsburg Mission was finally established. Reinforcements from Germany arrived in April 1878, including a third missionary Louis Schulze, plus Dorothee Queckenstedt and Wilhelmine Schulz, the fiancées of Kempe and Schwarz. They were the first white women to live in central Australia. Like Kempe and Schwarz, Louis Schulze also had a trade, as a tailor. The unsuspecting Arrernte were set to get clothes as well as religion.

Carving up the country: Charles Winnecke's trig stations

On 13 July 1877, a couple of weeks after pastors Kempe and Schwarz began building their new home west of Alice Springs, eight men left Adelaide on another mission. The South Australian Government had decided to send another surveying party to central Australia and put surveyors Henry Barclay and Charles Winnecke in charge of it. They reached the Alice Springs telegraph station on 16 November 1877.[33]

In the five years since the telegraph line was completed, wealthy southern investors had shown interest in the grazing potential of the region. The surveyors' first task was to establish a network of trigonometrical stations on elevated positions in central Australia so that cattle station boundaries, mining leases, etc. could be accurately mapped. Their second task would take them further afield. Ernest Giles, William Christie Gosse and Colonel Warburton had ventured into the desert west of the OT line in the early 1870s. Now it was time to examine the country east of the line. For this reason, the surveying party was officially tagged the Herbert River and North Eastern Exploring Expedition.

Trig stations are reference points whose latitude, longitude and height are known. The men made a start with Trig Hill, the rocky outcrop on the north side of the telegraph station. Calculating its latitude was straightforward but Barclay and Winnecke needed to know the exact time to work out its longitude. So Charles Todd transmitted accurate time signals up the line from Adelaide. With this done, Barclay split the party. He and four others headed north-east on 31 January 1878, towards the Queensland border. His aim was to find a route to the country along the Herbert-Georgina River, which was attracting squatters. Queenslander William Landsborough had come across this river in December 1861, while searching for Burke and Wills. Once there,

Barclay intended surveying the land and accurately determining the eastern boundary of the Northern Territory. He left the other three men behind to continue working in the Alice Springs area.

Winnecke climbed to the highest point on the range west of Heavitree Gap on 1 February 1878 to set up a second trig station. Undaunted by the summer heat, he climbed to the highest point on the eastern side the following day. He named them Mount Gillen and Mount Johns after John Mueller's two young telegraph operators, Frank Gillen and Ted Johns. Winnecke and his assistants established 50 trig stations across a wide area of central Australia in the next two years.

Barclay didn't make it to the Herbert-Georgina River. He followed the sandy beds of the Hale, Plenty and Marshall rivers but ended up in waterless country east of the Jervois Range. Provisions were running low by the end of May, two of the men were in poor health and Barclay was struggling with an internal injury he suffered in February. His horse had fallen on him, driving the butt of his rifle into his side. He got back to Alice Springs in late June and returned to Adelaide, leaving Winnecke in charge of the expedition.

Winnecke had no success on his own attempt to reach the Queensland border in the second half of 1878. Suffering from scurvy, he turned back after failing to find water at a soakage in the Tarlton Range, which Barclay had assured him was permanent. The men got back to the telegraph station in November and spent three months there waiting for supplies to arrive. The surveyor-general directed them to try again but this time to go up the OT line all the way to Tennant Creek and then head east across the Barkly Tableland. They left Alice Springs in February 1879 and got safely to their destination in September. They did not return to the Alice Springs telegraph station until December 1880. After a month spent there recovering, they began their journey home to South Australia on 7 January 1881. On his way south Winnecke carried out a check survey of the OT line. The work he'd done in the previous three years was crucial to the mapping of central Australia, facilitating white settlement and the carving up of the country the Aboriginal people thought belonged to them.

9

'The Giant of the Interior'

Ernest Ebenezer Samuel Flint was one of the original operators Charles Todd appointed to man the OT line. He was born in Richmond, Victoria, in 1853 and known by his second name. He was only 17 when he left Adelaide in September 1871 bound for Barrow Creek, blissfully unaware of the horrific events in store for him at that lonely outpost, near the geographical heart of the continent, a couple of years later. John Mueller was meant to take charge of the station but Todd transferred him to Alice Springs after Carl Kraegen perished in December 1871. Richard Watson went to Barrow Creek instead. Ebenezer Flint was destined to spend 16 eventful years on the line, the last nine as post and stationmaster at Alice Springs. He died there in tragic circumstances in 1887 with his young wife by his side.

Watson and Flint took up their posting in January 1872, living and working in a hut while Stephen Jarvis built them something more substantial. Jarvis was the former manager of the Mount Margaret pastoral run near Lake Eyre and sub-overseer to surveyor Alfred Woods who built the section of the line running through Barrow Creek. His stone masonry work has stood the test of time and the telegraph station still stands today, beside the Stuart Highway, 285 kilometres north of Alice. Jarvis finished the building shortly before their boss Todd visited on 16 August 1872, on his way south to Adelaide. An unnamed correspondent for the *South Australian Register* was on hand that day. He wrote an article for the paper describing:

a good substantial stone building, almost in the centre of Australia ... The white ensign is flying gaily in front, a flock of sheep are browsing quietly at the foot of Forster's Range, some well-fed horses are scampering about full of life and mettle, and a number of bullocks in the finest condition are looking peacefully on. In fact, as far as the country is concerned, a Stationmaster here might be another Rasselas in his Happy Valley; but at present the loneliness and isolation of the place must be very trying.[1]

Samuel Johnson's book *The History of Rasselas, Prince of Abissinia* was a popular fable about happiness, published in 1759. The telegraph station at Barrow Creek was designed as a potential fortress and just as well because the place was no Happy Valley when the local Kaytetye (kai-titch) people attacked it 18 months after Todd's visit.

The Barrow Creek 'outrage'

James Stapleton was the acting stationmaster at the time, relieving Richard Watson who had gone south to get medical treatment for scurvy. Stapleton was from Montreal in Canada and had worked on telegraph lines in Canada, USA and Central America.[2] He set up the telegraph instruments on the northern section of the line during the construction phase. Todd appointed him stationmaster at Katherine but he didn't enjoy the oppressive climate and was keen to return to his wife and four young children in Adelaide. In November 1873 he agreed to relieve Watson at Barrow Creek for 12 months, which enabled him to leave Katherine before the wet season.

The Canadian had a pet monkey named Jacko when he was based at the government's northern depot, 200 kilometres south of Port Darwin, in 1871.[3] One day it got off its chain and was found in the storeroom, pulling the corks out of medicine bottles, smelling each one and pouring the contents onto the floor.[4] Jacko's later life has not been recorded in the annals of Northern Territory history. It seems he didn't accompany Stapleton to Barrow Creek.

The evening of Sunday 22 February 1874 at Barrow Creek was very hot. Stapleton took his violin and sat on the verandah with the other staff and police trooper Sam Gason who had arrived at the station eight days earlier.[5] Around 8 pm a number of the local Kaytetye warriors crept down the gully behind the building and attacked. The Canadian was speared through the groin from close range. He was badly wounded but able to get inside the building. Lineman John Frank didn't make it to safety. He was speared through the chest and died soon afterwards.[6] Assistant operator Flint copped a non-fatal spear wound in the thigh while trooper Gason was hit by a blunt object thrown by one of the Kaytetye men. Jemmy, a young Aboriginal worker from the Peake in South Australia, was pulled into the building through a window after receiving three severe but non-fatal spear wounds. Lineman Alexander Murdoch, blacksmith James Maddock, and Chinese cook Si Jin were relatively unscathed. Grabbing their weapons, the men fired off a volley of shots, hitting a number of their attackers. Gason later said: 'There is not the slightest doubt that some of the natives were mortally wounded in the affray.'[7]

Exactly why the Kaytetye attacked that night is unclear but the resentment must have been building for some time. Watson had tried to keep the people at a distance but the Canadian showed confidence in them and supplied the old people with rations, as Todd had given his stationmasters the authority to do. Earlier in the day, around 11 am, a number of Kaytetye men had come to the station and asked for flour but were told only the sick and infirm, and those who worked, were entitled to it. Around 7.15 pm some boys and young men came and asked again for flour. They were told to come back in the morning. Most left but four hung around including one called Umpajama. Stapleton had endeavoured to make the Kaytetye useful by employing them. He asked Umpajama if he would accompany one of the linemen on a trip up the track; the young man agreed. Meanwhile, other Kaytetye men crept up on the station and attacked from the other side.

Despite being wracked with pain from his injury, Ebezener Flint was able to get word of the attack to telegraph operators at Alice Springs from where it was flashed to Adelaide. Charles Todd was soon advised and went to the Central Telegraph Office along with Dr Charles Gosse.[8] Dr Gosse's instructions on how the spear wounds should be treated were conveyed to Flint in morse code.[9] The Kaytetye warriors returned to the telegraph station at 7 am next morning but remained about 500 metres from the building. The men inside fired four shots and a couple of Kaytetye were seen to fall.

Todd reported the incident to Chief Secretary Arthur Blyth, and Commissioner of Police George Hamilton ordered punitive action. He sent a message to Gason telling him to secure the services of teamster Jack Bond and five of his men who were on the track south of Barrow Creek, heading north. Further help was available up the track from Tennant Creek stationmaster Charles Tucker and two of his linemen. The commissioner directed police trooper Fred Born, based at the Peake in South Australia, to obtain volunteers and assist Gason, but they didn't arrive until the end of March.

John Frank was buried at 9.30 am on Monday morning. Stapleton's condition deteriorated during the day as blood poisoning set in. He had a perforated bowel and there was discharge of both blood and faecal matter from his wound. In the afternoon Todd sent his carriage to North Adelaide to collect Mrs Stapleton. The folklore soon developed that it was the dying man who tapped out his final message to his wife. According to one account, he asked the others to lift him over to the morse key and transmitted the words 'God bless you and the children'.[10] He died at 9.45 pm that night.

There was another incident next day, Tuesday 24 February. Ebenezer Flint sent a telegram to Todd saying:

> At 1 pm natives attempted surround station. Three shots fired, killing one native. Fires all round station. Expect another attack. Strict guard kept. Please hurry relief.[11]

It arrived unexpectedly on the Wednesday evening when a stockman named Cowan and two others turned up at the station, on their way north with cattle.[12] Next day they went back down the track to tell Jack Bond and his five teamsters what had happened and warn them of the possibility of an ambush. Cowan's men had been with Bond's at Tea Tree Well that morning.[13] Charles Tucker and his two linemen reached Barrow Creek on the Thursday with W.T. Cook and two of his overlanding party. They were travelling north and happened to be with the telegraph men when Tucker learnt of the attack. The six of them covered the 130 kilometres from Dixons Creek in a little over 24 hours. They encountered armed Kaytetye men at Taylor Creek on their way and shots were fired.[14] Bond and his teamsters reached Barrow Creek the following Monday with Cowan's men. The next day Gason headed off with a party to scour the surrounding countryside and locate those involved in the attack. They shot several Kaytetye people at Taylor Creek. More were killed in the Hanson River near Central Mount Stuart in early April. Gason himself admitted to 11 being shot during and after the 22 February attack; other reports indicate up to 50 were killed.[15]

The graves of Frank and Stapleton can be seen today outside the old telegraph station at Barrow Creek but there are no tombstones engraved for the Kaytetye people who died. The events of 22 February 1874 and their aftermath were a significant turning point in the history of central Australia, with a hardening of attitudes towards Aboriginal people. An editorial in the *South Australian Advertiser* gives an insight into the emotions they stirred:

> We are glad that the Government have taken measures to deal with the difficulty at Barrow Creek ... This is the only way in which moral superiority can be maintained, and without that the residents at the Stations on the line would be in perpetual danger ... We can hardly expect that many arrests will be made, but a punishment will doubtless be given to the blood-thirsty rascals, which will be remembered for years to come. A heavy blow well struck now may prevent the striking of many blows in the future. We hope Trooper Gason is not hampered by too many instructions.[16]

Flint takes charge at Alice Springs

Ebenezer Flint recovered from his injuries and remained at Barrow Creek four more years. Todd clearly had a high opinion of him because he put him in charge at Alice Springs after John Mueller left towards the end of 1878. Frank Gillen called Flint the 'Giant of the Interior' in the diary he kept during his journey up to Alice Springs in 1875 to begin his own epic 24 years on the OT line.[17] It's unclear if he was referring to Flint's reputation, his size or both. There are no photos of him, to indicate one way or the other.

Ted Johns and Frank Scott were Flint's assistant operators when he took over at Alice Springs. Scott was there throughout Flint's eight years in charge. Ted Knight moved down from the north to replace Johns when he left at the end of 1879. His family has an interesting history in the Northern Territory. His architect father John George Knight was secretary to the government resident at Port Darwin from 1873 to 1875, as well as accountant and supervisor of works. He was subsequently chief warden of the goldfields, and filled a variety of other positions before becoming stipendiary magistrate, and finally government resident himself. In 1884, he built the town's first two-storey house, overlooking Port Darwin. He called it Mudville on the Sea but it became known as Knight's Folly. William Andrew took Ted Knight's place in April 1883 and Alice Springs acquired a fourth telegraph operator, John McKay, in 1884.

Two additional stone buildings were constructed during Ebenezer Flint's early years at Alice Springs: a separate house for the stationmaster and another building for the linemen.[18] The second one later became a battery room and meat store. With plenty of space now available for his staff and their equipment, Flint was able to make the original line party hut, in the north-east corner of the complex, available to Mounted Constable John Shirley in 1879.[19] He was the first policeman based at Alice Springs. The only police presence in central Australia up until then was at Charlotte Waters but the authorities decided it was time to beef it up. They also reopened the police post at Barrow Creek in June with the appointment of Mounted Constable William Garnet South. There was no policeman stationed there after Sam Gason left in February 1876.[20] Having a base at the telegraph station allowed John Shirley to communicate easily with the police inspector at Port Augusta but his main camp was south of the station, at a spot called Middle Park. He erected yards and bough shelters for his mounts near its semi-permanent waterhole.[21] Police stations, in the contemporary sense, were not built in central Australia in those days because the constables lived a life of constant patrolling.

Surveyor Charles Winnecke drew a detailed plan of the Alice Springs telegraph station in 1880, showing a grave on the eastern side of the river, seemingly the burial place of Thomas Fergusson whose death at the telegraph station on 19 January 1876 was reported by the *South Australian Advertiser*.[22] The paper gave no information about what happened or why he was there.

His death highlighted the need for a cemetery at Alice Springs and Flint had one built on the western side of the telegraph station. Fifty-two-year-old bushman Frank Hansen was the first person buried there, following his death from acute bronchitis on 1 November 1886.[23]

The missionaries at Hermannsburg struggle to save souls

The missionaries at Hermannsburg initially had more success increasing their own numbers than recruiting Arrernte people to Christianity. On the 19 March 1879 Wilhelmine Schwarz, the wife of Pastor Wilhelm, gave birth to a daughter Karoline Rosine Dorothea. She was the first white child born in central Australia. Twenty-two months later, their fellow missionaries Hermann and Dorothee Kempe gave thanks to God for the safe arrival of their little boy Johann Friedrich Georg. Heinrich and Catherine Juergens's son Hermann Friedrich Wilhelm followed in July 1881. Nine more children were born at the mission between 1882 and 1886.

Converts were harder to come by. The Arrernte mostly stayed away from the mission for the first couple of years while central Australia experienced above average rainfall. They continued to move around the MacDonnell Ranges and their adjoining country, as they'd done for millennia, hunting game and gathering their staple food and medicinal plants. Their traditional life had not yet been disrupted to the extent experienced by their countrymen further east at Alice Springs.

The missionaries had more success with their farming endeavours. In August 1879, the Commissioner of Crown Lands Thomas Playford asked Ebenezer Flint to go out to Hermannsburg and report. He had heard of cereal crops and other produce grown there. Flint found a number of solid buildings had been constructed, the main one being of stone, 'divided into three suites of apartments for the accommodation of the three resident missionaries, with their respective families'. His report said:

> The usual requisites of a sheep and cattle station are also to be seen, such as substantial sheep and cattle yards, woolshed, and large paddock recently fenced in. An attempt has been made by the missionaries to

grow cereals this year ... and judging by the result a most successful experiment it has proved. It must be borne in mind, however, that the past year has been a most exceptional one for rains, no such rainfall being experienced since 1872; and it remains to be proved whether in an ordinary season ... wheat, etc, can be produced. Of this the missionaries seem very confident, and intend next year laying down 100 acres of wheat, barley, etc. Should their prognostications be fulfilled, the time is not far distant when residents in Central Australia will be able to produce their own flour at less than one-half its present cost.[24]

Flint found only nine adult males living at the mission and was told the number fluctuated between three and 50. However, the situation changed as the good years of the late 1870s gave way to the drought years of the mid 1880s. Then the western Arrernte relied more on the mission for rations and also protection from police and pastoralists, retaliating to an increasing incidence of cattle spearing. Still, it was not until May 1887 that the missionaries baptised their first converts to Christianity.[25]

Flint and Shirley look for Ludwig Leichhardt

Policeman John Shirley was transferred to Barrow Creek in 1882 and William Willshire took his place at Alice Springs in August that year. Before he left, Shirley and Ebenezer Flint explored the country east of Alice Springs in May with an Aboriginal interpreter called Paddy and two Undoolya stockmen, Harry Price and F. Godlee. Their venture had a twofold purpose: to recover stock that had wandered off, and look for traces of Ludwig Leichhardt's lost expedition, one of the great unsolved mysteries of the time. It had been an issue of considerable interest to Todd and the men of the OT line from the time the construction parties set off into the unknown in August 1870.

In April 1848, Leichhardt and his brother-in-law August Classen left the Roma district of Queensland to cross the continent to the Swan River settlement in Western Australia. There were five or six men with them, depending upon which source you read, and they had 50–70 bullocks and 13–20 mules. No conclusive evidence of their fate and that of their livestock has ever been found. In March 1866, the *South Australian Register* published a letter about the matter from Stephen Jarvis who was managing South Australia's northernmost cattle station at that time.[26] It was headlined 'Leichhardt's Probable Fate' and said Aboriginal people had told him three months earlier of a massacre of white men at a river '30° east of north, from Mount Margaret head station'. The incident supposedly happened quite a few years earlier, when his informants were young, and Jarvis thought the white men might have been Leichhardt's party.

The inference was that the massacre occurred on the eastern side of the Simpson Desert. This was well east of the route chosen for the OT line but Todd asked his people to keep an eye out for any signs of Leichhardt as they worked their way through the centre of the continent in 1870 and 1871. Later, in October 1880, he wrote a long article entitled 'The Fate of Leichhardt', which was published in several Australian newspapers and evoked wide interest across the country.[27] In it Todd said:

> The fate of Leichhardt, and the rumour of one or more of his party living amongst the natives in the interior, were often discussed during the construction of the overland telegraph; and the late Mr. Jarvis, who for several years prior to 1870 had charge of the Messrs. Levi & Co's stations at Mount Margaret and the Peake, informed me that the natives in that part of the country had told him that a party of whites were murdered by the blacks many years ago, some distance east of the Dalhousie Springs, in the direction of the Mulligan River.

Todd ended his article by saying:

> In conclusion, I would suggest the exploration of the country between the Dalhousie Springs and the Mulligan as the most likely course to lead to the discovery of traces of poor Leichhardt and his followers. I need hardly say that any assistance this department can give to following up any clue as to the fate of the explorers will be readily and heartily given.

Todd subsequently received a letter from Ebenezer Flint at Alice Springs. Aboriginal people had told local cattleman Bill Benstead a similar story to the one Stephen Jarvis heard in the 1860s. According to Flint:

A native told Mr. Benstead, manager of the Undoolya cattle station, that a small mob of cattle was running on a creek some three days' walk (say 70 miles) from Love's Creek, 40 miles east of Undoolya head station, or 52 miles east of Alice Springs; and that some 50 or 60 miles east of that again there is a creek, on which a party of whites had been killed when he (informant) was a boy, about twenty-five years or more ago. He states that the natives on this creek killed the whites and their cattle. He volunteered to guide a party to the spot.[28]

Surveyor Charles Winnecke was winding up his three years work in central Australia when Flint wrote to Todd. It is safe to assume that Flint discussed the fate of Leichhardt with him at one time or other when the survey party were camped at Alice Springs. In 1878, Winnecke had come across some old dray tracks heading west along the Sandover River. He followed them for over 100 kilometres and examined them again when he was back there in May 1880.[29] There's nothing in his journal saying he thought the tracks were Leichhardt's but apparently he believed they were. He was unaware that the German didn't have a dray.[30]

Flint asked Todd's permission to go to the area with Bill Benstead, saying the journey would only occupy a few weeks. Todd approved but it wasn't until May 1882 that Flint was able to get away and investigate the story. Benstead had resigned as manager of Undoolya by this time and gone south to marry his fiancée Triphena Rains, who had waited patiently for four years, and John Shirley took his place.

The two men rode out to the Undoolya homestead and set off from there on 14 May 1882 with tracker Paddy and stockmen Price and Godlee. They went beyond the Ross River and Giles Creek, which drain into the Todd River roughly 100 kilometres east of Alice Springs, and five days later arrived at the Illogwa Creek. It runs in a south-easterly direction out of the ranges into the northern Simpson Desert. They came across a number of the wayward cattle, now quite wild, and the stockmen had no luck rounding them up. On Monday 25th the men met three Aboriginal men, relatives of Paddy, who acted as interpreter. Flint asked if they knew of any white men travelling through that area in the past. They went further east but turned back on 1 June having reached sand-dune country south of the Jervois Range. Flint telegraphed a report to Todd when he and Shirley were back at the Alice Springs telegraph station on 9 June:

I beg to report my return to station. Turned back through scarcity of water, lat 22° 45', long 136° 35'. About 100 miles east met friendly tribe of natives (Jerakwa), who corroborated the information as to the white men dying in that vicinity many years ago, and that the natives of the next tribe (Jerypoodna) could show me the spot. These tribes are on hostile terms at present; therefore they could not escort me into their opponents' country. The most valuable part of the information received from these natives is that they have given me some distinct idea of how long ago it is since the deaths occurred – a thing I was unable to accurately get at before owing to the inability of natives to convey a particular number of years past to a white's intelligence. I first met with two members of the Jerakwa tribe, men who were about twenty-five years of age, and these gave me to understand through an interpreter that the whites' deaths occurred before they were born. Shortly afterwards a grey-bearded native joined, and, pointing to him, they said that when he had just undergone the operation of being made a 'young man' these deaths took place. As this ceremony takes place when the lads are about fifteen years old and his present age is from forty-seven to fifty-two, the deaths of these whites may be reasonably supposed to be concurrent with Leichhardt's. They further informed me that at the time the Jerypoodna natives exchanged portions of blue blankets and tomahawks with them for weapons, &c. I then pushed on, but after travelling about eighty miles without seeing any traces of natives I reluctantly turned back through absence of water and running out of meat. Saw the wild cattle mentioned by the Alice Springs natives, but were unable to get near enough to shoot one for a fresh supply of meat. Had I obtained this I should have made another attempt to get amongst the Jerypoodna tribe by a more northern route. I firmly believe I was within reach of some clue of Leichhardt's fate. Country traversed useless for pastoral purposes, being very poorly grassed, and after leaving the Ross Creek, did not see a single permanent stock water, although by following the MacDonnell Range sufficient can be obtained at short distances for a lightly equipped party. Traces of iron tomahawks in natives' possession seen as far east as I reached. Journal, maps, &c, by post.[31]

John Shirley left Alice Springs in July 1882 for Barrow Creek, to replace Mounted Constable William Garnet South, but he died the following year in tragic circumstances. In October 1883, Harry Readford from Brunette Downs station on the Barkly Tableland was reported missing. Shirley formed a search party with seven other men and went looking for him. However, they got into difficulty in dry country in November and six of the men, including Shirley, died of thirst. Ironically, the man they were looking for was later found safe and sound. Readford, or Redford as he was sometimes known, had achieved notoriety in 1870, stealing a thousand cattle from Bowen Downs station near Longreach in Queensland and taking them to South Australia. Readford was the inspiration for the character Captain Starlight in Rolf Boldrewood's classic 1888 book *Robbery Under Arms*, first published in serialised form in the *Sydney Mail* between July 1882 and August 1883.

The first white woman at the telegraph station

The confidence Charles Todd showed in Ebenezer Flint was justified. He managed his responsibilities well and was highly regarded as the senior public servant and government representative in central Australia. In 1886 he responded to a request from John Langdon Parsons, the government resident in Darwin, to compile a detailed report on the non-Aboriginal population of the region, stock numbers, the potential for a horse-breeding industry, agricultural difficulties, and other problems associated with the uncertain rainfall. Parsons commended him on the quality of it.[32]

Flint became the first married man in charge of the Alice Springs telegraph station when he wed 21-year-old Florence Clementina Madeley; her brother George was a businessman at Port MacDonnell in South Australia. It's unclear how and where the couple met. The *South Australia Register* published a wedding notice on 21 February 1887:

FLINT-MADELEY, On the 26th January, at the Congregational Church, Alma-road, St Kilda, by the Rev. E. Handel Jones, Ernest E.S. Flint, J.P., Inspector of Telegraphs, South Australia, youngest son of Ebenezer Flint, of Brockley, Kent, late of Victoria, to Florence Clementina, youngest daughter of the late John Madeley, of Solihull, Warwickshire.

Flint didn't get back to Alice Springs with his new wife until late in May 1887.[33] While still on his honeymoon, he twice gave evidence to the Transcontinental Railway Commission in Adelaide in March.[34] It was set up in January to consider the best way to complete the railway from Port Augusta to Port Darwin. Work had begun in 1878 and rails were laid to Hergott Springs by December 1883. Surveyors pegged out a town four kilometres south of the springs and it was proclaimed Marree on 20 December 1883.[35] The first train steamed in with government supplies on 6 January 1884 during a raging dust storm.[36]

However, it was painfully slow progress from then on as South Australian politicians haggled about how to fund further work.[37] Governments were keen to see the expansion of both railways and telegraphy but not keen to reach into their own pockets to find the cash. While many South Australians believed their government should borrow money to build their great northern railway, others favoured its construction by private enterprise in return for land grants.[38]

The line was open for traffic to Coward Springs, 100 kilometres north of Marree, at the time Ebenezer and Florence were married. A month later the tracks were laid to Strangways Springs, south-west of Lake Eyre, and were used by the newlyweds in April on their way to Alice Springs.[39] Strangways Springs had grown from a telegraph station and sheep run to a little township. They found Chinese traders running a store and bakehouse, a bush pub was open to quench the thirsts of the railway workers, and there was a butcher, blacksmith and saddlery.[40]

The rest of their journey was a long, dusty buggy ride that took a couple of weeks. Ahead of them on the track was Graham Stewart, the superintending surveyor from the Engineer-in-Chief's department. He and his brother had left Strangways Springs early in April, with a string of 14 camels, to report on the feasibility of extending the railway line all the way to Burt Creek, 50 kilometres north of Alice Springs. They expected to be away for seven months determining the most suitable route in the country north of the Peake. It had been very dry the last couple of years but recent rain made travel along the parched track easier. Stewart submitted three progress reports in July, September and November 1887.[41] He recommended that the railway be laid to Alice Well and then go directly north to Alice Springs via the Ooraminna Range, rather than following the telegraph line westwards along the Hugh River, to Owen Springs.

Also on the track to Alice Springs at that time was Simpson Newland, a prominent member of the South Australian Parliament and chairman of the Transcontinental Railway Commission. He wanted to see for himself where the railway might go after it reached the Peake. He was travelling in a buggy driven by the legendary Joe Harding, a former teamster and manager of Crown Point station. Riding with them was an Aboriginal youth called Jim. Newland wrote of him, 'the silence of that boy is as the silence of the tomb'. They left the Peake after the Stewart brothers, at the end of April. Joe Harding clearly impressed his distinguished passenger. Newland extolled:

> It is not too much to say that Mr Harding is known to every inhabitant of the north from Hergott to Barrow Creek. To him everything is fit and beautiful, and as we jog along he expatiates upon the virtues of bush, herb or grass. Not a soul do we meet but he is accosted as an old friend, and not a horse is wanted that he will not lend.[42]

Joe Harding was two when he came to Australia with his English parents. He worked as a teamster between Port Augusta and the Peake from 1867 and later extended his operations further north. His bullocks and horses were contracted to carry government rations to the various telegraph stations and he hauled iron poles when Charles Todd began replacing the original wooden ones. By 1883 he had the mail contract between the Peake and Alice Springs. It was a monthly service using packhorses. He invested his money in cattle enterprises and, later still, stores and a couple of hotels.[43]

Newland was complimentary about Alice Springs in his report, declaring it 'undoubtedly the most interesting of all the stations on the overland line'. He was not, however, overly impressed with the telegraph station's garden:

There is an attempt at gardening, inasmuch as a piece of ground is enclosed and a pump erected over a shallow well adjoining, from which water is laid on. With soil, water, and climate in favour of the production of most vegetables and many fruits, the result appeared to me disappointing. Surely where so many are employed it would pay to keep a good gardener. The actual amount of rations saved by a continuous supply of vegetables would be considerable, to say nothing of the health of the community. It is a pity that something was not done years ago in planting vines and fruit trees, as well as attention paid to a kitchen garden, in a locality like this. Perhaps the authorities will take the hint and give instructions to have the matter attended to without further delay.[44]

Florence Flint was the first white woman to live at the Alice Springs telegraph station but her stay was brief. Her new husband died suddenly from rheumatic fever on Sunday 17 July 1887 and was buried in the little cemetery whose construction he had organised. He was the second person buried there. His obituary in the *Adelaide Observer* said:

He had been suffering from rheumatism for the past fortnight and was supposed to be getting on favourably. On Saturday he seemed to be a little better, but towards night began to wander in his mind and died at Alice Springs of acute rheumatism on Sunday morning about 6 o'clock. Dr. Gardner had prescribed for the deceased, and the medicine was made up at the station. Mr Flint had been married only seven months, and had his wife with him. No danger was anticipated, and therefore the news of his death came as a shock to the officers along the line and those engaged in the Adelaide office, as he was so universally respected. The funeral took place on Monday morning.

Telegraph operator Walter Randall had spent some time relieving at Alice Springs that year. He told the paper:

The unfortunate result is all the more to be deplored on account of his having only been recently married, and only arrived at his station about six weeks ago. The greatest sympathy is felt with Mrs Flint in her sad bereavement, she having arrived in the colony from England in December last only, and soon after her marriage accompanied her husband to Alice Springs, where buildings have just been commenced for private residence. It is expected that Mrs Flint will return to England as soon as her health permits, the sudden death having been a severe shock to her system. The sad occurrence has cast a gloom over the whole district, where he was universally respected and esteemed.[45]

Mount Ebenezer in the Basedow Range in the south of the Territory was named after him.[46] Some prospectors named Florence Creek in the East MacDonnell Ranges after her.[47] Florence eventually remarried in England on 26 April 1893, to Alan Bell, the son of a minister of religion.

10

Trouble brewing on the frontier

The industrious drover Alfred Giles stayed in the Top End after he delivered the sheep Charles Todd asked him to take north in 1873. Towards the end of the following year he received a telegram from his father saying Todd wanted him to shepherd another 5000 north. He promptly headed down the track and reached Charlotte Waters in late February 1875. There he heard about the sinking of the steamship *Gothenburg* in a cyclone off the north Queensland coast. The catastrophe sent shock waves through the Territory. Over 100 people had perished, including a number of the Top End's most prominent citizens. The ship hit the Great Barrier Reef on the evening of 24 February, a week after it left Port Darwin on one of its regular runs.[1]

Giles continued south towards Mount Margaret where the flock was grazing, along with 500 goats.[2] A bloke called Cotton had brought them up from Beltana but managed to lose 500 sheep on the way. Giles, unimpressed, went all the way down to Beltana searching for them and sent Cotton packing when he got back to Mount Margaret. Giles was a forthright character and he had a low opinion of this bloke. He took the sheep north to Alice Springs where the ewes dropped their lambs in a camp he set up on the southern side of Heavitree Gap.[3]

The first Northern Territory cattle stations, Undoolya and Owen Springs, were firmly established by this time on the traditional lands of the Arrernte people.[4] The arrival of the sheep in 1875 coincided with the first sale of cattle from central Australia. Drover Tim Nelson was taking 75 head north along the OT line to a butcher on the Pine Creek goldfields.[5] Alf Giles passed the bullocks near Barrow Creek in June and moved on to the Davenport Range. His decision to camp on Sutherland Creek, south of the Devils Marbles, was a mistake. He and his shepherds got a rude shock when they awoke next morning to find nearly 600 animals dead or dying. They'd camped on exactly the same spot, infested with poison pea, as the Milner brothers in 1870. Giles was aware the Milners had lost sheep but didn't know exactly where and what plant they ate. Warned of the danger, Nelson was able to drive his horses straight through the area without problem.[6]

Two of Giles's shepherds had a confrontation with Aboriginal people north of Tennant Creek and shot two men. There was another incident at Newcastle Waters when they brazenly drove the sheep through the middle of an Aboriginal camp. Not surprisingly, the Aboriginal people responded and the shepherds used their horses and stockwhips to drive them off. An entry in Giles's journal says the men's bodies were painted with red ochre and pipe clay, which suggests they'd gathered for ceremonies when the sheep appeared in their camp.[7] A new era had begun in the Northern Territory. Charles Todd had directed his OT people to maintain peaceful relations with the local Aboriginal people. Now there was now a new breed of men on the frontier. Clashes between black and white became inevitable once cattle and sheep were introduced, instigating a contest for land and water resources.

Several cattle stations were established in the 1870s and early 1880s, all by southern pastoral companies with money to invest and expectations of good profits. There were no winners. All these companies were destined to lose large sums of money, while the traditional owners of the land watched their waterholes emptied, their native vegetation denuded and their food sources decline.

The first of the new stations was Idracowra, on the lower Finke River. The South Australian firm F. & A. Grant and F.W. Stokes held the lease. Stephen Jarvis and Allen Breaden drove their first draft of 500 cattle up from South Australia and the animals were grazing along the Finke by May 1876.[8] Next came livestock for a large tract of land leased in 1876 to Englishman Edmund

Parke and a young stockholder named Charlie Walker. Parke was from Dorset in the south of England and he gave the name of his family estate Henbury to the land on the southern side of the James Range.[9] There were 400 cattle on it by August 1877.

In the same year, Ned Bagot, who had lost a fortune investing in goldmining in the Top End, sold Undoolya to Andrew Tennant and John Love of Port Lincoln. The new owners appointed a young stockman named Bill Benstead to manage it and their neighbouring property Loves Creek, acquired in 1876.

Grant and Stokes acquired a second property, Glen Helen on the headwaters of the Finke, and Allen Breaden delivered its first cattle at Christmas time 1878. Early in 1875 the company had sent Richard Warburton to check out this area west of Alice Springs. He was the son of explorer Colonel Peter Warburton and a member of his father's tortuous crossing of the Great Sandy Desert in 1873. He retraced the expedition's tracks along the northern side of the MacDonnell Ranges and penetrated into the heart of the ranges via Dashwood Creek, west of Mount Zeil. He explored the headwaters of the mighty Finke, which begins as four small watercourses: the Crawford, Davenport, Ormiston and Ellery creeks.[10] They merge to form central Australia's greatest river. He named the picturesque Glen Helen Gorge after Alexander Grant's eldest daughter. Allen Breaden managed Glen Helen station until early 1884 when James McDonald took over.

Dr Browne's great overlanding expedition

Alf Giles remained in the Top End for an extended time following his second overlanding trip with sheep for Charles Todd. He was at Barrow Creek in 1877, heading south to get married, when he received a telegram from his brother Arthur in Adelaide. It said that prominent South Australian pastoralist Dr W.J. Browne had asked Arthur to be part of an expedition to take sheep and cattle to the Katherine River; Alf Giles was also invited to participate. Surveyor Alfred Woods, who'd been in charge of the government parties building the central section of the OT line, would be leader and would scout ahead of the stock to determine the best route.

Alf Giles wired Dr Browne to say he would come to Adelaide for a meeting. In December they agreed he would overland 12,000 sheep, in three mobs of 4000, while his brother Arthur would drive 3000 cattle north in lots of 500.[11] It was an extraordinary venture. Some of the stock were purchased from a station on the Darling River in New South Wales, taken down the Murray River to Morgan and then north to Burra. Forty men were engaged from over 300 applicants and a large number of drays and wagons were loaded with supplies. This included a scoop to hollow out trenches then lined with tarpaulins to water the sheep. There was also a well-sinking team and a blacksmith equipped with forge, bellows and anvil.

Giles set off with the sheep in April 1878 and reached Charlotte Waters in August. He was welcomed by Frank Gillen, who'd recently taken charge of the telegraph station after three years at Alice Springs. They stayed while the sheep were shorn, from 13 August until 30 October 1878. His brother Arthur had hit the track north with the cattle eight months before the sheep but was overtaken between Charlotte Waters and Alice Springs. That stretch of country was very dry and so the brothers decided to park the cattle on the Finke River while the sheep went ahead to the MacDonnell Ranges. Alf Giles got them there safely and established a camp on Colyer Creek, north of the Alice Springs telegraph station.

He made no mention of it in his memoirs but it's likely Giles attended the inaugural Christmas race meeting at Alice Springs in 1878. The MacDonnell Range Turf Club was formed that year and its annual Christmas meeting became the biggest social event in central Australia in the years to come.[12] His men had been on the road for a long time and would have jumped at the chance to escape the monotony of their daily life and go on a spree. Sly grog sellers were regularly travelling the track, ensuring there was plenty of alcohol available to wet the parched throats of the local stockmen.[13]

Giles had a tough time getting the sheep from Colyer Creek further north to the safety of Annas Reservoir. They set off in the fearsome heat of mid January, travelling at night for nine days. The sheep went without water the whole time.[14] Fortunately, rain fell while they were at Tea Tree Well and he was able to send a message to the men on the Finke saying it was now safe to bring the cattle up the track. The leading mobs of sheep reached the Katherine River in June 1879 where Giles established Springvale station, the first pastoral settlement in the Top End.

An incident had occurred four months earlier resulting in a policeman being posted to Alice Springs. While he was shearing at Charlotte Waters, Giles received a message from Paul Foelsche, inspector of police in the Top End. Foelsche wanted him to find three Aboriginal men willing to go north and serve as black trackers. Two of them didn't make it. They were killed while camped at Temple Bar in February 1879. Some Arrernte men lured them away and their bodies were later found with spear wounds and their heads bashed in.[15] Ebenezer Flint, stationmaster at Alice Springs, had immediately called for a police presence. An Adelaide newspaper quoted Flint saying 'if the blacks find they can murder civilised natives with impunity, although under the protection of the whites, they will not be long in directing their attention to the whites themselves'.[16] In April 1879, Mounted Constable John Shirley was posted to the telegraph station.

More cattle and sheep arrive in central Australia

Late in 1879, teenager George Gilmour took 500 young cattle to land east of Henbury and started Mount Burrell station. It included a long section of the Hugh River. He'd checked out this country in 1877 on behalf of his father and partners Hendry and Melrose, sheep farmers from South Australia's Barossa. Young George built a homestead on the Hugh, 15 kilometres up river from the present-day Maryvale homestead, and stayed on to manage the new station. While they initially put cattle on the land, Gilmore, Hendry and Melrose intended making it a sheep station. They sent 1500 merino ewes up the track in 1881, but it was a year before they reached their destination.[17]

Also heading north was a well-to-do South Australian named Charles Chewings.[18] The 22-year-old set out with two camels from Beltana on 28 September 1881 heading into the drought-stricken north of South Australia to explore the grazing potential of the West MacDonnell Ranges. His wealthy father, sheep grazier John Chewings, had died two years earlier but provided him with both a good education at Adelaide's Prince Alfred College and a practical knowledge of the land. Charles Chewings reached Charlotte Waters at the end of October and enjoyed the hospitality of telegraph operators Gillen and King, plus Ebenezer Flint who was down from Alice Springs at the time. Chewings, full of confidence, took his camels north to Engoordina station on 'the famous underground river', his description for the Finke. The summer heat was building as he made his way along its tributary the Hugh River, to George Gilmore's homestead. The two got on like a house on fire. Chewings's next stop was Owen Springs, followed by Hermannsburg where he was welcomed by the missionaries, as visitors were in those days.

He managed to get the camels through Glen Helen Gorge despite its large, permanent waterhole. From there he explored the stunning, mountainous country to the north-west with Allen Breaden, manager of Glen Helen station. Chewings was back at Hermannsburg in early December intending to go on to the George Gill Range but his camels had sore feet. Instead, he followed the Finke downstream to Henbury station. The flies were dreadful and opening his cans of bully beef and eating was a challenge. George Gilmore, at Henbury when Chewings arrived, invited him to spend Christmas at Mount Burrell. The two celebrated New Year by climbing a hill at midnight with all the firearms they could muster and firing a volley of gunshots. Chewings commented that Mount Burrell had never heard the like before, and the Aboriginal people camped at the station bolted.

The final stage of his great trek was exploring the Palmer River area in early January 1882 with Charlie Walker, part owner of Henbury. Like the Hugh, it's a tributary of the Finke and they traced it to its source west of Henbury. They also explored a creek flowing into the Palmer. Chewings named it the Walker and said the country along its banks was 'clothed in some of the finest grasses I have ever seen, with cotton and saltbush as thick as they can grow together'. Well satisfied with what he had seen, he headed back towards Beltana and then to Adelaide.[19] He managed to establish his own station on the Walker Creek in 1885, in partnership with a number of Adelaide investors. He called it Tempe Downs and appointed Fred Thornton to manage it after Bob Coulthard stocked it with cattle.[20]

The sheep-breeding venture on Mount Burrell didn't prove a success. It cost too much to transport the wool to Adelaide where it failed to fetch a high price because the grease attracted so much Red Centre dust. They realised they weren't going to get a return on their money, got rid of their sheep in 1884 and sold the property to Thomas Elder the following year. He decided to breed horses and ship them to India for the army's remount service.[21] Elder purchased neighbouring Owen Springs in 1886 for the same purpose, following the death of its pioneering lessee Joseph Gilbert and the winding up of his estate.

The 4000 cattle grazing on Owen Springs were transferred to the unstocked Bond Springs lease of William Willoby, John Gordon and A.M. Youl, immediately north of the Alice Springs telegraph station reserve. Willoby was a pastoralist from Bordertown in South Australia; Gordon a solicitor and the mayor of Strathalbyn. They appointed the former teamster Tom Williams as their manager. Willoby and Gordon also held the Crown Point lease at the southern end of the Northern Territory, with two other partners. One was a member of the Heywood family, prominent South Australian pastoralists, and the other was former teamster Joe Harding. Harding managed to get 7000 cattle on Crown Point by 1886.[22]

Conflict between black and white in the 1880s

These pioneering cattlemen and sheep farmers were lured inland by the unusually good conditions that existed in the 1870s. It was a decade of above average rainfall, culminating in 1879 with one of the wettest years central Australia has ever recorded. Explorers Stuart, Ross, Giles, Gosse and Warburton encountered extensive areas of desert country in their travels but the Alice Springs area was different: good country clothed with a fine array of native grasses, saltbush and palatable shrubs on which livestock thrived. The German missionaries at Hermannsburg had success growing vegetables and sowing cereal crops in the late 1870s. They were confident their mission could be self-sufficient and their produce impressed Ebenezer Flint when he inspected the mission in late 1879. However, the good seasons didn't persist into the next decade. The mission's wheat, barley, oats and maize withered when rainfall failed in 1880 and cattlemen throughout the region realised the carrying capacity of the land was not what they'd come to believe.[23]

The first half of the 1880s was a sustained dry period in central Australia, with 1883 a particularly tough year. The 214 consecutive days without rain was the longest dry spell since the OT line was built. The sun beat down from cloudless skies, drying out the soil and shrinking waterholes. The stations had made no water improvements apart from sinking wells at their homesteads, so stock was confined to the same natural waters the Aboriginal people relied on for their survival. The new animals impacted on the plant foods the Aboriginal women had harvested for generations and the game the men hunted. They avoided the newcomers whenever they could in the 1870s, but by 1883 they were feeling threatened.

Still more cattle were brought to central Australia in that very dry year. An astonishing 5000 were on their way for a new station being established on virgin country north of Alice Springs. This was the largest movement of livestock since Dr Browne's sheep passed through in 1879. It was organised by Bill Benstead, now working for the newly formed Barrow Creek Pastoral Company.

The year 1883 marks a significant change in black–white relations in central Australia. Afterward there was increasing hostility between the old landholders and the new, as life got tougher for everyone. Instances of cattle spearing steadily increased and station managers in outlying areas felt vulnerable. The inevitable reprisals followed and the 1880s became a dark period in the region's history with many Aboriginal people dying at the hands of cattlemen and the police.[24] Bill Benstead's new station in the Barrow Creek area soon became embroiled in violence.

Benstead had come to central Australian six years earlier. He was a remarkably self-confident young man destined to carve a significant reputation as a cattleman, mining speculator and publican.[25] His parents migrated to New Zealand from Wales when he was four. Within a year they moved to South Australia, settling at Melrose near Mount Remarkable. Young Bill started work at the age of 11, on a hawker's cart belonging to a local firm. His passion for horses led him to become a stockman for Thomas Elder a couple of years later. He excelled in all aspects of the work and thrived on the continual round of mustering cattle, draughting, weaning, branding and grading stock for market, as well as being an excellent horse breaker. He resigned in 1877 when 22 and was in Adelaide for a break when he met Triphena Rains, just 16, and they became engaged. He wasn't out of work long. The pastoral firm of Tennant and Love asked him to manage the two leases they'd recently acquired in central Australia, Undoolya and Loves Creek. He took up the position in August, leaving his fiancée in South Australia.

It had been five years since the telegraph line was completed but the land South Australians called the Far North was still a wild place. Benstead wrote in his unpublished memoirs that 'the natives between Charlotte Waters and Alice Springs were very bad and treacherous'. Nonetheless, he confidently rode north on his own, with a second horse to carry his supplies and belongings. When he was one day overdue in Alice Springs, the telegraph operators sent a party down the track to make sure he was safe. They need not have worried. He proved capable and resourceful and happily managed Undoolya and Loves Creek for the next four years. He would have stayed longer had it not been for a courteous but discouraging response from his employers when he wrote to them to say he intended marrying Triphena and bringing her from Adelaide. They questioned the wisdom of taking a woman 'away from civilisation' and he replied impetuously: 'What on earth has that to do with you?' He put the station's affairs in order, went south and married her in July 1881. The new manager, Alec Ross, the son of explorer John Ross, was a single man when he took over from Benstead but wed Fanny Wallis in October 1885 – so Undoolya homestead soon had a woman in residence anyway.

It wasn't long before Bill Benstead was offered another job in central Australia. Adelaide businessman Andrew Wooldridge hired him to manage a huge expanse of Anmatjere land he was granted in early 1882. Wooldridge was a pioneer of the pastoral industry in the Gawler Ranges of South Australia. His new lease was one of the largest in Australia, totalling over 50,000 square kilometres east and west of the telegraph line at Barrow Creek. He formed the Barrow Creek Pastoral Company with two partners, David Murray and J. Brodie Spence, wealthy businessmen and members of the South Australian Legislative Council.

Benstead arranged for 3000 cattle to be driven north to Annas Reservoir in the Reynolds Range where he'd decided to locate the station homestead. The cattle travelled in four separate mobs with 18 camels to carry equipment and provisions, and the trip took 15 months.[26] The arrival of all this livestock in 1884 was a major shock to the Anmatjere people, whose lands had been largely unaffected by white settlement until then.

Unable to secure more cattle at a reasonable price in South Australia, the company agreed to purchase another 2000 cows from Ridley Williams of Bierbank station, near Quilpie in south-west Queensland. Drovers had taken cattle from Queensland to the Top End but never tried overlanding stock to central Australia along the route Williams proposed. It proved a remarkable feat of droving. Many long, dry sections lay between the Queensland border and Annas Reservoir, and some said the drovers would never make it when they set off in April 1883.

They headed north-west towards the Winton region. In early June, Ridley Williams got a worrying telegram from Charles Lowe, the stockman in charge, saying they were on the Diamantina and pleuro had broken out. He set off on 17 June to catch up with the cattle and inoculate them. He ended up going all the way to Annas Reservoir and didn't return home until the first week of February 1885.

From the Diamantina they pushed on to the Georgina River, but the manager of Glenormiston station doubted they would get the cattle through the sandy desert country further west of there. Williams established a depot in the Toco Range straddling the border between Queensland and the Northern Territory. He left the cattle there for some months while he went ahead to explore a route. The drovers eventually got them through to the OT line late in 1884, via the Marshall and Plenty rivers.[27] The route is now called the Plenty Highway.

The tension between the traditional landowners and the newcomers boiled over into open conflict at Annas Reservoir on 7 August 1884.[28] At 3 am, a large group of Anmatjere men attacked the homestead where stockman Harry Figg and cook Tom Coombes were sleeping in adjoining rooms. The Anmatjere entered Coombes's room, stuck eight spears into him and set fire to the thatched roof. The first indication Figg had of the attack was when he heard cries from his mate. The roof was well ablaze by this time and he rushed out into the open to avoid being burnt to death. He managed to grab his pistol and fired a number of shots, killing four of the attackers. However, he sustained a painful spear wound between the shoulders and bad burns. Coombes managed to crawl out of the blazing building despite his multiple spear wounds. He was also badly burnt. The Anmatjere withdrew enabling Figg to get his mate into a buggy and escape to the main stock camp 50 kilometres west of Annas Reservoir. It wasn't until around midnight that they managed to reach the six men at 32 Mile Camp. One of them, James Glynn, then rode 200 kilometres to Alice Springs to alert manager Benstead who was camped there at the time. Both Figg and Coombes recovered from their injuries.

Benstead went to the telegraph station to inform stationmaster Flint and his employers in Adelaide of the incident. He was also put in contact with a doctor and instructions for treating the men's wounds were relayed up the line. Port Augusta police inspector Brian Besley advised the commissioner of police, William Peterswald. He told the commissioner he'd telegraphed William Willshire at Alice Springs with instructions to 'organise strong party immediately, including four black trackers, and send me word when he can start and names of party'.[29]

Willshire went after the offenders with constable Charlie Brookes from Barrow Creek, two black trackers and four volunteers: Alec Ross, manager of Undoolya station, his stockman Harry Price and two other white men, Summard and McBeth. Brookes had been at Barrow Creek since December 1883, following the death of John Shirley in November while searching for Brunette Downs manager Harry Readford.[30] In mid September Willshire sent a telegram to Besley reporting that they had shot dead four Anmatjere men. He claimed: 'The natives were never fired at unless they commenced throwing spears and boomerangs first, and not even then until they were called upon in their own language to surrender.'[31]

There was another incident close to the Alice Springs telegraph station on 11 September. Ebenezer Flint sent Charles Todd a message saying 'Last night about twenty natives came in from a considerable distance west of the Mission Station. This morning they attacked my native shepherd within a mile of the station; he having a revolver defended himself, and shot one of the strangers'. None of the sheep were harmed and it turned out the attack was related to a dispute over a woman.[32] Cattle spearing was occurring in a number of places across central Australia. At the end of September, Willshire advised Inspector Besley that he had pursued a group of Aboriginal people with his tracker and Alec Ross in response to incidents on Undoolya station. He said three Aboriginal men were killed and four wounded.[33]

The Aboriginal people were being ruthlessly dispossessed of their land but one can understand the frustrations of the cattlemen. On 4 October James McDonald, the new manager of Glen Helen, was riding with two others when they found six of their cattle side by side with their tongues cut out. They followed tracks and found a large group of Aboriginal people camped in a gorge for ceremonies. They dispersed as the three riders came through the gorge but rolled rocks down on them, killing one of the horses. On reaching home McDonald got fresh horses and rode into Alice Springs to put the matter in the hands of the police. Willshire had gone to the Top End by this time to deal with problems near the Daly River, where four miners were killed in incidents in August and September.[34] So his newly arrived replacement Erwein Wurmbrand rode out to Glen Helen on 12 November with two white men, William Craig and James Norman, and four black trackers. James McDonald and Theodor Schleicher from the station joined them. Wurmbrand seized four Aboriginal men at Hermannsburg on 1 December but released one when the missionaries vouched for him. He chained the other three by the neck and took them up the Finke where he and his men shot them. He went on to pursue other suspects and reported shooting four more near Mount Sonder.[35]

Calls for a native police force

Central Australia had entered a phase of strained relations. The widespread cattle spearing led to calls for an increased police presence, with Bill Benstead at the forefront of this. Outraged at the August attack on his Annas Reservoir homestead he decided to go to Adelaide to consult with his employers seeking support for the formation of a native police force in the Territory to control the Aboriginal people. One of the station's owners, David Murray, provided him with letters of introduction to the chief secretary and the police commissioner.[36] They had already discussed the idea.[37]

The South Australian Government initially resisted the idea of native police because of the excesses perpetrated by them in Queensland and New South Wales. However, they eventually gave in to the pressure for action and in mid November 1884 gave Brian Besley approval to form a small force. Six 'blacks' were to be engaged under the leadership of William Willshire.[38] It was formed, however, in response to problems in the Top End rather than the recent events in central Australia. Willshire was directed to take his new recruits up there, despite the opposition of the local police inspector Paul Foelsche who was not in favour of a native police force. Willshire spent a year 'pacifying' the Aboriginal peoples of the Daly and Roper rivers before returning south early in 1886.[39]

While Willshire was busy in the north, his colleague Erwein Wurmbrand was involved with more killing in central Australia. Cattleman Bill Benstead was also in on this. Early one morning in April 1885 Aboriginal men surrounded the homestead at Glen Helen and threatened to burn it down and kill the cook Ben Rogers.[40] A station boy sounded the alarm and the attack was thwarted. Wurmbrand was advised and left Alice Springs immediately but took a circuitous route north-west via Annas Reservoir rather than heading straight for the station. He was hoping, he later said, to catch the culprits by surprise. Despite specific instructions that he was not to allow any station men to accompany him and his black trackers, Benstead and a stockman named Lennon joined them. His report said they followed the tracks of Aboriginal people for a couple of weeks in May. They made no arrests and Wurmbrand claimed they killed only one Aboriginal man. Lennon told the missionaries at Hermannsburg they had actually killed 17. Years later Benstead wrote in his memoirs:

What really happen (sic) that day! Well, it is a thing of the past, and of little use writing up now; but I am sure that seventeen out of this lot never killed or troubled anyone else. It was a lesson they never forgot. It instilled fear into their tribe for 200 miles around, and was the means of putting an end to their murderous attempts.[41]

Willshire was back in central Australia in March 1886 and the following month he oversaw the transfer of the police's nominal base from the Alice Springs telegraph station to Heavitree Gap, eight kilometres south. More substantial facilities were constructed at Heavitree Gap, including a lock-up for prisoners. The authorities in Adelaide had accepted the cattlemen's claims that having a single mounted constable stationed at each telegraph station was insufficient and a stronger police presence was needed in central Australia. Armed with rifles and revolvers, native constables under Willshire's command were soon conducting long patrols and acquiring a reputation for their treatment of Aboriginal 'offenders'.

11

The 'rush' to the East MacDonnells

As conflict simmered in the heart of Australia, a South Australian surveyor headed north late in 1885, totally unaware his discovery would significantly transform life there. David Lindsay and his six companions dismounted from their camels and set up camp at Dalhousie Springs on 23 November. This extraordinary place, 300 kilometres south of Alice Springs, is an oasis in some of the most desolate, featureless country Australia has to offer. Hot water and steam constantly percolate to the surface from the fractured earth a short distance east of the OT line. Alfred Woods came across this amazing sight in December 1870 and named them Edith Springs, after the wife of the governor Sir James Fergusson. She later asked that the name be changed to honour her father the Marquis of Dalhousie.

Lindsay was heading to the prime grazing country on the eastern side of the Barkly Tableland. His Great Central Exploration Expedition was assembled largely at his own expense but Hermann Dittrich, a plant collector, was funded by the Royal Geographical Society and the South Australian Government, with Sir Thomas Elder providing two camels for his use. The other members of the expedition were Lindsay's 18-year-old brother-in-law George Lindsay, Arthur Warman, Billy Glyde, Fred Leech and an Afghan camel handler named Joorak.[1] They were going to head up the Finke River and then ride around the northern fringe of the Simpson Desert in the oppressive heat of summer. This route would take them through the Plenty

River region where Queenslander Ridley Williams dared to take cattle the previous year, confounding all those who said he had no hope.

Lindsay had two things on his agenda before he crossed into the Northern Territory. The first was to solve a mystery about the Finke. This great ribbon of sand is one of Australia's longest rivers and reputedly the oldest in the world. It has followed much the same course for over 100 million years. People wondered if it ran all the way to Lake Eyre. Lindsay spent three weeks finding out and learnt it was normally a river to nowhere, petering out in a floodout area, several kilometres wide and surrounded by sand dunes. But once in a while, when the skies really opened up, the water went through this sandy country to the Macumba River, which runs into Lake Eyre.[2]

The second puzzle was the fate of lost explorer Ludwig Leichhardt. Adelaide's daily paper the *South Australian Register* drew attention to this on the eve of Lindsay's departure, retelling the tale an Aboriginal man had passed on to Stephen Jarvis in the 1860s:

> that when he was a piccaninny a party of white men came from the east, and that they had with them bullocks, horses and goats. The blacks were at first very much afraid of them, but kept following them up, and at last attacked them when they were swimming in a large creek near the Tirreawah. They drove on the stock from one tribe to the other until they all died.

The newspaper article said 'Mr Lindsay would try to solve the double problem' of the fate of the Finke and what happened to Leichhardt's party. Then he would proceed to the Herbert River blocks to undertake survey work.[3]

Tirreawah was supposedly east of Dalhousie. In 1880, Charles Todd had urged the government to send a party to investigate but his suggestion wasn't taken up.[4] David Lindsay was keen to see what he could learn but found no evidence of a large waterhole where Leichhardt's party might have been massacred. He concluded from his communications with Aboriginal people that Tirreawah was a word that had fallen into disuse and simply meant 'a very long way'. He didn't doubt the story that Leichhardt was killed but thought it must have happened much further away, to the north-east.[5]

After nearly three months in the Dalhousie area, Lindsay and his men headed north along the OT line in February 1886. Even though the 1880s were poor seasons compared to the 1870s, he wrote 'at times the vegetation was over our heads as we sat upon the camels' backs. The air was alive with the music of many birds, magpies, parrots of various sorts, pigeons, doves, diamond sparrows, and many others'.[6]

They left the line at Alice Well, turned north-easterly and struck the wide, sandy bed of the Todd River in late February, well downstream of the Alice Springs telegraph station. They were travelling on roughly the same course John Ross had taken in 1870. The days were hot and oppressive, with the camels showing signs of fatigue after several days without decent feed and water. The cameleer Joorak had sunstroke and Hermann Dittrich was also feeling faint.

On 2 March they entered a gorge in the spectacular East MacDonnell Ranges where they found permanent waterholes surrounded by reeds and bulrushes. Ebenezer Flint and Mounted Constable John Shirley had explored this area in 1882 on their quest for signs of Leichhardt and there was evidence of cattle. Three days further travel took them to the Hale River, named by Henry Barclay in 1878. Lindsay described it as 'another of those sandy rivers peculiar to Central Australia'. They followed it downstream until it entered a gorge where they made camp on the afternoon of 8 March.

In an address to the Royal Geographical Society in Adelaide on 29 June 1887, Lindsay said they came across 'a bar of granite completely studded with garnets' as they rode along the Hale. He added: 'Just above this point, when scratching for water under a rocky cliff, I found a quantity of beautiful gem sand, containing many garnets and some red stones of great brilliancy, which after careful examination, I believe to be rubies.' He said he told the other members of his discovery and they 'passed on to find a large deposit of these beautiful stones at the entrance to and in' a gorge, which he named Glen Annie after his wife.[7] This was a pivotal event in the story of Alice Springs. The establishment of the town, on the western bank of the Todd River, was the direct result of this discovery, followed by gold a year later.[8]

Lindsay pushed north-east but it was tough work for the camels, traversing rocky country, boulder-strewn creeks, dense stands of tea-tree and mulga scrub. Clouds built up and rain fell, providing temporary relief from the heat. 'What a misnomer!' he wrote in his journal when they reached the place Barclay had named Plenty Wells in 1878. It took eight hours of digging in a dry rockhole to get sufficient water to meet the needs of men and camels. They dug until 10 pm, removing 'ten tons of stone and sand' in the process.[9]

Lindsay found a way across the dry country that had defeated both Henry Barclay and Charles Winnecke a few years earlier and reached the prime grazing land straddling the border of the Northern Territory and Queensland. It was quite an achievement. They got a warm welcome from Mr and Mrs Farrar at Lake Nash station on 3 April 1886, along with a pile of letters and newspapers. Lake Nash is a stretch of water, several kilometres long, on the Georgina River. Queenslander William Landsborough found the headwaters of this river in December 1861, while searching for Burke and Wills, but he named it the Herbert.

Lindsay's party remained in the region for six months. He said, in a paper published by the Royal Geographical Society in 1889, 'We commenced to survey the boundaries of runs on the 12th April, and were occupied in this work over a wide district until October, by which time we had surveyed 550 miles of boundaries'. Two of the men headed back overland to South Australia with the camels while Lindsay and the others sailed from Borroloola to Port Darwin on the schooner *Ellerton*, and then to Sydney on the steamship *Tannadia*.[10]

The ruby rush of 1887–1888

Arthur Warman was quicker off the mark than his leader Lindsay in lodging a claim to the localities in the Hale River where they'd found the 'red stones of great brilliancy'. He told friends of the find and a syndicate was formed to reap the potential windfall. Richard Pearson, who became the public face of this syndicate, sent a letter to the Adelaide Lands Office, dated 4 April 1887, seeking four leases. Lindsay applied for three leases a couple of days later but the authorities felt it only proper that he be given the first choice of a block on the Hale. They granted him 40 acres straddling the river at the northern entrance to Glen Annie Gorge. The Pearson syndicate was granted mining rights to other land in the vicinity.

Pearson & Co. didn't wait for their application to be approved. They sent a party north in March 1887 and the men were back in Adelaide in mid June with a quantity of stones, which experts in Melbourne assessed favourably. The *Port Augusta Dispatch, Newcastle and Flinders Chronicle* carried news of their travels on 22 July, with a follow-up article four days later reporting on the ruby mania sweeping Adelaide: 'Everybody wants to take up M[a]cDonnell Range country and make a colossal pile out of precious stones.' It wasn't long before others were lodging applications for ruby leases in the rugged ranges east of Alice Springs.

Richard Pearson sailed to London on 11 August 1887 with a large number of stones to obtain expert opinion on their value.[11] In contrast, David Lindsay didn't leave for central Australia until 17 August when he boarded a ship for Darwin. After survey work in the north he rode down to Alice Springs, not reaching his lease on the Hale River until the end of November. His brother-in-law George left Adelaide five weeks after him and travelled overland with two other men.[12]

In the meantime there was further excitement in Adelaide. Word filtered through that in April an ex-teamster and camel-driver named Joseph Hele, with his mate Isaac Smith, had discovered alluvial gold at Paddy's Rockhole, not far from the ruby fields. Paddy's Rockhole is actually two rock basins, one above the other. The local Arrernte people call the place Arnerre-ntyenge (a-na-ra n-tung-a), 'stinking water'. Animals regularly get stuck in there and die. The area soon became known as Arltunga but it's unclear why. It has been attributed to difficulty pronouncing Arnerre-ntyenge but there's speculation it may be a corruption of *aldolanga*, a word meaning 'easterners', from the Kukatja language group west of Alice Springs.[13] The identity of Paddy is unclear. The *South Australian Register* and the *Adelaide Observer* each published an article in 1898 by W.H. Hardy describing the goldfields. Hardy spent a year in the area and wrote 'Arltunga gained its name (Paddy's Hole) originally from a huge rock hole containing splendid water, found by a man named Hill, who had been taken to the spot by a blackfellow called Paddy'.[14]

The man he called Hill was presumably Joseph Hele. It's likely Paddy was the Aboriginal man who travelled through the area in May 1882 with Ebenezer Flint and John Shirley in search of traces of Ludwig Leichhardt.

South Australia was in the economic doldrums with high unemployment. The great depression of the 1890s hit the colony several years before the rest of Australia, initiated by the onset of drought in the north. The collapse of the Town and Country Bank and the Commercial Bank of South Australia in 1886 forced companies into liquidation and depositors to lose their savings.[15] As a result, hopeful prospectors were hitting the track, in the hope they might scratch out a living in the MacDonnell Ranges.

There were 80 men on the mining fields by the end of 1887, when David Lindsay finally made it back to the area: 60 gathering rubies and 20 prospecting for gold or working claims near Paddy's Rockhole.[16] It was hardly a rush to compare with the ones that followed gold discoveries in New South Wales and Victoria in 1851. The movement of men to the East MacDonnells was more a trickle than a rush. However, the red stones Lindsay found in 1886 and the precious flecks Hele and Smith unearthed in 1887 gave South Australians hope they too might be on the crest of a golden age.

Stores open along the track to central Australia

Alice Springs telegraph station staff had always extended the hand of hospitality to travellers along the track but, reliant on an annual delivery of bulk supplies by camel train, they could not look after everyone heading to the East MacDonnells. The miners were fortunate that storekeeper Wesley Turton was operating in the Alice Springs area by the time word got out about the ruby and gold finds.

Wesley and his wife Effie are an intriguing couple in more ways than one. It appears they reached the area in mid 1886 with their young daughter Alice, the first white child to live in the area.[17] They hailed from Mount Gambier where they had married in March 1885. Wesley used the alias Rowland Bateman at the time and she was also known as Annie.[18] Details are sketchy but most likely they operated from a horse and cart when they began hawking their wares to the scattered residents of central Australia. They settled near the main track at the foot of Billy Goat Hill, halfway between the telegraph station and the new police camp at Heavitree Gap, well placed to attract the attention of travellers.[19]

South Australian politician Simpson Newland made a brief reference to the Turtons' pioneering business in the account he wrote of his buggy trip from the Peake to Alice Springs with Joe Harding in April and May 1887.[20] He didn't describe it or identify its proprietors but it was undoubtedly just a bough shelter, and unlicensed. The Turtons didn't construct a substantial building until 1889, on a new site, further north.

Joe Harding took Newland to Alice Springs via a shortcut pioneered by Frank Speed in the early 1880s and subsequently used by other teamsters, including Harding.[21] They left the telegraph line at Frances Creek, near modern-day Maryvale, and went north through the Ooraminna Range and across the Emily Plain, where the Alice Springs airport is now located. They passed through Emily Gap, and then turned west towards Heavitree Gap, along the northern side of the main range. Harding and Simpson Newland had passed two other newly opened bush stores on their way up from the Peake.[22] The first was at Bloods Creek, 30 kilometres south of the border, a popular camping spot with two waterholes and a government well;[23] the other at Horseshoe Bend on the Finke River, 160 kilometres south of Alice Springs. Its proprietor Ted Sargeant soon got a conviction for illegally selling grog.[24]

These facilities made travelling to Alice Springs a bit easier but it remained a daunting trip for the unwary or unprepared. The availability of water on the track became a major public issue once the good seasons of the 1870s gave way to the drier 1880s. Water wasn't a problem south of the Peake because of the reliable mound springs on the western side of Lake Eyre. It didn't taste the best but there was plenty of it. It was a different story north of the Peake. Charles Todd's telegraph department dug a number of wells along the OT line in the early days but there were still long stretches with no reliable supplies. This was troublesome for the cattlemen of central Australia. Moving stock to southern markets was never easy.

The South Australian Government was eventually stirred into action and in 1883 initiated a program to sink extra wells north of the Peake. A team was put together, led by Ned Ryan, and they commenced work in 1885 at Cecilia Creek near present-day Oodnadatta. They steadily worked their way north and were over the border at Charlotte Waters by December 1887.[25]

In the preceding months they'd regularly enjoyed the company of travellers bound for the mining fields of the East MacDonnells. Many of these hopefuls opted for the teamsters' shortcut to Alice Springs rather than sticking to the telegraph line. This meant following a line of camel pads through arid country but it saved them 80 kilometres. Ooraminna Rockhole was the only place they were likely to find water but it wasn't considered permanent.

Richard Pearson made it to London late in 1887 and sent letters home talking up the value of the gems gathered by his MacDonnell Ranges Ruby Mining Company. In March 1888 his shareholders accepted an offer of £200,000 from British speculators willing to buy the company's leases on the Hale River.[26] There were 260 people on the mining fields two months later but activity soon came to an abrupt end.[27] Word got through that Professor E.H. Rennie had read a paper entitled *On Some So-called South Australian Rubies* at a Royal Society of South Australia gathering in Adelaide.[28] The stones were not precious rubies, just high quality garnets. This wasn't a total surprise; others had said as much in recent months. The bubble promptly burst and the London speculators managed to wiggle their way out of the £200,000 deal with Pearson. The ruby rush may have come to nothing but that didn't put an end to all the activity east of Alice Springs. Attention turned to gold.

Ned Ryan's men pushed on and were 75 kilometres south of Alice Springs in mid 1888, sinking a 70-metre-deep well at the eastern end of the James Range, that became known as Deep Well. Instead of continuing north to Alice Springs, they were to go east to the mining fields for a couple of months to alleviate the acute water shortage. On their way they made a cutting in the Ooraminna Range at a difficult point called the Pinch to improve access to Ooraminna Rockhole, and they improved the water-holding ability of the rockhole.

12

A town is born

The 'rush' to the East MacDonnells in 1887 was the catalyst for a period of rapid development in the heart of Australia. Cattlemen saw new hope for their struggling industry, with the prospect of a larger population, hungry for meat. Entrepreneurs saw opportunities to open stores, pubs and other services. There were calls for a better mail service and completion of the transcontinental railway. A town was born in 1888.

In the second half of 1887, as this new era was dawning, Joseph Skinner took charge of the Alice Springs telegraph station. Charles Todd moved him down the line from Barrow Creek following the death of Ebenezer Flint in July. He had not turned 22 when he left Adelaide railway station on 2 April 1875 to take charge of Barrow Creek. The railway only went as far as Burra in those days and he faced a long horse ride. Frank Gillen, a couple of years younger and bound for Alice Springs, was his travelling companion. It was June before Joe Skinner reached his new outpost.[1] Most of his telegraph experience had been with the South Australian railways, starting at Port Adelaide railway station a few weeks short of his 13th birthday.

The OT line was very much a man's world in the early days but Cornelia Rains came into Joe Skinner's life at Barrow Creek in 1885. The Barrow Creek Pastoral Company's manager Bill Benstead thought it wise to build a new homestead following the clash with the Anmatjere people at Annas Reservoir in August 1884. He chose a site on Stirling Creek, 25 kilometres south of the

Barrow Creek telegraph station, and brought his wife Triphena and their three-year-old son Bertie up from South Australia to join him there. Half a continent had separated them for the first four years of their marriage. Triphena's 18-year-old sister Cornelia accompanied her to Stirling Creek and soon met telegraph operator Joe Skinner. The Bensteads travelled down to Hermannsburg for the birth of their second son Geoffrey in 1886. They were on their way back there a month later for the marriage of Cornelia and Joe on 15 November. Ebenezer Flint was his best man. Eight months later Flint was dead.

Joe Skinner's transfer to Alice Springs officially took effect from 1 September 1887. This also made him inspecting officer for the central section of the line, from Attack Creek south to the Peake. He and Cornelia moved into the two-roomed stationmaster's house built in the late 1870s. His predecessor and mate had drawn up plans for a new, bigger residence before he died suddenly in July.[2] It was constructed by a builder called Joseph Stead in 1888. The telegraph equipment was then relocated to the little house the Skinners vacated and the building converted into a kitchen for Cornelia.

The Barrow Creek telegraph station was a two-man job but Alice Springs had four operators. Frank Scott, William Andrew and John McKay were Joe Skinner's assistants until 1888 when both Scott and Andrew left. Their places were taken in 1889 by Bill Milne from Mount Gambier and Jim Field from Port Adelaide. Field went on to be one of the longest serving men on the OT line, working at Alice Springs and then Tennant Creek until 1907 when he transferred south to Streaky Bay.

Joe Skinner's brother-in-law decides to open a pub

Christmas 1887 was Joe and Cornelia's first at Alice Springs. They'd found life a lot busier there than up the track at sleepy Barrow Creek. There were 80 men out on the diggings in the ranges to the east by this time. The Todd's shady banks, south of the telegraph station, were now popular with campers. The Skinners had seen a steady stream of people arriving in recent months, enquiring about mail or seeking help with other matters. Business was good for Wesley and Effie Turton, who had moved to the Alice Springs area in 1886, and the annual Christmas race meeting was shaping as a great opportunity to make more money. They didn't have the market to themselves. The mining activity in the east was attracting a number of hawkers and slick operators.[3] One of them was a sly grog merchant named Palmer who turned up with 14 camels and lots of Christmas cheer. His activities soon attracted the attention of the police and he didn't stay long.[4]

Central Australia was thirsty country, a fact that did not escape the attention of Bill Benstead. In the months leading up to Christmas 1887, his attention turned from managing cattle to thoughts of opening central Australia's first hotel. He'd lived in the heart of Australia for 10 years and said in his memoirs that the years at Barrow Creek were the happiest of his life:

> We were free in a world of our own, myself contented and prosperous, my wife and her sister happy, not living for themselves alone, but continually doing good work for others in times of sickness and accidents. In fact in that, as in other respects, they were angels landed in an outlandish part of the world where there were no doctors to administer comfort.

However, his brother-in-law's transfer to Alice Springs and his wife's desire to stay close to her sister were the catalysts for a move and a career-change. He tendered his resignation to his employers in Adelaide and moved his family down to Alice Springs in September, living initially with Joe and Cornelia.

The Adelaide firm of Moulden & Sons had written to the Minister Controlling the Northern Territory on Benstead's behalf in August, with a proposal to build a hotel at Heavitree Gap. As well as a bar, it would include a dining room and eight rooms to accommodate travellers. He needed a permit to conduct business as a publican but he also wanted a grant of land. He had in mind an area of about 20 acres at Heavitree Gap, sufficient for keeping chooks and livestock as well as a vegetable garden. Moulden & Sons asked for a response within 10 days so the necessary application forms could be posted to the Licensing Bench at Palmerston, Port Darwin.[5] Optimistic to think the wheels of government might move this quickly! They didn't. Weeks passed. Bertie and Geoffrey played at the telegraph station and their dad checked what was happening on the mining fields.

He also changed his mind about where he wanted to build his hotel. His agents wrote a second letter on 19 October 1887, this time proposing to build the hotel at Middle Park, one mile south of the telegraph station. Joe Skinner was supportive of his brother-in-law's new business venture but didn't think Middle Park was a good idea. His boss Charles Todd in Adelaide concurred and later put his objection to this site in writing:

> If a public house is to be approved I strongly recommend that it should be at Heavitree Gap where it will be near the Police Station as originally intended I should very much regret to see it near the Telegraph Station.

Moulden & Sons lodged their client's plans for the hotel in November. His application for a publican's licence was tabled at the December meeting of the Licensing Bench at Palmerston, Port Darwin. The inspector of public houses later told local police officer Paul Foelsche that it would probably be granted at the 13 March 1888 meeting if there were no reasonable objections.[6]

Meanwhile Wesley Turton was keen to access about 40 acres between Billy Goat Hill and the Todd River. On 16 February 1888 he wrote to Adelaide seeking 'permission to buy or rent from the government sufficient land to start an experimental garden'. He got a favourable response in May 1888, provided the land was used solely for a garden and residence. The minister made it clear the site was not to be used to run any other business and Turton was to pay the costs of a special land survey.[7] However, Wesley's intentions were not for a market garden. Like Bill Benstead, he wanted to open a pub. On 21 May 1888, Adelaide solicitors Wigley & Bleechmore wrote to the minister on his behalf asking if he could pay a publican's fee and sell liquor until such time as he could be granted a licence. They said:

> Our client states that there is every probability that Alice Springs will shortly be the centre of an intensively populated District and with a view to accommodating the population he intend to proceed at once with the erection of additional accommodation.

They included two petitions signed by local residents declaring that he was a fit and proper person to hold a licence. The minister said no.[8]

A town is born

The number of miners in the East MacDonnells had swollen to 260 by May 1888. The ruby mania was about to come to an abrupt end but that didn't dull people's hopes that riches might be found in central Australia. Wesley Turton was not deterred by the minister's knockback and Bill Benstead had joined the growing retail sector.[9] He'd obtained a slaughtering licence and was busy ensuring the miners had fresh beef on their dinner plates.[10]

Active on the ruby fields was an intriguing character, former telegraph lineman Alexander 'Sandy' Murdoch. He had been at Barrow Creek when Kaytetye warriors attacked the telegraph station in February 1874. Now he was cashing in on the goldrush with a store at Florence Creek. He'd previously had a camp near Spencer Hill, south of the Alice Springs telegraph station, where he'd fed hungry travellers.[11] Things can't have been going too well for him, however, because he committed suicide at Florence Creek in August 1888, holding a gun to his head.[12]

The South Australian Government was under pressure to deal with the lack of proper facilities to serve the growing population of the heart of Australia. A deputation of prominent people, headed by William Horn, a member of the South Australian House of Assembly, met with the Minister Controlling the Northern Territory Mr J.C.F. Johnston on 17 May. Simpson Newland and David Lindsay were among those making the case for a township to be declared at Alice Springs. Johnston promised to consider their request favourably.[13]

David Lindsay had returned to Adelaide in March but intended going back to central Australia for a third time at the end of July. He had a number of mining leases to survey, including a mica claim in the Harts Range. Johnston decided to hire him to survey a town on the Todd River while he was there.[14] Wesley Turton's request to sell liquor in Alice Springs came while all this was happening. Minister Johnston decided he could wait until the government had formalised matters in the area. Once that was done, Turton could purchase a suitable block of land and apply for a licence in the usual way.[15] Johnston was adamant that Turton's garden site near Billy Goat Hill not be used for other business but Wesley was like a dog with a bone. In

June 1888 he sent another letter, posted from the Peake in South Australia.

> You agree to let me have a site for a garden and residence. Now Sir I am taking up a lot of Trees and Garden Seeds. I am going to a lot of expense in the matter and I ask one favour. Will you kindly let me carry on my little Store Business on the garden site until the Township is surveyed as I have a lot of goods and it will be a great inconvenience to me to camp any distance away trusting Mr. Minister I am not troubling you to much I don't wish to be any nuisance but simply ask this favour till the township is surveyed. Hoping to get a favourable reply.

Johnston gave in and approved this request, as a temporary arrangement. He made it clear he would cancel Turton's permission to use the land if any business, other than running a garden, was conducted on the site once the township was surveyed.[16]

David Lindsay caught a northbound train from the Adelaide railway station on 1 August. The new line was very slowly edging its way towards Australia's north coast, eventually reaching it in 2003! In 1888 it was open to traffic as far as Strangways Springs, south-west of Lake Eyre. Lindsay made it to Alice Springs before the end of the month and examined the campsites near the Todd River where the new town would be laid out. His instructions, sent by telegram, were to:

> Survey township of 100 half acre allotments immediately south of the Charles. Reserve land for railway 5 chains wide on each side of railway trial survey which is marked on ground with stakes and trenches.[17]

The 'railway trial survey' mentioned in the telegram was the route pegged out the previous year by Graham Stewart. He examined the country between the Peake and Burt Creek, north of Alice Springs, and recommended that the transcontinental railway cross the MacDonnell Ranges at Heavitree Gap. [18] Like fellow surveyor William Mills in 1871, Stewart had no idea that the gap (Ntaripe) was a sacred place for the local Arrernte people, with restrictions on who could pass through it.

The only major issue David Lindsay needed to resolve was whether the township should be on the eastern or western side of the proposed railway corridor. On 24 August he sent a telegram to Charles Todd in Adelaide saying:

> Cannot select better site I recommend blocks be surveyed on east side of railway line and extend to Todd Creek. Should streets be on meridian line or parallel with railway whose bearing is about 22 degrees east of north. Heavy acacia shrub over portion had to send 10 miles for suitable pegs will undertake survey one hundred half acre blocks and furnish plan for £85.[19]

He was keen to get out to the mining fields but surveyed the land Wesley and Effie Turton were occupying between Billy Goat Hill and the Todd River before he left. It turned out to be an area of 23½ acres, which he signed off on 26 August. He then met up with his brother-in-law George Lindsay and rode east next day.[20] The minister was happy with Lindsay's quote of £85 for the township survey but directed Charles Todd to contact Joe Skinner and make it clear the town was to be laid out on the western side of the proposed railway line, not the east. It's unclear who was advising him that this should be the case. Skinner replied by telegram on 15 September:

> Will communicate with Mr Lindsay as quickly as possible he is now out on field & I shall probably not hear from him under ten days Will get him to do work forward plans as soon as possible.

In fact, Lindsay responded in just a couple of days. Skinner wired Todd back, saying the surveyor strongly recommended the eastern side and felt it would be a mistake to do otherwise. Todd informed him on 29 September that the minister had changed his mind and was leaving the choice of site to Lindsay.[21]

He wasted little time in surveying the town site, signed his plan on 13 October and put it in the monthly mail to Adelaide. The new township was proclaimed on 28 November with the first sale of land held in Adelaide on 31 January 1889. His decision to site the 104 lots between Graham Stewart's railway corridor and the Todd River meant there was a Railway Terrace 40 years before the railway actually arrived.[22] He proposed three other terraces to form the northern, eastern and southern boundaries of the town. The government named them after explorers Wills, Leichhardt and Gregory, and decided that the town itself should bear the name of explorer Stuart. Of the four, John McDouall Stuart was the only one who'd come within cooee of the town site but even he got no closer than 50 kilometres away. South Australians regarded him as the greatest of all Australian explorers but the name Stuart never really caught on. The place continued to be known far and wide as Alice Springs and it wasn't until 30 August 1933 that the Commonwealth Government bowed to the inevitable and made that official.

Benstead opens his pub and Turton builds a brewery

Wesley Turton put down a well on the land near Billy Goat Hill, erected fencing and planted a large number of fruit trees. He wrote to the minister in November 1888 seeking to complete the purchase of the 23½ acres Lindsay had surveyed. To his surprise, the minister replied on 17 December that the government could no longer allow him to purchase that land because of its close proximity to the new town. Instead he would be reimbursed the money he paid Lindsay and could have a lease for 21 years 'of such portion as you may require for gardening purposes only'.[23] This was quite a shock. Like the young trees he'd carted up the track, his efforts and perseverance were not bearing fruit, but he wasn't about to chuck in the towel.

He had submitted plans for an Alice Springs hotel in September and placed an advertisement in the *South Australian Weekly Chronicle* advising of his intention to apply for a publican's licence at the December meeting of the Northern Licensing Bench at Port Augusta.[24] The minister had said no to his request to sell liquor back in May but he continued to harbour hopes the government would eventually relent and let him open a pub on the garden site. Being told now that he could not purchase that land was a major setback.

Bill Benstead, in contrast, was close to achieving his objective. Contrary to expectations at the end of 1887, the Palmerston Licensing Bench did not grant him his coveted liquor licence at its March 1888 meeting. This was because the Bench ruled it had no jurisdiction over the Alice Springs region.[25] Instead, they deferred his application to the September 1888 meeting the

Northern District Licensing Bench at Port Augusta. That one duly approved it, on the condition he build three extra bedrooms, erect a verandah around the building and improve the toilet arrangements. Police inspector Brian Besley vouched for Benstead's good character and said it was better for diggers on the mining fields to purchase alcohol in the regular way rather than from sly grog sellers. The Bench gave Benstead six months to build the hotel and then he would receive his licence.[26] The one drawback was the government not granting him the 20 acres of land he'd sought at Heavitree Gap. Instead, he was told to purchase a suitable site in the new township.

The government reserved eight of the 104 blocks in Stuart for its own use. Only five of the remaining ones were purchased at the first land sale in Adelaide on 31 January 1889. Bill Benstead bought adjoining lots 78 and 79 in Todd Street for his hotel while the aptly named stonemason Fred Stone bought lot 77. He came to central Australia with the Hermannsburg missionaries in 1877, the same year Benstead arrived. His building skills would be put to good use in the coming years. Stone was the first person to actually hand over his money and so has the honour of being the town's first title holder.[27] Wesley Turton didn't bid for any blocks but sent a telegram to the minister a week later, on 6 February 1889, expressing interest in lot 99. It was near the river at the corner of Leichhardt and Gregory Terraces. He'd been assured he would receive compensation for the improvements he'd made on the land near Billy Goat Hill.[28]

The minister said he could use this new block of land and make improvements until the next public sale of land when he would be able to purchase it. Wesley got to work sinking a well and building a substantial stone building with unusually high, thick stone walls and a narrow passage down the middle.[29] It was to be a brewery. He'd seen the writing on the wall and realised his dream of a pub of his own was unlikely to happen. If he could not stand behind a bar and sell beer to the locals then he could brew the stuff for the bloke with the licence. The Northern District Licensing Bench was due to meet at Port Augusta on 12 March 1889. His application for a liquor licence was on the agenda but he withdrew it.[30]

Also on the agenda was the finalisation of Bill Benstead's licence.

Beaumont Moulden, his solicitor, produced receipts for the two blocks his client had purchased in January. He advised that a contract had been let to build the hotel and work was progressing satisfactorily. Inspector Brian Besley had no objections, remarking that the hotel was needed and the sooner it was open, the better for the public.[31] Benstead had always had friends in high places and this worked in his favour. He originally intended calling his establishment the Great Northern Hotel but changed his mind after the town was named Stuart. It became the Stuart Arms Hotel.

In subsequent years Wesley Turton was listed as a brewer on the electoral roll. He clearly built a good working relationship with Bill and Triphena Benstead because some years later they made moves to go into the hotel business together in Western Australia.

Turton got the title to lot 99 after the second sale of land in July 1889. Lot 57 on Wills Terrace attracted the attention of the Wallis family but they didn't buy it until the following year. Tom and Hannah Wallis, and their sons Frank and Albert, were based at Claraville, on the goldfields a few kilometres north of Paddy's Rockhole. Frank had a storekeeper's licence but his main interest was a camel transport business established a couple of years earlier.[32] His brother Albert was keen on cattle. Their sister Fanny was married to Alec Ross who managed Undoolya station in the 1880s after Bill Benstead quit. They were running the hotel at Saltia near Port Augusta in 1889.[33]

Frank Wallis started building a store on lot 57 before he actually got the title to the land early in 1890. The government allowed people to occupy and improve lots on the condition they purchased them at the first available opportunity. However, he didn't hang onto it for long. In 1891 he sold to Bob South, the younger brother of local policeman Bill South.[34] Bill South had been based at the Heavitree Gap police station since March 1888.

Wesley Turton and his wife developed another garden on their new block of land but their marriage didn't prove a long and happy one. He petitioned for divorce on 11 October 1891 after Effie ran off to Adelaide with Frank Wallis in 1890, taking young Alice with her.[35] The affair didn't blossom but added spice to life in the new town. Wesley hung around for a few more years, brewing beer.

The town of Alice Springs was originally named Stuart.
Scotsman John McDouall Stuart opened the door for the
settlement of central Australia with his three epic journeys
through the heart of the continent in 1860, 1861 and 1862.
[NTAS NTHP 553 National Trust Collection]

Englishman William Whitfield Mills
arrived in Australia in 1866 with £4
in his pocket. Five years later, he chose
the site for the most important repeater
station on the line, by a waterhole he
named the Alice spring.
[NTAS ASTS 1651 Mortlock Library Collection]

Charles Todd is a giant of Australian history. His OT
line was Australia's first big infrastructure project. Only
those familiar with the country it crossed can truly
appreciate the magnitude of his men's achievement.
[NTAS ASTS 858 Miscellaneous Collection]

About 200 Arrernte people lived in the Alice Springs area when the telegraph station was built. The site was criss-crossed with dreaming tracks but the people showed remarkable tolerance of their uninvited guests.
[NTAS ASTS 41 Bradshaw Collection]

The hum of the wire was a familiar sound to travellers plying the track through the heart of the continent. A second 'singing wire' was added to the poles in 1898–1899.
[NTAS ASTS 424 Wutke Collection]

Surveyor Edwin Berry's 1873 sketch is the earliest known image of the Alice Springs telegraph station. He also produced the first sketch of Uluru (Ayers Rock) exploring the country west of the telegraph line that year.
[NTAS ASTS 1351 Miscellaneous Collection]

Joe and Cornelia Skinner's baby Maud was the first white child born at the Alice Springs telegraph station. This 1889 image taken by telegraph operator Bill Milne is one of the earliest photos of the place.
[NTAS ASTS 841 Miscellaneous Collection]

Frank Gillen spent 24 years working on the OT line. In the 1890s the telegraph station became the site of groundbreaking research in anthropology, by Gillen and his friend Baldwin Spencer, from Melbourne University.
[NTAS ASTS 1561 Mortlock Library collection]

Amelia Gillen shared her husband's genuine concern for the Aboriginal people's welfare and interest in their culture. Dolly and Polly helped her with the endless housework and cared for her little boys Brian and Jack.
[NTAS ASTS 185 Gillen-Meldrum Collection]

Ted Johns visited the telegraph station in November 1897 with Llew Griffiths from the Engineer's Branch. They installed duplex equipment and instructed the staff on its use. This enabled them to send signals simultaneously in opposite directions on the one wire.
Back: Vaughan Jagoe, Jack Besley, Phil Squire
Front: Llew Griffiths, Frank Gillen, Ted Johns, Jim Field
[NTAS ASTS 555 Gillen-Meldrum Collection]

Drought gripped central Australia – and much of the continent – in 1902. Tom and Attie Bradshaw provided Christmas dinner for 167 Aboriginal people that year.
[NTAS ASTS 1568 Bradshaw Collection]

Alice Springs wives and children in 1903.
Back: Doris Bradshaw, Ernie Allchurch, Bessie Williams, Nellie French, her baby Eugene,
John Meyers, Annie Meyers, Don Bradshaw, Attie Bradshaw nursing baby Edna
Front: Mort Bradshaw, Dorothy Meyers, Jack Bradshaw, Consie Bradshaw
[NTAS ASTS 1571 Bradshaw Collection]

Mort Bradshaw was decorated for bravery as a stretcher-bearer in France in 1916. He died from
wounds sustained in the disastrous May 1917 action at Bullecourt which cost Australia 10,000 men.
From left: Doris, Mort, Consie, Jack, Don and Edna Bradshaw in 1905
[NTAS ASTS 9 Bradshaw Collection]

Amelia (centre) and Runge (right) worked with the Bradshaw family throughout their years at the telegraph station and were significant figures in the lives of the children. Runge was one of many Aboriginal people who died when influenza swept across Australia after the return of troops from the First World War.
[NTAS CCNT 2017 Bradshaw Collection]

The Alice Springs telegraph station was a busy little village but only its substantial stone buildings survive today. Ernie and Bessie Allchurch lived in a thatched cottage following their marriage in 1905.
[NTAS CCNT 2020 Bradshaw Collection]

The telegraph station, looking east towards the river, in July 1908 shortly before the Bradshaw family departed for a new life in Moonta.
[NTAS CCNT 2009 Bradshaw Collection]

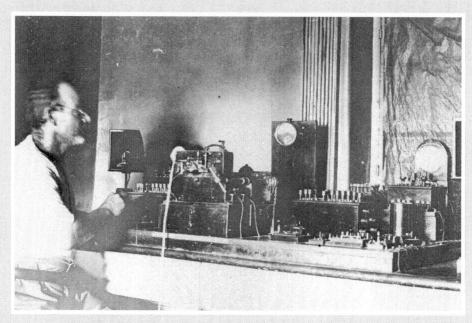

High-speed machine telegraphy was in use on the line by Fred Price's time.
However, his considerable responsibilities affected his health and this conscientious
man died in Adelaide in 1924 on his first holiday in eight years.
[NTAS ASTS 1310 Powell-Price Collection]

There was extraordinary rainfall at the start of the 1920s, filling the waterhole that
William Whitfield Mills named the Alice spring. Then followed one of the
worst droughts in central Australian history.
[NTAS ASTS 209 Powell-Price Collection]

Ernie Allchurch was a much loved character, up and down the line. He was a source of countless stories about the early days in central Australia but never got the chance to complete the book of reminiscences he had begun writing.
From left: Bessie, Ernie, Maisie and Jessie Allchurch
[NTAS NTHP 182 National Trust Collection]

The discovery of gold at Arltunga in 1887 was the pivotal event in the establishment of the town of Stuart, now Alice Springs. A shortage of water was a perennial problem on the goldfields. Prospectors used dry blowers to extract flakes of gold from river sand.
[NTAS ASTS 56 Bradshaw Collection]

It is ironic that the first buildings in town were a brewery and a pub, given the alcohol problems now afflicting Alice Springs. Wesley Turton built the brewery in 1889 but it was the home of the Meyers family in the early 1900s.
[NTAS ASTS 133 Bradshaw Collection]

Central Australia's first pub, the Stuart Arms Hotel, was built across two blocks in Todd Street in 1889. It survived until 1960 when gutted by fire.
[NTAS ASTS 236 Wutke Collection]

Most of the town's buildings were located along Wills Terrace, at the northern end of town, in 1901.
[NTAS ASTS 1494 Horn Expedition Collection]

Charlie Meyers set up a saddlery at the southern end of Todd Street in the early 1900s. There was the pervading smell of leather with bridles, harnesses and whips hanging from the ceiling, plus saddles in various stages of construction or repair.
[NTAS CCNT 1981 Cavanagh Collection]

The little township of Stuart in 1908, looking north-west across the Todd River towards the rocky outcrop now known as Anzac Hill.
[NTAS ASTS 1551 Bradshaw Collection]

Stonemason Jack Williams was busy building a new police station and gaol in 1908. The gaol still stands today, thanks to legendary heritage advocate Doreen Braitling and the National Trust. The small stone quarters built for the warder became the town's first schoolroom when teacher Ida Standley arrived in 1914.

[NTAS ASTS 151 Bradshaw Collection]

Ida Standley's first class was a diverse group.
Back: Dempsey Hong, Gordon and Malcolm Stott, Tessa Betts, Katie Williams, Don Stuart, Mort Conway, Tom Williams
Middle: Dick Gillen, Maude Smith, Leslie and Doreen Crook, Claude Nicker, Cameron Stott, Jack Cooper, Ada Hong, Essie Simpson, Amy Colley, Eileen Cooper
Front: Willie Smith, Ben and Margaret Nicker, Agnes Stott, Kathleen Crook, Emily Smith

[NTAS NTHP 498 National Trust Collection]

The Commonwealth Government began taking children of mixed descent from their Aboriginal
mothers in 1914. They placed them in the care of Topsy Smith (second from the left.)
Their shabby 'home' behind the Stuart Arms Hotel was known as the Bungalow.
It went west to Jay Creek in 1928.
[NTAS NTHP 540 National Trust Collection]

Sleepy little Stuart grew considerably after the arrival of the railway.
The first passenger train rolled in shortly after 2 pm on 5 August 1929,
hauled by one of the Commonwealth Railway's new NM class steam locomotives.
[NTAS NTHP 220 National Trust Collection]

Jay Creek was just a temporary location. In 1932 the Commonwealth Government built a corrugated-iron dormitory at the old telegraph station to accommodate the children. Other buildings were converted to a dining room, bathrooms, schoolroom and nurse's clinic.
[NTAS NTHP 794 Boehm Collection]

The children's dormitory in the 1930s was stinking hot in summer and freezing in winter. Overcrowding soon became a problem as the number of inmates at the home grew from 73 children in 1932 to 114 in 1933.
[NTAS ASTS 723 Chettle-Robb Collection]

Hetti Perkins was a stable figure in the lives of the Bungalow children, at both Jay Creek and the old telegraph station. She took over from Topsy Smith, running the kitchen and looking after the smallest children. Her son Charlie was born at the Bungalow in 1936 and twins Ernie and Gary in 1938.
[NTAS NTHP 825 Boehm Collection]

The Bungalow children identify as members of a stolen generation.
Back: Ruby Webb, Milly Woodford, Tilly Tilmouth, Melva Palmer,
Myrtle MacDonald, Nellie Stirling, Hilda Stirling
Front: Jessie White, Daisy Pearce, Mavis Webb, Nora Meyers, May Perkins,
Millie Glen, Lorna Nicker, Netty Pearce, Lorna Purvis, Sporty Pearce
[NTAS ASTS 714 Chettle-Robb Collection]

Wally Boehm was in charge of the Bungalow School from 1938 until 1941.
He secured funds to purchase woodworking equipment so the boys could receive proper
technical training. It was installed in the blacksmith shop early in 1939.
[NTAS NTHP 813 Boehm Collection]

A favourite game of the
boys at the Bungalow in
the 1930s was racing old
tyres with smaller boys
curled up in the rims.
[NTAS ASTS 709
Chettle-Robb Collection]

Beatrice (Grac) Moore taught domestic arts at the Bungalow from 1939 until 1941. The girls received instruction in cooking, sewing, knitting and crochet as well as practical tasks such as setting a table, making a bed and household hygiene.
From left: Millie Glen, Molly Stone, Nora Meyers, Rona Glynn, Lorna Nicker, Nettie Waters, Lily Kunoth, unknown girl
[NTAS NTHP 815 Boehm Collection]

Schoolteacher Wally Boehm established a drum and fife band at the Bungalow. Its leader Joe Croft was a clever boy who was awarded a bursary enabling him to attend All Souls Anglican Boarding School at Charters Towers.
[NTAS NTHP 799 Boehm Collection]

World War II was a major turning point in the history of the Northern Territory. The army took over Alice Springs and established a camp between Anzac Hill and the river. There were 2500 troops in town by January 1942.
[MacCormac Collection, courtesy of Prue Crouch]

13

Rough justice on the frontier

The government dispatched its geologist Henry Yorke Lyell Brown to the East MacDonnells as 1888 was drawing to an end. He reached the diggings in November but found work had largely come to a standstill even though good reefs had been found.[1] The problem was a shortage of water. Paddy's Rockhole had dried up completely and Brown saw conditions were little better for the miners working claims 13 kilometres north, at Claraville. Ned Ryan's well-sinkers were there when Brown arrived. Ironically, good rains fell not long after they started digging, flooding the Hale River and temporarily stopping their work. So they moved over to Paddy's Rockhole and started another well there.

The entrepreneurial Joe Harding was at Paddy's Rockhole. The former teamster and cattleman figured there was more money to be made selling things to the miners than wielding a pick and shovel. His business was a simple affair but it wasn't long before he built a proper store and a separate butcher's shop with a cellar. The government geologist was cautious about the future prospects for the goldfields but believed they would pay if steam-driven machinery was erected and there was a reliable water supply. He made regular trips to central Australia in the following years to check on the progress of the field, where he was known affectionately as 'Geology Brown'.

The first photographs of central Australia

Mineral exploration parties ventured into other parts of central Australia in the years that followed. The first of these was an 1889 expedition under the auspices of the South Australian Branch of the Royal Geographical Society of Australasia. Its leader, William Tietkens, was second in charge to Ernest Giles during his desert explorations between 1873 and 1875. Tietkens was born in England and attended the same London school. He migrated to South Australia in 1859 but went to the Victorian goldfields the following year. He returned to Adelaide to study after his travels with Giles and passed the South Australian Licensed Surveyors Examination 1878.

In 1886, he gave a lecture to the Royal Geographical Society. He was unemployed and angling to be given command of an expedition to the Lake Amadeus district in the south-west of the Territory. He argued that this great salt lake was bound to have a supply channel, probably coming from a chain of hills that he and Giles had seen to the north-west in 1873. He thought this might open a reliable route to Western Australia.[2] The Society began planning an expedition the following year in conjunction with the Victorian branch. However, they couldn't raise sufficient funds and a private company was formed, the Central Australian Exploring and Prospecting Association Ltd. Investors, attracted by the prospect of mineral discoveries and new grazing land, helped them reach their target of £5000.[3]

Tietkens, David Beetson and cameleer Frederik Warman reached the Alice Springs telegraph station on 28 February 1889 and went on to Bond Springs station where manager Richard Taylor had their supplies. They were heading west, along the northern side of the MacDonnell Ranges, by mid March with an Alice Springs police blacktracker called Billy and an Aboriginal boy referred to as Weei.[4] Unlike earlier expeditions to central Australia, they had a camera to photograph their discoveries.

They prospected in the West MacDonnells where Tietkens and Billy climbed Mount Sonder, one of the most beautiful and iconic peaks in the ranges. The expedition headed west to the Cleland Hills and then to the Kintore Range, which Tietkens named after the new governor of South Australia. They were fortunate, 1889 had a lot of autumn rain. They discovered a large expanse of salt, straddling the border of Western Australia and the Northern Territory, and rode around it. It contained shallow water at the time and Tietkens named it Lake Macdonald.

Then they turned south-east towards Lake Amadeus where Tietkens had been with Giles in 1874. He mapped its shores before heading on to Mount Olga, Ayers Rock and Mount Connor, taking the first-ever photographs of these places. The expedition increased knowledge of the geography of central Australia and Tietkens was made a Fellow of the Royal Geographical Society. The geological specimens they collected enabled Geology Brown to compile a geological sketch of the country between Alice Springs and the West Australian border, but no mining activity resulted.

Meanwhile back in the east, the ever-resourceful and versatile Bill Benstead was venturing from meat to mining, as well as establishing his Stuart Arms Hotel. The Wheal Fortune Gold Mining Company was floated in 1889. The company purchased a Huntington mill and erected it at Claraville to crush ore from its reef six kilometres away, the most promising claim on the mining fields. The mill began crushing in August 1889 but a shortage of water brought its operations to a stop in November. The well Ned Ryan's men dug earlier in the year needed deepening and the directors persuaded the government to pay for the work. Bill Benstead erected another battery at Paddy's Rockhole to crush quartz from the Round Hill claim but the well there went dry at the end of January 1890. Again the government agreed to pay the cost of rectifying the situation. It was deepened to yield 1500 gallons a day but the water supply was still insufficient for the constant running of Benstead's machine.[5] His pub, in no danger of running dry, was better at accumulating the diggers' gold.

A child is born at Stuart and another at the telegraph station

Bill Benstead's employers had expressed misgivings in 1881 when he wrote to say he intended bringing his fiancée Triphena to join him on Undoolya station. They doubted it was a fit place for a woman, yet alone children. The only white women in central Australia in those days were the missionaries' wives at Hermannsburg.

It's too easy to overlook the contribution of women in the early days of white settlement. Young, unsung heroines like Triphena Benstead worked their fingers to the bone and put up with the kind of life most men would baulk at: a life of never-ending household drudgery and the demands of childrearing. Their comforts were few, their worries many, and loneliness a constant challenge. The lack of medical facilities was particularly telling.

Fortunately, Hermannsburg's Wilhelmine Schwarz and Dorothee Kempe were competent midwives who opened their doors to the other pioneering women of central Australia.[6] Alec Ross, Bill Benstead's successor at Undoolya, drove his wife Fanny 150 kilometres to the mission for the birth of their first child Alexander on 18 September 1886. Geoffrey Benstead arrived safely a month later, after his parents made an even longer buggy journey down from Barrow Creek. On 28 February 1887 the Hermannsburg baptismal register recorded the christening of Graham Wells, though it doesn't say where his parents Bob and Catherine Wells were living or the work Bob was doing.[7]

Maud Dorothy Skinner has a special place in the history of the Alice Springs telegraph station. She was the first white child born there, making her entry into the world on 12 June 1889. Triphena Benstead helped her sister Cornelia through the birth while husband Joe Skinner used the telegraph to keep in touch with a doctor at the Central Telegraph Office in Adelaide.

Triphena had given birth to a daughter of her own, three months earlier on 8 April 1889 in the fledgling township of Stuart. The little girl was named after her mother but nicknamed 'Queenie'.[8] She did not live long. The *South Australian Register* recorded her death in a hospital in Adelaide, of croup and bronchitis, when she was only five months old.[9] It said nothing of the unbearable heartache that gripped her mother.

Maud was luckier. She lived in the relative comfort of the telegraph station for nearly two years before her parents moved to Adelaide early in 1891. A blurry image of the family on the verandah of the stationmaster's house in 1889 is one of the earliest photos of the place. It was taken by Joe Skinner's fellow telegraph operator Bill Milne, who arrived with a camera that year.

Years later, Lucelle 'Lulu' Benstead claimed she was the first white child born in Stuart when in fact it was her unfortunate sister Queenie. Lulu made her first public appearance at the Stuart Arms Hotel on 5 February 1891. She made many more in future years because she was blessed with an extraordinary singing voice and became a renowned performer in London and Paris during the Great War.

Voting rights for whites but rough justice for blacks

A number of significant events happened in 1890, a noteworthy year in the history of central Australia. On Saturday 19 April, an election was held for the South Australian House of Assembly and white men north of the 26th parallel of latitude chose their own representatives for the first time. The *Northern Territory Representation Act* allowed them to elect two members and the successful candidates were J.L. Parsons and V.L. Solomon. The electoral reform didn't extend to Cornelia Skinner or the other women of central Australia. Female franchise was still six years away.

John Langdon Parsons had been a member of the House of Assembly from 1878 until 1884, representing the people of Encounter Bay and then North Adelaide. He was Minister for Education and Minister Controlling the Northern Territory from 1881 until 1884 but then sailed north to become the Northern Territory's fifth government resident. A street was named after him when the new town of Stuart was created in 1888. He stood down from the position to contest the 1890 election.

Businessman Vaiben Louis Solomon was elected on the back of a campaign advocating a white Australia policy. He'd lived at Port Darwin since 1873 when he became editor of the *Northern Territory Times* at the age of 20. He was a prominent figure in the north, nicknamed Black Solomon after painting himself black and walking naked through the streets of the town, following a dare. In 1899 he became South Australia's shortest-serving premier, holding the position for one week from 1 December to 8 December. The federal electorate of Solomon in the Northern Territory is named after him.

There was a more contentious issue than electoral reform on everyone's lips by the middle of 1890. It was the Swan-Taplin inquiry into the ill-treatment of Aboriginal people in central Australia. Information had steadily been filtering through to the missionaries at Hermannsburg since 1883 about disturbing incidents involving police, cattlemen and Aboriginal people. They'd seen enough with their own eyes to be concerned about the situation.

Pastor Hermann Kempe raised the matter with the authorities in Adelaide in 1885 when he and his wife were in the city so their son Johann could have an eye operation. He met with the chief secretary, commissioner of police and the protector of Aborigines, accompanied by Pastor Georg Heidenreich from the Barossa Valley who was the general secretary of the Lutheran Mission Society. Kempe specifically raised the issue of Constable Erwein Wurmbrand shooting three prisoners the previous November, though he declined the option of making it a criminal case.[10]

The 'pacification' of the Aboriginal people continued but things came to a head on the afternoon of 9 January 1890 when Pastor Wilhelm Schwarz spoke at a meeting at the YMCA Parlour in Adelaide. It was a small gathering of people interested in Aboriginal welfare, chaired by Friedrich Krichauff who was a member of the Legislative Council and long time supporter of the mission. Schwarz had left Hermannsburg the previous August, worn down by years of hard work. Speaking in German (translated by the German speakers present) he gave details of police shootings in response to cattle spearing and said cattlemen were using Aboriginal women 'for shameful purposes'. He remarked: 'There was hardly a station on which there were not half-caste children.' The *South Australian Register* reported the missionary's statements next day.[11] The Aborigines' Friends' Association called on the government to initiate an inquiry. It appointed Henry Swan, a magistrate, and Charles Eaton Taplin to investigate the charges, plus counter charges the police and cattlemen made against the missionaries.[12] Taplin had heard what Pastor Schwarz had to say and was a key figure in the call for an inquiry.[13]

The two men took a train from Adelaide on 20 June 1890 to Warrina, at the end of the line and a short distance south of the Peake. The rest of the journey was 550 kilometres on the back of a camel.[14] Pastor Georg Heidenreich and Inspector Brian Besley rode with them. Heidenreich had insisted on going along to represent the interests of the church. Besley was responsible for all policing in the Far North, including the Alice Springs district. His officer William Willshire was the prime focus of scrutiny. He and his native police had been based at Boggy Hole on the Finke River since August 1889. Willshire's notorious colleague Erwein Wurmbrand was no longer a serving officer by this time. He had been transferred to the Top End in May 1888 and resigned the following year.[15]

Henry Swan and Charles Taplin got to Hermannsburg on 19 July 1890 to begin their inquiry. There they took evidence from Willshire and the missionaries, followed by others around the region in the ensuing weeks. All told, they heard from 23 people; not a single one was Aboriginal. Their report presented to South Australia's parliament on Tuesday 23 September 1890 was a whitewash.[16] Amazingly, the two commissioners said Pastor Schwarz's charges were unproven and they did not believe Aboriginal people were being treated inhumanely. They also found the claims cattlemen kept Aboriginal girls solely for immoral purposes could not be supported. The report exonerated Willshire of wrongdoing and endorsed him as 'the right man for the work' in central Australia. They declared: 'We are convinced there is no foundation for any charge of his being guilty of shooting down blacks ...'

The findings were humiliating for the missionaries who were accused of making 'their statements without careful consideration, and acting upon reports from the natives without testing their accuracy'. These stunning conclusions make you wonder about Taplin's role. Was he bullied into putting his name to its findings? Within a year a very different story would be told about police treatment of Aboriginal people in the heart of Australia.

Two months after Swan and Taplin visited the telegraph station to take evidence from Joe Skinner, he faced a calamity. On 10 October 1890 a fire swept through the roof of its oldest building. Getting it under control was a nightmare, with no pumps or hoses to direct water at the flames. There are no accounts of this catastrophe in Adelaide's daily newspapers, so it's unclear exactly what happened. It seems the fire started on a verandah with brush and dry grass packed on top to provide insulation from the heat. Alice Springs is not normally a windy place but October brings frequent swirling willy-willy winds – not a time you want to have a building catch fire. The situation was made worse by the lack of rain.[17] The roof had to be removed and a new one built. Rather than being able to quietly wind down to Christmas, Joe Skinner had his hands full dealing with the disaster. Procuring new roofing iron and sawn timber from Adelaide, plus a tradesman capable of restoring the barracks, took a lot of time and effort.

Another town is born

The miners on the goldfields had worries of their own as 1890 drew to a close. The year had not been a wonderful one for them. Geology Brown made his second visit to Arltunga in midyear and found men struggling. No great fortunes had been made or big nuggets found since his first visit in November 1888. The goldfields were not as rich as South Australians originally hoped. He found only a small number of people working the creekbeds for alluvial gold. The directors of Wheal Fortune, one of the few reefs being worked, were also looking to the government for help. Their subsidy of £1000 did not prevent them giving up the mine.

A number of men drifted north to the Harts Range during 1890. Some prospectors, including Bill Benstead, discovered mica there that year but the market for this mineral was unreliable. They gradually returned to fossick for gold. One of the few bright spots for them that year was the government's decision to open a post office on the goldfields and introduce a better mail service. It commenced operating in a building made of mulga logs at Paddy's Rockhole on 1 January 1891, with storekeeper Joe Harding acting as postmaster.[18] The place was officially known as Arltunga from that point onwards but it never developed into a town in the usual sense of the word.[19] Its long-suffering residents were scattered far and wide.

Progress was slow on the railway, the people's great hope to spur Northern Territory development, and 1890 saw it extended only 90 kilometres, from Warrina to Angle Pole – a point on the parched gibber plain where the OT line changed direction and took a more northerly course. A town was surveyed a short distance south of it and given the name Oodnadatta, from the Aboriginal *utnadata*, meaning blossom of the mulga. It was hardly an idyllic location but this sun-baked patch of flat country had a reliable supply of artesian water for the boilers of steam locomotives. A large bridge was needed to span the Neales River at Algebuckina and carry the rails on to Oodnadatta. Construction of this impressive steel structure fed the story, false but often repeated, that it was intended for Murray Bridge in South Australia and erected in the north because of errors in design.[20]

The new railhead was officially opened on 7 January 1891 but the people present that day had no idea nearly 40 years would elapse before the line advanced further. The economy was in the doldrums by 1891 and showing no signs of recovery. The government was afraid of getting further into debt and work stopped. Despite the high hopes of South Australians when work began in 1878, their Great North Railway was a railway to nowhere. People who travelled on this narrow-gauge line before its demise in 1980 have an idea what nowhere looks like.

A major realignment of the southern section of the OT line was undertaken as the railway advanced north towards Oodnadatta. Long sections of wire between Port Augusta and Strangways Springs were pulled down and relocated alongside the new railway, facilitating line maintenance. The wire kept to its original route north of Strangways Springs but the Peake telegraph station closed in 1891 and was replaced by an office in Oodnadatta 75 kilometres further north.[21]

The railways added their own telegraph wire all the way to Oodnadatta and provided voice communication, using an early type of telephone called a phonopore. Credit for the invention of the telephone is disputed, as with other influential breakthroughs such as the light bulb, radio, television, and computer. Several inventors were experimenting with voice transmission over a wire and improving on each other's ideas. American Alexander Graham Bell was the first to be awarded a patent and so he usually gets the credit. Experimental lines were being trialled in both Sydney and Melbourne by January 1878. The phonopore was an English design, developed by Charles Langdon-Davies of London, in the mid 1880s. He built on the discovery made by Belgian professor of physics François van Rysselberghe that incorporating high inductance coils into the circuit enabled a telephone to use existing telegraph lines without interfering with the telegraph messages. This saved postal authorities and railways a lot of money because it meant they didn't need to install separate lines. Phonopore literally means 'sound channel'. It is derived from the Greek words *phone* (meaning voice or sound) and *poros* (passage).

Camel trains to the Alice and beyond

The country takes on a very different look once you cross the 26th parallel of latitude and enter the Northern Territory. The hard gibber plains of South Australia's Far North are replaced by countless red sandhills, though the country improves dramatically as you approach the MacDonnell Ranges. The track to the Alice in the early days featured many tortuous crossings of dunes and dry creek beds. This was the realm of the turbaned camel drivers known collectively as Afghans. Camel trains became a regular site as central Australia's population swelled in the late 1880s. There were 30 Afghans on the mining fields east of Alice Springs in July 1888 delivering supplies for the diggers and carting south what little reward they could ply from the hard ground.[22]

Different books will give you different stories about the cameleers' origins. Some came from regions that are now part of Iran, Pakistan or India but most were actually from mountainous landlocked Afghanistan.[23]

A strong Afghan community developed on the north side of Hergott Springs (Marree) after the railway reached there in 1883. It was a major crossroads from which long strings of camels headed up the dusty track to Alice Springs and beyond, or along the Birdsville track into the south-west corner of Queensland. The people living in the lonely outstations, as far up as Newcastle Waters, depended on them for their hardware, clothing, flour, tea, sugar, tobacco and other commodities they couldn't procure locally. A ghantown formed on the north-western side of Oodnadatta after it was surveyed in 1890. A visitor to this area might see 400 camels in the four decades it was the terminus of the Great Northern Railway.

The Afghans mostly came to Australia on three-year contracts and worked for wages that were considerably less than white teamsters expected.

Some went home again when their time was up but many stayed longer, like the brothers Faiz and Tagh Mahomet from Kandahar. Thomas Elder lent them money to start their own camel business in 1888. They sailed to Karachi and travelled north and west, buying animals and recruiting drivers. Their big break came in 1890 when they won the first of a couple of contracts to supply the telegraph stations north of Oodnadatta: a total of 29 tonnes carried to Charlotte Waters, Alice Springs, Barrow Creek and Tennant Creek.[24]

Moving this amount of freight required between 70 and 100 animals. A large bull camel is strong enough to carry 600 kilograms but loads were generally between 250 and 400 kilograms, depending on the age of the camel and the nature of the freight.[25] Transporting non-perishable food, clothing, kerosene and hardware was relatively straightforward but bulky or awkward items such as building material and furniture were more challenging. The camel trains spent long days on the track but were slow, compared to a horse and buggy. Everything needed to be unloaded each night and repacked next morning. They took six to eight weeks to cover the distance from Oodnadatta to Alice Springs, not conducive to carrying perishable items such as fruit and vegetables.[26] Despite being slow, the Afghan drivers earned a reputation for reliability and their arrival at their destination was always warmly welcomed.

Faiz and Tagh Mahomet headed to Western Australia in 1892. They set up a major operation on the Coolgardie goldfields and bases further west at Geraldton, Mullewa, Daydawn and Cue to serve the Murchison goldfields. In 1896, Tagh was murdered at Coolgardie while his brother was on the Murchison goldfields. Faiz kept the business going on his own but later got into financial difficulties after being cheated of a substantial amount of money by another Afghan. He returned to his homeland and died there in 1910.

Christopher Bagot of Oodnadatta was the successful tenderer for camel cartage to the four central telegraph stations for most of the 1890s. He also serviced Arltunga. The former OT line cadet surveyor died in 1899 but his widow Ada Annie Bagot kept the business going in her own name.[27] Frank Wallis was the other major player in the camel transport business in central

Australia, starting in 1887 when he headed for the Kimberley goldfields with a string of camels. His young brother Albert joined him. On the way, they met a number of disappointed diggers at Attack Creek who said the gold had petered out and they were going to Queensland. So the brothers turned around and went across the Barkly Tableland with them instead. They followed the Barkly stock route to Anthony Lagoon and then took the camels north along the McArthur River to the Gulf of Carpentaria, loading at Port McArthur before heading south to Brunette Downs station. They returned to Port McArthur and loaded up again. After selling everything they returned to Alice Springs via the telegraph line. The ruby rush was in full swing in the East MacDonnells by this time and so they headed out there with their camels. In time Frank Wallis owned 200 animals, earning the epitaph 'the camel king'. He set up a successful operation that served the people of central Australia until the railway eventually made it to Alice Springs in 1929.[28] It seems his fling with Mrs Turton in 1890, and being named in her colourful divorce case, didn't harm his reputation at all.

Leaving Alice Springs

Joseph Skinner officially held the position of Postmaster at Alice Springs until 30 November 1892, but he actually left early in 1891. He'd spent 16 years on the OT line. He and Cornelia were given a warm send-off by the sturdy souls with whom they'd shared nearly four years at Alice Springs. People waved goodbye as Joe drove their buggy through the embryonic town of Stuart. Ahead of them was a bumpy 10-day ride to Oodnadatta to catch the fortnightly train to Adelaide.

Skinner worked in the Central Telegraph Office in the city for 18 months until appointed Postmaster at Port Lincoln. Stints at Port Pirie and Norwood, where he retired in 1918, followed. He'd served a record 52 years and 7 weeks. His family grew, with three sons born in South Australia. Maud, the first child born at the Alice Springs telegraph station, married Allan Freeth in September 1925 when she was 36. Sadly she died in childbirth the following year.[29]

Bill and Triphena Benstead stayed in central Australia until late 1891.

Bill lost faith in the Arltunga goldfields and began looking further afield. He leased the Stuart Arms Hotel to Thomas and Mary Ann Gunter and the family headed south, with Western Australia their ultimate destination.[30] It was a while before they got there but they turned up at the right time. Arthur Bayley and William Ford struck gold at Coolgardie on 17 September 1892. Some had been discovered at Southern Cross, 200 kilometres east, in 1888 but nothing like this new find. Nine months after Bayley and Ford's windfall, Irish prospector Paddy Hannan filed a claim on 17 June 1893 for a discovery he'd made at Mount Charlotte with his mates Dan Shea and Tom Flanagan. This area became known as Kalgoorlie and proved an even richer goldfield. Bill Benstead claimed he was among the first at Coolgardie, pegging out an allotment and putting up one of the town's first buildings.[31] He opened a butcher shop, became the first postmaster, and later built a hotel, as well as pursuing mining interests. His musically talented family entertained the people on the mining fields. They prospered in the west but moved to England in 1910 to further Lulu's singing career.[32]

14

'Gillen time'

Frank Gillen called Ebenezer Flint the 'Giant of the Interior' in 1875 but there is no bigger figure in the annals of the OT line than Gillen himself. This son of Irish immigrants took Joe Skinner's place managing its most important repeater station; he was also effectively the administrator of central Australia with the responsibilities of special magistrate and sub-protector of Aborigines. He left a prodigious record of his times in letters, diaries, photos and museum artefacts. He achieved worldwide fame through the pioneering anthropological books he co-wrote with his great friend Professor Walter Baldwin Spencer but was 'always extremely modest about his own achievements'.[1]

Alice Springs writer Shirley Brown aptly described Frank Gillen as 'a boisterous, genial Irishman, earning him, all too often, the disapproval of his superior, Sir Charles Todd. Clean-shaven but for a bushy moustache, he wore a wide, flat-brimmed hat stuck at a jaunty angle. Photographs taken of him in Central Australia reveal twinkling eyes reflecting a life very much to his liking'.[2] His daughter Clare described him as 'impetuous, generous, witty and bubbling over with energy'.[3] Frank Gillen was a genial character who liked meeting people, enjoyed a drink and loved to have a chat while sucking on his pipe. He was an inveterate gambler and fan of horse racing but also interested in politics and world events. Like so many of his contemporaries living in the far-flung outposts of central Australia, he was well read, with a thirst for knowledge despite limited schooling.

The *Australian Dictionary of Biography* says 'his genial administrative efficiency in the Centre's senior command, combined with a sense of justice for Aboriginal people, made him a celebrity'. The respected historian Dick Kimber has written of senior Arrernte men using 'Gillen time' as a reference to their parents' and grandparents' times. Dick Kimber said 'these men never once talked of Gillen in other than respectful terms'.[4]

This man who spent a quarter of a century in the heart of the continent was an authentic Australian but never lost sight of his Irish Catholic roots. Indeed, his friend Mounted Constable Ernest Cowle called him the 'Pontiff'. Frank's parents migrated to South Australia in 1855 and he was born later that year, at Little Para, north of Adelaide. The family settled in the Clare Valley in 1862. Frank wasn't the only one who made a name for himself. His brother Peter Paul Gillen was elected to the South Australian House of Assembly in 1889 and held the ministerial position of Commissioner for Crown Lands for four years. Their youngest brother Thomas Philip Gillen was a respected storekeeper in the main street of Clare for 45 years and mayor from 1910 until 1912.

Eleven-year-old Frank became a telegraph messenger at the Clare post office in 1867. He mastered morse code and was appointed a junior operator in Adelaide on 1 October 1871, while Charles Todd's men were completing the central section of the line. He was on duty in Adelaide's Central Telegraph Office on 23 February 1874 when James Stapleton transmitted his last message to his wife half a continent away after Kaytetye men had attacked the Barrow Creek telegraph station. This harrowing experience didn't dull the young man's desire to work at one of Todd's northern stations and he got his chance the following year.

He left Adelaide in March 1875 and made his way to the Beltana telegraph station in the Flinders Ranges. Another young operator, Joe Skinner, caught up with him there on 7 April. Six days later they set off together on horseback.[5] It took them until 6 June to reach the majestic MacDonnell Ranges, stretching east and west as far as the eye could see, beneath a brilliant blue winter sky. Alice Springs operators Ted Harris and Hugh Conlon met them at Fenn Gap, 25 kilometres from the telegraph station. Conlon was relieving at Alice Springs because the stationmaster John Mueller had gone south for his first holiday after three-and-a-half years on the line.[6] Skinner went on to Barrow Creek while his younger mate remained at Alice Springs.

Todd transferred Gillen down the line to the much less picturesque Charlotte Waters in 1878. What a stark contrast to Alice Springs, perched on a bare stony rise in one of the driest parts of Australia. An early resident called it Bleak House, after Charles Dickens' novel of the early 1850s, but Frank spent 12 years working there, 'years free from care of any sort and of absolute content'.[7]

Early in 1891, Todd moved him back to Alice Springs to take charge of the station.[8] He fitted in easily. The other three operators John McKay, Bill Milne and Jim Field knew him well, as did Walter Randall and Jack Besley at Barrow Creek. They were familiar with one another's habits, moods and quirks. Gillen was good at his job and respected by the others who worked with him at Alice Springs in ensuing years: Frank Juncken, Phil Squire and his younger brother Edward, Vaughan Jagoe, Sid Middleton and Jack Besley.

The Pastoral Lands Commission visits Alice Springs

Frank Gillen wasn't long in his new job at Alice Springs when five members of parliament landed on his doorstep. Despite the huge area of land at its disposal, these were bleak times for the South Australian pastoral industry. Rather than expanding into new areas, grazing land for cattle and sheep was actually being abandoned. Leaseholders were struggling to move their stock the long distances to markets and faced low prices for the meat and wool once they got them there. The government decided to appoint a Royal Commission to enquire into the best way of dealing with the situation. Its members travelled widely in the first half of 1891, inspecting pastoral lands and talking to people.

Robert Caldwell, John Warren, Frederick Holder, John Robert Kelly and Robert Kelly got off the train at Oodnadatta on 25 March, with the Royal Commission's secretary Edwin Derrington. Camels were on hand to take them to central Australia. They visited Mount Burrell, Undoolya and Bond Springs stations, as well as the Arltunga and Harts Range areas. Rain greeted them on the way, the first decent fall for quite some time. They quizzed people about the nature of the country, stocking rates, rainfall, wells and the cost of freight. They were particularly interested in sheep. Again and again, they raised the issue. What was the local experience and what were the prospects for the future?[9]

The total stock numbers for central Australia by the end of 1888, Australia's centennial year, was estimated to be 50,000 cattle, 4500 horses and 10,000 sheep.[10] The missionaries at Hermannsburg had half of the region's sheep. They hung onto their large flock right through the 1890s while others gave them away.

Charles Todd had told the South Australian Parliament in 1884 there were 3400 sheep at the Alice Springs telegraph station at that time, with less at Charlotte Waters, Barrow Creek, Tennant Creek and Powell Creek.[11] The station employed Aboriginal people to keep an eye on them, especially to watch out for dingoes. However, the total for the four central telegraph stations was down to 1600 by 1889.[12] Alice Springs significantly reduced its flock after Willoby, Gordon and Youl stocked their Bond Springs lease with cattle and horses in late 1885. The sheep had been grazing on this land, north of the telegraph station reserve, and the new owners wanted them removed. A couple of pastoral leaseholders also tried sheep grazing in the early days but the cost of carting the wool to southern markets was prohibitive.

The Pastoral Lands Commissioners conducted a formal session with Frank Gillen at the Alice Springs telegraph station on 15 April 1891. He impressed them with his knowledge of the region. He pointed out the sheep at the central telegraph stations were kept for meat, not wool. They gave the wool away because they couldn't sell it. He showed his concern for the Aboriginal people saying the 'squatters' had 'not always treated them so well as they should have'. He said 'Government should provide rations for the old and infirm, who are in a chronic state of starvation, and appoint a sub-protector. A reserve of 250 square miles should be made round each telegraph station for use of the blacks; a suitable reserve might be set apart on the Finke river'.

Next day the commissioners met with Bill South at the Heavitree Gap police station. He commented on the poor state of most of the wells along the track. He expressed similar sentiments to Frank Gillen in relation to the Aboriginal people, discounting the suggestion they were troublesome. He said: 'They are very useful; I do not know how their services could be dispensed with.' The parliamentarians then climbed aboard their camels and headed back to South Australia, stopping at Crown Point station on the way to talk to the new manager Alec Ross.[13]

The governor drops in and discusses Irish politics

A couple of weeks after the Pastoral Lands Commission departed, Frank Gillen and his staff were called on to entertain the governor of South Australia. The government had asked Lord Kintore to investigate the prospects for settlement in the north of the Territory and generate some much needed publicity for the place.[14] He caught a ship to Darwin, disembarking there on 31 March 1891 with Dr Edward Stirling, director of the South Australian Museum, and his collector, Thomas Cornock. They spent a week inspecting the colony's most distant outpost and then took the train to the end of the line at Pine Creek. They started south by horse and buggy on 9 April.

Their guide was telegraph line inspector Alf Pybus, who had been in the Top End since the OT line was constructed. His uncle Harry Pybus was one of the stockmen who made the epic overland trip with the Milner brothers and their sheep in 1870 and 1871. Seven other men travelled south with the governor: two drivers, a cook, three Aboriginal men, plus Mounted Constable Charles Brookes from Burrundie, on the railway north of Pine Creek. Charlie Brookes had previously served at Barrow Creek.

Frank Gillen met them at Burt Creek, north of Alice Springs, on 7 May and escorted them to the telegraph station next day. The governor sang Frank Gillen's praises when he got back to Adelaide. The telegraph station didn't look its best, with the roof off the main building following the fire the previous October. However, the visitors enjoyed the chance to relax in comfortable surroundings and imbibe the warm hospitality of their genial host. They were particularly impressed that his staff lit up the ranges around the telegraph station with bonfires on their first night.

The governor's party stayed the weekend and then headed south through

Heavitree Gap and the Ooraminna Range towards Charlotte Waters. They received another cordial welcome there and a bigger one when they reached the new railhead and fledgling township at Oodnadatta. There was a race meeting in their honour following the speeches of welcome, and a special train was waiting to take Lord Kintore to Adelaide.

The governor duly reported on the state of the Northern Territory. He was impressed with the MacDonnell Ranges country and its potential but didn't see much future for the Top End. He recommended to the Secretary of State for the Colonies in London that the border of South Australia be shifted to the 21st parallel of latitude, north of Alice Springs, or perhaps to the 20th parallel. The Northern Territory had been entrusted to South Australia in 1863 but the arrangement could be revoked by the Colonial Office at any time. South Australia wanted permanent possession of the southern portion but considered the less productive north a burden. Lord Kintore recommended it be hived off.[15]

Gillen shocked his boss Charles Todd a couple of years later when he replied to a farewell telegram the Scottish-born governor sent him early in 1895. Lord Kintore's message ended with the Irish greeting *slianthe* and Gillen messaged back that he trusted his 'sojourn in Australia had made him a good Home Ruler'. He told his friend Baldwin Spencer in a subsequent letter 'I have heard since that old Sir Chas. Todd saw the wire and nearly fainted at what he termed my audacity'.[16]

In the months after Lord Kintore's tour of the north, the *South Australian Register* and its companion weekly the *Adelaide Observer* published a series of articles entitled 'Our Undeveloped Territory'. One article focused on Alice Springs and reported:

> The telegraph station buildings were severely damaged by a fire last year, and at the time of our visit some men were engaged rebuilding. This is the chief telegraph station on the line and has the largest staff of operators. Although the repeating is done by automatic repeaters the operators have their time fully occupied.[17]

Getting a new roof on the fire-damaged building was one of Gillen's pressing tasks when he took over from Joe Skinner. He was familiar with this building having lived in it as a young operator between 1875 and 1878. The new roof constructed in 1891 had a lower pitch than the original. There was more building work in the months that followed. A separate storeroom with a cellar was constructed at the western end of the store and a flour shed added at the eastern end. However, verandahs on its western and eastern sides, to shield the stone walls from the fierce heat of summer, were not added for another decade.

The 1891 trial of Mounted Constable William Willshire

The Pastoral Lands Commission had visited in April 1891, followed by Lord Kintore's visit in May. An even bigger event was just around the corner: the trial of William Willshire. The *Adelaide Observer* reported: 'It is some years since a trial in the Port Augusta Court has excited so much general interest.'[18] The matter was freely discussed in the Adelaide newspapers and even more so around dinner tables and camp fires in central Australia. Willshire was the first policeman ever arrested there and faced the prospect of hanging if convicted at the trial set for July. Frank Gillen JP had charged him with murder.

While the 1890 Swan-Taplin inquiry had exonerated Willshire of any wrong doing in his treatment of Aboriginal people in the 1880s, the authorities in Adelaide were in no doubt his actions, and those of his native police, warranted careful scrutiny. So Inspector Brian Besley and the police commissioner William Peterswald must have cringed when he advised them of the deaths of two more Aboriginal men, known as Roger and Donkey, at Tempe Downs station on 22 February 1891. Neither Besley nor Peterswald was inclined to take action but South Australian Attorney-General Robert Homburg felt an investigation was necessary. It took a while before the matter came to his attention but he acted decisively after reading the file.[19]

In April he directed his secretary to send a telegram to Constable Bill South at the Heavitree Gap police station, making it clear there was to be an inquest and, if possible, the bodies were to be exhumed so the bullet wounds could be examined. The only issue was who should conduct the investigation. Homburg thought either of his fellow parliamentarians Robert Caldwell or Frederick Holder might do it. Neither was keen. They and the other members of the Pastoral Lands Commission were winding up their investigations in central Australia at that time and about to head home. They suggested Frank Gillen, senior government official in central Australia and a justice of the peace. Willshire's past was about to catch up with him and he would be up against a man concerned that Aboriginal people be treated justly.

Aided by South, Gillen conducted an investigation into the deaths of Roger and Donkey, commencing with Willshire's sworn testimony on 19 April.[20] Unlike the Swan-Taplin inquiry the year before, Gillen interviewed Aboriginal people. The result was Willshire's arrest on the evening of 27 April 1891, charged with ordering the shootings at Tempe Downs. He was put in the lock-up at Heavitree Gap he had helped build. Bill South went so far as to question his fellow officer's sanity in a letter he wrote to Inspector Brian Besley a couple of days later. Willshire began his journey to Port Augusta gaol on 3 May.[21] Five days later Frank Gillen escorted the governor Lord Kintore from Burt Creek to the Alice Springs telegraph station. It had been a torrid couple of weeks.

The court was convened in Port Augusta on Thursday morning 23 July with Justice Henry Bundey presiding. Pastoralists throughout the colony had contributed money to engage its top barrister, Sir John Downer QC, to defend Willshire. It was a circus. The *Adelaide Observer* reported:

> The Court was crowded to excess, and several ladies sat the proceedings out. The sympathy of the town's people appeared to be entirely with the accused, and it is said that the funds for his defence were provided by voluntary subscription. A good number of people came up from Adelaide to hear the trial, and judging from the number who went to the telegraph-office to send down the result as much interest was felt in the city as in the country over the matter.'[22]

The much anticipated trial deteriorated into a farce lasting only a day. The native police retracted statements they'd made to Frank Gillen. It was clear they'd killed Roger and Donkey, and then burned the bodies, but their statements were considered unreliable. Willshire was behind the killings and everyone knew it but the process was flawed. People had convinced themselves he was just doing his duty. Gillen wasn't called to Port Augusta to give evidence. The judge said in his summing up that 'it would be a serious discouragement to the interests of justice if officers of the law in the execution of their duty were not supported'. The jury retired late in the afternoon and came back 10 minutes later with a verdict of not guilty. The crowd broke into cheers.

Willshire remained in the police force but did not return to central Australia. His post at Boggy Hole was closed and his native police force split between Barrow Creek and Alice Springs. Greater scrutiny of police activities brought an end to a destructive period in the region's history, though the incidence of cattle spearing and white retaliation had already declined by this time. A couple of witnesses told the Pastoral Lands Commission earlier in the year that the Aboriginal people were no longer causing trouble. A notable exception was the Tempe Downs area where cattle spearing continued until a police station was opened nearby at Illamurta in 1893.

Relations between black and white were already entering a new era before Willshire's arrest; an era of of increasing accommodation. The Aboriginal people had little choice. Their traditional lands, food supplies and water resources were being degraded by the hard-hooved animals the white men introduced. Their numbers were declining markedly. The respected researcher Dick Kimber has estimated that 500, and quite possibly upwards of 1000, Aboriginal people were shot in central Australia in what he called 'the bad old days' from 1871 to 1894. Add to this the deaths from new diseases such as influenza and typhoid; he estimates 20 per cent of the Aboriginal population of the Centre succumbed to disease in that same period.[23] Applying words like invasion and genocide to central Australian history is a vexed issue but there's no denying the wholesale usurping of land and the significant loss of Aboriginal life.

The Aboriginal people increasingly gravitated towards the station homesteads. There was the prospect of white man's flour, tea, sugar and tobacco in exchange for work, as well as offcuts of beef, though often it was largely the offal and fatty bits the whites didn't want when they carved up a carcass. The advent of another drought in 1890, extending into 1894, accelerated this movement towards white outposts. For their part, the whites became increasingly dependent on black labour. Both Frank Gillen and Constable Bill South had raised this in their submissions to the Pastoral Lands Commission in April 1891 when they said the station owners could not get by without their help. The white men also needed Aboriginal women. Wealthy South Australian landholders had invested in central Australia in the 1870s but realised by the end of the 1880s that they had overestimated the carrying capacity of the land and its ability to generate income and employ workers. Also, the markets were just too far away. Most disposed of their leases with heavy financial losses leaving the country to men with more modest expectations, hopes and dreams. They needed Aboriginal people who would work for meagre rations.

Willshire ridiculed Gillen after his acquittal but the episode enhanced Gillen's reputation with Aboriginal elders. The government aimed at bringing the rule of law to the region and ensuring Aboriginal people better treatment by, firstly, establishing a court in central Australia to allow charges to be heard locally, rather than hundreds of kilometres away in Port Augusta. The governor issued the necessary proclamation on 30 August 1892, to take effect from 30 September 1892. Court would sit at the Alice Springs telegraph station on the first Wednesday in the months of November, January, March, May, July and September.[24] Frank Gillen was appointed a special magistrate so he could preside over the court cases. The second initiative was the appointment of a local sub-protector of Aborigines. Constable South proposed this when he gave evidence to the Pastoral Lands commissioners and they made it a recommendation in their report.[25] Once again Frank Gillen was appointed to the position, in October 1891, with an extra salary of £20. His district was defined as the country between Charlotte Waters and Attack Creek to a limit of 80 kilometres either side of the telegraph line. When ration depots were established in the early 1890s at the Alice Springs, Barrow Creek and Tennant Creek telegraph stations, plus Illamurta police station, they were entrusted to his supervision.[26]

Gillen marries

Amid all the drama of the Willshire trial, 35-year-old Gillen was making plans to marry 22-year-old Amelia Maude Besley from Mount Gambier. The wedding was set to take place there on Wednesday 5 August 1891, so Gillen could easily have given evidence at Willshire's trial on the way past. It's interesting that the court chose not to hear what he knew of the case.

Amelia's uncle Brian Besley was the police inspector at Port Augusta. Her extended family included a number of telegraph operators so it's not surprising she met Frank. Amelia's brother Jack had been at Barrow Creek since 1887; another brother Dick was an operator in South Australia. She had a stepbrother Patrick 'Pado' Byrne on the OT line in the Top End until 1883 when he moved to Charlotte Waters as Frank Gillen's offsider. Pado's widowed mother Catherine married John Besley in 1865 and Amelia was born a couple of years later. Her cousins Jim and George Field also spent time on the OT line. Jim Field met the newly married couple with a buggy when they got off the train at Oodnadatta and escorted them to Alice Springs.[27]

Amelia shared her husband's interest in the Aboriginal people and his genuine concern for their welfare. They treated them with greater respect than most other whites of their time and this was recognised and appreciated by the Aboriginal people. The Gillens employed Aboriginal people as assistants, recognising them as individuals, and endeavoured to learn their language as well as teaching them English. Amelia also taught the girls dressmaking.

Dolly, a young Arrernte woman, worked as a 'housegirl' for a number of years and helped Amelia with her sons Brian and Jack, born in 1893 and 1895. An older woman Polly was another regular in the Gillen household, along with her husband Solomon. She rated regular mentions in Frank Gillen's correspondence and clearly played a significant part in family life at the telegraph station. She had a couple of light-skinned sons, fathered by lineman George Hablett, but contributed the condition to eating too much white man's flour.[28] Dolly worked for Mrs Bradshaw, after the Gillens left, along with another girl Tryff. Old Polly's employment ended with the Gillens' departure. Their house may have been the most palatial in central Australia but it lacked flyscreens and this made meal times a challenge. Doris Bradshaw recalled many years later:

> One day a portly matron named Polly, aware of the problem, offered her services as fly-swisher-in-chief during meals. She demonstrated her technique with a leafy bough and pressed her claim for the job by saying, 'All-day me bin shepherd'em flies longa Mitta Gillen.' But father declined with thanks.[29]

Amelia Gillen shared her husband's social tolerance and progressive views. She got the chance to express them via the ballot box during her years at the telegraph station. Women over the age of 21 in South Australia and the Northern Territory were the first in Australia to gain the vote. The colony's upper house, the Legislative Council, passed the *Adult Suffrage Bill* on 18 December 1894. New Zealand women had won the right to vote the previous year. As far back as 1885, Dr Edward Stirling had been raising the issue in the South Australian parliament. Six men who had pledged to vote for female suffrage were returned at the 1893 elections and the issue gained momentum from there. Northern Territory representative Vaiben Solomon made no bones about his opposition to the notion but he was in the minority by the time the issue came to the floor of the House of Assembly.[30] Northern Territory women got their first chance to vote in the April 1896 election and Amelia Gillen was one of 70 who turned out to have their say.

The Horn expedition

Central Australia was recovering from drought when a distinguished group got off the train at Oodnadatta on 4 May 1894. They were members of a scientific expedition financed by William Austin Horn, a former South Australian stockman who'd made a fortune from copper and silver mines. Their intention was to thoroughly examine the belt of country between the fledgling town of Oodnadatta and the MacDonnell Ranges. The governments of the colonies of South Australia, Victoria and New South Wales had responded favourably to the idea and agreed to release some of their leading academics.

There was Ralph Tate, professor of natural science at the University of Adelaide, and Dr Edward Stirling from the South Australian Museum. Stirling's main interest on this expedition was ethnography, the study of people and cultures, and he was keen to collect Aboriginal artefacts. The University of Melbourne sent its dapper young professor of zoology, Walter Baldwin Spencer, sporting a distinctive walrus moustache. From New South Wales was mineralogist John Alexander Watt of the Sydney Geological Survey Department. Victorian ornithologist George Keartland and Horn's brother-in-law F.W. Belt were engaged as collectors and taxidermists. Belt was an Adelaide solicitor and amateur naturalist.

Horn employed surveyor Charles Winnecke to organise the logistics of the expedition, as well as being its meteorologist. He was an experienced explorer who knew the region well after surveying a large expanse of central Australia between 1877 and 1881. Winnecke was waiting at the railhead when the train pulled in. He had gone ahead to organise camels, handlers, a cook and Aboriginal assistants. Horn was partly motivated by the possibility of new mineral discoveries along the way and so the party also included two prospectors.

Horn accompanied the expedition as far as Idracowra station on the Finke River. The local cattle industry was in trouble, with its inherent problems exacerbated by drought. The men found the homestead abandoned, apart from the few Aboriginal people camped there. The South Australian pastoral firm of Grant and Stokes had given up on central Australia. They began investing money in the region in 1875 but it was rumoured they'd lost over £100,000. They put their three stations Glen Helen, Idracowra and Macumba up for auction in 1893. Alexander and Fred Stokes returned to Europe, leaving William Grant to wind up their affairs.[31]

The expedition went on to Horseshoe Bend but continued along the Finke instead of following its tributary the Hugh and the OT line to Owen Springs. They visited the new police station at Illamurta, manned by constables Tom Daer and Ernest Cowle, and then went west to Tempe Downs station, now owned by Fred Thornton. He bought it from his employers in 1893. The Tempe Downs Pastoral Association, like Grant and Stokes, had lost a lot of money.

The party split at this point because Horn wanted photographs of Ayers Rock and Mount Olga. Constable Cowle escorted a small group to the south-west while the others went north to Haast Bluff, near the western end of the MacDonnell Ranges. Baldwin Spencer, the expedition's photographer as well as its zoologist, went off with Cowle. While they were away Winnecke and Stirling coerced an Aboriginal man to reveal the location of a cave in the Haast Bluff area containing a large number of sacred ceremonial churingas. They removed a number of these precious objects, some of them stone tablets and others carved from wood. In exchange, they left behind items of hardware such as axes and knives, clearly insensitive to how significant the churingas were to their Aboriginal custodians.[32]

The men all met up again in late June at Glen Helen station, abandoned now, like Idracowra. From there they followed the Finke River down to Hermannsburg Mission, to be greeted by temporary caretaker Louis Heidenreich. The founding missionaries Hermann Kempe, Wilhelm Schwarz and Louis Schulze had left, defeated by years of exhausting work and despair. The Lutheran Church's Immanuel Synod was taking over the mission, having paid £5000 for it. A young pastor, Carl Strehlow, ordained at Light Pass in the Barossa Valley after completing his seminary studies in Germany, was coming in a couple of months to take charge.

The expedition stayed a week at Hermannsburg and then headed east to Alice Springs, arriving on 15 July. The bulk of the party replenished their supplies and set off south towards Oodnadatta a couple of days later, examining the Ooraminna Range on the way. Watt stayed behind so he could have a look at the mining fields of the East MacDonnells. Spencer accepted Gillen's offer of accommodation. He was keen to do fieldwork around Alice Springs, including investigate a large spider which barked, according to the locals. Gillen's brother-in-law Jack Besley was working at the Alice Springs telegraph station by this time and he spent a night in the bush with the professor in a vain attempt to hear the noise. Spencer suspected the sound was made by quails living in the same habitat but couldn't prove it.

He and Gillen spent their evenings having long discussions on a range of subjects, most notably the Aboriginal people of central Australia. Watt's evenings in the east weren't quite so comfortable. He found only a small number of men working the diggings of Arltunga and Claraville. Three years of drought, commencing in 1890, had made life difficult on the goldfields. There was little financial return for their hard work but the miners had no other option because South Australia had descended into a major economic depression. A decent fall of rain soaked their parched landscape in December 1892 and significant rains, nearly 400 millimetres, fell in six weeks early in 1894.[33] However, the water seemed to evaporate as quickly as it dropped from the sky and it was clear this was a land where only the hardiest and most persistent souls could prosper.

Central Australia's native fauna was still largely intact when the Horn Expedition visited, despite two decades of land degradation. Their reports included a reference to brushtail possums being 'everywhere amongst the eucalypts which border the riverbeds'. The fast-moving mala, the smallest member of the kangaroo family, were common in the sand country. Burrowing bettongs and bilbies were also doing well but they were about to come up against the Spanish rabbit, a fierce competitor for food and living space. Rabbits were running wild across the country, after being imported to a Victorian farm in 1859, and they reached Charlotte Waters in 1894.

Among the Horn Expedition's achievements was collecting and describing a large number of new plant and insect species. William Austin Horn's experts were the first to collect fishes from central Australia. He was not rewarded with lucrative mineral discoveries but the money he contributed resulted in a better understanding of the geology of the region, particularly its fossil-bearing rocks. Hundred of photographs were taken. Add to all this, the genesis of a remarkable partnership between the balding, pot-bellied telegraph operator Frank Gillen and the young professor from Melbourne, Walter Baldwin Spencer.[34]

'The best man I ever had'

Amelia Gillen went south to Mount Gambier for the birth of her first child Brian in 1893 but was confident enough to remain at the telegraph station for the arrival of their second, Jack Besley Gillen in January 1895. By July mother and baby were ready to handle the long buggy ride to the railhead at Oodnadatta and holidays in the south with her family in Mount Gambier. While they were there, Frank ducked across to Melbourne on the train and spent a couple of days with Spencer. They had lots to talk about.

While in Adelaide, the couple engaged the services of Mrs Connor, a widow who would help with the running of the house. She travelled back to Alice Springs with them in October and stayed nearly two years.[35]

Mrs Connor was a fair age and very deaf but that didn't worry the station's handyman and blacksmith George Hablett. He took a fancy to her and worked overtime to win her favour. George was an Englishman who served in the Royal Navy before he came to South Australia in 1876. He was one of the OT line's great characters and a distinctive figure in the English cloth cap that rarely left his head, small gold gypsy earrings, grey beard, and pipe hanging from his mouth. He was an immensely strong man and looks a serious, no-nonsense chap in photos from the 1890s and 1900s. Not so! Rather, he was kind and loveable, and had a propensity for mixing up his words. His loud voice boomed like a foghorn across the telegraph stations of the OT line for 33 years. Everybody on that section of the line knew George Hablett. He started as a casual labourer in 1881, or thereabouts, and finished as foreman for No. 8 Line Party (NT), a team of three constantly on the track between Oodnadatta and Attack Creek, carrying out routine maintenance. He moved to the Barrow Creek area when his line party days were up, at the age of 65, and ran Neutral Junction station with George Hayes, another former lineman. He died in Adelaide on 5 April 1924.[36] Frank Gillen told his friend Baldwin Spencer that George was 'the best man I ever had'.

George Hablett was lovestruck. Frank kept his friend the professor informed of the developing relationship in his regular letters to Melbourne. 'Hablett and Mrs Conner have shifted their spooning perch to the fence', he wrote one day and 'the old girl grows younger daily'. He added that George 'has taken to buttoning his shirt collar on Sundays. This more than anything else convinces me that his attentions are serious'. By the middle of 1897 they were engaged to be married and she left for Adelaide. George followed her south in October. However, the engagement was soon called off when he found she had a weakness for the bottle. It turned out she was an alcoholic who had gone to Alice Springs to dry out. When she got off the train in Adelaide she also got off the wagon. Amelia Gillen was shocked when she heard this because Mrs Connor came with splendid references and never accepted a drink when offered one during her time at Alice Springs. Gillen was afraid the embarrassed fiancée might not return for fear of being ridiculed. He did so, telling his friends at the telegraph station 'Billy blowed if she ain't the rummest woman I've ever had time to look at, I'm puffektylgusted with her'.[37]

The pioneering work of Gillen and Spencer

The evenings Baldwin Spencer spent with Frank Gillen in his den at Alice Springs in July 1894 were the genesis of a close and enduring friendship. The young professor impressed the genial stationmaster and Spencer was similarly taken with Gillen. The discussions they had as the Horn Expedition was winding up were followed by a continuous exchange of letters for nearly 20 years, until Gillen's premature death in 1912. Together they developed their common interest in anthropology and forged a productive partnership. The Alice Springs telegraph station became the site of groundbreaking collaborative work through the remainder of the 1890s and the early 1900s that would bring world renown to them both.[38]

For years Gillen had been collecting Aboriginal artefacts, including sacred churingas, before he was fully aware of their significance to the Aboriginal people. He was mortified when he realised. Though never a fluent speaker of Arrernte, he'd been keenly observing and recording the language. Edward Stirling wrote the section of the Horn expedition's report covering anthropology and recognised Gillen's worth:

> This gentleman, from his long acquaintance and sympathetic dealings with the natives, has had opportunities of witnessing ceremonies and gaining information concerning them that have fallen to the lot of few white men.[39]

For example, it was Frank Gillen who introduced the term dreamtime as a loose translation of *alcheringa*, the creation era, though he and Baldwin

Spencer recognised the contribution of missionary Pastor Hermann Kempe of Hermannsburg.[40]

The couple of days Gillen spent in the professor's Melbourne home in August 1895 cemented their relationship.[41] Guided by questions that Spencer sent him in the months that followed, Gillen intensified his investigations in central Australia and began posting carefully written pages of notes.[42] One of his significant informants was Unchalka (or Ntyarlke), the senior cultural man in the Alice Springs area.[43] His totem was the emu bush caterpillar whose spirit ancestors are associated with the creation of the Alice Springs area and its key sacred sites. Gillen called him the 'royal brother' or 'King Charlie'. He was the same important man who, according to local folklore, was at Temple Bar in 1871 when the first white men came through the region.

Spencer returned to Alice Springs in the summer of 1896–1897 when he and Gillen conducted intensive fieldwork adjacent to the telegraph station. Day after day the two men lived in a wurley in temperatures exceeding 40°C. In mid 1896, Unchalka and the senior man of the Achilpa (western quoll) dreaming had begun arranging a major cycle of ceremonies, called an Engwura (or Angkwerre).[44] Many of these ceremonies were pertinent to a western quoll dreaming site called Imarnte, 100 kilometres south of Alice Springs on the Hugh River. It was a testament to their high regard for Gillen that they arranged this for him and that a large number of Arrernte people travelled to the telegraph station to take part. Not only did they allow him and Spencer to watch a constant succession of ceremonies, they also let the men photograph them. The ceremonies performed during the Engwura had never before been witnessed by uninitiated men.

The ceremonies commenced before Spencer arrived and continued until January 1897.[45] They had only just begun when Gillen received the terrible news that on 22 September his brother Peter Paul Gillen MHA had died on the steps of Parliament House. His rheumatic fever as a child had left him with a heart problem. He was accorded a State funeral but Gillen was unable to attend.

The work he and Spencer did that summer is generally perceived to be the most significant anthropological field research conducted in Australia in the 19th century.[46] Gillen did further fieldwork on his own after Spencer left Alice Springs. Spencer had no doubt the knowledge Gillen was accumulating warranted publication.[47] Their documentation of the Engwura ceremonies formed a large part of their classic book *The Native Tribes of Central Australia*, published in January 1899.[48] The information flowed mainly from the pen of Frank Gillen but Spencer's literary ability and skilful editing assured it became an influential work. While working hard during 1897 to get a first draft, Frank Gillen was faced with a major dilemma. The South Australian premier and attorney-general, Charles Kingston, offered him the position of resident stipendiary magistrate in Port Augusta. It was a wonderful opportunity and Amelia wanted him to accept it. However, to her disappointment, he declined, telling Spencer that he didn't want to leave Alice Springs 'until our work is through the press'.[49]

Frank Gillen and the Wheal Fortune mine at Arltunga

Frank Gillen left school at the age of 11 but he was an educated man. He went to night school in Adelaide when transferred to the Central Telegraph Office and the courses he took at the South Australian School of Mines and Industries, combined with his appetite for reading, gave him a broad education, including knowledge of geology and an interest in mining – which he pursued when he moved back to Alice Springs in 1891. An inveterate gambler on the horses and buyer of lottery tickets, it was inevitable he would dabble in the share market as well. Regrettably he was a loser but this didn't stop his irrepressible optimism that one day he would make enough money to ensure his children a good education and a start in life.

The most promising sites for hopeful miners in the East MacDonnells in the early 1890s were Claraville, north of Paddy's Rockhole, and the Wheal Fortune reef to the north-east.[50] The Wheal Fortune Gold Mining Company was floated in 1889 with Bill Benstead one of its directors. They purchased a Huntington mill to crush their ore but the returns were not good enough to justify their investment and keep the company afloat. They gave up on the mine and in 1893 their manager sold the mill for £13, even though it was worth around £700. He was owed backpay and sold off assets to recover it.[51]

When Geology Brown visited the goldfields in April 1896 he found only a few men on the diggings. There had been little progress since his last visit in 1891 but, in spite of this, he recommended the government erect a 10-stamp battery and a small cyanide plant for treating tailings. The politicians agreed, giving heart to the miners and the ever hopeful Frank Gillen. He formed the MacDonnell Ranges and Arltunga Gold Mining Syndicate in 1896 to work the Wheal Fortune reef and also the Star of the North. His brother-in-law Jack Besley, Amelia's stepbrother Pado Byrne, and policeman mate Ernest Cowle chipped in. Byrne went to Adelaide in August that year to raise capital but, fortunately for him, had second thoughts about the venture and the good sense to unload his shares a few months later. The returns were poor and Gillen lost a lot of money over the next couple of years. However, it took a while before his folly was crystal clear.[52]

The erection of the new government battery proved a mammoth task. The machinery reached Oodnadatta by train early in 1897 and then had to be hauled the remaining 600 kilometres by teams of horses. It took a year to settle on the best site and assemble the equipment, plus build the sheds to house it all. Fifty residents at Arltunga watched Frank Gillen turn on the steam and officially open the battery on 8 February 1898. He had faith in the future. As if to welcome the new plant and reassure the government it had not wasted its money, Henry Luce had discovered new reefs in the White Range area at the end of 1897. They were the richest discovered to that date.[53] A prospector and well sinker, John Byrne (regrettably not Pado Byrne), had discovered alluvial gold in the creek beds on the eastern side of the White Range but it was Henry Luce who realised where it came from. Luce was one of the few people who made a lot of money at Arltunga but he didn't live long to enjoy it, dying at the age of 39 in 1903.[54] In contrast, Frank Gillen's dreams for his wife and children came to nothing.[55] The Wheal Fortune mine proved a disastrous investment. He ultimately had to sell his extensive collection of Aboriginal artefacts to the National Museum of Victoria for £300 in 1899 to recover some of his losses.[56]

Two-wheeled travellers along the track

April is invariably a delightful time in central Australia as the summer heats ebbs away and the chilly nights of winter are still a few weeks off. On a Friday evening in April 1897, a notable visitor arrived on Frank and Amelia Gillen's doorstep. Irishman Jerome Murif was on his way to Port Darwin by bicycle. He had left the coastal suburb of Glenelg in Adelaide on his own, without fanfare, on 10 March, and made good progress over the rough track along the telegraph line.[57] He was warmly welcomed and happy to enjoy a few days rest and the company of the genial postmaster and his fellow telegraph operators. He later wrote an account of his travels in which he described the little township of Stuart as:

> All shade and silence and tranquility! It seemed as I came upon it to be the veritable 'Sleepy Hollow' of romance, with appropriate Catskill-y surroundings. The supplies for Arltunga goldfields, the mica fields, neighbouring horse station and cattle ranches, and the telegraph stations up north, all pass through here. It is a terminus of townships; beyond it lies the undeveloped.

He was impressed by Gillen describing him as 'a genial officer who, in addition to controlling this most important repeating station on that Transcontinental line which links Australia and Europe, has acquired during a long residence a profound knowledge of the aborigines of Central Australia, their languages, their customs, and their folklore'.[58] Before heading north the following Monday, Gillen took his photograph and, unbeknown to the intrepid cyclist, wrote an article for the *South Australian Register*:

> Both Murif and his machine were looking in the best of trim. On leaving here he was carrying a fair amount of dunnage, including waterbag, &c. The quartpot strapped underneath the saddle whilst travelling does duty as a storage-room for his tea and sugar. On his back he carries a small knapsack full of provisions, his chief nourishment being a small capsule of compressed beef tea, about the size of an almond, which he makes in his quartpot. This he finds a capital beverage and very refreshing after a hard day's ride. On his belt he has a small pouch for pipe, tobacco and

matches. He smokes very little during the day, and when short of water dispenses with the pipe until such times as he can afford to indulge freely. He converts his lampstand into a rack for his revolver, which article all travellers north of here carry, although it is some years since the natives attacked a white man on the road. However, prevention is better than cure. Murif, unlike most cyclists, prefers to travel in loose pajamas, using clips, rather than the knickers, the former being cool and comfortable in this semi-tropical climate.[59]

Murif found he was a national celebrity when he arrived in Darwin on 21 May, 73 days after leading Adelaide.[60] He made his way back to Adelaide by coastal steamer and train and found a large gathering of people waiting for him when he stepped off the express from Melbourne, including the mayor Mr Tucker and other dignatories. He was escorted to the South Australian Hotel where Mr J.A. McPherson MP proposed a toast declaring 'they were meeting a man who had successfully completed a trip that had never before been attempted by a white man, and which was beset, as they all knew, by innumerable dangers'. In rising to respond Murif was loudly cheered and said he had not had the slightest idea there would be such a gathering to meet him.[61]

Murif's feat aroused the spirit of competition. Soon after he reached Port Darwin, the Dunlop Rubber Company and Austral Cycles announced they would send two riders there, to ride south and better his time.[62] Charles Greenwood and Tom Coleman started from Port Darwin on 20 June but Greenwood pulled out at Adelaide River after two days hard riding against the prevailing south-easterly wind that blows at that time of year. It was reported he was suffering from a fever. In July, Alf Mather, a cycling journalist, was dispatched to take his place.[63] Coleman and Mather started on 11 August and reached Adelaide on 15 October, bettering Jerome Murif's time. But their journey was plagued with problems. At one stage Tom Coleman cut the telegraph wire to get help for which he later received a bill for £49 9s 2d to repair the line.[64] Mather praised Murif's effort after the trip but said he would only ever do it again in a balloon or with a vice-regal party.[65]

Central Australia was slipping into a new and prolonged dry spell when Jerome Murif, Tom Coleman and Alf Mather were pedalling their way into cycling folklore. The Federation drought of 1897–1903 was one of the worst in Australian history, affecting virtually the whole of the country. Sheep numbers across the continent dropped from 100 million to half that figure and central Australia's last big flock went during this period. Hermannsburg Mission had persisted with large numbers through the 1890s when everyone else had called it a day. Charles Todd's department purchased animals from the mission whenever it needed extras to supplement the small ration flocks it maintained on its telegraph stations. During 1899, a particularly dreadful year, the Hermannsburg shepherds were compelled to cut branches off shrubs to keep their animals alive. Their flock had fallen from 5000 at the end of the 1880s to less than half that number when the mission decided to sell most of them in 1901. Carl Strehlow thought it a waste of effort to continue running so many sheep. Shearing was an ongoing problem and the exorbitant cost of carting wool to southern markets meant they made little profit. Joe Harding travelled to the mission in September 1901 and took away all but 200 of the 2400 remaining at Hermannsburg.[66]

A very dusty little township at the end of the 1890s

Goat was the meat on most dinner plates in the township of Stuart as the 19th century drew to an end. People preferred beef or lamb but the hardy goat could survive the toughest of seasons and deliver good supplies of milk as well. Stuart only had a dozen permanent residents but the goat population was substantial, with 2000 roaming around.[67] It was just a speck on the map but had a steady stream of visitors passing through and blokes from the bush craving the pleasures of the pub and a hot dinner.

Its handful of buildings nestled among a shady expanse of river red gums, thanks to the foresight of the town's first greenie, policeman Bill South. Stationed at Alice Springs from 1888 until 1895, he had prevented the first residents from cutting down all the young trees for building and fencing material.[68] David Lindsay's 1888 town plan featured a square grid of streets, intersecting at right angles, and 104 lots. When offered for sale they attracted little interest. There were no footpaths, kerbs and guttering, street signs or streetlights. Todd Street and Wills Terrace were discernible but the rest of Stuart existed only on paper.

The Stuart Arms Hotel sprawled across two lots in Todd Street and was the town's main drawcard. It was built from stone, with shady verandahs to provide relief from the oppressive heat of summer, and it stood for over 70 years until gutted by fire in 1960. Bill and Triphena Benstead left town at the end of 1891, leasing it to Thomas and Mary Ann Gunter.

There was a butcher shop of sorts at the northern end of Todd Street but it had been vacant since its operator Edgar Pavey died in 1895. Three general stores served the needs of the local district. The most substantial was the one owned by Frank Wallis and built by stonemason Fred Stone in 1894, opposite the vacant butchery. It had a north-facing verandah where customers could stand and chat. A bit further west was Wallis's original store, run by Charlie South, nephew of policeman Bill South, since 1893. The third general store, a dark, windowless place built from wooden slabs, was in Todd Street, just south of the pub. The proprietor Fred Raggatt had made money working as a teamster along the OT line in the early days and obtained a storekeeper's licence in 1894.

A Chinese man was also established in Todd Street. Ah Hong grew vegetables and kept chooks and a few goats. He regularly carted garden produce out to the miners in the Arltunga area with Bulabaka, the son of his Aboriginal wife Ranjika. Details of his early life are sketchy but it seems he was born in Canton, now Guangzhou, around 1857. His descendants believe he came to Australia sometime in the 1870s and worked on the Pine Creek goldfields and the North Australia Railway before moving to central Australia. He was a cook at Bond Springs station and had a brief stint at Arltunga before setting up in town.

There was a newly married couple living near the river. Pastor John Bogner from Hermannsburg had officiated at the marriage of saddler Charlie Meyers and Annie Williams on 23 May 1897 at the Stuart Arms Hotel, where she was working for the Gunters. They were from the Cornish copper mining community of Moonta on the Yorke Peninsula. Wesley Turton had recently left for Western Australia, leaving his place on lot 99 vacant. Charlie and Annie Meyers eventually bought it but not for brewing beer.

No rain worth talking about fell in 1897 and, by the end of the year, duststorms were making life miserable. Enormous dark clouds would roll over the ranges covering everything with gritty red dust. The land either side of the Todd River was denuded of vegetation as hungry goats stretched up the trunks of trees and shrubs to nibble on bark and leaves. Someone complained to the authorities in Adelaide about the goats, which elicited a letter from Mounted Constable Alfred Kelly, Bill South's successor at Heavitree Gap. He defended the locals:

> I beg to state if the residents of the town of Stuart were compelled to do away with their goats it will inflict great hardship upon them as they cannot get beef from the cattle stations and sheep are not procurable. Goat mutton is all they have to depend on just now. We are suffering from a severe drought in this country and the goat is the only animal that keeps its condition.

Publican Thomas Gunter and storekeepers Charlie South and Fred Raggatt also wrote defending themselves:

> We are informed by MC Kelly that a complaint has been made in reference to our goats running near the Township of Stuart ... The residents here are without a Butcher and meat is almost unprocurable ... If there was any reliable way of obtaining meat, we should be first to do away with goats.[69]

One last year in central Australia

While the residents of Stuart were dealing with the challenges of goats and dust in late 1897, Frank Gillen and his staff were familiarising themselves with the biggest improvement in telegraph technology on the OT line since the introduction of automatic repeaters. Duplex working enabled signals to be transmitted simultaneously in opposite directions, a necessity with the volume of traffic being transmitted. Former Alice Springs operator Ted Johns was an expert on it.[70] It was installed on the southern half of the line first and Johns was sent to Alice Springs in November 1897 with Llew Griffiths, of the Engineer's Branch, to instruct staff on the various instruments and their operation.

Frank Gillen's last full year in Alice Springs was 1898. It got off to a good start with a decent fall of rain at the end of January, which greened the country for a while. At the gala day at Arltunga in February he presided over the official opening of the new government battery and cyanide works. Frank reported to Baldwin Spencer in March that he had never known the flies to be so bad. Many of the Aboriginal people had bung eyes.[71]

Early that month the government announced a decision to add a better performing copper wire to the poles of the OT line at a cost of £50,000.[72] The old galvanised-iron wire still worked well but the superior electrical characteristics of copper allowed faster transmission – and the introduction of mechanical telegraphy. Transmission on the iron wire was limited to hand-speed morse.[73] This major upgrade provided the opportunity to complete the replacement of the remaining wooden poles with iron ones in 1898 and 1899. In central Australia, it also meant the line could finally be re-routed to run directly north from Frances Well to Alice Springs, via the Ooraminna Range and Heavitree Gap, following the railway corridor surveyed by Graham Stewart in 1887.

The advent of drought made travel more challenging but the mail contractor Bob Wells continued to deliver letters, parcels and newspapers using the high-seated open buggy that locals called the mail coach. Stagecoaches of the type used by Cobb & Co in the eastern states never operated on the Oodnadatta track. A more frequent service commenced in April 1898, enabling Alice Springs residents to get a reply to a letter one month after they posted it. Drivers left Alice Springs and Oodnadatta simultaneously, met at Horseshoe Bend, exchanged mails and then returned to their respective starting points.[74] Special magistrate Gillen was put in an awkward situation that same month when forced to sentence the youngest son of his old friend Unchalka to six months hard labour in Port Augusta Gaol. He reported to Spencer:

Our old friend the King is terribly upset ... As soon as the old fellow heard the sentence he stalked off to his camp, burnt off his beard and destroyed all his weapons and even his blankets. I have never seen a blackfellow take anything so much to heart. This young scamp has given a good deal of trouble during the last twelve months and on three occasions he has been allowed to go unpunished when he richly deserved gaol ... The King with his scraggy burnt beard and troubled face is a real object for pity and I have just returned from the Camp where I have been trying to Comfort the old chap, who in all the years I have known him, has never, so far as I know, done a dishonest action.[75]

The dry conditions prevailing through 1898 didn't stop another adventurous bloke deciding to ride a bicycle across the continent from north to south. However, the Gillen family wasn't on hand to see Albert MacDonald when he passed through Alice Springs. Frank had accumulated leave he wanted to use ahead of an anticipated transfer south in 1899 and so they set off for South Australia on 23 August. Amelia was pregnant with their third child and did not plan to return to her home of seven years. A considerable portion of Frank's collection of Aboriginal artefacts was packed up and dispatched south, along with the family silver, paintings and other valuables. Albert MacDonald was waving goodbye to friends in the Top End as the Gillen family was preparing to depart Alice Springs for the train at Oodnadatta.

MacDonald was a telegraph operator, like Gillen, and also due for a new posting in South Australia. He'd spent over five years working in the north, stationed first at Port Darwin and then down the line at Powell Creek. Rather than catching a coastal steamer south, he decided to pedal his bike, clearly undeterred by the bad experiences of Tom Coleman and Alf Mather the previous year. At first light on 22 August 1898 he left the Port Darwin post office bound for Adelaide and ultimately Melbourne. The Melbourne-based Austral Cycling Agency Ltd agreed to repay him the cost of a Swift bike on a 'no result, no pay' basis, provided he completed the full journey in five weeks.

Friends from the North Australian Cycling Club, including his brother, accompanied him to Adelaide River. The prickly, spinifex country between

Newcastle Waters and Alice Springs turned out to be a hard slog. Worse was to come crossing the many sandhills between Alice Springs and Charlotte Waters but he was lucky, opportune rain had firmed the sand, making pedalling somewhat easier. He rested at Pado Byrne's telegraph station for a day and calculated he needed to average 100 miles (160 kilometres) a day from then on to get to Melbourne on time. He hadn't achieved this rate to date.

He made a fresh start at daylight on 12 September and travelled 101 miles to the Macumba cattle station homestead, arriving a little after dark. It was the first time he'd topped the magic ton. From there he had to negotiate the stony gibber country between Oodnadatta and William Creek. On 18 September he managed 107 miles (171 kilometres) to Wilmington. A strong wind behind his back the next day enabled him to cover an amazing 187 miles (300 kilometres) and pull up outside the Adelaide GPO at 9.45 pm. A large and enthusiastic crowd had gathered, blocking King William Street. He had not expected such a welcome, nor to be hoisted shoulder high and carried around the Central Telegraph Office where he'd worked as an operator in 1892 and early 1893. He'd covered 3000 kilometres in 28 days. He rode on to Melbourne as fast as his legs could take him, completing the entire journey in 34 days, one less than the target his sponsor had set.[76]

Meanwhile Frank Gillen was being feted in Adelaide for his knowledge of the Aboriginal people. Early in September he was interviewed by a reporter from the *South Australian Register* about the Aboriginal people of central Australia. He mentioned the book he was working on with Baldwin Spencer. He was scheduled to give a lecture entitled 'The Native Tribes of Central Australia' for the Royal Geographical Society on 23 September 1898. The newspaper article excited a lot of interest and people turned up in droves. It didn't take long for the meeting room above the Albert Hall in Pirie Street to be packed and so everyone was asked to grab their chairs and move downstairs to the main hall itself. The lecture included a description of the Engwura conducted at the Alice Springs telegraph station the previous year.[77] Meanwhile, in Melbourne, Spencer was preparing to board a ship for London to secure publication of the book.

Frank returned to Alice Springs in October leaving his pregnant wife and young boys with her family at Mount Gambier. December 1898 was oppressively hot and made worse by an outbreak of measles at Alice Springs that killed a number of Aboriginal people, including one of Unchalka's daughters and his mother-in-law. Frank received a telegram from Charles Todd that month saying the position of postmaster at Moonta was about to become vacant and urging him to take it. Another option was to go to Mount Barker, which was closer to Adelaide, but the Moonta job paid a higher salary. He reluctantly applied for it in the hope that he might be able to transfer to one of the large Adelaide suburban post offices later on.[78]

'I shall go with regret'

Early in 1899, Frank Gillen made one last trip up the line to Attack Creek in his role as senior inspecting officer. The country was very dry and it turned into a pretty crook year, rainfall-wise. People looked hopefully to the skies but little came. For years he'd experienced problems with haemorrhoids and he reported to Baldwin Spencer '800 miles in the saddle and piles nearly all the time. So you can imagine what sort of a trip I've had – Per loot I did splendidly'. Aboriginal groups to the north had been expecting him for months and he was able to collect a lot of artefacts and anthropological information.[79] He was back in Alice Springs by early March, ready to conduct a handover with his successor Tom Bradshaw. In the meantime, Amelia had given birth to daughter Eily Catherine Gillen on 28 February. Copies of the great book also arrived.

The Native Tribes of Central Australia quickly achieved the status of an anthropological classic. All 1500 copies were promptly sold, as were another thousand printed in 1938.[80] The book demonstrated that the supposedly primitive Aboriginal people had a well-ordered social structure and a complex spirituality, closely linked to the natural world in which they lived.[81] Dick Kimber said in 2002: 'Much as this book can be criticised for the Darwinian perceptions of the era it nonetheless was revelatory about Aboriginal culture. It is probably the most famous book ever published about Aboriginal culture.' His assessment of Frank Gillen is equally laudatory. Gillen achieved 'a status in Arrernte society that probably no other outsider has ever achieved'. He was trusted to such an extent that the people called him Akngerrepate (or Oknirrabata). The name means great teacher and is a title given to old men who are learned in customs and teach others.[82]

One of Frank Gillen's last tasks, on 14 April 1899, was to officially open the new copper wire now strung all the way to Alice Springs via Heavitree Gap. The next day he wrote a final letter to Baldwin Spencer telling him:

> I was to have started South tomorrow but my successor funked the mail journey, they are sending him through per buggy. He will arrive next week. I shall leave on the 30th and be in Clare on the 18th May ... Hanley is here with the Copper wire which I *officially!* fixed to the terminal pole amidst whiskey and rejoicing yesterday evening. Today we are working through to Adelaide on the new wire and without the aid of another repeating Station. This wire will quadruple the carrying capacity of the line ...[83]

Workmen were dismantling the old section of the OT line that deviated west along the Hugh River to Owen Springs.[84]

It was months since he had seen his family and he was looking forward to getting to South Australia and meeting his baby daughter. At the end of the month he left a drought-stricken place with people doing it tough, particularly his many Aboriginal friends who were saddened to see him go. He wrote in that last letter to Baldwin Spencer 'I am all eagerness to get away but when the time comes for me to leave I shall go with regret and I don't mind admitting to you that I shall feel parting with the blacks more than with the whites'. He was greatly missed. From his new posting at Moonta, he would periodically write to his successor Tom Bradshaw asking about his old Aboriginal friends and sending money for their wellbeing.[85]

Was Charles Todd jealous of Frank Gillen's fame?

Frank Gillen's status in academic circles was sky high following the publication of *The Native Tribes of Central Australia* in January 1899. In January 1900 he was given the honour of being president of the ethnology and anthropology section at the Congress of the Australasian Association for the Advancement of Science, held in Melbourne.[86] Later that year, Sir James Frazer of the University of Glasgow, the Scotsman considered one of the founding fathers of modern anthropology, organised a petition that was signed by a number of British academics and prominent figures. It called on the South Australian and Victorian governments to release Frank Gillen and Baldwin Spencer from their official duties for a year so that they could continue their anthropological research.

Both men were granted a year's leave of absence on full pay and the South Australian government contributed £400 towards the cost of an expedition across Australia. David Syme, proprietor of Melbourne's newspaper the *Age*, contributed £1000 in exchange for regular newspaper articles. Baldwin Spencer's father also provided money. They caught the train to Oodnadatta in March 1901 and set off on a journey that would take them along the OT line to Newcastle Waters and then north-east to the remote township of Borroloola on the Gulf of Carpentaria.[87] Travelling with them were two Aboriginal men Gillen knew from his years in the Northern Territory: Parunda, known by the English name Warwick or by his skin name Perrurle, and Erlikilyika (Alyelkelhayeka), who also went by the name Jim Kite. Policeman Harry Chance was the fifth member of the party: driver, cook and handyman. He looked after all the practical arrangements, such as food supplies at various points along the route.

Their plan was to observe and record the customs and ceremonies of a number of Aboriginal groups, primarily Arabana, Arrernte, Anmatjere, Kaytetye, Warramunga and Jingili, plus the Binbingka, Anula and Marra peoples of the Borroloola area. They had the latest in sound-recording apparatus: an Edison Concert Phonograph with which they pioneered the recording of Aboriginal songs and speech onto wax cylinders. They also had a Cinematograph camera, which they used to shoot some of the earliest moving pictures of indigenous people.

They stayed a fortnight at Charlotte Waters (until 10 April), over a month at Alice Springs (until 25 May), six weeks at Barrow Creek (until 19 July) and nearly a month at Tennant Creek (until 18 September.) Shorter stopovers followed at Powell Creek telegraph station and Newcastle Waters. They left the telegraph line there and headed east to Beetaloo station and then north-east to McArthur River station. The final leg of the journey was 65 kilometres downstream to Borroloola, which they reached on 2 November. This little riverport town had a pub, store, courthouse and, amazingly, a library. It was gazetted in 1885 and serviced the surrounding stations. Nine days after they got there, the man who was purchasing most of their horses and wagon arrived with some unwelcome news from Postmaster Little at Port Darwin, transmitted down the line to Powell Creek. The coastal steamer that was going to take them south was lying at the bottom of the sea.

Parunda and Erlikilyika returned to their country on 16 November, going overland with two riding horses and two packhorses. Spencer, Gillen and Chance were stuck at oppressively hot Borroloola for three months. They sat out the wet season under the floorboards of the courthouse, waiting for another boat to turn up and rescue them. Floodwaters from the monsoon storms had cut them off and they had no way of communicating with anyone outside the town. In January, Spencer's wife talked to the premier of Victoria to see what could be done. The Queensland government sent its small river steamer *Vigilant* around the coast from the pilot station at Karumba at the mouth of the Norman River and Gillen, Spencer and Chance happily climbed aboard on 8 February 1902. It took them to the hotel at Normanton but another three weeks passed before they could get to Thursday Island and a steamer down the east coast to Melbourne, eventually berthing on 17 March 1902. The results of their year's work filled the pages of a second book *The Northern Tribes of Central Australia* (1904), along with the results of a brief trip they made in 1903 to study the Arabana people at the Peake.

Frank Gillen's last years were difficult despite the worldwide acclaim his work with Spencer achieved. He was unhappy at Moonta and his subsequent appointment to Port Pirie in 1908. He wanted and felt he deserved a position in Adelaide where his children could receive a good education and he could enjoy the intellectual stimulation from close proximity to the centres of learning. He'd given a quarter of a century of faithful service in the Far North, which he believed warranted special treatment. He told Spencer in 1902 that

Moonta was 'drearily dull'.[88] He'd made a similar comment in 1901 when they passed through his old posting of Charlotte Waters: 'I know no drearier aspect except perhaps the surroundings of Moonta.'[89]

His disappointment at ending up in these out-of-the-way places was compounded by his failing health. He was suffering from a form of motor neurone disease known as Lou Gehrig's disease. His family attributed the condition to the deprivations of his many years in the bush and a lack of vitamins but the cause of the disease is unknown.[90] He ended up in a wheelchair, dependent on the nursing of his faithful wife. The accidental shooting death of his 18-year-old son Brian in Port Pirie in 1911 left him very depressed. He died on 5 June the following year and was buried in the Gillen family plot at Sevenhills, in South Australia's Clare Valley.

Frank Gillen's second son Jack became a doctor, as did his grandson, Robert Spencer Gillen. Robert Spencer Gillen raised the issue of his grandfather's relationship with Charles Todd in the preface he wrote for *F. J. Gillen's First Diary 1875*, which was published in 1995. He felt Todd was jealous of Gillen's fame, writing: 'Although Gillen was read, and quoted, by an international audience (including Sigmund Freud), for the rest of his life he was kept in the obscurity of a minor country post office position.'[91] The noted Spencer and Gillen scholar John Mulvaney also addressed this issue in the 1985 book he co-wrote with J.H Calaby, *So Much That Is New, Baldwin Spencer 1860–1929, A Biography*: 'Both Gillen and Spencer sensed that despite Todd's unstinting support for their fieldwork, he had become jealous of Gillen's extra-postal fame.'[92]

The Royal Geographical Society hosted a lecture by Frank Gillen at the Adelaide Town Hall on 24 July 1902 entitled 'Life of a Central Australian Aborigine'. Gillen wrote to Baldwin Spencer a couple of days later from Moonta:

Todd was too unwell, he said, to attend the lecture. The old begger didn't say one word by way of congratulation, which rather nettled me. Millionaire Brookman gave a lunch on Friday to celebrate the 40th anniversary of Stuart planting the flag on North Coast. Four survivors of the party were there including a nice modest fellow, a surveyor named Stephen King. I sat opposite to Todd and I fancy the old chap did not approve of his subordinate being placed in such close proximity to him. I had a long chat with him in the morning on official matters and he distinctly promised to recommend me for appointment to the first big office becoming vacant about the city, so this is satisfactory if he doesn't forget all about it. I told him that I thought my long service in the Interior and my ethnological work entitled me to some special consideration at the hands of the Government and he was good enough to say that was his opinion.[93]

John Mulvaney endeavoured to be fair to Charles Todd and suggested there may have been reasonable explanations for Gillen's failure to get a city posting. Another issue this respected academic raised is more puzzling:

> If prime appointments did not come Gillen's way, neither did honours. Spencer was made a Companion of the Order of St Michael and St George in 1904, but there was no honour for Gillen in the same list ... Spencer raised the anomaly directly with Prime Minister Deakin, who blamed a federal–state dispute concerning nominations of awards.[94]

It was to no avail. The anomaly wasn't corrected and Frank Gillen was never recognised in an Imperial Honours List. Perhaps his Catholicism and the sectarian prejudices of the time had something to do with this. Who knows? If ever there was a case for a posthumous Order of Australia then surely this Giant of the Interior deserves it.

15

The Bradshaw era

One cold morning in May 1899, a mother and her four young children caught the 6.30 suburban train from Glenelg to the Adelaide railway station. It was the first leg of a journey to the centre of the continent. Her husband was already there, as the new man in charge of the Alice Springs telegraph station. Attie Bradshaw was was born on the migrant ship *Atalanta* as it rounded the Cape of Good Hope on 10 March 1866 on a voyage from Plymouth, England. She grew up by the sea at Glenelg and married telegraph operator Tom Bradshaw in April 1890. Nine years on, she was bravely following him into the great Australian nothingness. Tom had worked night shift at Adelaide's Central Telegraph Office for a number of years and needed a change. The job was wearing him down and his doctor suggested he might benefit from a long sea voyage. Instead, he headed to the bush, leaving Adelaide on a hot morning in March, for a handover at his new posting with the departing stationmaster Frank Gillen.[1]

A slight, fair-haired girl in her early twenties met Mrs Bradshaw and the children at the Adelaide station that cold May morning. Bertha Easom had answered an advertisement in the *South Australian Register* a couple of weeks earlier.[2] It didn't say much: 'Wanted Alice Springs (Far North) Lady as Companion and Governess.' It gave Mrs Bradshaw's address, said references were required and that she could be contacted in the evenings. There weren't many applicants for the position but Mrs Bradshaw was impressed by the young woman's good education and bright disposition. She seemed unfazed by the prospect of a spending a year in the middle of nowhere, with only modest pay. She ended up staying two years and the two women became close friends. They corresponded regularly for the next 30 years, until Mrs Bradshaw's death in 1929, at the age of 63.

Bertha helped get the children settled on the train that would take them to the Mid North town of Terowie. Doris was eight years old, Mort was six, Consie three, and Jack an active toddler of 18 months. They changed trains at Terowie, boarding the wooden rattler that ran once a fortnight on the narrow-gauge line to Oodnadatta.[3] The train to 'Oodna' wasn't renowned for speed, class or comfort. Passengers sat on two long seats running the length of the carriage and were constantly thrown sideways. There was no dining car and no sleeping berths. The crew pulled up each night and the passengers got off to stay at a hotel. The train wouldn't leave next morning until everyone had finished their breakfast. The two women had plenty of time to get to know each other, though it was hard to chat in the noisy carriage as the train rattled its way north.

Quorn in the southern Flinders Ranges is a pleasant little town but Mrs Bradshaw and Bertha Easom must have wondered what they'd gotten themselves into when they pulled up the second night at Hergott Springs, on a flat, sunbaked saltbush plain that was hot and dusty in summer, cold and windswept in winter. There was a substantial two-storey hotel and a well-built stone telegraph station but little else. The town was mostly an assortment of galvanised-iron dwellings inhabited by the Afghan families whose camel trains supplied the lonely outposts of the inland. The government named it Marree but the railways and post office continued using the original name Hergott Springs. David Herrgott discovered a dozen mound springs in the area while exploring with John McDouall Stuart in 1859. It was a significant find and a shame the mapmakers misspelt his German name. He did not live to see the railway reach the area in December 1883. He'd died in Melbourne in 1861 at the age of 36.

The two women were very relieved when the train made it to Oodnadatta. The novelty of the trip had well and truly worn off by the end of the third day. South Australia's most northerly town, on another bleak stony plain, had a substantial railway station, an interesting name and mobs of camels. Nonetheless, the unpretentious, low-roofed Transcontinental Hotel was a welcome sight and Tom Bradshaw was there to meet them. Telegraph lineman George Hablett was with him, plus driver Bob Crann and two Aboriginal helpers. They'd been in town for a couple of days to allow the horses a decent rest before setting off next day on the 470-kilometre journey back to Alice Springs. They'd brought the telegraph station's buggy and a buckboard to carry the luggage and camping gear. They'd also brought plenty of spare horses so that the teams hauling the vehicles could be changed regularly. The track to Alice crossed some challenging country, most notably the infamous Depot Sandhills, north of Horseshoe Bend on the Finke River.

Bob Crann took a fancy to the young and attractive governess. He headed for the blacksmith shop when they pulled into the Charlotte Waters telegraph station, spending all their time there fashioning a brooch for her from coins.[4] There's a Crann Street in Alice Springs but precious little is recorded about the man, other than his tragic end 18 months later. He perished while riding from Dalhousie station to Oodnadatta in very hot weather.[5]

Big shoes to fill and a difficult transition

Thomas Andrew Bradshaw was born in Bedford, England, on 28 February 1859 and migrated to the Portland district in Victoria with his parents as a child. Charles Todd quickly rose to pre-eminence in Australian telegraphy but it was actually Samuel McGowan who pioneered it in this country. McGowan, a Canadian engineer trained by Samuel Morse, brought batteries and instruments with him to Australia in 1853 with the intention of establishing a private company. Instead he was appointed superintendent of the Victorian Government's new Electric Telegraph Department and oversaw the creation of a network across that colony. By 1857 it included a line to Portland near the border with South Australia. Young Tom Bradshaw joined the telegraph office in Portland but saw a better future in Adelaide, and got a position there in June 1878.

He had over 20 years telegraph experience under his belt when he went to Alice Springs in 1899. He had a fair bit else under his belt. His daughter Doris recalled: 'He was a short, stocky man with dark hair and brown eyes, a moustache, and a developing corpulence that the Aranda tribesmen dignified with the name Adnutta.' Attie was somewhat similar. Doris said her mother was 'as plump as mothers of four children should be, with beautiful brown hair she had allowed to grow. She was courageous and practical, an able seamstress and a good cook'.

Frank Gillen and Tom Bradshaw had very different personalities; one effusive, boisterous and fun loving, the other a reserved man of few words. Doris admitted her father could be 'slightly irritable'.[6] Bradshaw was bookish and content to spend his free time reading in an armchair. A period of readjustment was inevitable for the staff; Gillen's letters to his friend Baldwin Spencer make this clear. Gillen was critical of his successor at times. Even before his replacement arrived, he wrote to Spencer saying 'Great soreness in the line about the appointment of Bradshaw'.[7] He gives no indication why there would be apprehension about the new man; it's possible the off-hand remark reflected his own mixed feelings about leaving central Australia. You have to feel sympathy for Bradshaw, who was stepping into the shoes of a popular figure with a huge reputation.

On 28 April 1902, Tom Bradshaw drove the telegraph station buggy down the road to Stuart, bound for Oodnadatta and the fortnightly train. With him was Herbert Koschade, a young telegraph operator sent up to relieve at Charlotte Waters and Alice Springs for a couple of months.[8] Koschade, who needed surgery in Adelaide to relieve pressure on his brain, made a full recovery.[9] While he was in the city, Bradshaw enquired about the possibility of a transfer back to South Australia after three years in Alice Springs. This didn't happen and Gillen continued to pass on negative comments about him to Spencer. He said he disliked and distrusted his predecessor, and that he was at loggerheads with his staff.[10] However, Bradshaw got on with the job and ended up staying another six years. He earned the respect of the white people of the region and administered justice with a strong sense of fairness and compassion for the Aboriginal people. Ironically, when he eventually got a transfer south in 1908, it was to replace Frank Gillen at Moonta.

Attie's brother Ernie Allchurch joined them at Alice Springs in September 1902. He was also a telegraph operator. The Bradshaw family expanded to seven children during their nine years at the telegraph station. Three little Centralians were born there: Don, Edna and Alan. We know more about the Bradshaw era than any other in the station's history because of the many photographs he took and the wonderful book his daughter Doris co-wrote with journalist Douglas Lockwood in the 1960s. Their story of the family's time at Alice, on the line, became a bestseller.

Bradshaw and the Aboriginal people

It's clear that stress was a factor in Tom Bradshaw's decision to give up night duty in Adelaide and seek a new life in Alice Springs. So it's understandable that he wasn't happy, initially, to be saddled with the extra responsibility of being sub-protector of Aborigines. This should not be construed as disinterest in the plight of the Aboriginal people or lack of empathy for them, even though Frank Gillen voiced that opinion. He wrote to Baldwin Spencer from Moonta, a year after he left Alice:

> McKay who arrived from Barrow Creek lately tells me that my successor, Bradshaw, takes little or no interest in the blacks. He dislikes the duties of Protector and is trying to have the protectorship transferred to the local Police. The Country up there is in an awful state, at the Alice they lost all their little herd of about 90 cattle but this, I consider, is simply the result of bad management.

Three weeks later he continued to stir the pot:

> The Alice Springs staff are not a very happy family. Neither Bradshaw or his wife are liked: he dislikes the duties of Sub Protector, has hunted the Niggers away from the Station to Middle Park Gap and wants the Govt to relieve him of his duties and appoint the Officer in Chge of Police, Brooks, Protector – No man more unfitted than Brooks could be found in the Country. When not drunk he's suffering a recovery.[11]

However, at that very time, Bradshaw was demonstrating his concern for the Aboriginal people and his willingness to support them. He took the decisive action of forbidding whites from entering Aboriginal camps between sunset and sunrise.[12] He then wrote to the authorities in Adelaide on 8 June 1900 advising them what he had done:

> I beg to respectfully attach a copy of a notice which I thought necessary to exhibit in the Township of Stuart, and on the notice-board of the local Post-Office. Aborigines have complained to me that White men – in certain states of Excitement consequent upon a free indulgence of stimulants – have disturbed their camps during the night, and endeavoured to entice young girls therefrom. I am not sure whether my appointment entitles me to issue such as notice, as I am unable to find any Act of Parliament, or Regulation, defining the duties and powers of a Sub-Protector, and therefore I respectfully submit this notice for your approval or otherwise.

> NOTICE
> I hereby give notice that after this date, all white persons visiting or entering any camp occupied by Aborigines, between Sunset and Sunrise, will be prosecuted – unless such visits be made for reasons of Extreme Urgency – when the circumstances connected with such visit must be reported to me within 24 hours thereof, by the person or persons so visiting.
>
> T.A. Bradshaw, sub-protector of Aborigines

Asked for its opinion, the attorney-general's department said Bradshaw didn't have the power; he had overstepped his authority. He was advised of this. Nonetheless, the exercise demonstrates he took the role of sub-protector seriously, and was willing to take Aboriginal complaints on board.

It's clear the first couple of years were difficult for him as the staff adjusted to new management and a personality so different to Frank Gillen's. The situation was no doubt aggravated by the stress caused by the long Federation drought.[13] There was a good fall of rain in mid 1901 but its effects were shortlived, and by early 1902 a tonne-and-a-half of flour had to be sent to Barrow Creek to save the lives of starving Aboriginal people.[14]

Keeping the telegraph station's livestock alive was minor concern compared to the heartache Tom and Attie Bradshaw felt as they saw the Aboriginal people struggling to survive. It's clear he and his wife had the same, genuine concern for the people as the Gillens. His report as sub-protector for 1901 said there were 98 Aboriginal people living near the Alice Springs telegraph station that year. This number increased as conditions worsened the following year. The couple personally provided Christmas dinner for 167 Aboriginal people in 1902.[15] Attie Bradshaw's obituary in the *Advertiser* gave an insight into the relationship she developed with the Aboriginal people:

> Mrs Bradshaw showed great resource as a nurse, and became loved by the community because of the friendly interest she took in those who needed care. Her kindness to the blacks who came into the telegraph station, especially during drought periods, for rations and blankets, inspired their devotion. Wild blacks used to come into the settlement with those partly civilised, and the pitiable condition of the frightened, sick, and starving creatures caused Mrs Bradshaw great distress. Having no trained medical knowledge, she could do little for the sick natives, for whom her invariable prescription was a mixture of ground ginger, sugar, and hot water. She comforted herself with the thought that it could do them no harm. The blacks who could speak English pronounced it very good.[16]

A stark difference between Tom Bradshaw and his predecessor was their attitudes to Christian missionary activity. Gillen was never a big fan of Hermannsburg and the Lutheran efforts to convert the people to Christianity. Despite his obvious empathy for the Aboriginal people, he was convinced, like Baldwin Spencer, that they were doomed to extinction. He wanted to observe and record as much of their culture and beliefs as possible while there was still time. In contrast, Tom and Attie Bradshaw admired the work of the Hermannsburg missionaries and saw Christianity as providing hope for the people.[17] Bradshaw conducted a service at the telegraph station on Sunday mornings and his wife led Bible study and provided religious instruction to Aboriginal women and children, as well as her own brood.

Bradshaw upheld the law and followed established sentencing guidelines as special magistrate. He sentenced many cattle spearers to six months hard labour in the Port Augusta gaol. However, he had doubts about the effectiveness of this and would have preferred an alternative form of corrective service. He wasn't long in the region when first confronted with the pitiful sight of Aboriginal prisoners on their way south, chained at the neck. His daughter Doris recalled: 'Once or twice I saw men who had walked so far in lawful custody that they had no skin left on the soles of their feet.'[18] He wrote to the Minister Controlling the Northern Territory on 16 September 1902 saying:

> I beg to respectfully say, that in my opinion, the present system of sending Aborigines convicted of stealing, to Pt Augusta jail, is costly, ineffective, and to some extent cruel ... I respectively submit my opinion that Aborigines committing offences of this nature, should be punished locally, and if the punishment be by imprisonment with hard labour, there is plenty of work for them to do in this neighbourhood, whereon they could be very usefully employed, such as improving and repairing roads etc etc.[19]

He tried to treat people fairly and was prepared to let an offender off with a warning, as happened in December 1901. An Aboriginal bloke called Sambo had broken into the store and stolen a sizeable quantity of flour, tea, sugar and a butcher's knife. It was the height of the drought and Bradshaw sent him to Barrow Creek with some food after the stolen goods were recovered.[20] In October 1903 he wrote a letter to the editor of Adelaide's daily the *Register* defending Aboriginal people after earlier comments of a very critical nature by Mounted Constable French. French had arrested an Aboriginal man Cattylundie at Crown Point for the murder of a white man William Lange. He described 'the aborigines of the interior as being utterly savage and incapable of the finer instincts of humanity'. Bradshaw replied: 'On behalf of the much-maligned aborigines of this portion of the state, I strongly protest against such an extravagant, cruel and misleading statement.'[21]

The small police lock-up at the Heavitree Gap police station made from rough, bush timber was an unsatisfactory structure to incarcerate prisoners for any length of time, especially in the stifling summer heat. An incident occurred at the Finke River in 1905 that set off a string of events leading to the construction of a new town gaol. Mounted Constable Fred Phlaum and his trackers arrested eight men in August 1905 on suspicion of cattle killing. The police tied them to a tree and gave them a hiding. They took them to Hermannsburg and then to the lock-up at Heavitree Gap where they were beaten again with a stockwhip doubled up. Two of the prisoners, youths aged 14 and 16, were released after 14 days detention.[22] The incident cost Phlaum his job. He was asked to resign.

The six older men escaped on 1 December while working about a kilometre from the Heavitree Gap lock-up. The warder Jim Grant was knocked unconscious and suffered a broken rib. The men fled west leaving most of their prison clothing a few kilometres away, along with one discarded neck chain. They were back in detention by early January 1906 and committed for trial in Port Augusta. Bradshaw preferred local punishment but the crown solicitor advised that he must commit the men to a higher court. They escaped once more on the night of 24 January, along with another prisoner. They'd managed to pick open a large padlock connecting their neck and foot chains to a much larger one and removed one upright log from the wall of the lock-up. Six of the seven were subsequently recaptured and dispatched to Port Augusta in March.[23]

Stonemason Jack Williams came to town in 1907 to start work on a new and much larger gaol. The final cost totalled £1368 2s 6d and resulted in more humane conditions for prisoners, most of whom were Aboriginal. It meant those on relatively minor charges were no longer despatched to South Australia, at considerable cost in both money terms and police time. Bradshaw had pointed out to the authorities a few times that sending those charged to Port Augusta wasn't an effective deterrent anyway. 'A trip to Pt Augusta is regarded by most Aborigines as being more pleasure than punishment', he wrote in 1902.[24]

Last gasp for the goldfields

The discovery of a gold reef at White Range at the end of 1897 and the opening of the government's battery and cyanide works in 1898 gave hope to the long-suffering diggers in the East MacDonnells. There was a steady output of gold at the turn of the century but nothing to compare with the fortunes made at Bathurst, Ballarat and Bendigo. Arltunga was no El Dorado. A shortage of feed for horses, as drought gripped the country, made it difficult to get the ore from the various diggings to the government works. Calamity struck towards the end of 1901. The Star of the North Well, providing water for the battery, started to fail and clearly needed deepening. Then the boiler collapsed, overcome by corrosion of the internal plates. A new horizontal engine and Cornish boiler were brought up to Oodnadatta on the train in February 1902, but hauling them the extra 600 kilometres to Arltunga was a mammoth task. Particularly challenging was crossing the fearsome Depot Sandhills between Horseshoe Bend and Alice Well. Teamsters Steve Adams, Fred Raggatt, Charlie South and Larry Rosenbaum combined to do the job. It wasn't until July 1902 that the new equipment was installed at Arltunga and gold processing resumed.[25]

This was opportune timing because a major new discovery in October 1902 raised hopes that a gold bonanza was imminent. A prospecting party led by John McNeil reported a new reef about six kilometres south of a waterhole in the Hale River known as Winnecke's Depot. They called it Paddy's Goose and before long there were 160 men on the new field. Burton Corbin, manager of the government works 40 kilometres away to the south-east, was so enthusiastic that he resigned in November and formed his own mining company.[26]

The best way to get to the new field was to head up the rough track north of the telegraph station and then go east, rather than use the established southern route through Undoolya. Doris Bradshaw remembered the invasion of new miners:

> There were men in buggies, drays, sulkies, and on horseback. There were men with packhorses and others humping their blueys; there were even men who pushed handcarts carrying their belongings all the way from Oodnadatta – and if that wasn't the ultimate in doing it the hard way I'd like to know what was. Alice Springs was transformed almost overnight. The population doubled and then trebled. Whereas we usually saw a new

face one a month, sometimes only once in three months, we now had more than we could readily identify.

It was a proper goldrush, compared to the steady trickle of earlier days. The population reached 300 in February 1903. A calico village of tents and bough shelters appeared from nowhere. Merchants were operating from tent-stores, and the Winnecke Hotel opened for business in a rough structure of wooden posts, rails and hessian, with a roof of compacted spinifex grass. This fair dinkum shantytown looked like it would blow away in the first dust storm. Tom Bradshaw drove the station buggy out there on 13 March 1903 to investigate requests for a post office. He recommended one be opened but six months elapsed before the authorities in Adelaide made it happen.[27]

The South Australian Government decided a second official was needed on the goldfields for a while, someone 'more conversant with the law relating to goldmining' than John Mueller, who had been appointed warden in 1895. A state of chaos existed, not helped by Mueller's frequent bouts of insobriety. Lionel Gee of the Department of Mines left Adelaide in March 1903 with 150 prospectors on the fortnightly train and reached his destination 21 days later. He got a taste of what lay ahead when he stopped for a night at Ted Sargeant's store at Horseshoe Bend, telling the *Register* many years later there were 'Plenty of tough citizens and sly grog; the place seemed to me a veritable sink of iniquity'. Things were much the same when he finally reached the government works at Arltunga on 5 April: 'Found Mueller there, rather drunk, black gins, unsavoury place.' Heavy rain fell during the journey, after significant falls the previous November. More was to follow in April, breaking the long Federation drought and ushering in the best season since 1889.[28]

In July 1903, the high point in the goldfields' history, there were 350 on the diggings, by Lionel Gee's count. English newspapers were talking of 'rivers of gold'.[29] However, an outbreak of typhoid fever followed the rains. It was rampant around Alice Springs and at Winnecke by this time, though the situation wasn't so bad further south at Arltunga.[30] People contracted it by drinking contaminated water and it took a heavy toll in the primitive living conditions. Sick men were simply lying down under bushes because there were no medical facilities or suitable accommodation for them.[31]

A doctor was sent up from the Flinders Ranges to deal with the outbreak. Patrick Shanahan left Hawker on 23 June 1903 accompanied by Mr J.F. Bishop, who acted as dispenser of medicines, nurse, dentist and general handyman. They drove at breakneck speed in a light buggy, drawn by two resilient Timor ponies, and stayed in central Australia until September. Dr Shanahan had tents set up a kilometre from Stuart township, and patients were taken there. People were drawing water from soakages and wells where cattle, horses and goats were also congregating and animal droppings were contaminating the water. The doctor also reported to the Board of Health in Adelaide that toilet pans were being emptied into the sandy bed of the Todd River close to the town. He directed the locals to boil all their drinking water.[32]

Winnecke had a meteoric rise but the high was also short-lived. Men starting drifting away in the second half of 1903 when they realised the high cost of carting ore 40 kilometres to the battery at Arltunga. The owners of the Winnecke's Junction and Coorong reefs knew they had to crush their ore locally to be profitable. They formed the New Coorong Crushing Company in 1904. The government gave them a subsidy of nearly £2000 to erect a 10-stamp battery at Winnecke but it didn't start crushing until mid 1905. The government took over the Coorong battery in 1908 by which time the bustling shantytown had gone with the wind. There was only a handful of people left on the goldfields and little ore being crushed. The prospects were better in Western Australia. The Arltunga battery operated occasionally in the next couple of years but the hiss of steam from the boiler, the whirring of wheels and the loud clattering of its stampers ceased altogether in 1916. There was no one sending stone and so it was mothballed.[33]

Pioneers of education in the Alice

Frank Gillen and Baldwin Spencer were camped at Abminga Creek in northern South Australia on 27 March 1901. They'd just begun a year of fieldwork that would take them north to Borroloola and culminate with the publication of their second book, *The Northern Tribes of Central Australia*. The flies had been dreadful, driving men and horses crazy. During the day they'd called into the Bloods Creek store where they found half a dozen men, including the proprietor Harvey, somewhat inebriated. Gillen was not impressed with the miserable place, writing in his diary that they 'put up with their hiccoughs and blasphemy for about 10 minutes and then moved on to the creek' to eat lunch. They travelled further north in the intense afternoon heat before camping for the night in a forest of gidgee trees.

Around 5.30 pm the southbound mail coach came down the track. Gillen's brother-in-law Jack Besley and a young woman with a pretty face were on their way to Oodnadatta to catch the fortnightly train. Besley was returning to South Australia after more than 13 years as a telegraph operator on the OT line to marry Florence Ruthven in Adelaide. He didn't introduce the young woman on the coach during their brief stop.[34] It was Bertha Easom, also heading south for a new life, after spending two happy years with the Bradshaw family as governess to the children.

She'd just turned 22 when she went north with Mrs Bradshaw in 1899. Her father David Easom ran a successful business manufacturing farm machinery until the depression and banking crisis of 1893. Bertha's friends were from well-to-do families in Adelaide but she found many of them didn't want to know her when her father lost his fortune.

There was no school in the little town of Stuart and so Mrs Bradshaw employed governesses. She set up a schoolroom next door to the staff dining room, which doubled as a courtroom on the first Wednesdays of January, March, May, July, September and November. Doris was eight when they left Adelaide and already had a couple of years of formal education. Bertha had no training but she was able to build on this and teach Mort and Consie the basics of reading, writing, spelling and arithmetic. She also provided lessons in history, geography and playing the piano. The ability to teach piano was the one qualification Mrs Bradshaw expected of the four governesses she employed. The Bradshaw children were more fortunate than the four young Brookes children living eight kilometres away at Heavitree Gap. Ruth, Dolly, Jessie and Henry Brookes had no prospect of a formal education, other than what their parents Charlie and Albina could pass onto them. Mounted Constable Brookes took charge of the Heavitree Gap police station the year before the Bradshaws arrived. His previous posting was Burrundie in the Top End, with a spell at Barrow Creek before that, in the 1880s.

Bertha was employed as a governess on a sheep station near Mildura after her time in the Territory. She married a local man, Murray Forster, and had five children of her own. Elsie Conigrave took her place at Alice Springs and became romantically involved with telegraph operator Alec McFeat. They married at her parents' home in Adelaide in August 1903.[35] Louisa Cornock, the only trained teacher the children had during their years in Alice Springs, then filled the position for a year. The family had grown by that time. Stuart MacDonnell Bradshaw, known as Don, was born in November 1900 and a third daughter, Edna, arrived two days after Christmas in 1902.

Mrs Bradshaw and the children headed south on 12 September 1904 for their first holiday in Adelaide in over five years. Mrs Cornock travelled south with them, as did her predecessor Elsie, pregnant with her first child. Doris Bradshaw wrote:

> For almost a year we'd been under the thumb of an experienced teacher, Mrs Louisa Cornock, a widow who had come to us from Adelaide. Our previous governesses had been pleasant and easy-going but academically unqualified. The result must have been obvious in the standard of knowledge, for Mrs Cornock was frankly horrified, and said so ... We were worked as we'd never been worked before.[36]

Tom Bradshaw stayed behind in Alice Springs a couple more months, until January 1905. Frank Scott from Barrow Creek acted as stationmaster while he was on leave. The family didn't return until June 1905. A new governess was waiting on the platform when they got to the Adelaide railway station for the first leg of their journey back to Alice Springs, 27-year-old Mabel Taylor, a self-confident young woman from a reasonably privileged family. On arrival she made herself a divided skirt to wear while riding a horse. Never before in Alice Springs had a woman been seen riding astride rather than side-saddle. She was less of a disciplinarian than Mrs Cornock and her more casual attitude is evident in a letter she wrote to family on 17 September 1905, describing Doris as 'an exceptionally nice girl and we are great chums'. She admitted to having 'no knowledge of mathematics' but Mr and Mrs Bradshaw were clearly content with her because they asked her to stay a second year.[37] She arranged for Doris and Mort to have art lessons by correspondence from the Adelaide School of Design.

In April 1906 a teacher arrived on a camel with the fortnightly mail. The young Englishman Harry Hillier was on his way to the school at Hermannsburg Mission. Mabel Taylor wrote to an aunt:

> We had his company for the greater part of Sunday & liked him very much. He was very frank & lively – not one scrap like the conventional idea of a missionary & tried to convince us that he was going to do the work, merely because he liked it & the country suited him, & that there was no virtue or self denial in it at all. We were rather hard to persuade however that anyone could undertake such monotonous & discouraging years of work without some deep and abiding enthusiasm. He talked in the most matter of fact way about staying either five or seven years before visiting the south again.[38]

Mrs Bradshaw was unable to secure a replacement for Mabel when she eventually returned to South Australia in March 1907. Doris wrote years later 'there just weren't any takers for the position; either the Australian spirit of adventure was waning or governesses had discovered the value of money and wanted more than my father was able to pay'.[39] She was nearly 16 by this stage and took over the tutoring of her younger siblings for the remaining time they lived in Alice Springs. Mabel had no plans for the future when she packed her bags to leave. Doris and Consie asked her why she couldn't stay another year but she was keen to get home and spend time with her family. She'd contracted tuberculosis but did not indicate to anyone that she was unwell, if indeed she knew herself. She was admitted to the Kalyra TB hospital at Belair in the Adelaide Hills in August 1907 and died at home in January 1909, aged 34.[40]

Kindly men and much-loved Aboriginal housegirls

The OT line was in its heyday when Tom Bradshaw took charge at Alice Springs, with four assistants to handle the post and telegraph work: Jim Field, Phil Squire, Vaughan Jagoe and Sid Middleton. The other operators in the Bradshaw era were Jack Supple, Alex McFeat, Pat Moore, Wally Harris, Harry Dixon, Phil Bastard, Ernie Allchurch, Bill Perry, Evan Outerbridge, Les Spicer, Charlie Lamshed and Bill Wilson. Unlike many residents from the early days of Alice, these men are not forgotten, thanks to their boss's interest in photography.

Les Spicer made a notable contribution to the sporting life of Alice Springs. He joined the telegraph staff in 1905, shortly after the Bradshaw family returned from holidays in Adelaide. Their new governess Mabel Taylor wrote to her mother that he was 'intensely quiet' but they shared a love of tennis.[41] A court was pegged out between the barracks and the weather station, with a firm surface of crushed termite mounds. It lacked a fence, so players got plenty of exercise running to retrieve balls. Another tennis court was built in the township of Stuart in 1906.[42]

The station's handyman George Hablett was a favourite of the Bradshaw children. He opened their eyes to a world very different to the one they'd left behind in the heart of Adelaide. The Englishman with a voice like a foghorn provided endless fascination for the wide-eyed children: introducing them to campfire cooking on the way north from Oodnadatta; singing them sea shanties from his Royal Navy days; and contorting his sentences. They followed him around the telegraph station, visited him in the men's hut, and watched him work in a blacksmith shop on cold winter days. He was always kind and patient, as was the bushy-bearded Billy Crick and the easygoing stockman Harry Kunoth.

The three men were officially designated linemen but elderly Billy's time was mostly occupied tending the garden and maintaining the batteries that powered the line. Politician Simpson Newland had been impressed with the telegraph station when he visited in 1887 but not the state of the garden.[43]

The situation was much better by 1899 with Billy Crick producing excellent vegetables, except for potatoes which were never a success in the warm climate.[44] Doris Bradshaw described him as 'a kindly old man – small, gnarled, weatherbeaten'. Mabel Taylor said he was 'very quiet, peaceable, inoffensive ... with no vices, which is saying a good deal in this country'. He lived in 'a tiny little humpy in the garden of kerosene cases roofed with grass thatch' and had his meals in the barracks with the other men.

The extensive vegetable beds he lovingly tended were located on the riverbank, close to the blacksmith shop, men's washhouse and well with its solid, brass hand pump. They were surrounded by pepper trees, which survive to this day in silent testimony to Billy's labours. In central Australia the sun shines day after day from a vivid blue, cloudless sky and the little man constantly carted water to keep the soil moist and productive. There were no taps, hoses or sprinklers, just buckets, shoulder yokes and watering cans. His work was never ending. He reached the compulsory retiring age of 65 in July 1906 and reluctantly handed over his garden to a new man. Mabel Taylor expressed her thoughts on the matter in her diary on 1 August 1906:

> It seems a very arbitrary rule in a case where a man is able and willing to perform his work as any new-comer could be. We do not know who his successor will be as yet. Mr Bradshaw has had several applications, several of which have a distinctly humorous side. The most notable of these is a man who is at present in gaol for 'contempt of court', and who in addition is about as lazy as it is possible for a man to be. Another applicant has three times been tried by Mr Bradshaw, once for cruelty to blacks, and twice for cattle stealing. What do you think of these two in a government position? They have plenty of self confidence to try, at all events, but I do not think they have the least expectation of being appointed. It would be a pity if they had.

The job went to Arthur Kunoth, known as 'Sonny', who arrived at the opportune time with drover Humphrey Pepperell and a mob of 550 cattle. Pepperell's party had been on the track for 16 months, slowly moving south from one waterhole to another, trying to find feed and steadily losing animals. The men nearly perished and the cattle frequently went mad for want of water. Mabel Taylor wrote: 'Cattle droving is not the rosy life that city boys longing for the bush are apt to imagine it. There is hardly anything worse, unless it is camel driving.'[45] Billy Crick didn't live long after departing the OT line where he'd spent a large chunk of his working years. He died in Adelaide aged 67.[46]

Sonny's older brother Harry had been in the Alice Springs area since 1898.[47] It was a time when just about every man in Australia had a nickname and his was 'Trot'. Their father Henry worked on the extension of the railway to Oodnadatta in the 1880s and then settled there with his wife Caroline. Mabel Taylor wrote of Harry Kunoth: 'He is about the squarest man I have ever seen, in face and figure both, a sort of German giant without the height.'[48] His daily duties mostly involved managing the horses, cattle, sheep and goats. He was an excellent driver. Doris Bradshaw said his 'handling of the horse teams was a delight to watch'.[49] He accompanied her father on his tours of inspection up and down the line and happily took the Bradshaw family on picnics to favoured spots such as the nearby Wigley Waterhole or further afield to Simpsons Gap. Tom Bradshaw always avoided picnics if he could. He'd rather spend quiet time at home on his own with a book. Harry Kunoth turned to managing cattle stations after his telegraph days. He was approaching the ripe old age of 78 when he died in 1955.

Alf Lloyd was the first of three cooks employed to feed the staff during the Bradshaw family's nine years at Alice Springs. He got the job after a decade as storekeeper at Arltunga's government battery and cyanide works.[50] Alf wasn't much of a cook, though he looked the part, in his big apron and cap. He took over from George Medworth, cook at the end of the Gillen era. The children liked him but the men found the food he dished up lacked variety and taste. He made good bread and buns but was notorious for the bland sago he served as 'puddin' night after night. It was made with sugar and water but nothing else. They called it slide because it wobbled like jelly and would readily slip off the plate.[51]

Sid Stanes was in charge of the kitchen in 1904 and 1905. He came to central Australia with his father and Ted Harris in 1902. Sid Stanes senior was the tradesman engaged to install the replacement Cornish boiler at Arltunga after the original one collapsed in November 1901. He only had one sound leg and rode a camel from the railhead at Oodnadatta while his son and young Harris walked the whole way. He returned south when the job was done but the other two remained in central Australia. Young Sid had a variety of jobs in the early 1900s including manager of the Stuart Arms Hotel in 1907 when the owners Charlie and Luna South went south for a break. In 1911 he was granted a lease on land on the northern side of the MacDonnell Ranges. He went into partnership with Ted Harris and they established Hamilton Downs station in 1913.

Jim Rodda was the third cook in the Bradshaws' time. He and his wife Meta Alvine had been hotel keepers out on the goldfields before that. She was a ventriloquist with two dolls, named Nelson and Wellington, after two of the great military figures of British history. They were slightly the worse for wear, from bouncing around as the couple travelled from Queensland to the Kimberley and down through central Australia. However, she was the life of the party at social gatherings.[52]

Doris Bradshaw noted: 'The native staff included a rather elastic number of houseboys, shepherds for cows and sheep, hewers of wood and carriers of water, scullerymaids for the staff kitchen, and two housemaids and a nursegirl in our home.' Her mother inherited housemaids Dolly and Tryff from the Gillen family and they were followed by Runge and Amboora. Runge won a very special place in the hearts of the Bradshaw family. Doris called her 'a dear old soul' and the family was very sad when they learned years later that she was one of many who died as influenza swept across Australia after the return of troops from the Great War:

> When Mother was not feeling well, Runge would put her arms around her protectively and say, 'You go longa bed, Quei; me shepherd 'em piccaninnies.' And shepherd us she did, with all the gentleness and affection of one of our own relatives.[53]

Amelia was another significant figure in the lives of the children. Like Runge, she was with the Bradshaw family all the years they lived at Alice Springs. Amelia was the granddaughter of Unchalka, Frank Gillen's old friend and principal informant on ceremonial matters. Her father was Englishman

Edgar Pavey, one of the earliest residents of the township of Stuart. He acquired a block at the top end of Todd Street at the second land auction in Adelaide on 24 July 1889 and opened a butcher's shop. Amelia was a pretty girl who looked after the young children and was companion as well as nurse. She was heartbroken when the family eventually left in 1908 and the Bradshaws seriously considered her request to go south with them.[54] However, they realised it would be a mistake to take her away from her people and her land. She married Harry Kunoth and was a much-loved figure in central Australia when she died on the last day of 1984. The *Centralian Advocate* published a long article about her life a year later, ending with the sentences:

> Most speak of her as a woman who exuded love, and was willing to give love, asking nothing in return. Her home on Railway Terrace, where the new K-Mart is being built, became a refuge for anyone in need. Her death leaves a hole which can never be filled, but the strength of her love lives on in her descendants.[55]

Tom Bradshaw's telephone and other developments

Tom Bradshaw set off for Barrow Creek in May 1904 with Harry Kunoth on one of his regular trips to inspect the line. They soon ran into heavy rain making the ground so soft the horses were unable to pull their buggy through the bog. The prolonged Federation drought had ended 12 months earlier and the two men spent three nights sleeping in the vehicle with a tarpaulin pulled over them to keep them dry. When they finally reached Tea Tree Well they had run out of food and were feeling miserable. That night Tom Bradshaw spoke to his family 190 kilometres away in Alice Springs. He had his own private telephone, a phonopore, which he attached to the old iron telegraph line.

His children were eating in front of a log fire when called to the telegraph office that cold night.[56] Doris Bradshaw, at 13, was hearing someone speak on the telephone for the first time. While new to her, the telegraph operators had been using them for a couple of years to chat to Barrow Creek and Charlotte

Waters when the line was free of telegraph traffic. Phonopores were also being used along the railway line south of Oodnadatta to communicate with fettlers' camps and train crews.

The government didn't supply the OT stations north of Oodnadatta with phonopores so a few of the operators, like Bradshaw, bought their own. Doris could vaguely remember the first time the Alice Springs staff talked to their counterparts in the Port Darwin office. A special hook-up was organised on 5 May 1901 with extra batteries to ensure a strong enough signal. Alex McFeat put the phonopore in circuit with six Meidinger and two Leclanché cells; the operators at Port Darwin wired up four extra Leclanché cells. The men were amazed that they could hear each other clearly with so little battery power.[57]

In 1907 the Commonwealth Government coughed up the cash to erect five extra iron poles and run a branch line to Wallis's store at the northern end of Todd Street. A phonopore was installed in the store by 21 June so the town's people could send or receive a telegram without travelling four kilometres to the telegraph station.[58] The manager George Wilkinson could phone their words through to an operator who would then transmit the message for them.

The stores down the line at Horseshoe Bend and Bloods Creek also got phonopores. Another was installed at Alice Well, 135 kilometres south of Alice Springs, when the police station at Illamurta was closed in May 1912 and relocated there. The Johannsen family got one too at Deep Well, between Alice Springs and Alice Well, after they took over the property from the Hayes family in 1911.[59] The phonopores enabled communication over distances less than 150 kilometres. A telegram remained the only reliable option for long distance communication.

Improvements were made to the buildings at the telegraph station during Tom Bradshaw's time in charge. Verandahs were finally added to shield the eastern and western walls of the barracks. Photographs Bradshaw took show new washhouses, one near the well, and another on the south-western side of the stationmaster's house with ready access to hot water from Mrs Bradshaw's kitchen. In the early days, the station's bachelor staff had used the barracks courtyard to sit in a tub and spruce up. More class and modesty was needed in the early 1900s with wives, governesses and young girls around.

Attie Bradshaw missed the wedding of her brother Ernie Allchurch to Bessie Williams, younger sister of Annie Meyers. The ceremony took place at Hermannsburg in March 1905 while the Bradshaw family was in Adelaide. The men had built a distinctive log cottage with a thatched roof on the south side of the stationmaster's residence to accommodate the newlyweds.

The first motor car to cross the continent

In the lead-up to Christmas 1907, a 20-horsepower English Talbot car with Henry Dutton and Murray Aunger behind the wheel came puttering into the telegraph station. Dutton, from a wealthy South Australian family, and Aunger, a mechanic who'd clocked up road and track records as a cyclist, left Adelaide in November with the intention of being the first to drive a car across Australia to Port Darwin. Dubbed *Angelina*, the vehicle proved remarkably durable in the tough conditions she faced despite lacking the advanced technology of modern off-road vehicles. Instead, her drivers had a shovel, a hand-operated winch, some rolls of coconut matting, and an extra set of wheels, called Stepney wheels, which could be bolted onto the car's existing ones to give more traction when needed. She also had steel-studded rubber tyres to reduce the likelihood of punctures.[60]

The men carefully planned refuelling stops along the way and arranged for petrol to be carted ahead of them and left by the track. However, the plan came unstuck at the end of their first week of driving. They pulled up at Coward Springs railway siding on the western side of Lake Eyre where there was a pub and store, a cluster of date palms and a railway siding. It was the height of summer and their drums of fuel had been left in the sun. A number had burst as the pressure built up. They had no option but to put the car on a train to Oodnadatta where their fuel was hopefully stored more safely.

Angelina coped amazingly well with the stony gibber plains of northern South Australia and the many dry creek beds but the two men found it hard going in the open vehicle with no protection from the harsh sun. John Bailes's store at Bloods Creek was pretty rough but they were pleased to pull up there. Ahead of them in the Northern Territory was the prospect of multiple crossings of the Finke as it wound its way across sandhill country. Their coconut matting enabled them to negotiate these but they were beaten by the dreaded Depot Sandhills north of Ted Sargeant's store at Horseshoe Bend. The wheels spun hopelessly in the fine red sand and the men had to organise a team of donkeys to pull them through to Alice Well.

Stuart residents and the Alice Springs telegraph station staff gave them a warm welcome when they finally reached the MacDonnell Ranges in the mid December heat. They were on the road again after a day's rest, facing a 20-kilometre horror stretch through the ancient hills north of the telegraph station to the start of the vast mulga plains in the centre of the continent; then on to Barrow Creek, dodging termite mounds and tyre-piercing mulga stumps hidden by long grass. Monsoonal rain began to bucket down, the red earth turned to bog, and *Angelina* started to show the strain. She got them to Edinburgh Creek, between Wauchope and Tennant Creek, just before Christmas, but transmission trouble followed. She'd go no further until repairs could be done but the necessary spares were 2000 kilometres away in Adelaide.

The telegraph operators had warned Dutton and Aunger against cutting the telegraph line if they got into trouble, telling them instead to throw a wire over the line and wait for help. Bill Perry from Tennant Creek soon appeared with old-fashioned horsepower. *Angelina*'s driver and mechanic made their way back to Oodnadatta and caught a train to Adelaide but weren't planning to abandon their faithful car.

They set off again at the end of June 1908 in a new model Talbot christened *The Overlander*. It had a bigger engine and improved suspension. They reached Alice Springs without mishap on 22 July and night-time temperatures below zero, very different conditions to the extreme heat of the previous December. Change was in the wind with the Bradshaw family preparing to return south after nine years at the telegraph station. They picked up a passenger, Mrs Bradshaw's brother Ernie Allchurch, with a portable morse kit to tap the telegraph line if they got into difficulty this time around.

The three men met another adventurer on the grass-covered Burt Plain 50 kilometres north of Alice Springs. Adventurer Francis Birtles was riding a bicycle from Darwin to Adelaide. He'd left Sydney in August 1907 and was now on his way back home, completing an amazing feat that took him 13 months.[61] Remarkably, there were three other cyclists on the track too, but heading in the opposite direction to Birtles: Fred Blakeley and the O'Neil brothers Jim and Dick accompanied by Jethro the dog. They'd set out from White Cliffs in New South Wales and were bound for Darwin; they reached Alice Springs the day before *The Overlander* got there.[62]

Dutton, Aunger and Allchurch found *Angelina* safe and sound at Edinburgh Creek on 31 July 1908, still covered by the tarpaulin they'd secured to her. It was clear from the number of Aboriginal footprints that the people had taken a keen interest in her but were content to just look. Murray Aunger had brought spare parts from Adelaide and soon got her going. Both vehicles were then driven north to the telegraph station at Tennant Creek. They had no trouble crossing the dense lancewood and bullwaddy scrub south of Newcastle Waters because the OT linemen kept a 20-metre corridor clear of vegetation either side of the poles and wire. Their next challenge was to safely negotiate the Sturt Plain where tall grass concealed deep cracks as the black soil dried out under the cloudless dry season sky. They faced a number of river crossings north of the Daly Waters telegraph station before they got to the safety of Pine Creek where the North Australia Railway ended in those days. They needed rolls of cane matting to cross the dry creeks of central Australia but now it was tarpaulins tied over the front of the cars to prevent their engines stalling as they ploughed through the water. *Angelina* was put on a train from Pine Creek to Port Darwin but *The Overlander* completed the south–north crossing under her own steam, arriving on 20 August 1908, 55 days after leaving Adelaide. Each night Ernie Allchurch had tapped into the OT line to report their progress.

Harry Dutton and Murray Aunger wrote a new page in the annals of Australian motoring. Amazingly they only had three punctures in the process. They didn't chance their luck by going home the way they came. They put both Talbots on a ship and sailed to Adelaide. Ernie Allchurch joined them for the voyage and then took the train to Oodnadatta. The final leg of his trip home to Alice was on the back of a camel.[63]

Life after Alice

The Bradshaw family was nearing Oodnadatta when Murray Aunger, Harry Dutton and Ernie Allchurch reached Port Darwin. They'd left Alice Springs on 11 August after a sad farewell from a community that had grown to love them dearly, despite the early misgivings of Frank Gillen. Once more they were following in the Gillen family's footsteps. Frank Gillen was leaving Moonta for Port Pirie and Tom Bradshaw was to take his place at the Cornish copper mining town. There was a family connection. Tom and Attie's sister-in-law Bessie Allchurch and her older sister Annie Meyers were both from Moonta. Attie and Annie had become close friends, supporting each other through childbirth and childraising, each enjoying the companionship of the other in good times and in bad. Saying goodbye was tough.

The sadness at leaving Alice Springs was compounded the day after they departed. They were preparing their midday meal when an Aboriginal man rode into the camp with a telegram. Mrs Bradshaw's 73-year-old mother Anne Allchurch had died suddenly around the time they were leaving the telegraph station. The family received bright letters from her when they reached Oodnadatta, saying how much she was looking forward to seeing them all soon.[64] She hadn't yet met her youngest grandchild Alan. Attie Bradshaw gave birth to an eighth child, Sheila, a year after they left Alice Springs. It was hard for her growing up hearing countless stories of the family's life in Alice Springs and she always felt left out.[65]

Tom Bradshaw spent three years at Moonta, then was Postmaster at Gawler, Port Pirie and finally suburban Norwood. His 51-year career ended in July 1924. He had passed the normal retirement age of 65 but wanted to keep working. The Commonwealth Public Service Board said no, Bradshaw objected and the matter ended up in the High Court in Melbourne which ruled against him.[66] He died a decade later on 28 August 1934, five years after his wife Attie.

16

Thirty-two years on the line

John McKay was a telegraph operator in the heart of Australia for 32 years but details of his life are hard to find and he seems to have escaped the photographer's lens. In this regard he is typical of most of Charles Todd's telegraph operators. Much of his life was devoted to maintaining the country's tenuous but crucial connection to the rest of the world but he was rarely in the public eye. History is as much about ordinary people doing ordinary things, as it is about larger-than-life characters doing extraordinary things.

John McKay was born on 28 January 1857. He was a well-educated young man, attending the Stanley Grammar School at Watervale in the Clare Valley before joining Todd's telegraph service at Port Augusta when not quite 17.[1] Official records date his appointment 'on the Port Darwin line' from 1 April 1876, 30 months later. The man in charge at Alice Springs was also senior officer for the long section of line between the Peake and Attack Creek. He allocated staff to the four stations along this section and moved them around as circumstances required. The postmaster at Port Darwin did the same for the northern stations.

It seems young Mack had a term at Charlotte Waters and was at Alice Springs between 1884 and early 1891.[2] Joe Skinner gave him the honour of laying the foundation stone for the new stationmaster's house in January 1888. 'JOHN MCKAY ESQ' is inscribed above the name of the builder Joseph Stead. He bought a block of land in town at the July 1889 auction but never built anything on it.[3] His next posting was in charge at Barrow Creek from the middle of 1891, and he remained there until appointed Postmaster at Minlaton, on South Australia's Yorke Peninsula, in 1900.

He witnessed some interesting developments during his first 24 years in central Australia: the stocking of the country; the comings and goings of diggers to Arltunga; the birth of a town with its own brewery to quench the local thirsts; the first women and children to live on the line; and the uneasy accommodation between black and white. Alice Springs has always been a place where there's something happening.

His stay on the Yorke Peninsula was brief. He married Ida Smythe in May 1901 and got a transfer to the post office at suburban Unley. The groom was 44, the bride 37. Their only child John Ross Stuart McKay was born at Unley in 1904. Eight years after leaving, he took his family north to succeed Tom Bradshaw at Alice Springs. His previous long spell in the Northern Territory clearly hadn't dulled John McKay's appetite.

The residents of Stuart in 1908

John McKay noticed the town hadn't changed much since he left central Australia. It was still just a handful of buildings, spread along dusty Todd Street and Wills Terrace, but ownership of the Stuart Arms had recently changed hands. Claraville pastoralist Tom Wallis purchased the pub in July and put Jim Baker in to run it.

The telegraph station received a major loading of supplies once a year from Oodnadatta but Ida McKay could call on a couple of local businesses if in need. Ben Martin had a butchery at the northern end of Todd Street, though the telegraph station killed its own meat. George Wilkinson, manager of Frank Wallis's store, had come from Sydney in 1896 to work as a bookkeeper at Arltunga but was told his services were no longer required when he got there. He gave mining a go and then bought camels to earn money as a carrying agent and met Frank Wallis, who offered him the job of running his store.[4] Wilkinson, who bought the business off Wallis in 1914, willingly provided credit when people needed it and helped anyone down on their luck. The town's people erected a monument across the road in his honour when he died in 1933.

Charlie South's store was no longer open but Fred Raggatt's was still operating in Todd Street. Manager Fred Freer was living in the cottage next door with his wife Zoe and their young child.[5] Raggatt now lived at Glen Helen station, preferring the company of cattle after a decade tending customers. His wife Annie died during the 1903 outbreak of typhoid fever that took a toll on the local population.[6] He sent his six-month-old daughter Molly to Oodnadatta to be cared for.

Ah Hong's market garden was prospering in Todd Street and he'd also produced a family. His Aboriginal wife Ranjika bore him three children: Dempsie, Ada and Gloria. The Hong place wasn't flash but it was popular with bush men needing a good feed when they came into town. He was a well-regarded figure in an era of considerable prejudice against Chinese.

Charlie Meyers's saddlery at the southern end of Todd Street was a simple structure with whitewashed stone walls, thatched roof and a verandah of wooden packing cases. Bridles, harnesses and whips hung from the ceiling, with saddles in various stages of construction or repair and the pervading smell of leather. Charlie lived a short distance away near the river, with his wife Annie and children Dorothy, Jack and Gwen. The couple had lost an infant, Henrietta, a few years earlier. Life wasn't easy for the handful of resilient women scratching out a living in central Australia in those days. Unfortunately the marriage was not a happy one and the departure of the Bradshaw family in August 1908 was a blow to Annie. She and Attie Bradshaw were close friends and she decided to leave too. In 1909 she packed up her things and took the children south for schooling. Charlie could look after himself. She didn't return until 1924.

The rest of the town's established buildings were perched along the northern margin of the town, Wills Terrace. Alec and Fanny Ross lived in a house next door to the store owned by her brother Frank Wallis. The couple moved into town in the early 1900s when Alec got a government job in charge of the local well-sinking team. He'd previously managed Undoolya, Crown Point and Dalhousie stations, plus had a spell as a publican in South Australia. Their 22-year-old son, Alexander junior, was working for his uncle Frank as a camel driver in 1908.

Ben Walkington had a little cabin next door to the Ross place but didn't spend much time in town. He ran the Crossroads Store out at Arltunga. He was not the tidiest of men but had training in bookkeeping, was a JP, and always willing to help anyone who could not read or write.

Visitors to modern-day Alice Springs soon notice the lack of old buildings. Bricks and mortar, sawn timber and roofing iron were hard to procure and expensive until the railway came to town in 1929. Skilled tradesmen were also scarce. Swede Bill Segerman, nicknamed 'Lightning Bill' because he was so slow, was one of the few. Telegraph operator Syd Leesong joked 'it took Lightning several days to get up a ladder and several more to get down again ... Even the effort of standing up, turning around and answering a friendly gesture took him several minutes'.[7] Ernie Allchurch's daughter Jessie Wolfe remembered him as 'such a kindly good man' and said 'the big gentle swede' was 'truly mourned' by those in town when he died in 1926. She said a coffin was made for him from 'packing cases one of which had "keep away from Boilers" printed on it'. Her father, a long-time friend, went through his effects after he died and found a letter from Bill's brother, a 'Baron von something or other'. It turned out Lightning was of aristocratic blood and had left home when he was young after committing an indiscretion.[8]

Stonemason Jack Williams was busy in 1908 constructing a police station, gaol and warder's hut at the corner of Hartley and Parson streets. He hailed from the Isle of Man and had been on the job for a year. Danny Maher and the brothers Tom and Jim Turner were his labourers. Tom Turner came from New South Wales in 1903 looking for work, found there was plenty and sent word back home to the rest of the family. Jim and Alf made their way over by bicycle in 1904 and a fourth brother Dick followed later. The first officer to reside in the new police station was Mounted Constable John Dow, who arrived in October 1908 with his wife Anna to take over from Corporal Charles Nalty. They lived in the old police station at Heavitree Gap until the new one was completed in 1909. Afterward Jack Williams's building skills were put to good use on various cattle stations. The Turners turned to raising cattle.

Jack Williams didn't install plumbing in the new police house. Everyone relied on private wells. Doing the weekly washing, having a bath and maintaining a garden were laborious tasks, as was looking after the goats relied on for milk and meat, the chooks down the back of the yard, and the faithful nags that provided transport. Water was always on the minds of the town's people, and particularly challenging for travellers along the track.

Ned Ryan's men had sunk a well for the police at Heavitree Gap in 1889 but there was no public well in the town itself or facilities for drovers passing through with cattle. Early in 1909, the town's people discussed the matter with Alec Ross, foreman of the well-sinking party. A petition was handed around and he promised to take the matter up with the authorities. The request was received favourably and a suitable site selected on the south side of town in November, between Billy Goat Hill and the river.[9] The skies opened up in March 1910, shortly after the well was completed, with 147 millimetres of rain falling in 24 hours: the biggest flood experienced in town until the 1980s.

The disturbing case of the postmaster's horse

Like his predecessors Frank Gillen and Tom Bradshaw, John McKay was the senior government representative in the heart of the continent, with a wide range of responsibilities beyond the post and telegraph office. He received an annual income of £317: £285 salary, £64 district allowance, less £32 for rations. The four telegraph operators at the station when he arrived in 1908 were experienced and reliable men. Ernie Allchurch, Charlie Lamshed, Les Spicer and Bill Wilson monitored the station's automatic repeaters 24 hours a day in six-hour shifts. They tested the batteries weekly and assisted McKay with the mail when it arrived once a fortnight. There were no changes until 1910 when Bill Wilson left and was not replaced. Joe Johnston, from the Inspection Branch in Adelaide, had recommended a reduction in staffing on the OT line after visiting all stations from Port Darwin to Oodnadatta the previous year. Traffic on the line had declined since cables were laid across the Indian and Pacific oceans in 1901–1902. He believed Alice Springs could afford to lose one man, suggesting each assistant work a seven-hour shift and McKay man the instruments for the remaining three hours of the day.[10]

Ernie and Bessie Allchurch packed up in 1911 after nine years in central

Australia and headed south with their four-year-old daughter Jessie. He was a popular and respected figure in the Alice Springs district but an allegation of evesdropping McKay made against him the previous year soured their relationship. The complicated issue arose out of a horse duffing case McKay dealt with in his role as special magistrate. On 15 March 1910, an unhappy McKay wrote to the commissioner of police about suggestions a grey gelding he received was a bribe to go easy when he heard the case. Mounted Constable John Dow, the senior policeman in the area, had raised the matter with McKay as well as discussing it with others. McKay declared it 'an absolute lie' and demanded a written retraction from Dow.[11]

Charlotte Waters lineman Alex McKinnon, who had delivered the gelding to McKay, was one of two men accused of horse duffing. The other was Robert Sharpe, a young labourer from Bloods Creek south of Charlotte Waters. It was alleged that on 5 October 1909 they unlawfully branded a filly and colt belonging to Horace Cowan, the owner of Crown Point station. Cowan's manager Richard Taylor noticed the filly with Sharpe's brand, a diamond and 47, but recognised it as the progeny of a station mare. He questioned Sharpe about it but the young bloke claimed he got her from Alex McKinnon as payment for some shearing. The colt was spotted at McKinnon's camp at Charlotte Waters bearing his brand, AMK over L1.

Special magistrate McKay committed the two for trial in the Port Augusta Circuit Court and they faced the music on 8 March 1910. Both were found guilty. The jury recommended mercy for Sharpe on account of his youth; he got nine months hard labour and McKinnon a sentence of 18 months; the judge declaring 'his conduct had been disgraceful and brazen'.[12]

One night, around the time of the court proceedings in Port Augusta, McKay had a 'conversation' by telegraph with Harry Kearnan, Alex McKinnon's boss at Charlotte Waters. It was about the grey gelding McKinnon had delivered to McKay. Charlie Lamshed and Les Spicer were in town that evening but Ernie Allchurch was home at the telegraph station. Next day at the police station, McKay was astonished to learn that Constable Dow seemed to know what he had discussed with Kearnan. He jumped to the conclusion Ernie Allchurch must have talked to Dow and accused him of creeping up to the telegraph office and evesdropping. Allchurch was indignant and wrote to Dow on 24 April so he could be cleared of 'a mean and contemptible charge'.

McKay formally apologised to Allchurch the next day and said he believed it was a ruse on Dow's part to see if Kearnan had spoken to him about the subject. Dow was suspicious about the extra horse but it actually had no connection with the duffing of the filly and colt.

The grey gelding actually belonged to the telegraph department. Kearnan had asked McKinnon to take it up the line for McKay's personal use. McKay was to send another horse back with McKinnon.[13] As well as souring Ernie Allchurch's relationship with his boss, the whole business caused bad blood between McKay and Dow and affected their later interactions.

Herbert Heritage moved down from Darwin to take Ernie Allchurch's place in July 1911 and worked at Alice Springs for two years. Other operators who served at the station during McKay's time in charge were Dudley Adamson, Syd Chalken, Syd Leesong, N.C. Octomann, Vince Schrader and F.H. Sharley.

A new family moves into the Allchurch wurley

British couple Bill and Rose Crook worked at the telegraph station during the McKay era and their daughter Doreen became a revered figure in Alice Springs. 'The less said of old Bill Crooks the better', according to long-time cattleman Bryan Bowman, 'but his wife and two daughters were some of the finest women ever and are worthy to take their places alongside the pioneers of the Centre'.[14] Bowman lived in the Centre for over 60 years and knew the bush people well. Despite his bold assertion that 'old Bill would do nothing but give advice', the former soldier did make a go of things.

Rose's uncle, Fred Raggatt, had encouraged them to try their luck in Australia on a visit back to England after his wife Annie died in 1903. The Crook family spent a year at Glen Helen station but Uncle Fred was not an easy person to get along with. Bill found work at neighbouring Hermannsburg Mission where they lived for another year.[15] At the end of 1911 they moved to the Alice Springs telegraph station and lived in the wurley vacated by the Allchurch family a few months earlier. Bill became the yardman, taking over from Keith McDonald who'd replaced Sonny Kunoth in 1909. Rose replaced Jim Rodda as staff cook.

The Crook family headed up the track in 1915 to try their luck on the wolfram fields of Hatches Creek.[16] Then they moved on to Wycliffe Well where their job was to provide water for mobs of cattle being driven from the Top End to southern markets. It was hard work, pulling up 55-litre buckets and pouring the water into a cattle trough. Poddy calves left behind by the drovers helped the family establish Singleton station. Bill and Rose's marriage didn't survive and she eventually returned to England with daughter Kathleen. Doreen Crook married drover and war veteran Bill Braitling in 1932 and they established Mount Doreen station north-west of Alice Springs on the edge of the Tanami Desert. In her latter years, she became a strong advocate for heritage conservation in Alice Springs.

A contemporary of the Crook family was the colourful Will Fox who came to Alice Springs in 1912 and got Harry Kunoth's job at the telegraph station when he joined the police force in October 1913.[17] After working for a number of years as a lineman, rising to the rank of line inspector, Will bought a team of camels and began carting goods from the railhead at Oodnadatta. A drapery business followed, in a tiny shop in Todd Street opposite the Stuart Arms, after the railway was extended to Alice Springs in 1929. He married an Aboriginal woman whose father, according to him, was 'the proper king of Centralia'. He reasoned this put him in a lawful line of succession to the 'Aboriginal throne' but the Commonwealth Government failed to respond to this claim. According to local legend, he decided to seek retribution one night after consuming numerous rums at the Stuart Arms. The story goes that a policeman spotted him behind the home of the government resident with a case of gelignite he was about to detonate.[18]

The Northern Territory's transfer to the Commonwealth in 1911

John McKay's years in charge at Alice Springs included a major turning point in the administration of the Northern Territory. South Australians had high hopes when they acquired it in 1863, but they were not realised. Rather than reaping economic prosperity, the vast lands in the north became a burden of successive governments in Adelaide. A transcontinental railway alongside the OT line was their great dream but there was never enough money to pay for it. A great chunk was missing between Pine Creek in the north and Oodnadatta in the south. By the 1890s, many in Adelaide were convinced they should cut their losses and get rid of the Northern Territory, or at least the top end of it. South Australians were more favourably disposed to keeping the more productive Alice Springs region.

A couple of months after Federation, South Australian Premier Frederick Holder offered the Territory to the Commonwealth.[19] Tom Price, the leader of a subsequent Labor Government, thrashed out a deal with Prime Minister Alfred Deakin in February 1907. A key part of it was a promise to build a railway from the Top End to the South Australian border, though no date was set and nearly a hundred years passed before the first train from Adelaide rolled into Darwin. Both houses of South Australia's parliament passed the *Northern Territory Surrender Act 1907* but there was a hiccup at the Commonwealth level. Alfred Deakin's government collapsed and the new one was less enthusiastic. It was a couple more years before the Commonwealth's *Northern Territory Acceptance Act 1910* was passed.[20]

The land South Australians were so keen to get in 1863 became the responsibility of the Commonwealth of Australia from 1 January 1911. The Commonwealth Government was based in Melbourne at that time, with Canberra still populated by sheep rather than politicians and public servants. To mark the transfer, the name of Australia's heat-stupefied northern outpost Palmerston was changed to Darwin on 3 March 1911.

The white population of Australia was five million in 1911 but only 1729 of them lived in the Northern Territory. The Aboriginal population was anyone's guess but possibly 50,000.[21] Aboriginal people weren't included in the census in those days. The prime minister of the day, Andrew Fisher, formed a scientific mission to investigate the potential of the Northern Territory. It was to report on the health, productivity and living conditions of the population, as well as the prospects for agricultural, horticultural, pastoral, and mineral development. Fisher chose Melbourne University professor Baldwin Spencer to lead it. Spencer's friend and and professor of veterinary pathology at Melbourne University, Dr John Gilruth, joined him. Dr Anton Breinl, director of the Australian Institute of Tropical Medicine at Townsville, and Sydney University geologist Walter George Woolnough made up the rest of the team. They went north on a coastal steamer in June 1911 and were there until August checking out the place and formulating recommendations in their respective areas of expertise.[22] The government also asked Walter Campbell, a retired NSW agricultural administrator, to advise on suitable sites in which to test the Territory's agricultural possibilities and he suggested three for experimental farms. At the same time Henry Barclay was asked to report on a stock route from Newcastle Waters to the Victoria River District. The trip fired Dr Gilruth with enthusiasm for the economic development of the Territory and in February 1912 he accepted the position of its first administrator.

It was April 1912 before Gilruth started work in Darwin and set up a new Northern Territory Administration. These new political arrangements didn't much affect John McKay and his fellow telegraph operators at Alice Springs. They had been under Commonwealth administration for more than a decade. The six colonial postal and telegraph departments had been transferred to the control of a Commonwealth Postmaster-General in March 1901. Their departmental heads were each designated Deputy Postmaster-General and continued to run things as before. The exception was the greatly respected South Australian Sir Charles Todd who was allowed to continue using his old title of Postmaster-General until he retired in 1905.

Ornithologists Samuel and Ethel White

Some unusual visitors dropped into the telegraph station one day in 1913.[23] Samuel and Ethel White were ornithologists, while he was also an established correspondent for Adelaide's newspaper the *Register*. The previous year they had travelled through the Gawler Ranges in a buggy collecting bird skins as well as recording their observations of reptiles, mammals, fish, insects and the botany of the region. John and Ida McKay were out when the visitors arrived but telegraph operator Charlie Lamshed and Rose Crook made them a cup of tea while they waited. Dinner that night with the McKays was a welcome change from the usual fare of salt beef and damper. They were able to relax in comfortable armchairs and listen to the latest music on the telegraph station's pianola.

They had caught the fortnightly train to Oodnadatta in July with a vast array of collecting equipment, bottles, specimen jars, boxes and other odds and ends courtesy of the South Australian Museum. Much of the continent was in drought and the view from the train was of bare brown country. Frank Marsh, mayor of Oodnadatta, met them when they got off the train. White described him as 'a most energetic man' who 'speaks and moves quickly, and never stops still for more than a few minutes at a time. He has many business irons in the fire … and is always ready to help to do one a kindness'. Frank Jones, the manager of Fogarty's store, had camels and supplies for them. A cameleer would accompany them north, along with two Aboriginal 'boys' and a dog called Jack.

They were warmly welcomed throughout the Territory, starting at Charlotte Waters telegraph station. Next stop was Crown Point station on the Finke, managed by the Henderson family, and then Allen Breaden's homestead at Henbury, further up the river. At Hermannsburg they met Pastor Carl Strehlow and his wife Frieda. After weeks of roughing it, the mission was a haven and they enjoyed soaking in a warm bath, putting on clean clothes, sitting down at a table and sleeping in a bed. German-born Strehlow had chalked up close on 20 years at Hermannsburg. Frieda Keysser followed him to Australia, married him on arrival in 1895, and accompanied him to Hermannsburg. She gave birth to five sons and a daughter in the ensuing years. Carl was a gifted linguist who learned to speak the Arrernte language, translated the New Testament and Lutheran hymns into Arrernte, and created an extensive language dictionary. In 1910 they travelled back to Germany for a year and left their children to be educated in German schools, except for the youngest Theodor.

The next stage of the Whites' journey was east towards Simpsons Gap and the Alice Springs telegraph station. On their first night out from Hermannsburg, they had a visit from a rather tame butcherbird, said by the local people to be a Christian. This great songster had made a habit of turning up at church on Sunday mornings, frequently drowning out the preacher's voice with its melodious flute-like call. Eventually Strehlow banished it to the soak where the Whites had unloaded their swags that afternoon.

They rode east to Undoolya station after their stay at Alice Springs and dined with Bill Hayes. Members of his family were now the major landholders in the district. His parents William senior and Mary ventured into central Australia in 1884 with three bullock wagons, hardware and equipment to construct fencing and do other work for Thomas Elder on his property, Mount Burrell. The family took on other contracts, including sinking wells and hauling iron telegraph poles as the last of the original wooden ones were replaced in 1890 and 1891. Drought forced Elder to put Mount Burrell on the market in 1894 and the Hayes family invested their earnings in the land. They later acquired the Undoolya and Owen Springs leases, as well as land at Ellery Creek. In 1912 the old couple was living at Maryvale, 18 kilometres south-east of the original Mount Burrell homestead, with their daughter Mary and her husband Steve Adams.

The glory days of the Arltunga goldfields were well and truly over. Constable Matthew Dowdy, at Kangaroo Well, served the Whites a cup of tea and shared his knowledge of the area. The country looked barren courtesy of years of timber-felling to feed the boilers, which drove the batteries, which crushed the hard, gold-bearing quartz the miners extracted from their diggings.

They camped the night at Arltunga's Glencoe Hotel run by the colourful character Alexander (Sandy Myrtle) McDonald who'd been a member of the Northern Territory's gang of wannabe bushrangers, the Ragged Thirteen. This motley bunch met up in 1886 and travelled together to Halls Creek in north-western Australia, where gold had been discovered the previous year. They helped themselves to other people's property along the way, though never at gunpoint. Despite their brazen exploits, no charges were ever laid against them. McDonald opened the pub in 1910.

Next morning they headed back towards the OT line calling into Loves Creek station on the way. Its owner Lewis Bloomfield was away, taking a mob of horses to market in Adelaide. However, they received a hearty welcome from a stockman pleased to have company at the lonely outpost. Bill Cavanagh, the manager of the government battery and cyanide works at Arltunga, rode in while the Whites were at Loves Creek. They hadn't called at his place so he'd ridden over to say g'day.

Next stop was Maryvale where they found William Hayes senior sitting in a deckchair, complete with a long white beard reminiscent of Father Christmas. The elderly pioneer was taken ill after they left and his family took him down to Oodnadatta. They put him on a train to Adelaide but he died a few days later.

The Whites returned to Adelaide in October with the largest collection of inland bird skins made to date, over 2000 specimens of insects, and significant numbers of other animals and plants.

17

The 'half-caste' problem

Australia's vibrant heart has a complicated history with black and white still struggling today to determine their common future. The first stage of black–white relations in central Australia was mostly avoidance. John McDouall Stuart's encounters with Aboriginal people were few and far between when he passed through the region. In 1870, Charles Todd was adamant that the men constructing the OT line treat the Aboriginal people with respect, there was to be no interference with their property, and no one was to visit Aboriginal camps without permission. He didn't say it but it was obvious some of his enthusiastic young workers might be tempted to seek sexual favours from the women. The governor's wife had given them Bibles and hymn books to entertain them in their spare time but the superintendent of telegraphs was no fool.

Perhaps the Arrernte people saw no threat to their traditional way of life initially, believing – or hoping – the OT men might just pass through, like Stuart did in the years 1860 to 1862. A couple of kilometres south of Atherreyurre (Alice Springs), the senior man of the dingo dreaming performed a ceremony to get rid of the newcomers. He rubbed the sacred dog rock and sang its special songs to get the local dingoes to drive the intruders from central Australia.[1] The alarm bells were clearly ringing when more white people arrived with mobs of horses and cattle, which they plonked on the waters of sacred Anthwerrke (Emily Gap). Then more cattle came, and sheep, spreading far and wide, not just on Arrernte land but also on that of neighbouring groups.

The second stage of black–white relations was the simmering conflict in the 1880s as the region entered a sustained dry period. A battle for water and other natural resources left both sides feeling edgy and threatened. That decade is notable as a savage period when a significant number of Aboriginal people were killed by the police and others who took the law into their own hands. The situation improved following the 1890 Swan–Taplin inquiry and 1891 trial of Constable William Willshire but the killings did not end.

By the 1890s, black and white people were entering a third phase, with more interaction and increasing mutual dependency. The cattlemen began involving Aboriginal 'boys' in stock work and their interest in the women increased. There was a common saying that Aboriginal women would work all day in the stock camp and all night in the swag. The Aboriginal people, for their part, found it was often safer to spend time around the homesteads than to roam in remote areas where they might be labelled as cattle killers and feel the blast of a gun.

Initially the central Australian stations were established by wealthy southern businessmen who invested capital and employed managers. Drought and depression put an end to this type of pastoral enterprise in the 80s and 90s, with most of the big landholders relinquishing their leases after losing large amounts of money. Central Australia then became the preserve of the small squatter who lived an existence more akin to subsistence farming than rural aristocracy. They realised that cheap Aboriginal labour was essential to their survival in a tough environment. The Aboriginal people were increasingly dependent on the whites and the rations they handed out, as their country was eaten out by cattle, their waterholes degraded, and native plants and game declined.

The abortive ruby rush and the discovery of gold in 1887 brought an influx of white people who willingly engaged with the Aboriginal people. Before long there were many Aboriginal people on the diggings and white interest in black women rose sharply. It became an acceptable thing for white men to live with black women and an increasing number of 'half-caste' children resulted. The 'half-caste problem' would continue to be an issue in central Australia for decades to come.[2]

Constable Dow takes on sub-protector McKay

Like his predecessors Frank Gillen and Tom Bradshaw, John McKay carried the added responsibility of sub-protector of Aborigines. Constable John Dow was critical of his performance of this role. Dow was posted to the Alice Springs district in October 1908, a few weeks after McKay's appointment to the telegraph station. The horse duffing case involving Alex McKinnon and Robert Sharpe put the two men at odds and their relationship remained caustic. On 14 June 1910, Dow sent a long and significant letter to his superior Inspector Thomas Clode in Port Augusta concerning the treatment of the Aboriginal women and children in the district. He singled out Harry and Sonny Kunoth for a special mention, plus John McKay.[3] Constable Dow reported there were 'about 94 half castes and quadroon children of all ages in The Ranges irrespective of those at Arltunga'. He said most of the children:

> live in the black's camp in a state of uncivilization, and the sooner something is done for the benefit of these unfortunates the better ... At the present time there are many half castes and quadroons in the camps without clothing (with the exception of a torn old shirt) some of these little ones are motherless and it is a pitiable sight on these cold nights to see these little children (as white of skin as Europeans) huddling up with dogs to try and keep their little bodies warm; and more often than not they go to their sleep supperless ... I am sorry to have to say that the native half caste females in my opinion get little protection from the present Sub-Protector of Aborigines at Alice Springs (Mr John McKay) who is also the Post Master.

He pointed out that McKay had a 15-year-old 'half-caste' son of his own, also named John McKay, who was with Constable Matthew Dowdy at the Arltunga police station. The boy's mother was an Aboriginal woman from Barrow Creek. Dow said:

the ordinary bush person has little to fear from the present Sub-Protector as is proven by the fact that when I came to Alice Springs 18 months ago two brothers employed as Yard-man and Line-man under the Postmaster ... kept two young half caste girls about the place for immoral purposes. I questioned their age and spoke to the Sub-Protector, but nothing was done in the matter.

The two brothers he referred to were Harry and Sonny Kunoth. Harry had an ongoing relationship with Amelia Pavey who had looked after the Bradshaw children and now did laundry for the telegraph operators and other single male staff at the station. Amelia's first child had died as an infant and she was pregnant again. Harry's younger brother Sonny was involved with Mary Earwaker, who had a seven-month-old daughter he'd fathered. However, he left his job at the telegraph station after the birth.[4] Dow recommended that something be done speedily for the benefit of these girls and their children.

Nine months later, on 18 February 1911, John McKay reported 'things pretty good, no probs and apart from the moral aspect Aborigines couldn't be better looked after – station people do their best too'. However, by the end of that year he was decrying the behaviour of many white men and his inability to prevent the sexual exploitation of Aboriginal women. He wrote to his new Commonwealth bosses on 22 November 1911:

I regret that my efforts up to the present to discourage and prevent this happening have been futile through interference from those who should have supported me, instead of encouraging these men in their immoral practices, and at the same time privately and officially casting slurs on my administration. I earnestly urge that steps be immediately taken to prevent the employment of Aborigines and half caste females by white men, unless under the care and protection of a respectable married white woman, and that they should be treated as children in law and that no age of consent be recognised. Unless I have laws to assist me in protecting the natives the title of sub-Protector is a misnomer and had better be abolished. An early answer would oblige.[5]

Bob Stott takes over as sub-protector of Aborigines

Robert Stott arrived at the end of 1911 to take over from John Dow as the senior police officer in central Australia.[6] He had joined the South Australian police in 1882 and was transferred to the Top End the following year. His wife Mary died in February 1901 and their five-week-old daughter the following month. He married Agnes Heaslop in 1902 and they had six children: Malcolm, Gordon, Robert (who was known by his second name Cameron), Agnes, Duncan and Mavis.[7] The family moved into the stone police house Jack Williams had built at the corner of Parsons and Hartley streets. In those early days of Commonwealth administration, Bob Stott was also the mining warden, administered the affairs of the lands department, and was the stock inspector. More significantly, he took on the responsibilities of sub-protector of Aborigines, previously exercised by the telegraph stationmasters. John McKay was happy to relinquish a role that had caused him a lot of pain.

The welfare of Amelia Pavey was an ongoing concern and became an issue between him and Stott. McKay had eventually challenged Harry Kunoth over his relationship with her. The lineman promised he would end it but then another child was born. McKay declared he had no faith in Kunoth's promises and said he wanted her sent to Hermannsburg rather than remain at the telegraph station. Kunoth then appealed to Stott who agreed with him that the mission was not a suitable place for her. Instead, he granted Harry Kunoth a licence to employ her and Kunoth in turn promised to look after her and the child. He erected a dwelling for her at the telegraph station, which further inflamed the situation because he had not sought McKay's approval to do this.

McKay sent a letter to the Department of External Affairs in 1912 about the matter in which he said 'I regret that there has been some misunderstanding between MC Stott and myself'. He laid out the history of the case and referred to correspondence Stott had posted off. He wrote 'Kunoth is continually visiting the camp whether for immoral purposes I am not in a position to say'. He followed this with the unfortunate words 'To me Stott's letters seem so unwarranted that I can only surmise the trouble with his head and attack of Malaria has made him act as he has done'. The comment was unlikely to promote congenial relations between the two.[8]

Harry Kunoth quit his job at the telegraph station the following year and had a spell as a policeman, with Bob Stott. A couple of years later he married Amelia. They spent their life together managing stations: Bond Springs, Tempe Downs and then, briefly, Hamilton Downs. They later owned Utopia station with Harry's brother Sonny.

The 1911 Commonwealth Aboriginals Ordinance

Two bills concerning Aboriginal people were presented to the South Australian parliament late in 1908; one covered those in South Australia, while the *Northern Territory Aboriginals Act* was applicable to people in its Northern Territory. This was passed eventually in 1910, only weeks before South Australia handed over responsibility to the Commonwealth Government on 1 January 1911.[9] The Commonwealth quickly adopted this legislation and enacted its own Aboriginals Ordinance to be read as one with the Act.[10]

The prevailing view at the time was that the Aboriginal people were a dying race and the legislation provided protection for them, with the appointment of a chief protector and sub-protectors. Adelaide doctor and anthropologist Herbert Basedow got the nod as the first chief protector but he didn't last long, resigning in August 1911 after only 45 days in Darwin. He had an overblown opinion of his own importance and spent most of his time pushing for better conditions for himself. His brief tenure is remembered for his infamous suggestion that Aboriginal people be tattooed for identification and administrative purposes.[11]

Frank Gillen's close friend and collaborator Baldwin Spencer agreed to take Basedow's place for a year from 1 January 1912. He'd been in Darwin from June to August leading a scientific mission to investigate the potential of the Northern Territory and hadn't expected to be back so soon. His brief was to commence implementation of the 1911 Aboriginals Ordinance and recommend what needed to be done about Aboriginal welfare.[12] The Commonwealth Government wanted him to provide them with a blueprint for future policy in the Northern Territory and that is exactly what he delivered.[13] The decisive, energetic professor arrived back in Darwin by ship on 15 January 1912 and immediately set about using the considerable power the Ordinance gave him.

While intended to protect Aboriginal people, the Ordinance was based on the premise they were an inferior race. It gave the chief protector and sub-protectors control over their lives and where they would live. In particular, it allowed the Commonwealth Government to take charge of any Aboriginal person in the Territory if this was deemed to be in their best interests.[14] Spencer turned his attention to the two dirty and decrepit camps occupied by the Larrakia people in Darwin. One on the top of a cliff was known as King Camp; Lamaroo Camp was on the beach below.[15] In their place he established the Kahlin Compound for the Larrakia people and it became the blueprint for urban concentrations of Aboriginal people. He felt each town in the Territory required such a compound and it would be compulsory for the people to live there. Their nocturnal movements would be restricted and non-Aborigines banned from going there without permission.

Baldwin Spencer presented his recommendations to the government on 20 May 1913.[16] One of the professor's concerns was the increasing number of children resulting from relationships between white men and Aboriginal women. Some fathers accepted parental responsibility but most did nothing to provide for the welfare of their offspring and left them to be raised by their Aboriginal relatives. He believed it was in the children's best interests to take them from their mothers and educate them in special schools so they might aspire to a place in white Australia. He told the Commonwealth Government:

> It must be remembered that they are also a very mixed group. In practically all cases, the mother is a full-blooded aboriginal, the father may be a white man, a Chinese, a Japanese, a Malay or a Filippino. The mother is of very low intellectual grade, while the father most often belongs to the coarser and more unrefined members of higher races. The consequence of this is that the children of such parents are not likely to be, in most cases, of much greater intellectual calibre than the more intelligent natives, though, of course, there are exceptions to this. No half-caste children should be allowed to remain in any native camp, but they

should all be withdrawn and placed on stations. So far as practicable, this plan is now being adopted. In some cases, when the child is very young, it must of necessity be accompanied by its mother, but in other cases, even though it may seem cruel to separate the mother and child, it is better to do so, when the mother is living, as is usually the case, in a native camp.[17]

So began one of the most infamous government policies in Australian history, its patron one of the most esteemed figures in Australian anthropology.

Administrator Gilruth and his chauffeur go for a drive

Baldwin Spencer's friend and fellow academic Dr John Gilruth took up the position of Administrator of the Northern Territory in April 1912, a couple of months after Spencer began his year as special commissioner and chief protector. Gilruth was a farsighted but abrasive man whose time in Darwin came to an inglorious end when the locals sent him packing after the so-called Darwin rebellion of December 1918.[18] His suitability for the position of Administrator might be questioned but certainly not his desire and vision to develop the Territory.

Gilruth's 15-horsepower Napier car was landed in Darwin in August 1912, along with his chauffeur G.H. Cowper. It was the first car many Territorians had seen since Dutton and Aunger's *Angelina* and *The Overlander* in 1908. On 2 September, Gilruth and Cowper set off for the Barkly Tableland with Baldwin Spencer in the back seat and an Aboriginal assistant, Billy Shepherd, reputedly the son of George Goyder who had led the government survey of Port Darwin in 1869.

Their plan was to drive down the OT line to Newcastle Waters, then head east to Anthony Lagoon and up to Borroloola. From there they would head back to Katherine via the Roper River. Gilruth was undaunted by the prospect of driving off the beaten track. It was a truly adventurous endeavour for those days and the car made it, though not without incident. They had to be towed by horses when they ran out of petrol on the Barkly Tableland.

Gilruth and Cowper set off again in 1913, to inspect stations on the

Barkly Tableland and the MacDonnell Ranges. This time the two men took a different car, a Talbot, with a more powerful engine than the Napier. They drove from Cloncurry to Powell Creek and then down the telegraph line to Alice Springs. The Talbot was left at Barrow Creek on the way home to Darwin when tyre troubles and wet weather forced them to complete the journey on horseback.[19] During the time he was in Alice Springs district, the Administrator quickly became aware of the increasing number of 'half-caste' children. He wrote in his annual report:

> During my visit to the MacDonnell Range district recently I was impressed by the large number of half-caste, and even quadroon, children in the native quarter at Alice Springs, growing up without education or any moral control. One half-caste mother had five quadroon children – four of school age – yet, although white in complexion, these children are developing under conditions worse than those of their native ancestors and disgraceful to their Europeans relatives. It is hoped this may be early remedied, the first step being the establishment of a school with a qualified teacher who, although primarily required for the white children previously denied a State School education, will also hold classes for the quadroons and half-castes.[20]

The Bungalow is established

At the time Dr Gilruth visited Alice Springs, there was a woman living at Arltunga who would play a major and positive role in the lives of local children for years to come. Topsy Smith is a significant figure in Alice Springs history, and it's fitting that an aged-care facility for Aboriginal people was named in her honour, following a life of caring for others.

Her gravestone at the Alice Springs General Cemetery says she was 86 when she died on 6 April 1960, implying she was born in 1874. Her mother Mary Kemp was of Arabana descent, from the country around the Peake telegraph station.[21] Her father, policeman George White, did not play a big part in her life. Mary's white partner Arthur Evans was more like a father to her.[22] Arthur and Mary had a variety of jobs, including minding the store Frank Marsh established in 1889 at Alice Well, 135 kilometres south of Alice

Springs. Regrettably, Arthur later 'got respectable', left Mary and married a white woman.[23]

Topsy married Welsh-born Bill Smith. They headed north to the Arltunga goldfields in the early 1890s and the first of their 11 children was born there in 1893.[24] Bill was a good father, unlike so many white men in central Australia who used Aboriginal women but took no responsibility for the offspring that resulted. For 11 years from 1899, he and his partner Patterson worked the Great Western Mine, one of the most productive on the goldfields. He was also involved with the Joker Mine.[25]

Bill died on 20 May 1914, at the age of 48. Life at Arltunga was tough for the family those last few years with gold increasingly hard to find. Topsy wanted to return to Oodnadatta where her children could attend school. She packed the family's belongings onto a dray and the older children followed behind her with their herd of several hundred goats. Arltunga policeman Matthew Dowdy helped them move. Stuart was as far as she got but the town held the promise of a better life for her children than Arltunga. Bob Stott put up a tent for them on land reserved for government purposes, diagonally opposite the police station in Hartley Street, adjacent to the town's tennis court, behind the Stuart Arms Hotel. The big Scots-born policeman was a tough man but respected by the local people and he took his role as sub-protector of Aborigines seriously. Topsy's goats grazed on the edge of town, in the vicinity of a prominent outcrop, which came to be known as Billy Goat Hill. She gave birth to her last child in October, five months after the death of his father.[26]

Stott recommended to Administrator Gilruth that the area where Topsy was camped be reserved for 'half-castes'. Money was found and a galvanised-iron shed erected.[27]Sixteen children were living there by November 1914 with Topsy and another woman, Mariah McDonald who had four children. Numbers rose as other light-skinned children were picked up from Aboriginal camps and placed there.[28] They bore some well-known surnames because Stott enforced the rule that children be given their father's name.[29] He had a young family of his own and took a paternal interest in these children. Two additional iron sheds were later added. The place became known as the Bungalow but it's unclear who came up with that name or exactly when. It conjures up a homely image but the place soon degenerated to a wretched hovel.

The town of Stuart finally had a schoolteacher by this time. Bob Stott and Sam Nicker had lobbied the Commonwealth Government and Mrs Ida Standley reached the dusty little village in May. Ida and her husband George separated in 1897 and she worked as a teacher in bush schools in South Australia to support her children. By 1914 they were old enough to fend for themselves and she accepted the offer of a new life in central Australia. She caught the fortnightly train to Oodnadatta where Stott's offsider Harry Kunoth and Alice Springs lineman Will Fox were waiting to escort her up the track with a police buggy and a telegraph station wagon. There was no house for her to live in so she moved into the police house with the Stott family. Her schoolroom was a stone hut at the side of the gaol, originally built as a dwelling for the gaol warder. Stott had been using it as an Aboriginal rations store but had it renovated for Mrs Standley. Kunoth and some Aboriginal workers added windows and cut timber to build a verandah.

Mrs Standley had no formal training and so was paid less than qualified teachers in South Australia.[30] In February 1915 it was suggested she take on the extra responsibilities of matron of the Bungalow. She would be paid £50 per year, on top of the £150 salary she was receiving for teaching the local children. Topsy Smith would stay on as houseparent and look after the children when they weren't in school with Mrs Standley. This meant she was on duty for much of every day because the Bungalow children's time in school was restricted to an hour and a half each afternoon. The suggestion they attend lessons with the other children was vetoed by parents.[31] Topsy received no pay, just her keep, and was never compensated for her goats, which became the property of the home.

Living conditions at the Bungalow were far from ideal, despite the love and best efforts of Topsy Smith and Ida Standley. Topsy worked hard to keep the place clean and scrounged whatever materials she could find to make clothes for the children. Food was limited and the children would hang around the nearby Stuart Arms Hotel, looking for scraps. Toilet and washing facilities were primitive and there were few proper beds. They slept huddled together on the floor in winter and camped outdoors under the trees in summer. Mrs Standley was praised for the job she did but Topsy's contribution was largely overlooked, with only the barest mention of her in government records of the time. She worked constantly to the point of exhaustion, in the toughest of conditions, and was truly one of central Australia's great unsung heroes.

The Great War

The Commonwealth Government was kidding itself if it seriously believed putting children in an institution like the Bungalow was better than leaving them with their Aboriginal mothers. Its failure to allocate more money to improve matters was similarly hard to comprehend. Regrettably for the children, the politicians' attention was focused on events unfolding on the other side of the world.

On 28 June 1914, Gavrilo Princip stepped onto the running board of the open car carrying Archduke Franz Ferdinand and his wife Sophie through the streets of Sarajevo, capital of Bosnia. The archduke was heir to the Hapsburg throne of Austro-Hungaria. The 19-year-old Bosnian Serb fired two shots, one at the archduke and the other at his wife. The assassin was part of a group intent on freeing Bosnia from Austrian control and securing its integration with neighbouring Serbia. Austria had annexed Bosnia from the Ottoman empire of Turkey in 1908. The murders triggered a chain reaction of political and military manoeuvring and 37 days later Europe was engulfed in war. Once Britain launched her forces into the conflict on 4 August, all her dominions, including Australia, were expected to get involved. Europe had been on a steady path to conflict for a number of years, its countries engaged in an arms race and forming complex political and military alliances. It seems now that almost everyone was itching for a fight that most thought would be over by Christmas.

John McKay and his staff were well aware of the growing tensions but their more immediate concern was securing a better supply of water for the telegraph station. Since the mid 1870s they had drawn their water from a well near the blacksmith's shop. It was equipped with a brass hand pump. Water for their stock was hauled into troughs from waterholes in the riverbed, using a hand-operated whip, called a *shaduf* by the Afghans. A large water tank would make life easier.

In March 1914 the Commonwealth's Department of Works made arrangements to install an Alston gearless windmill at a new well, a couple of hundred metres south of the buildings. The water would then be piped to a steel tank on a stone base behind the blacksmith shop. The windmill was in place by late August and it was then up to the men of the No. 8 Line Party to assemble the tank, ensure it was watertight and get the windmill pumping. The work was completed on New Year's Eve.[32] Europe was hellbent on destroying much of its infrastructure while the residents of the telegraph station were improving theirs.

Ida McKay advocates for Aboriginal people

Ida McKay became a prominent advocate for Aboriginal rights after the family returned to Adelaide in 1916. She was one of a number of white women who became vocal campaigners for the reform of Aboriginal policy in the years after the Great War. She joined the Women's Non-Party Association, which was affiliated with the Australian Federation of Women Voters. Members identified the treatment of Aboriginal women as one of the most pressing issues and were very critical of conditions at the Bungalow.

On 12 September 1924, she addressed a gathering in Adelaide, strongly criticising the Commonwealth Government and charging the 'authorities with inhumanity in their treatment of the aborigines and aboriginal half-castes in the Territory'. Her speech, reported in one of Adelaide's major newspaper the following Monday, raised the ire of former Alice Springs police officer John Dow who had clashed with her husband when he was in charge of the telegraph station. The paper reported:

> Mrs McKay, an executive member of the Aborigines' Friends Association, delivered her remarks before the Women's Non-party Association in Adelaide. She claimed that Aboriginal women had performed an

invaluable part in the development of the Northern Territory and had received little but abandonment from white men in return. Her comments drew an immediate response from another former Territorian, John Dow, who said her allegations 'were not fair to the hundreds of decent and clean-living men in the bush'.[33]

In 1927 the South Australian Government appointed Ida McKay to its advisory council on Aborigines; she remained a member until 1939. Along with others involved in the Women's Non-Party Association, she called for action in 1928 to protect Aboriginal women during the extension of the railway from Oodnadatta to Alice Springs. The Association proposed that the line be declared a prohibited area under the Aboriginals Ordinance and that two women be appointed protectors to distribute food in drought-affected areas so Aboriginal women had no need to go near the construction camps. The government agreed to the first suggestion but not the second.[34]

Ida McKay was part of a long tradition of South Australian humanitarians advocating for Aboriginal people against the prevailing negative attitudes of the day. The longest established group was the Aborigines' Friends' Association formed in 1858. The advocacy of Ida McKay and like-minded individuals resulted in a significant shift in community attitudes by the 1930s, partly driven by revulsion about events such as the Forrest River massacre in the Kimberley in 1926 and the Coniston massacre in the Northern Territory in 1928. Her place in Territory history, running against the tide of entrenched ideas, has been obscured by the colourful and controversial figure of Miss Olive Pink who first appeared in Alice Springs in 1930. Ida McKay deserves greater recognition for her efforts to gain a better deal for Aboriginal people.

She died at Serpentine in Western Australia on 22 June 1946.[35] Her husband John died a decade earlier, on 26 April 1936 at Henley Beach in South Australia.

18

Worn out by the work

Like Frank Gillen and Tom Bradshaw before him, Fred Price left a rich photographic record of his years in charge of the Alice Springs telegraph station; and like Doris Bradshaw, his own daughter Pearl wrote a book detailing the family's life at the telegraph station. The Price photographs and *By Packhorse and Buggy* tell the story of a happy and close family who were keen to make central Australia their permanent home. However, a photo of Fred Price at work in 1923 shows a man seemingly older than his years. The long hours of work seriously affected his health and he died the following year aged 57.

Fred Price took over from John McKay at a challenging time during the Great War with less staff than in previous eras. The Postmaster-General's Department was depleted as young operators went to fight on the bloodsoaked battlefields of Belgium and France or ride with the Light Horse in the Middle East. He was a conscientious man, perhaps too much so for his own good. His daughter Pearl said that he was never away from the station for a full night in the eight years he was there. He never took sick leave or a holiday, believing he was responsible for the place at all times. If there was telegraph traffic at night needing attention, he would get out of bed to attend to it, leaving the junior operators to sleep.[1]

His father was a schoolteacher in the South Australian farming community of Whyte-Yacowie and 14-year-old Fred became a messenger there in 1880. He qualified as a telegraph operator and Charles Todd sent him to Farina in 1887. A year later he was posted to the Central Telegraph Office in Adelaide where he gained valuable experience of the fast-developing technology. Todd transferred him to Port Darwin in June 1891 where he met a young English girl, Isabelle Violet Hesketh (known as Ivy from her initials I and V), who had sailed to the tropics to visit her sisters. The couple married on 5 March 1898.

Fred was transferred back to Adelaide in 1904, by which time Ivy had given birth to three children. Tragically, two of them, Ivy and Cyril, died of meningitis in infancy. Early in 1912 he was promoted to Postmaster at Hergott Springs (Marree), on the OT line, but his wife struggled in this desolate little town on the featureless gibber plains. It was as different to her native Nottingham as a place could be. At the end of year she returned to Adelaide with their young children Hilda, Molly, Pearl and Alf, and it wasn't until October 1913 that Fred was able to join them. Their last child Ron was born in Adelaide in 1914.

Fred Price was a gifted man. A fine singer and accomplished piano player, he played a leading role in various church choirs in Adelaide. When war broke out in Europe and the cream of Australia's youth answered the bugle call to arms, he performed in benefit concerts to raise money for troops serving overseas. By 1916 he and Ivy had agreed to have another crack at life in the outback and he was appointed Postmaster at Alice Springs from July 1916, unaware it would be his last posting. The family joined him in February 1917, except Hilda, who had started work as a milliner. However, a new and exciting life beckoned for the younger ones.

They arrived in the middle of another protracted drought affecting much of the continent. The Alice Springs telegraph station no longer kept sheep for meat by the time the Price family arrived, relying instead on goats. They seemed to find enough to eat even in the worst conditions. Most of the station horses were allowed to roam free in the hills to find whatever grass and water they could but a number died, as was the case across central Australia. The very dry conditions also affected the Price children's education. Fred was reluctant to let young Molly and Pearl walk the four kilometres into town along the dry Todd River to attend Mrs Standley's school next to the gaol. Instead, Len McLean, a young telegraph operator relieving at the station, supervised lessons prepared by the teacher.[2]

The drought lasted until December 1919 when the heavens finally opened and the Todd River ran again.[3] Two years of unusually high rainfall followed. As the country recovered, the telegraph station was restocked with cattle brought down the line from Barrow Creek.[4] The Price children enjoyed working with the livestock and their parents contemplated taking up land in the region when Fred's time at the telegraph station came to an end.

Staff members in Fred Price's time

The addition of a copper wire to the OT poles in 1898–1899 enabled the Wheatstone system of machine telegraphy to be used on the line.[5] Large offices like Adelaide had equipment that punched holes in paper tape, in a precise pattern corresponding to dots and dashes. The perforated tape was then fed into a transmitter, which sent messages much faster than an operator could achieve manually. The Alice Springs telegraph station had a Wheatstone receiver during Fred Price's time, driven by a clockwork mechanism.[6] An inker built into the receiver recorded the incoming signals onto another roll of paper tape. This was a boon during the war years when the station was shortstaffed.

Syd Chalken, Vince Schrader and Dudley Adamson were stationed at Alice Springs when Fred Price arrived. Adamson went off to the war in 1917 and it seems Len McLean came up to relieve him, though his name is absent from official staff lists. Syd Leesong also spent time at Alice Springs during the war, though his nominal position, from 1915 until 1917, was Charlotte Waters with Harry Kearnan.[7] It was one of the loneliest places on the line and Kearnan happily transferred to Alice when Syd Chalken finished in 1919. Dud Adamson returned from overseas service in 1920 and John Cain also arrived that year. Bill Wutke replaced Vince Schrader in 1922. He was a keen cricketer who appears in a few photos from the early 1920s padding up on the grassless recreation ground at the northern end of town.

Arthur Neale loomed large in the daily life of the Price children, just as English handyman George Hablett had done with the Bradshaw children a decade earlier. It seems he came to central Australia in 1911 and worked as a stockman at Bond Springs. His duties were diverse. He looked after the station's livestock but was also responsible for anything that needed fixing or carting. He was adept at blacksmithing, saddlery and wheelwright work. Fred Price's daughter Pearl remembered him as 'a man of few words, strong in the arms but gentle in his manner'. She said 'he showed great patience in handling both men and animals'. He lived in the wurley built for Ernie and Bessie Allchurch in 1905 and used by the Crook family between 1911 and 1915.

Pearl summed him up as 'a quiet, generous man, a hard worker and very reliable', going on to say 'I know that Dad thought very highly of him and relied on his judgement in many matters'.[8] He died in Alice Springs on 20 June 1933, aged 55.

Miss Beatrice Fitzpatrick cooked for the staff throughout the eight years the Price family lived at the station. She took on that role when Rose Crook left in 1915. Mrs Price cooked for her own family but employed two Aboriginal women, Maude and Jenny, to help with housework. Maude's husband George worked as a stockman with Arthur Neale. However, he was the wrong skin group for her and the Arrernte people did not approve of their relationship. Consequently she was 'sung' as punishment by the older men, became listless and died.[9]

There were about 300 Aboriginal people living close to the telegraph station but family groups came and went. They were issued with rations once a fortnight from the station's supplies: flour, tea, sugar and tobacco plus blankets and occasionally clothes. They were also given meat when a beast was killed. The quantity was recorded in a large ledger as they received their rations, and took Fred Price all morning. He thought it better to issue rations weekly, rather than fortnightly, because they had no way of storing food and it was all consumed or spoilt within a couple of days . However, his bosses in Adelaide said no to this request, on the grounds it would take up too much of his time.[10]

Centralians who went to war

Young men across Australia rushed to enlist for Europe's war, though eight months elapsed before anyone in central Australia left to sign on the dotted line. It's easy these days to lose sight of the isolation of men living in the stock camps of the outback in those days. There were no daily papers to fill their heads with the latest news from Europe, even though the OT line's copper wire was constantly singing with all sorts of information and secrets. It was an era of nationalistic fervour, fed by racial prejudice and narrow-mindedness, but most of the men who enlisted were driven by a spirit of adventure and the prospect of a free trip to Mother England. Their promised pay of six shillings a day was more than the basic wage in Australia and earned them the tag 'six bob a day tourists'.

Disillusionment invariably crept in but that wasn't yet the case when 29-year- old stockman Bill Heffernan packed his bags and headed to Adelaide to sign up for the war. He enlisted at Keswick in April 1915, four days before the landing at Gallipoli. He joined reinforcements for the 3rd Light Horse Regiment made up of men from South Australia and Tasmania. Across the globe, earlier recruits to the regiment left their horses behind in Egypt and were preparing to land on the peninsula to fight as infantry. They went ashore on the night of 12 May and were deployed in one of the areas of fiercest fighting, between Courtneys Post and Johnstons Jolly. Bill Heffernan boarded HMAT *Star of England* and left Adelaide to join them in September. He didn't make it into battle, falling ill on the island of Lemnos in November and being evacuated to a hospital at Alexandria in Egypt. He wasn't released until January 1916 by which time all the ANZACs had withdrawn from Gallipoli. He spent the rest of the war fighting the Turks in Sinai and Palestine, where he suffered shell shock. He was one of over 300 men of the 3rd Light Horse who contracted malaria in October 1918, was admitted to hospital and spent a number of weeks in a rest camp, by which time the war was over. He returned to the Territory, taking up land around Tea Tree Well on the OT line where he established a store, as well as a cattle station.

John Dow was living in South Australia when war broke out, after lengthy service at various police posts in the Northern Territory between 1893 and

1912. He also signed up for the 3rd Light Horse Regiment, three months after Bill Heffernan. He enlisted as a private but was promoted to 2nd lieutenant in January 1916. He was 45-years-old and did not go overseas, presumably because of his age. Instead, he served as a recruitment officer.

Alice Springs telegraph operator Dudley Adamson tried to enlist around the same time as Bill Heffernan but was not allowed. The 20-year-old was classified as working in an essential service but wrote to Prime Minister Billy Hughes and was eventually given permission. He signed on at Tanunda in August 1915 and was sent to signals school. However, an attack of peritonitis in December following surgery for appendicitis prevented him being posted overseas with the AIF and he was discharged on medical grounds in April 1916. He returned to Alice Springs but was allowed to re-enlist 16 months later when fully recovered. He embarked for Egypt on board HMAT *A38 Ulysses* in December 1917. After a couple of months in the Signals Office in Alexandria, he joined the 1st Signals Squadron of the Anzac Mounted Division as a sapper in August 1918. The war ended three months later and he returned to the Alice Springs telegraph station in 1920.

Sonny Kunoth quit his job as a lineman with No. 8 Line Party (NT) to enlist in Adelaide. He signed up in October 1915, a few days before his 30th birthday, and served with the 4th Division's artillery, both as a gunner and driver. He sailed for Egypt in November and then to France the following July to fight in the Battle of the Somme. The 4th Division was subsequently involved in the battles of Bullecourt, Messines, Polygon Wood, Hamel, Epehy and Amiens. He got home in May 1919 and returned to central Australia. He and Bill Liddle took up grazing leases in the country north of the George Gill Range and Kings Canyon.

Leslie Spicer had less trouble enlisting than his fellow telegraph operator Dud Adamson but getting to the recruiting office posed a challenge. He was offered a ride to Oodnadatta on one of two camels belonging to Commonwealth surveyor Jack Waldron, who was heading south after a couple of years survey work. Just before they set off at the end of 1915, two other blokes asked to join them. It turned out one was ill with tuberculosis and Les let him ride the camel while he walked the entire 470 kilometres to the railhead.[11] Not surprisingly, he had no trouble convincing the army he was fit for duty when he presented for a medical examination in Adelaide in December. The 33-year-old embarked for Egypt as a signalman for the 9th Light Horse Regiment on board HMAT *A68 Anchises* in March 1916. It comprised South Australians and Victorians but late that year he was transferred to the 3rd Light Horse to join other men from the Territory. The remarkable level of fitness he exhibited on the Oodnadatta track did not continue overseas. He suffered repeated bouts of illness during his service in the Middle East. He returned to Adelaide in August 1919 and then moved to the post office at Renmark, on the Murray River.

Alf Turner, a 28-year-old stockman working cattle on the Waite River north-east of Alice Springs, enlisted in Adelaide in April 1916 and was another to serve in the 3rd Light Horse. He left for Egypt on RMS *Mooltan* in August. During the campaign in Palestine, he volunteered to swim the flooded River Jordan one night in March 1918 and attach a rope to the other side so the engineers could build a pontoon bridge, an act of great bravery. He knew he had little chance of surviving if the Turkish snipers spotted him in the water. He contracted malaria later in the year and was admitted to hospital in October, like his mate Bill Heffernan. He was discharged from the army in September 1919, and returned to central Australia to take up the Alcoota station lease.

Jack Swanson enlisted late in the war. He'd grown up in a farming family in Victoria but was working in central Australia when he joined the AIF in June 1918. He was not quite 20 and left behind a teenage wife and a child. Dolly was a gifted singer and friend of the renowned Nellie Melba. He boarded HMT *Gaika* in Adelaide in August 1918 bound for London. Originally attached to the 43rd Battalion, he served as a gunner with the 5th Brigade Field Artillery. The couple spent the rest of their lives in the Territory apart from a spell in Adelaide during the 1939–1945 war. He was a jack-of-all-trades who ended up running a taxi business in Alice Springs.

The tragedy of war and its terrible aftermath

As Mrs Price and her children settled into their new home in the first half of 1917, their predecessors the Bradshaw family were confronted with the unbearable heartache that the Great War brought to so many Australian families. Tom and Attie Bradshaw's eldest son Mort died in hospital at Rouen in France on the 20 May from wounds he sustained in action at Bullecourt earlier in the month. This disastrous attack in a snowstorm cost Australia 10,000 men. Tom Bradshaw, in charge of the post office at Port Pirie, suffered a broken heart. Father and son had always been close.

Mort was a 20-year-old bank clerk at Kadina, on South Australia's Yorke Peninsula, when war broke out in 1914. We should consider him the first man from central Australian to enlist, rather than Bill Heffernan, even though he was living in South Australia at the time. He'd grown up at the Alice Springs telegraph station, five years old when his father took charge and 14 when the family left in 1908.

He joined the 7th Field Ambulance in March 1915 and served with distinction akin to the legendary Simpson of the 3rd Field Ambulance. Like other young Australians, Mort felt he was off on a great adventure when his unit sailed from Sydney in June 1915, aboard HMAT *Clan McEwan*. Mort's unit landed at Gallipoli in September 1915 and six months later headed to France where they fought in the vicinity of the Albert-Pozières-Bapaume road during the bloody Battle of the Somme. He was awarded the Military Medal for bravery under fire on 5 December 1916. His citation said:

> This man was stationed at Goose Alley, north-west of Flers on 7 November, 1916. While a heavy barrage was being maintained on the area he set out to assist a wounded man who was observed some 200 yards from the dressing station. He rendered first aid, dressing his wounds, and carried him back to the aid post. He was under shrapnel fire the whole time, the personal risk he ran was great, and his action is worthy of the highest praise.[12]

He survived another six months in the slaughterhouse that was the Western Front before his luck ran out. He is buried in St Sever Cemetery, Rouen.

A second man born in the country's heartland died on the Western Front five months after Mort Bradshaw. Alex McKinnon's story is intriguing because his enlistment papers say 'Aboriginal half caste' in the section relating to complexion. Aboriginal Australians had few rights in those days, could not vote and were not included in the census. Many tried to join the war effort but were rejected on the grounds of race. The regulations prevented men from enlisting in the AIF if they were 'not substantially of European origin or descent'. There were, of course, Aboriginal men who did manage to enlist. Some simply slipped through the net or claimed an 'acceptable' racial identity, such as Italian or Portuguese. Others who knew the local recruiters managed to circumvent the regulations and there was the occasional officer who ignored the rule. However, restrictions were cautiously eased in 1917, when the casualty list was reaching staggering proportions and new volunteers harder to find. A new Military Order in March 1917 stated:

> Half-castes may be enlisted in the Australian Imperial Force provided that the examining Medical Officers are satisfied that one of the parents is of European origin.

Alex McKinnon enlisted before this date. He was a station hand from the Charlotte Waters area and somehow signed up in Adelaide on 3 May 1916. His father, the telegraph lineman of the same name, had been embroiled in the infamous 1909 horse duffing case during John McKay's time in charge of the Alice Springs telegraph station. Young Alex was born at Charlotte Waters in 1889, his mother an Aboriginal woman from Mount Dare.

He sailed to England on board HMAT *A70 Ballarat* in August 1916 and was assigned to the 43rd Infantry Battalion. He was killed at Broodseinde Ridge in Belgium on 4 October 1917 during the third Battle of Ypres. His name was inscribed on the Menin Gate Memorial at Ypres because his body was never recovered. His war medals were eventually sent to his father's wife Mrs Mary McKinnon at Kadina. She wrote to the army in 1921 saying she'd only just heard of his death but didn't know his right age or when he enlisted. She said both his father and mother were dead.

A third child of the OT line failed to return home. Harry Havelett died on 8 July 1918 from wounds he sustained the previous day, in fighting east of Amiens in France. He was also of Aboriginal descent. His father was telegraph lineman George Hablett and his mother the beloved Arrernte woman Polly, who worked as a housemaid for the Gillen family in the 1890s.[13]

He gave his age as 19 years and one month when he enlisted at Mitcham in Adelaide on 24 January 1917 and his occupation as stockman. He must have been working at a station in the Marree area because his name was later listed among local war dead on a monument outside the Marree post office. His father was retired and living on Neutral Junction station, near Barrow Creek, when Harry was killed. His son's service records include a letter written to the army on George's behalf in September 1918. It mentioned 'the deceased going south and receiving education at Quorn or Craddock and becoming known by the name of Havelett'.[14]

The young recruit was assigned to the 50th Infantry Battalion and headed overseas in February 1917, on board HMAT *A48 Seang Bee*. The men disembarked in England and went to France in August. Later that year Harry Havelett was charged with desertion while on active service and court martialled in the field on 29 October. Missing for 10 days, he pleaded not guilty but was sentenced to 10 years imprisonment, commuted to two years, and taken to a military prison in France. There he contracted a severe bout of pneumonia in 1918 and was transferred to a hospital in Calais on 30 March. The 50th Battalion participated in the now-legendary attack on Anzac Day 1918 to dislodge the enemy from Villers-Bretonneux. He was sent back to prison in May but a major advance against the Germans was underway by that time and all available resources were swung into action to finally end the war. So, sentence suspended, he was released on 21 June and rejoined his unit. The 50th Battalion engaged with the enemy east of Amiens. Harry Havelett was wounded in action on 7 July 1918 and died the next day. He is buried in the Daours Communal Cemetery, east of Amiens.

Jack Meyers lived in Alice Springs at the same time as Mort Bradshaw but had better luck than his childhood friend and managed to survive the war. He was born at Hermannsburg in 1899, the son of Annie and Charlie Meyers, and was working as a postal assistant at Adelaide's General Post Office when he signed up with the 48th Infantry Battalion in January 1918. He sailed for London on board HMAT *A54 Runic* in March and went to France in August.

However, he was detached from his battalion and sent to the 12th Brigade Signalling School in October, not rejoining his unit until three days before the war ended. They remained in France for several months after which he was posted to London to undertake more telegraphy training, from March 1919 until mid June. He got back to Australia at the end of August 1919 but did not pursue a career with the post office. Instead he was back in central Australia by 1921 working as a stockman.

The war ended in November 1918 but not the tragic loss of life. In March 1919 the Price family was shocked to receive word that their eldest daughter, 19-year-old Hilda, had died in Adelaide. She'd been married barely a year and was pregnant with her first child.[15] She was a victim of the virus known as Spanish flu, which was spreading rapidly around the world as soldiers headed home from the killing fields of Europe. It would claim an estimated 50 million lives worldwide and 11,552 in Australia by the time it had run its course at the end of 1919. The pandemic swept across the world in three waves in 1918 and 1919. It tended to affect an area for 12 weeks and then suddenly disappear, almost as quickly as it arrived, only to return several months later.[16]

The first Australian case of Spanish flu was reported in Melbourne on 22 January 1919 and it reached epidemic proportions between February and July. People in the cities were compelled to wear face masks but the disease was not confined to the closely settled areas. Hundreds of Aboriginal people died in central Australia.[17] The exact number is unknown because they were not counted in any Australian census until the 1967 referendum brought about a change in the constitution. The drought during the war years had already pushed many Aboriginal people to the limit of their resources, lowering their resistance to the disease.

Rev. John Flynn decides to build a hospital in Alice Springs

The people of central Australia lacked access to medical care at this time. With the nearest doctor hundreds of kilometres away, they had to rely on their own experience and their basic supplies of medicine. In emergencies a doctor could be called into the Central Telegraph Office in Adelaide and advice transmitted up the OT line but much was left to the resourceful women of the outback. One hot night in January 1921 a stockman from the Bond Springs cattle station, 20 kilometres north of the telegraph station, arrived with a message from the manager Alf Draper. His baby son Maxie was having convulsions and his wife Vera desperately needed Mrs Price's help. She rode north on her horse as fast as she could but was too late to help save the little boy, who had died not long after the stockman had ridden off to summon help.[18]

There were too many lonely graves along the dusty outback tracks. Reverend John Flynn of the Presbyterian Church was determined to do something about it. He was superintendent of the church's Australian Inland Mission (AIM), set up in 1912. Flynn, based in Sydney for much of his working life, travelled regularly to far-flung places. He began his work to improve the lives of people in central Australia in November 1913 when he sent a young padre named Bruce Plowman to Oodnadatta with £160, saying 'Buy some camels, find out what to do, and do it'. Plowman worked for Flynn until 1917, travelling up and down the track between Oodnadatta and Tennant Creek, ministering to the needs of the people as best he could, both spiritually and in material ways. He didn't receive a wage, just reimbursement for his expenses.

He later wrote a book about those years with his faithful offsider Dick Gillen. One of his stories in *The Man from Oodnadatta* is the tragic tale of young William Hayes, the two-year-old son of Ted and Ann Jane Hayes. They were managing the Hayes family's Mount Burrell property when their son became mysteriously ill in 1914.[19] The nearest medical help was the AIM's nursing sister Jean Finlayson at Oodnadatta. The nearest doctor's surgery was much further away at Port Augusta, though the railway employed a doctor who went up and down the line between Oodnadatta and Hergott Springs (Marree).

Ted rode 50 kilometres from Mount Burrell to the Alice Well police station and a telephone to get a message to the Alice Springs telegraph station. The operators sent a telegram to Adelaide but the anxious father got word back saying the doctor needed more information before he could diagnose the problem. So he rode back to Mount Burrell to talk to his wife. He returned to Alice Well next morning and rang through to Alice Springs with more information to be passed on to the doctor. The reply came back: 'Not enough data. Can you give more detailed particulars?'

The exhausted father rode the 50 kilometres to check on the condition of his child and talk to his wife yet again. He returned to Alice Well next morning and the operators at Alice Springs sent off a third telegram. This time the reply was: 'Sorry, cannot diagnose. Better bring the child down.' His parents rushed him by buggy to the railhead at Oodnadatta, which took a week. Sister Finlayson examined the unconscious child but shook her head and admitted she did not know what was wrong. The family reached a hospital in Adelaide after a three-day train journey but William died shortly afterward.

Sister Finlayson's heart went out to the Hayes family and all the others living up the track with no access to medical help. She offered to spend a year working in the Alice Springs district as soon as someone could replace her at Oodnadatta. She began ministering to the needs of the local people in August 1915. Policeman Bob Stott and his wife Agnes offered accommodation at their house, with schoolteacher Mrs Standley.

Eventually alternate accommodation became available: a slab cottage on Wills Terrace, owned by Ben Walkington. He spent his time at Arltunga where he ran the Crossroads store and the place was occupied by Ann Jane Hayes's mother Lizzie and her husband Sam Nicker. The Nickers were in the process of establishing themselves on the land around Ryans Well, 100 kilometres up the OT line, but Sister Finlayson could move in when they vacated it. The cottage became known as Sister's Hospital.

Interestingly, Lizzie Nicker was the one the locals called for help in the years before Sister Finlayson appeared. She had no medical training but had acquired skills and experience during her many years living in the bush. She was often away from home, delivering babies or tending the sick, and was known to ride through the night on rough tracks to render assistance to someone in need. Patrol padre Bruce Plowman lauded her efforts in *The Man from Oodnadatta*:

In the annals of our race there have been recorded from time to time the names and noble doings of great women. In the lonely places of the vast Australian continent there are women whose names and deeds are worthy of record in these annals. One is Mrs Sam Nicker.[20]

Sister Finlayson's time in Alice Springs was a boon for the locals while it lasted but they needed a permanent medical facility. Plowman's replacement, Reverend Skipper Partridge, got the ball rolling. He took over as patrol padre after Bruce Plowman's health deteriorated in 1917. One night in August 1918, while still new to the job, he dropped in on a group of men playing cards in George Wilkinson's store at the top end of Todd Street. His boss, Rev. John Flynn, had a vision of a network of hospitals for the people of the inland, each staffed by two skilled nursing sisters. Partridge said the AIM wanted to build one in Alice Springs and the men passed around the hat. The padre walked away with £25. The townspeople formed a fundraising committee, which soon took the tally to £200, quite a large sum of money in those days. The only hiccup was when Flynn asked them not to run raffles because this offended some prudish, southern church members. The Presbyterian Young People's Association of South Australia was a major contributor to Flynn's hospital in Alice Springs. They organised a fete in the Adelaide Town Hall, which raised £532 in December 1919. As a result, Flynn proposed calling the building Adelaide House.

Early in 1920, the locals sent a message to Flynn in Sydney saying that a stonemason in town could begin work on the building. They pleaded for him to be employed. It could be years before someone else with his experience came along. Flynn agreed and in April 1920 let a contract to 70-year-old Jack Williams to construct the stone walls and concrete floor for the sum of £800. He had built the Stuart Town Gaol around the corner, between 1907 and 1909, and the police house next door to it. Williams worked hard but the project was plagued with delays. He was unable to get good help and worked single-handedly for much of the three years he was on the job. He quarried his own stone and burnt his own lime but had trouble getting sawn timber for boxing the concrete and steel for reinforcement. The project came to a standstill in 1923, with the walls up but no roof and the concrete floors unfinished. The cost was blowing out and Flynn was strapped for funds. He wasn't able to get it finished and open until June 1926, two years after Fred Price left the telegraph station for an extended holiday. Price was exhausted and unwell by 1924, and destined never to return to central Australia.

Mail men and Afghan cameleers in the Price years

Central Australia was a land where people learned to wait. By Fred Price's time, camel trains delivered bulk supplies to the Alice Springs telegraph station twice a year, in May and November.[21] Small items could be procured via the fortnightly mail service but there was no guarantee they would survive the journey. The war years were very dry, for the most part, compelling the mail contractor to use camels rather than a horse and buggy. Two teams travelled the track simultaneously, one trudging south from Alice Springs while the other headed north from Oodnadatta. They timed their trips to arrive at Horseshoe Bend on the same day. The mail packets were exchanged and each camel train returned after a rest.[22]

Claude Golder brought the mail to Alice Springs for seven years until 1922 when he gave up the contract to take over the pub at Oodnadatta. Ex-serviceman Jim Lackman then became the mail contractor. Lackman was new to the region. Born in Victoria he served in the Middle East with the 9th Light Horse Regiment during the latter months of the war. He was suffering from tuberculosis and came north hoping his health would improve in the warm climate. Central Australia had enjoyed a couple of good seasons by the time he took over the mail run and he was able to switch back to a horse and buggy. This happened at the urging of three senators who visited the region in June–July 1921 as members of the Sectional Committee of the Commonwealth Parliamentary Standing Committee on Public Works. They recommended a buggy mail service be instituted at once because it was difficult for women and children to travel on the camels.[23] By 1925 central Australia was again in the grip of a severe drought and camels were reintroduced.

People north of Alice Springs had to wait six weeks for mail, a service only introduced in December 1914.[24] It wasn't considered profitable to use a contractor on the route and so, for many years, the mail was simply entrusted to anyone reliable who happened to be travelling along the track. Eventually the government agreed to employ an extra lineman to travel between the Alice Springs and Powell Creek telegraph stations with the mail. A small Cornishman named Sammy Lynch took on the job in 1922, accompanied by Jimmy, the brother of his Aboriginal wife Elsie. Sammy did it for a number of years using a plant of 16 horses.

Sammy and Elsie Lynch lived in the old line-party hut in the north-east corner of the telegraph station. He had a five-day break between successive trips to Powell Creek and would go on a glorious four-day binge, drinking fortified wine, usually referred to as 'fourpenny dark'. He was always happy, never aggressive or abusive, and Mrs Price referred to him as the gentleman drunk. Her daughter Pearl said:

> She saw to it that, when it was time for him to start out north again, she had a big pot of soup ready. It helped him to sober up and he really appreciated her concern. Sammy only drank on these brief holidays; the rest of the time he was as sober as a judge. He spent the last day of each break checking the harness and packs for his next trip, making sure that each pack saddle was well greased to keep it soft and pliable. The same applied for the straps and hobbles …[25]

Like stockman Arthur Neale, the Price children adored him.

A permanent Afghan community developed on the south side of the town during the Price period. Saleh Sud-Ud-Din – better known as Charlie Sadadeen – was a key figure in this. Born in Peshawar around 1846, he was the first Afghan cameleer to buy land in the town. He'd been carting goods between Oodnadatta and Alice Springs since the turn of the century. He kept his camels among the coolibahs and saltbush on the eastern side of the Todd River, sheltered by a rocky ridge later named the Sadadeen Range. In 1913 he purchased lot 89 in Todd Street, immediately south of the two blocks used by market gardener Ah Hong. He sold the house and land to publican Len Browne in 1921, purchasing miscellaneous lease 53, further south on Todd Street, that same year. This block was one of five extending to the river.

Other Afghans settled permanently in the town and a small mosque was built on Sadadeen's block. He established an extensive garden irrigated by two windmills of which he was very proud.[26] The Alice Springs Town Council named the area Nishan-e-Afghan ('centre of Afghans') Park in 2000.

Renewed moves to complete the railway to Alice Springs

The Commonwealth's agreement to take over the Northern Territory included a commitment to complete the transcontinental railway, but nothing much happened for 10 years. In 1920 there was a gap of 1650 kilometres between Oodnadatta in the south and Katherine in the north. That year, adventurer Francis Birtles had the audacity to offer to move things along. Amazingly Prime Minister Billy Hughes accepted. He said he would provide a detailed report on the country between Oodnadatta and Katherine if the government would loan him a suitable Hudson motor car and contribute £1000 toward his expenses. Billy Hughes personally approved the project and Francis Birtles agreed to photograph the country, prepare charts, collect samples of plants and minerals, plus provide advice on suitable sites for airstrips along the way.[27]

This intrepid and irrepressible man had ridden a bicycle solo from Sydney to Darwin, via Brisbane, and then south through central Australia in 1907 and 1908. In 1912 he made a name for himself when he sat behind the wheel of the first car to cross Australia from Perth to Sydney.

No one had driven a car all the way from Oodnadatta to Katherine since Harry Dutton, Murray Aunger and Ernie Allchurch in 1908. Administrator Gilruth and his chauffeur G.H. Cowper ventured south from Darwin in 1912 and 1913 but ran into trouble both times. Joe Breaden from Todmorden station, near Oodnadatta, bought a new Dodge in 1917, and travelled to his second property Henbury, on the Finke River. He had recently injured his hip and couldn't drive, so was chauffeured by Cyril Woodward. They needed donkeys to pull the vehicle over a number of sandhills and across the Finke. In 1920 three Victorian pastoralists, McKinnon, Manifold and Peck, drove another Dodge from Adelaide to Alice Springs and back – but they also needed help.[28]

Francis Birtles left Oodnadatta on 31 December 1920 with Roy Fry and a blue cattle dog called Dinkum. They took more than three weeks to get to the Alice Springs telegraph station, averaging only 20 kilometres a day, because exceptional rains had waterlogged the country between Oodnadatta and Charlotte Waters. The country north of Charlotte Waters was drier but they had to coax the Hudson over sand dunes and large expanses of spinifex. Showers of the sharp-pointed seeds flew over the windscreen into their open vehicle and choked the radiator. The exhaust pipe occasionally became red-hot during prolonged periods of slow, low-gear driving. It would have been near impossible to prevent the vehicle's drums of spare petrol from exploding if the grass had caught fire. North of the MacDonnell Ranges were vast mulga plains, numerous termite mounds and long grass concealing fallen timber.

Eventually they crawled into the Katherine River where construction of the railway from Darwin had come to a halt in 1917. They were able to get petrol for the return journey but disaster struck before they managed to get far. Pushing slowly through long grass on Old Elsey station on 24 May, the car hit a hidden stump and came to an abrupt halt. It was quickly engulfed by flames when the grass caught alight, their ruptured petrol tank exploded and flames roared 15 metres into the sky. Both men and the dog were badly burnt. They managed to walk to an Aboriginal camp a few kilometres away and someone ran to Mataranka station for help. It was noon the following day before a horse-drawn buggy arrived to take them to the Maranboy tin fields. Rev. John Flynn's Australian Inland Mission had established a small hospital there with two nursing sisters who gave them morphine to ease their pain. Roy Fry, close to death on a couple of occasions, was slowly nursed back to health. It was a number of weeks before either man was well enough to board a steamer in Darwin Harbour and return south. Their adventure, if you could call it that, was soon followed by two more parties of intrepid motorists.

On 10 June 1921, three members of the Sectional Committee of the Commonwealth Parliamentary Standing Committee on Public Works arrived in Oodnadatta for their own investigation of the proposed railway extension: Senator Simpson Newland (SA), Senator Harry Foll (Qld), and Senator

Jackson (Tas.) With them were three Commonwealth public servants: Gerald Whiteford, G.A. Hobler and surveyor Jack Waldron. Three new Buick cars were waiting in Oodnadatta to take them to Alice Springs.[29]

Not long afterward, two Dodges had a trouble-free run all the way from Adelaide to Darwin. This was a private trip organised by Harry Dutton who took his wife Emily with him, giving her the distinction of being the first woman to cross the continent by car. The second vehicle was driven by a bloke called Breally. Their trip took 17 days, actual running time, and the only trouble they had was a puncture and a broken front spring when one of the cars hit a termite mound obscured by long grass.[30]

The first aeroplane lands in Alice Springs

Despite his horrific experience in May, Francis Birtles was back in the Northern Territory before the end of 1921. This time he was aboard the first plane to land in Alice Springs.[31] He'd persuaded aviator Frank Briggs that a flight to central Australia to film the area would prove profitable, as well as enabling him to complete the investigation of the proposed railway route. No one had previously flown to central Australia. They set off from Melbourne early on 26 September with mechanic George Bailey in a de Havilland Airco DH-4 biplane. Birtles was armed to the teeth with cameras and film.

They touched down in a swirling cloud of dust on 5 October. The locals had cleared a patch of ground west of the town and everyone came out to meet them: 27 white people plus an unrecorded number of intrigued Aboriginal people. The three aviators climbed into a two-horsepower buggy and headed to the Stuart Arms Hotel to celebrate. John Laver had recently taken over the place from Len and Vivian Browne who ran it from 1917 until 1921. Mrs Browne was the youngest daughter of schoolteacher Ida Standley. The pub wasn't too flash and John Laver's son Bob recalled years later that his 'mother, when she saw this dilapidated, broken down looking building, she just stood and cried'.[32] The men stayed two weeks giving Birtles time to inspect the surrounding country. This was his third visit to the town and he thought it should be the site for the nation's capital, though few agreed with him. Bob Laver remembered the place:

The police Station, two stores ... the Stuart Arms Hotel, a boarding house run by Mrs McGowan, a stone house structure known as the Hostel (just the foundation and walls, no roof), a stone house belonging to Jim Shannon, George Wilkinson's residence near Anzac Hill (then known as View Hill), 'Myrtle Villa' the little cottage where Mrs Standley lived, another small cottage nearby (Ben Walkington's home), a broken down thatched roof building of Charlie Meyers and his saddler's shop. There was also a gaol built of stone ... a wood and iron building more like an iron shed which was called the Bungalow, housing the half-caste children and their half-caste caretaker, a small stone building in between the Police Station and Anzac Hill Stables, a wood and iron structure used as the school on the Police Station property, a blacksmith shop almost falling down, and Norm Jones residence.[33]

In 1922, Murray Aunger made his second crossing of the continent. He and his brother Cyril organised three Dort cars to carry them and four other South Australians to Darwin: Tom McCallum, a member of the South Australian Legislative Council, and his brother Donald, ornithologist Samuel White, and a man named Crowder. The McCallum brothers were wealthy landholders and wanted to assess the suitability of central and northern Australia for investment. They were also pressuring the Commonwealth to complete the railway which was essential if they were to get a healthy return on their money. White was compiling a new checklist of Australian birds.

The men left Adelaide on 6 May 1922, drove to Quorn and then on to Marree, Oodnadatta and Charlotte Waters. They pulled into Alice Springs on 17 May and then drove all the way to Darwin without drama.[34] Murray Aunger had the South Australian franchise for Dort cars and the widely-publicised journey was good for sales.

The death of Pastor Carl Strehlow

These pioneering motor trips gave local people the confidence to buy cars of their own. Both Gerhardt Johannsen of Deep Well and Ted Hayes of Undoolya station purchased a Dodge 4, converted into a utility to better suit their purposes. Sergeant Bob Stott acquired a Ford Model T a bit later. It was the first police car in central Australia but he was a dreadful driver, according to his son Duncan.[35] None of these vehicles were purchased in time to save the life of Hermannsburg's pastor Carl Strehlow in October 1922.

Twenty-eight years had elapsed since the small Immanuel Synod of South Australia took over the struggling mission and sent Carl Strehlow north to run it. The synod's meagre funds meant the place was always understaffed and Strehlow and his wife Frieda worked to the point of exhaustion. Early in September 1922 the Lutheran authorities received a telegram from Alice Springs informing them that their pastor was very ill and needed to go south for medical treatment. He'd been sick since July. Strehlow originally thought it was influenza but realised by September that he had suffered an attack of pleurisy and then dropsy had set in, with asthma on top of it.

It was unlikely his health could withstand a rough trip to the train at Oodnadatta in a horse-drawn buggy. He asked the mission board to send a car to Hermannsburg. The only one in the region at that time was Joe Breaden's Dodge way down at Todmorden station but Breaden doubted it could make the trip. Sergeant Stott sent a telegram to Pastor J.J. Stolz, the chairman of the mission board, suggesting they hire a car and drive it up with a nurse. Stolz consulted Murray Aunger who said 'because of the extremely poor roads and the sandy creek crossings of the interior at least two cars would have to be sent, and that the cost could be well in the vicinity of £500'.[36]

The mission board baulked at this and Strehlow got word he should trust in the Lord and come by buggy. However, a few days before he was due to depart he learnt that church member and wheat farmer Gotthold Wurst had offered to put his car on the train to Oodnadatta; he and Stolz would then drive as far north as possible. They got to Oodnadatta on the night of 13 October by which time Carl Strehlow had left Hermannsburg with his wife Frieda and 14-year-old son Theo.[37] The build up of fluids in the desperately ill missionary's body made breathing difficult and lying in a bed was painful. His lower legs were so swollen that he was forced to spend the nights sitting upright in a chair.

Unfortunately, the car only made it as far as the Stevenson River. The Alberga had pretty well knocked the car out and the Stevenson finished it off.

Joe Breaden then decided they should see if his car could make it up the track. Strehlow managed to survive 10 arduous days bouncing around in the buggy but died at Horseshoe Bend on Friday 20 October. Not long before he died, the telephone rang on the wall of the pub with the news, relayed up the line from Charlotte Waters, that Breaden's car was held up at the Alberga River by an unexpected flood. It might be a week before it could hope to get across.[38]

The unexpected death of Fred Price

In April 1924, Fred Price decided he needed a break from the work that was taking its toll on him. He left operator Dudley Adamson in charge without waiting for a replacement to come up the line to take his place. He and Ivy were committed to returning to central Australia. He'd taken up the lease on Harper Springs station, south-east of Tea Tree Well, and the adjoining block on the western side of Harper Springs. He could see a great future in central Australia and intended retiring there. They packed up their household belongings, including his cherished piano, and arranged for them to be stored with friends in town. Their horses, goats and the various family pets were left at the telegraph station. Ahead of them lay the 12-day buggy trip to Oodnadatta and three days on the train to Adelaide.

The children noticed their dad was quiet and listless on the trip; they didn't realise he had only a couple of months to live. Within a few days of arriving in Adelaide he was admitted to hospital where he struggled for two weeks to recover from the stress of the previous eight years. The family travelled by train to Sydney for an extended stay with Mrs Price's sisters but the trip was too much for Fred and he was admitted to hospital on arrival. Two weeks passed before he was well enough to be released. Fred was once again hospitalised for a few weeks when they returned to Adelaide. This time he did not leave, dying there on 12 August 1924 aged only 57.[39]

19

'Make it an Allchurch!'

The death of Fred Price while on leave in 1924 brought one of the line's most popular men back to Alice Springs after an absence of 14 years. Attie Bradshaw's younger brother Ernie Allchurch jumped at the chance to return to the place where he'd spent nine contented years from 1902. He and Bessie Williams were married at Hermannsburg in 1905 and their first daughter Jessie May was born in Moonta two years later. Their second child, Maisie, didn't come along until 1919.

Bessie was short like her sister Annie Meyers but Ernie was tall, and solid in body and nature. Liked and respected by people up and down the line, he loved the life in the heart of Australia even though he'd grown up by the sea at Glenelg. He didn't follow his father into the police force but, like his father, earned a high level of esteem among his work colleagues and those he served.

Ernie's telegraph career began shortly before his 14th birthday when he left home to commence work as a messenger boy at Macclesfield, a town 50 kilometres from Glenelg. Three years later he was transferred to Adelaide's Central Telegraph Office to complete his training in morse telegraphy. He was promoted to operator and posted back at Glenelg four months short of his 18th birthday.[1]

Bessie was pleased to get a move to Adelaide in 1911 but Ernie vowed to return to Alice Springs one day. They made it halfway in 1916 when he was put in charge at Hergott Springs for six years. The town was officially named Marree when it was gazetted in 1883 but the telegraph and railways departments continued to use its old name Hergott Springs until anti-German hysteria forced a change in 1918. Bessie considered it 'a dreary desolate place' but enjoyed meeting their old friends from the north as they passed through the little town.[2] Two years in the senior job at Kapunda followed and then the unexpected death of Fred Price in August 1924 saw her husband's long-held wish come true.

Ernie Allchurch was known up and down the line as a convivial man who enjoyed sharing stories and a drink. Motorist Penryn Goldman wrote of him in 1929:

> His name is common property up and down the country, for when he offers you a drink, he pours half the bottle into the glass. So, when anyone wants a long drink and a friend is doing the pouring, they always say 'Make it an Allchurch'.[3]

He was a source of countless stories about the early days in central Australia but never got the chance to complete the book of reminiscences he had begun writing. Like his predecessor he died unexpectedly at a relatively young age. The 16 January 1932 edition of Adelaide's *Advertiser* carried a lengthy report of his death:

> After undergoing a minor operation on his throat in Calvary Hospital on Thursday, Mr Ernie Allchurch died suddenly yesterday afternoon at the age of 61. His position as stipendiary magistrate at Alice Springs made him virtually the 'King of Central Australia' and although it was his duty to try many of the aborigines for cattle spearing and other misdemeanours, he was regarded by them more as a guide, philosopher and friend than the stern representative of the law. The experiences which this position put in his way, combined with his skills as a raconteur, made him a man well worth meeting, and his personality endeared him to a wide circle of friends ... There in a country of big men, he became one of the biggest. He was interested in all sports and was invariably a popular figure at the Oakbank meeting, which he usually contrived to fit into his annual leave. The suddenness of his death was a shock to his many friends. He was very ill when he came down on sick leave, and seemed to have lost about 4 st. in weight. Three days ago, however, in a conversation with 'Rufus' of 'The Advertiser', he said he was much improved and had only to undergo a minor operation to his throat to be all right.[4]

Port Augusta's weekly paper the *Transcontinental* expressed similar sentiments:

> Mr Allchurch was a genial soul, with a flexible outlook on life, and beloved
> by those living outback ... he listened to and smoothed out the troubles of
> the residents in a most engaging manner.[5]

Technological change and telegraph staff in Allchurch's time

Telegraph technology had advanced significantly in Australia and abroad
by 1924 when Ernie Allchurch took charge at Alice Springs. That year the
Postmaster-General's Department adopted the high-speed telegraph system
Murray Multiplex, the brainchild of New Zealander David Murray. It allowed
eight telegraph channels to operate simultaneously on a single wire using
a five-unit code rather than traditional morse signals. It was used between
state capitals and some major regional centres but not on the OT line. Monday
9 September 1929 saw another breakthrough with the first commercial
transmission of photos by telegraph between Sydney and Melbourne.
Producing picturegrams involved scanning photos by an electric eye with the
shade and intensity of the image transferred along the wire. At the receiving
end a roll of photographic film recorded the impulses being transmitted.

Alice Springs was still a busy telegraph station in the 1920s but
international traffic was declining because the OT line was no longer
Australia's sole link with the outside world. It had lost that status in 1889
when the Eastern Extension, Australasia and China Telegraph Company
laid a cable from Java to Broome, giving rise to the name Cable Beach, now a
tourist mecca. A new telegraph line was built down the west coast to carry
international messages to Perth. In 1901 the company invested in another
cable, which ran from Durban in South Africa to Perth's Cottesloe Beach,
via Mauritius, Rodriguez and the Cocos Islands. It laid a connecting cable
around the south coast, from Cottesloe to the Adelaide suburb of Glenelg.
Australia was linked to North America in 1902 by a cable across the Pacific
from Southport in Queensland to Vancouver. It went via Norfolk Island, Fiji
and Hawaii.[6]

These new cables bit into traffic on the two older cables. The cable station
at Broome closed in March 1914 because of reduced traffic but also due to

defects in the cable itself. Darwin continued to operate but the OT line's most glamorous days were over. Its demise was hastened on 30 April 1930 when a radio-telephone system began operating between Sydney and London and Prime Minister Jim Scullin spoke directly to his counterpart Ramsey MacDonald in England, ushering in a new era in communication.

Harry Kearnan, Dudley Adamson, Jack Cain, Bill Wutke, Maurie Fuss, Frankie Pearce, Claude Galpin and Bill Duncan worked alongside Ernie Allchurch during his years in charge at Alice Springs. The 1931 electoral rolls include a Donald Frederick Hancock whose occupation is recorded as postal clerk. This reflects the station's changing role, with staff time increasingly being devoted to post office duties as opposed to operating the telegraph equipment. Maurie Fuss is credited with introducing golf to the town when he returned from his holiday one year with a set of clubs.

Dudley Adamson had four separate spells at Alice Springs between 1913 and 1946, clocking up over a quarter of a century of service. He'd met attractive young Mabel Wilkinson in Alice Springs after he returned from the war. Her father Frank Wilkinson was working with his brother George who owned Wallis's store, at the top end of Todd Street. Mabel said years later that her father came up from Sydney on his own and 'stayed eight months to see if it was suitable for all of us to go there and live for a few years. I was 15 and still going to school in grade seven and learning piano. We had a very comfortable home and my mother had a few regrets about leaving her home but my brother and I thought it would be a great adventure'.[7] Dud and Mabel married in Adelaide in 1923.

Cook Beatrice Fitzpatrick and stockman Arthur Neale, staff members during the Price years, stayed on at the telegraph station into the Allchurch years. Mrs Jessie Roper took over as staff cook from Miss Fitzpatrick in 1929 and subsequently opened a guesthouse in town in the early 1930s. Others who worked for Ernie Allchurch include lineman Tom Barrett and Tim Golder in the battery room. There were also Aboriginal employees, regrettably anonymous for the most part, though one of Bill Duncan's photos from 1931 shows 'mess servants Katie and Mabel' standing next to a water tank, with Katie smiling brightly.[8]

Central Australia and the town of Stuart in 1924

The Allchurch family's move back to the Alice Springs telegraph station in 1924 was accompanied by the return of Bessie's sister Annie Meyers. Her marriage to Charlie was not a happy one and she'd taken her three children Dorothy, Jack and Gwen south in 1909 to be educated. Jack had already returned after serving overseas in the army in the last year of the war. While Bessie was settling into the substantial stationmaster's residence at the telegraph station, Annie was moving back into her old house by the river in town. Having her sister nearby once again was a bonus for Bessie.

The pioneering recorder of local history, Adela Purvis from Woodgreen station, described Annie Meyers as 'a little dumpy lady, of the figure 8 variety' but she was a keen tennis and croquet player.[9] She was also a shrewd businesswoman with plans to turned her place into a guesthouse and eventually open a second hotel in town. She soon developed a large vegetable garden, with many fruits trees, and a sizeable poultry run. Her Stuart Guest Home opened in 1926, two years after her return, and quickly acquired the reputation for serving the best food in town.

Her estranged husband Charlie had been living out at Haast Bluff since 1911 running cattle on land he held in partnership with telegraph operator Les Spicer. He would come into town from time to time to do saddlery work at his ramshackle thatched-roof workshop in Todd Street. He was short, like his wife, but cut a distinctive figure when dressed in hunting jacket, white riding britches and knee-high black boots to serve as clerk of the course at picnic race meetings. His home brew ensured his abode was a popular nighttime alternative to the Stuart Arms Hotel. However, he was also renowned for being a very hard man from whom to extract money.[10]

Central Australia in 1924 was still a sparsely populated region, with fewer than 400 white people living between the South Australian border and Newcastle Waters, 1000 kilometres to the north.[11] Sleepy little Stuart was the only town between Oodnadatta and Newcastle Waters. North, south, east and west of it were small clusters of hardy people scratching out a living in fairly primitive conditions. Motor vehicles were venturing along the track from Oodnadatta but the one heading north was very rough.

There was no serious attempt to turn it into a proper road until the 1930s.

There were two modest stores up that rough north track. Sam and Lizzie Nicker had one near Ryans Well, 120 kilometres from Alice, while war veteran Bill Heffernan had opened another at Tea Tree Well, 70 kilometres further on. There were a couple of telegraph linemen based at Barrow Creek and no town at Tennant Creek, just the staff at the telegraph station. Hermannsburg Mission was still plugging along but it had struggled since the death of its pastor Carl Strehlow in October 1922. It wasn't until April 1926 that German war veteran and Iron Cross winner Friedrich Albrecht arrived to take his place.

Getting stock to southern markets was a challenge for local cattlemen. Like so many battling farmers in southern Australia colloquially called 'cockatoos', they scratched out a very modest living. It was also a bleak time for the mining industry. A few diggers poked around on the Harts Range mica fields, north-east of Alice Springs, but mining had petered out at Arltunga by 1914. It was a similar story on the wolfram fields of Wauchope and Hatches Creek north of Alice Springs. The Great War had created a demand for this mineral, the source of tungsten, used for toughening steel. The European armaments industry paid good prices then for central Australian wolfram but demand declined once the war was over and there was no production between 1923 and 1929.

Bessie Allchurch recalled in a letter she wrote to Adela Purvis in 1954 that the township of Stuart had changed very little between 1911 and 1924. The one change she mentioned was motor vehicles replacing the horse and buggy.[12] The population had risen to 40 white residents but they had few creature comforts or conveniences. They still carted their water from wells, lacked decent toilet facilities and had no electricity. The town was still just a pub, police station, gaol, two stores and the saddlery. Once a month a camel train brought provisions for these stores from the railhead at Oodnadatta but the range of goods they stocked was limited.[13] Fruit and vegetables were grown in backyards, irrigated by water drawn from wells. Most of the town's houses would be called shacks these days. Building materials were scarce and expensive, because of the high cost of haulage on the back of a camel, and the few skilled tradesmen. One significant addition since 1911 was the children's home behind the pub but it was just a couple of shabby sheds. The other was Adelaide House, John Flynn's uncompleted medical facility in Todd Street.

The town was quite a different place when Ernie Allchurch died eight years later. Rapidly improved transport was the trigger for its transformation. In 1925, Sam Irvine pioneered a motor mail service between Oodnadatta and Alice Springs and the storekeeping firm Wallis Fogarty Ltd started a fortnightly transport service with trucks. War veterans Billy McCoy and Phil Windle were their first drivers, carrying goods between Oodnadatta and Powell Creek in 30-cwt trucks. In 1927 work finally began on extending the railway to Alice Springs and aeroplanes were increasingly seen in the sky. Those last few years of Ernie's life were a time of rapid change for the far-flung residents of Australia's heartland.

Flynn of the Inland

Reverend John Flynn is a figure closely associated with Alice Springs even though he was based in Sydney. His design for Adelaide House featured a cellar with ducts taking cool air up to the various rooms and a staircase leading to a second storey. There'd been nothing as substantial as this built in town since the Stuart Arms Hotel in 1889. Flynn had run short of cash and couldn't get things moving again until October 1925 when he hired builders Bert and Angus McLeod from Adelaide to finish the job; there was simply no one in town capable of handling the building's large roof span.

Flynn is a remarkable figure in the history of outback Australia. He worked tirelessly for 40 years to improve the lives of people in the bush, building hospitals rather than churches, employing more nurses than ministers, and giving away more books and magazines than Bibles. His priority was to meet the social and physical needs of the people, rather than preaching and evangelising. His practical Christianity made him a legend in his own lifetime and earned the respect of people who might never go near a church. More monuments were built to honour him after his death in 1951 than any other Australian of his time.

The town didn't actually get a church until 1926 and it was travelling missionaries Erny and Effie Kramer who built it, not Flynn. The Kramers and their children settled in town in January 1924, before the Allchurch family returned. Their first venture to central Australia had been in December 1919. They spent the next two years imparting Christianity to the Aboriginal people from a caravan with the Biblical words 'Behold I come quickly' painted on one side. Locals smiled because their donkeys were slow movers. The church they built on Gregory Terrace was called the Ebenezer Tabernacle.

Adelaide House was the ninth in a network of 14 medical facilities established by John Flynn's Australian Inland Mission. They were part of the 'mantle of safety' he envisaged for the people of the outback. However, he was well aware of the agony patients suffered travelling long distances to his bush hospitals and the tragedy of many others who never got help. He knew that radio and aeroplanes were the answer and dreamed of a system of two-way radios in isolated outposts, with flying doctors to help people when and where they needed it. That vision came closer to reality on 24 November 1926, five months after Adelaide House was officially opened.

On that day Flynn and electrical engineer Alf Traeger sent a telegram by radio from Hermannsburg to Alice Springs, the first transmission of a telegram by a field radio in Australia. The power came from a bank of heavy batteries transported out to the mission specifically for that experiment. Something simpler and better was needed but this event heralded the most significant advance in communication and social development for people in the outback since the introduction of the postage stamp. By 1929, Alf Traeger had developed a simple generator driven by bicycle pedals, leaving the operator's hands free to tap out a message on a morse key. Next came a keyboard that automatically transmitted a message in morse code. It was later replaced by a microphone and loudspeaker, and the bush had a voice.

Central Australia becomes a separate Commonwealth territory

A radical change to the administration of the Northern Territory was enacted in January 1926. A bill presented to the Commonwealth parliament in Melbourne, Australia's temporary capital, aimed to split the Territory into two separate administrative entities. The dividing line was the 20th parallel of latitude, 50 kilometres south of the Tennant Creek telegraph station.

The town of Stuart became the administrative centre for the new territory of Central Australia; the top half became Northern Australia. The governor-general gave assent to the *Northern Australia Act 1926* on 4 June, though the actual division didn't happen until 1927. Residents in Central Australia would have their own form of local government with a government resident and a four-man advisory council to represent the area's interests to the faraway politicians.[14] John Charles Cawood from New South Wales came to town to take up the new position from 1 March 1927, when the new arrangements came into place.[15]

There was no house for him and his wife Alice in 1927 so they took up residence in the Stuart Arms Hotel. A builder, Emil Martin, came to town from Mount Barker in South Australia at the end of the year and built them a place officially called The Residency. Locals called it 'the palace in the Alice'. Martin also built a house next door for the government secretary Vic Carrington and his young wife Pearl. Their offices across the road weren't completed until the end of 1928, so the town's top officials ended up spending a lot of time at the pub. Stuart was surely the most inauspicious capital on the planet and was destined to enjoy only five years of glory. The Act was repealed on 11 June 1931 and Central Australia ceased being a separate entity – however, locals did not relinquish its capital C.

While the Commonwealth Government didn't provide official accommodation for its senior man for more than 18 months, they did rig up a telephone for him. His new phone equipment arrived by camel in June 1927 and was operational a few weeks later.[16] The elderly phonopore installed at George Wilkinson's store in June 1907 was the town's one and only telephone until then. The locals had to wait until 1932 to get a subscriber phone system that allowed a lucky few to talk to each other. John Cawood couldn't make long-distance calls but he could contact Ernie Allchurch's staff at the telegraph station to get messages to his bosses down south. The phones at regular points between Alice Springs and Oodnadatta were only good for communication over a short distance. Central Australians had to wait until

World War II for a trunk-line service enabling them to make long-distance calls to southern cities.[17]

Matters were on the up by 1927 when 80 members of a special tour group organised by Victorian Railways visited during the winter. The Reso tour set off for Central Australia on 2 August, travelling by rail and road for 18 days. They had 16 new Dodge cars, with two Dodge service cars and a one-tonne truck. Motoring pioneer Murray Aunger looked after the vehicles and Rev. John Flynn acted as a tour leader. The group included prominent representatives of pastoral, financial and manufacturing interests.[18] The focus was on the economic potential of the region but the 1927 Reso tour effectively marks the beginning of organised tourism to the region. It seems that Pioneer Tours, run by Alf Withers, also sent a group that year, as did Bert Bond, an established South Australian tour operator.[19] However, trouble was looming. A significant event at the end of 1928 focused adverse attention on the region, and painted its residents in a very poor light.

Black–white relations hit rock bottom

The arrival of John Cawood and the new administrative arrangement brought an end to Sergeant Bob Stott's reign as the benevolent, uncrowned king of Central Australia. The short, burly policeman who ruled the town with a firm hand for 16 years was a tough man but respected by the local people. The story is told of Victorian governor Lord Stradbroke visiting in 1924 and addressing local children. When asked if they could name their king, they all replied 'Sergeant Stott'. He stayed in town for a year after the government resident took over many of the diverse responsibilities that had previously fallen on his broad shoulders. He retired in April 1928 and moved to Adelaide but was killed on 5 May 1929 when hit by the Glenelg train at a level crossing in Wayville.

If Bob Stott was still in town it's possible that a very dark event in the region's history might have been avoided: the massacre that followed the death of Fred Brooks on 7 August 1928 at Yurrkuru soak on Coniston station, 230 kilometres north-west of Alice Springs. The experienced sergeant might have taken a more cautious and restrained approach in tracking down Brooks's killer than did George Murray, the constable based at Barrow Creek.[20]

John Cawood had not been in his job for long when he began hearing stories of unruly blacks and cattle killing in the north-west, an area not stocked until the eve of World War I and during the postwar years. There had been tension there, with the Aboriginal people unhappy about the cattlemen trespassing on their land, entering sacred sites without approval, and taking over key waterholes, and the station people feeling threatened. Matters boiled over after Warlpiri man Bullfrog Japanangka murdered Fred Brooks. He was a longtime friend of Randall Stafford, and had helped him establish Coniston station on Warlpiri land in 1917. Stafford was heading down to Tea Tree Well when the incident occurred, and Brooks had left the homestead with a couple of camels on 2 August to do a bit of dogging. The Commonwealth Government paid good money for the scalps of dingoes, which were regarded as vermin. Two Aboriginal station hands, Skipper and Dodger, accompanied him and they set up camp at Yurrkuru soak. A number of Warlpiri were also camped there; drought had forced people to retreat to refuges such as Yurrkuru where the water supply was reliable.

Brooks negotiated with Bullfrog for two of his three wives to do his washing and other domestic chores. He promised tobacco and rations in exchange. Bullfrog wanted to move on a couple of days later and was getting tired of waiting for Brooks to come up with the goods. He was enraged when he woke up on the morning of 7 August and noticed his young third wife wasn't at his camp. She'd gone off to get water but Bullfrog assumed Brooks had enticed her away while he was asleep. Approaching his camp, he called out to the two wives there to hold the man's arms and then he struck him on the head, killing him. They shoved the body down a hole that someone had dug out while rabbiting, took tobacco and food from the camp and left. Skipper and Dodger were off rounding up the camels and came back to see Brooks dead. Other Aboriginal people camped near the soak were helping themselves to various items. The two young blokes took off to the station homestead.

It wasn't long before the body was discovered. Paddy Tucker was camped nearby and travelling towards Yurrkuru with his camels the morning Brooks was killed. He saw the rabbit hole and a protruding leg but kept going to Ryans Well to report what he'd seen. Another man came upon the scene that day. Alex Wilson, a stockman from the neighbouring property owned by William (Nugget) Morton, also left the body as he found it and raced to the Coniston homestead, arriving late that night. A third man in the vicinity, 20-year-old prospector Bruce Chapman, also known as Henry Bruce Farrington, learnt what had happened when he got to Coniston on 8 August. He subsequently went to the soak, removed the body from the rabbit hole and buried it. Randall Stafford didn't get the message his mate was dead until 11 August, but was back at the station four days later.

Charles Noblet was the senior police officer in Central Australia, following the retirement of Sergeant Bob Stott. John Cawood didn't send him to investigate the death, instead directing George Murray, the policeman at Barrow Creek, to go after the Aboriginal people involved. Murray was a veteran of Gallipoli and the fighting on the Western Front, and been wounded four times. He and Cawood talked via the phone at Ryans Well. The government resident would have been aware there was a prevailing view around the region that the authorities needed to 'teach the Aboriginal people a lesson'. Unfortunately he did not foresee how Murray and his black constables Police Paddy and Major would interpret his order to go after the culprits. Many innocent Aboriginal men, women and children died in the days that followed.

Murray, Paddy and Major rode west from Coniston on 16 August with Randall Stafford and station workers Jack Saxby, Billy Briscoe, Alex Wilson and Dodger. They came across a camp of 20 to 30 people, shots were fired and deaths resulted, including a young woman. More confrontations and shootings followed in the next couple of days. Murray reported this to Noblet and Cawood in Alice Springs on 1 September. They were alarmed at what he told them. Cawood sent a telegram to the Department of Home Affairs & Territories and informed them that 17 Aboriginal people had been shot. Missionary Annie Lock soon got word of the killings at her camp at Harding's Soak, east of Coniston. She'd come to Central Australia in March 1927 and was living there with about 50 Aboriginal people, who were frightened by the course of events. The Adelaide press first got news of the matter on 11 September. Bullfrog was not among the dead. He and his wives had escaped Murray's patrol and were nowhere to be seen.

Murray led a second patrol in the first half of September with more shootings. There is no written account of this, of who was involved or how many died. A third patrol followed later in the month, involving just three white men: George Murray, Nugget Morton and Alex Wilson. They returned to Morton's station in mid October after three weeks in the bush. In the course of the official inquiry held a couple of months later, Murray admitted that 14 were killed during this patrol but he and Morton both said that Wilson was not involved in the shootings.

Murray was soon on his way to Darwin for the trial on 7 November of two men he'd arrested and charged with Brooks's murder: Padygar and Arkirkra. He had brought them to Alice Springs in September to appear before magistrate Ernie Allchurch for committal.[21] Annie Lock attended the proceedings in Darwin, in the course of which Murray admitted that he shot to kill. The trial was well publicised and this statement shocked people in the south. The jury found Padygar and Arkirkra not guilty after deliberating for only 15 minutes.

Prime Minister Stanley Bruce and his ministers were inundated with calls for an official inquiry. The events at Coniston were hot on the heels of the 1926 Forrest River massacre in the Kimberley, which had generated outrage in the south. The heat was on from church groups, the Aborigines' Friends' Association, and other concerned people. A.H. O'Kelly, police magistrate from Cairns, chaired the three-person panel formed to review what had happened. The other two members were South Australian police inspector P.A. Giles, whose area covered Port Augusta to Oodnadatta, and John Cawood. Missionary Erny Kramer was given approval to be present throughout the inquiry and allowed to question witnesses, as was George Murray. They travelled widely from 30 December 1928 until 16 January 1929. The inquiry was formally closed on 7 February 1929 when a summary of the panel's findings was presented. It was a whitewash.

The panel said that the shootings were justified. Police Paddy was the only Aboriginal person to give evidence. Alex Wilson was not called but years later said: 'They never got off their horses. They shot them down in cold blood.' While Murray admitted to 31 deaths, the numbers bandied around the bush ranged from 70 to 200. The Coniston massacre brought publicity of a very different sort to that generated by the Reso tour the previous year. It focused national attention on the treatment of Aboriginal people and Central Australia's black history.

Bullfrog Japanangka was never arrested and died of old age at Yuendumu in the 1970s. George Murray remained in the police force and served in the North Australia Observor Unit, known as the Nackeroos or Curtin's Cowboys, during World War II.[22] Nugget Morton withdrew from the country north-west of Alice Springs in the 1930s and moved to the eastern side of the telegraph line, establishing Ammaroo station on Alyawarr land by the Sandover River. There have been allegations he and Murray were involved in the deaths of 100 Aboriginal people there, following the spearing of cattle. Termed the Sandover massacre, it supposedly included putting the poison strychnine in a soakage on the Sandover River.[23] Randall Stafford remained on Coniston until 1946.

Drought and devastation for native wildlife

Central Australia was in the grip of one of its worst-ever droughts when the Coniston massacre happened. The drought followed an extraordinarily wet 1919/1920 summer, and a second one of above average rainfall 12 months later. The Todd River flooded a number of times and vegetation sprouted across the previously parched heart of the continent. This fuelled widespread bushfires, devastating large areas in 1922 and leaving pasture lands bare once more.[24] Waterholes were shrinking by 1924. By the 1925/1926 summer, cattle were dying all the way to Oodnadatta.[25] It was similar in western New South Wales. The year 1928 was the toughest with only 61 millimetres of rain recorded at Alice Springs and 86 millimetres at Barrow Creek.[26]

The term drought is often misunderstood by people living on the edges of the continent, where rainfall is consistent. It is defined as a period when rainfall is significantly below average for a sustained time but doesn't mean there's no rain at all. The sky may open up occasionally, even during the toughest droughts. One such deluge came out of the blue in the middle of the 1920s. Dark clouds built up early on the afternoon of 19 March 1926. There were brilliant flashes of lightning and rain poured down for half an hour. There was another fantastic cloud formation at daybreak. It began falling again about midday with practically no let up for five days. It was widespread, flooding the country as far south as Oodnadatta, but it came too late to save thousands of stock. Another, long dry spell followed, with all the moisture evaporating and no sign of relief on the horizon.[27]

The 1920s drought had a worse effect on the native fauna than any other episode in recorded history.[28] It forced a number of small mammal species to the brink of extinction, though the larger kangaroos and wallabies survived. The fate of the centralian brushtail possum is a good example of its impact. These animals are the same species as their southern cousins *Trichosurus vulpecula* but smaller, with a less bushy tail and colouring differences. They also spend a lot more time on the ground where they're surprisingly quick. Possums were 'everywhere amongst the eucalypts which border the riverbeds' in the 1890s, according to Professor Baldwin Spencer. Only a few isolated populations survive today and the 1920s drought was virtually their last gasp.

Droughts are a regular feature of the climate in the centre of Australia. Many animals die when times are tough but their numbers recover when conditions improve. The introduction of cattle, sheep, horses and camels made survival a bigger challenge but the possums, in diminished numbers, managed to compete for the limited food available in the tough years of the 1880s and the Federation drought of 1897–1903. However, the 1920s drought was the first major dry spell in which they had to compete with voracious rabbits. Descendants of the Spanish rabbits introduced into Victoria in 1859 crossed the border into the Northern Territory in the 1890s. The telegraph operators at Charlotte Waters saw them for the first time in 1894. They spread across the land as it recovered from the Federation drought and they were well established by the beginning of the 1920s.

Gerhardt and Ottilie Johannsen left the Barossa Valley in 1909 to work at Hermannsburg Mission and took up the land around Deep Well in 1911. Their son Kurt wrote years later of desperately hungry rabbits climbing three metres up mulga trees and stripping them of their leaves.[29] The possums never had a chance against this competition and their numbers declined dramatically. Many rabbits also perished, of course, before the drought finally broke, but their quicker rate of reproduction, compared to native mammals, gave them a distinct advantage. The rabbits simply outbred the natives when better seasons returned in the 1930s. They took over the burrow systems that bilbies and burrowing bettongs had previously occupied, along with crevices in rocky outcrops that possums used. The 1920s drought pushed possum numbers to a critically low level. The small numbers that managed to survive those years were steadily picked off later by crafty feral cats and foxes. Bushfires may also have been a factor in their demise. The prevalence of large fires increased after traditional Aboriginal burning practices were disrupted with the usurping of their land.

The railway arrives and the town takes off

The *Northern Australia Act 1926* was a key event in the region's development but one of considerably greater interest to the local people happened four months earlier. On 18 September 1925 the Commonwealth reached an agreement with the South Australian Government to finally extend the railway across the north of the state, to Alice Springs. A further 16 months elapsed before the ceremonial turning of the first sod at Oodnadatta on 21 January 1927, but at last there was action. Officials dug the ground with the same polished shovel used at Port Augusta way back in January 1878 to inaugurate the Great Northern Railway. The Commonwealth gave an undertaking to complete the transcontinental railway when it took over the Northern Territory in 1911 but had never said when. Politicians now pledged to complete the extension to Alice Springs by 30 June 1929, and they kept their word. The last rail was laid at Alice Springs on the afternoon of 29 June 1929.

The first passenger train rolled into the town's new station shortly after

2 pm on 5 August 1929, hauled by one of the Commonwealth Railway's new NM class steam locomotives. It was a gala day for the locals. Never before had so many white people gathered in the one spot in the Territory. The operator on duty at the telegraph station was one of the few people not there to share in the excitement. Once all the passengers had alighted, wide-eyed bushies clambered aboard to get a peek at the novelties aboard this new train, tagged the Flash Ghan. It was a luxury train for those days with its dining car and lounge attracting attention.[30] It was also fast, averaging over 25 kilometres an hour and reducing the journey to Adelaide to two days and two nights!

Over 800 men were involved in the extension of the final section of the line to Alice Springs in 1929.[31] John Cawood was concerned about the impact of an influx of railway workers on the local Aboriginal people, particularly the women. A new camp had been established a couple of years earlier, outside the town boundaries, along the Todd River east of Billy Goat Hill. Cawood had proudly reported at the time:

> The camp has been laid out in blocks, subdivided by streets, and the natives have vied one with the other in building up-to-date wurlies. They cleaned up the deserted camp and now take a pride in their new surroundings. They have been instructed in modern methods of sanitation.[32]

He now thought it wise to move the camp's residents to fresh camping grounds away from the railway line and declare a prohibited area '10 miles' either side of the line. A number of people were sent to Hermannsburg and the remainder distributed between Bond Springs and Undoolya cattle stations where rations were issued.[33] It wasn't necessary to keep the Aboriginal people so far away once the construction work was completed and they were permitted to return to their former areas.[34]

The arrival of the railway was a pivotal event in the history of Alice Springs, accelerating its transformation from a dusty little village into one of Australia's most romanticised towns. The population jumped from 90 in 1928 to 560 early in 1930. The Shell petrol company built a fuel depot at the end of the new railway line in July 1929, and a petrol pump was installed outside George Wilkinson's store at the top end of Todd Street.[35] Phil Windle acquired land further down the street to open a garage and service the increasing number of motor vehicles puttering about the place. Father Jim Long arrived in May 1929 and built a Catholic Church, which was open in time for Christmas services. Another Christmas present for the town was the appointment of the town's first doctor, Bruce Kirkland, in December 1929. John Cawood ensured the town finally got a proper school, which opened in Hartley Street in September 1930. Pearl Burton had taught the town's children in Tom Turner's shed in Todd Street since arriving in May 1929 to take over from the legendary Mrs Ida Standley. New shops included a bakery and Kilgariff's General Cash Store opposite the pub. It was the first one in town to have a front window for shoppers to see items on display. Meanwhile both Annie Meyers and the Underdown family from Oodnadatta were making plans to open a second pub in town and guarantee the growing population did not die of thirst. The social life of the residents got a boost with the construction of a town hall on stilts, on land set aside as a recreation reserve on the northern side of Wills Terrace.

The global economy was plunging into deep depression but this was a go-ahead time for the Alice Springs region. New opportunities were unfolding, though the town's sizeable Afghan community was uncertain what the future held for them. The extension of the railway had brought to an end camel haulage between Oodnadatta and Alice Springs. However, they continued transporting goods further up the track and servicing outlying stations.

Latter-day explorers Cecil Madigan and Donald Mackay

Adelaide University geologist Cecil Madigan was a regular visitor to Alice Springs in the late 1920s and 1930s. He went to Antarctica as a 21-year-old meteorologist with Douglas Mawson's Australian Antarctic Expedition of 1911–1913. They set out to map the 3000 kilometres of coastline directly south of Australia. After a spell in Sudan, where he gained experience in desert fieldwork and handling camels, Madigan turned his attention to the geology of Central Australia.

On his first trip to the Alice Springs region in October and November

1927 he accompanied Mawson to check out a mineral deposit in the West MacDonnell Ranges. A local had taken a sample to Adelaide, thinking it might have something to do with oil. Some Aboriginal people had shown him how it made a fire blaze if you threw it in the coals. It was saltpetre and the two geologists decided to go north and assess its economic potential for a local syndicate. Alice Springs driller Harry Wolfe was a member of that syndicate and he met them with a car at Oodnadatta. Another member, Georgian miner Simon Rieff, joined them at Alice Springs. Harry Wolfe held the record for the fastest trip between 'the Alice and the Oodna', taking only 10 and a half hours.[36] He'd arrived from Queensland in 1925 and worked as a bore contractor. The saltpetre deposit turned out to be of limited extent and no commercial value. The two geologists then accompanied him on a quick trip up the track to Barrow Creek where he had an interest in a copper mine.

Harry Wolfe married Jessie Allchurch, the older daughter of Ernie and Bessie, in December, after his travels with Mawson and Madigan. He won the government contract to put down all the bores between Oodnadatta and Alice Springs when the railway was extended north. Jessie went with him when he began this work in 1928 and lived in the boring camps. They left Central Australia in 1930.[37]

With aeroplanes quite reliable by the 1920s, government authorities and academics saw the advantages in using them for aerial photography and surveying. The Royal Australian Air Force formed a fulltime flight crew in 1927 to map large areas of land with the Survey Corps. In 1929, Cecil Madigan won the support of the South Australian Branch of the Royal Geographical Society of Australasia and the Commonwealth Government for the first systematic attempt at overlapping aerial photography in Australia. The RAAF put two of their new Westland Wapiti aircraft at his disposal in August 1929, complete with crews and photographers. They flew from Melbourne to Broken Hill and on to Marree, traversing the eastern half of South Australia's horseshoe of salt lakes: Frome, Callabonna, Blanche and Gregory. From Birdsville they made the first of three long survey flights over the vast desert that stretched from south-west Queensland into the Northern Territory and South Australia. No white man had ever crossed it or seen it in its entirety, though various explorers had nibbled at its margins, beginning with Charles Sturt in 1845. The first flight took them diagonally across the desert to Alice Springs. Then they flew eastwards across its northern edge and back again. The third flight was down the western edge of the desert from Alice Springs to Oodnadatta. In between these second and third traverses, Madigan conducted a geological survey of the MacDonnell Ranges from the air, taking numerous aerial photos.[38]

This desert had never been officially named, though people loosely referred to it as the Arunta Desert. Madigan proposed it be called the Simpson Desert after the South Australian president of the Royal Geographical Society, Alfred Allen Simpson of washing machine fame. The Commonwealth Department of the Interior agreed and the name became official. In May 1936, pastoralist Ted Colson from Bloods Creek in northern South Australia became the first white man to cross the desert. He had camels and was accompanied by Peter Aines, a young Aboriginal man from the Musgrave Ranges. The French Line, created in 1964 and now a popular track used by tourists in four-wheel drive vehicles, is close to Colson's route. Madigan led an expedition across the desert with camels in the winter of 1939, claiming his route was closer to its geographical centre.

Cecil Madigan's pioneering work south-east of Alice Springs in 1929 was a significant step in completing the exploration of the heart of the continent begun by John McDouall Stuart in 1860. Sixty-year-old philanthropist Donald George Mackay decided to finance aerial mapping of other unknown sections of the outback. He was motivated by the forced landing of Charles Kingsford-Smith's famous plane *Southern Cross* near the north-west coast in March 1929 and the loss of the crew of the *Kookaburra* who went looking for the *Southern Cross*. Smithy, Charles Ulm, Tom McWilliams and Hal Litchfield had left Sydney on Easter Saturday 30 March 1929 bound for England. They headed towards Wyndham, rather than using the safer route to Darwin, but lost their radio antenna soon after take-off. Rather than returning to the ground and replacing it, they flew on even though they were not carrying adequate emergency supplies. A huge storm developed over the Kimberley and they lost their way trying to fly through it that night. Running low on fuel, they were forced to put the plane down on swampy ground on Easter Sunday. They didn't know exactly where they were and had no option but to wait for someone to find them. The newspapers later criticised them for their foolhardiness.

A number of planes went looking for the missing aircraft, including Keith Anderson and Bobby Hitchcock in the *Kookaburra*. They reached Alice Springs on Tuesday 9 April, more than a week after the *Southern Cross* had put down in the Kimberley. They headed off across the Tanami Desert next day with lots of fuel but very little water and no radio; engine trouble forced them down in thick scrub. They fixed the problem but were unable to get the plane airborne again. The four men on board the *Southern Cross* were found safe and sound on 12 April but Anderson and Hitchcock perished.

Donald Mackay knew that better aeronautical maps of the outback might prevent tragedies like this happening again. He began in 1930 by financing an aerial survey of the south-west corner of the Territory. He leased two planes from Australian Aerial Surveys of Melbourne, along with pilots and two aerial photography specialists. He engaged former Royal Navy officer Harry Bennett as navigator and surveyor. Mackay, from a wealthy pastoral family with a property at Yass, near Canberra, was farewelled with his party from the new national capital on 23 May 1930 by Prime Minister Jim Scullin. They flew to Hermannsburg, where fuel had been trucked in advance, and then on to the Ehrenberg Range 250 kilometres further west. Mackay had engaged Bob Buck from Middleton Ponds station to clear an airstrip there and create a base for them. Buck chose a spot near a soak called Ilpilla, which had a reliable supply of water.[39] He hired Ali Mahomet and Akbar Khan to transport aviation fuel, stores and other requirements out there with their camels.

Radio time signals from the Melbourne Observatory enabled Commander Bennett to determine their exact position on the earth's surface. In June they systematically triangulated 5000 square kilometres around Ilpilla with 15 flights over 24 days. This included the Lake Amadeus area and a new salt lake they discovered, which turned out to be the second largest in Australia. The Commonwealth Government named it Lake Mackay. The expedition finished in Adelaide on 28 June 1930. In 1933, Mackay financed an aerial survey of a large expanse of inland Western Australia, west and north-west of the Petermann Ranges. A survey of the Nullarbor Plain followed in 1935 and then the Tanami in 1937.[40]

The search for Lasseter's reef

As Donald Mackay was preparing to fly to Alice Springs in May 1930 he received a letter from one of the most controversial and enduring characters in Australian history.[41] Harry Lasseter asked for a seat on one of his planes so he could peg out gold leases. Mackay told him there were no spare seats and the object of his expedition was topographical mapping, not prospecting. Undeterred, Lasseter turned up in Alice Springs on a cattle train two months later. Mackay's men had finished their work at Ilpilla by that time.

The town's residents knew Harry Lasseter and other members of the Central Australian Gold Exploration Company were heading their way but no one turned out to see them get off the train.[42] They were on a quest for a fabulous gold reef Lasseter claimed he found in 1897 in the desert about 500 kilometres to the west. His story was that when 17 he rode a horse from Cloncurry in western Queensland to the OT line and then down to Stuart to search for rubies in the Hale River. He got supplies at the Alice Springs telegraph station and went overland to Western Australia after he learned the rubies were only garnets and of little value. He said he ended up in Carnarvon, finding the fabulous reef along the way. His horse died but he was rescued by an Afghan camelman and taken to the camp of a surveyor named Harding. He claimed that he and Harding located the gold reef about three years later but were unable to get financial backing to mine it.[43]

Lasseter told his story to John Bailey, president of the Australian Workers Union, early in 1930. Although initially sceptical, Bailey was eventually convinced Lasseter was fair dinkum and affairs moved quickly. The Central Australian Gold Exploration Company was formed and thousands of pounds worth of shares sold, even though there was a global economic depression. In charge was Fred Blakeley, an experienced bushman and prospector who rode a pushbike in 1908 from Farina in South Australia to Darwin with the O'Neil brothers Jim and Dick. His own brother Arthur was a minister in the

Scullin Labor Government in 1930. The company purchased a Gypsy Moth biplane named the *Golden Quest*. The British company Thornycroft loaned one of their six-wheeled trucks and Blakeley hired Alice Springs carrier Fred Colson to transport their supplies and equipment west to Ilpilla. The company had decided to use Donald Mackay's airstrip as their base camp.

The vehicles were packed and ready to go on the afternoon of 24 July 1930.[44] The plan was to drive to the northern side of the MacDonnell Ranges and then go west to the Ehrenberg Range and Ilpilla. There was still no proper road north in 1930. Travellers followed the well-worn track alongside the Todd River to the telegraph station and then wound their way through the rocky hills to the vast mulga plains of the north. It took a couple of hours to negotiate, even though it was only 20 kilometres as the crow flies.

The expedition didn't get far before running into trouble. Their heavily laden Thornycroft got bogged less than a kilometre from town crossing the sandy bed of the Todd River. A small crowd of locals gathered to help them dig it out of the creek. It was a minor mishap but perhaps an omen of what lay ahead. Ernie Allchurch, waiting for them at the telegraph station, wasn't convinced about the gold reef story having picked up on details Lasseter described about Alice Springs in 1897. They conflicted with his own memories of the place, dating back to September 1902 when he'd first arrived. He had shared a few drinks with Fred Blakeley and the *Golden Quest*'s pilot Errol Coote the previous night. Ernie Allchurch told Blakeley he 'was a fool to believe anything the fellow said'.[45]

The plane never made it to Ilpilla, crashing on the way. The company quickly organised a replacement, the *Golden Quest II*. The men left Ilpilla and headed further into the desert, towards the area where Lasseter said he'd found the reef in 1897. It was a fruitless trip, with the Thornycroft struggling to cope with the sand dunes and spinifex grass. Fred Blakeley became increasingly frustrated that Lasseter could give them no clear directions and was unable to recognise landmarks in the area. He said they must be too far north.

The new plane arrived in September and Lasseter was taken up into the air to check out the country. They flew south-west towards the Petermann Ranges and then back to Ilpilla. Lasseter claimed he'd seen the reef but Fred

Blakeley had his doubts. The two men were arguing incessantly by this time. They couldn't get the Thornycroft to the area where Lasseter now claimed the reef was located and Blakeley suspended the search. He decided to return to Alice Springs to contact the company directors for fresh instructions, but Lasseter wanted to stay in the desert. A young German dingo trapper Paul Johns had turned up at Ilpilla with his five camels and two Aboriginal men from Hermannsburg. Lasseter insisted that Blakeley hire Johns and the expedition leader drew up a contract for Johns to work with Lasseter for two months from 13 September.[46]

Lasseter and Johns headed south with the camels, crossed Lake Amadeus and then went on to Mount Olga and Ayers Rock. They turned west from there, over the border into Western Australia to the Rawlinson Range and Lake Christopher. Lasseter left Johns for a couple of days at one stage. When they rejoined, he said he'd found the reef while on his own. An argument occurred with Johns calling Lasseter a liar. Low on supplies by this time they headed back to Ilpilla, arriving at the end of October. The two men agreed Johns should go east to Alice Springs for fresh camels. Lasseter gave him a letter for the company saying he was returning on his own to peg the reef, and he urged the other members of the expedition to follow without delay. Johns tried to persuade him to wait at Ilpilla but to no avail and Lasseter was not seen alive again.

Bob Buck from Middleton Ponds station found his body and notebook on 29 March 1931.[47] According to it, Lasseter pegged his reef before Christmas. He then headed across the border into the Northern Territory. He was stranded at the end of December when his two camels took fright and ran off. It was the height of summer and he took refuge in a cave next to the Hull River in the Petermann Ranges. The local Aboriginal people gave him food. He attempted to reach Mount Olga but perished near the Shaw Creek on 30 January 1931. According to Lasseter's notebook, he'd marked the location of the reef on a map he buried in the sandhill where the camels bolted. The map and the reef have never been found.

20

From telegraph station to children's home

The clicking of morse instruments was heard at the Alice Springs telegraph station for the last time in 1931. For four years the Postmaster-General's Department (PMG) had been under pressure to give up the place and move into Stuart, allowing the children living in town at the back of the pub to move to the buildings.

The police had been steadily rounding up light-skinned children since the war and placing them in the care of Ida Standley and Topsy Smith.[1] Their shabby accommodation, known as the Bungalow, had grown from a tent in 1914 to three tin sheds, two primitive toilets, a basic bath house and a garden. The place copped a lot of criticism from humanitarian groups, ministers of religion and journalists but nothing much happened as the years rolled on.

In 1922 the Administrator of the Northern Territory suggested relocating the children to the Hermannsburg Mission but this idea went nowhere.[2] The following year there was a proposal to build a new home next to the old police station at Heavitree Gap, but the Commonwealth was unwilling to commit the necessary money.[3]

Journalist Malcolm Ellis of Sydney's *Daily Telegraph* passed through the town in August 1924, saw the conditions in which the children were living and wrote a scathing article entitled 'The Alice Springs Bungalow. A Place of Squalid Horror'. It appeared in a number of capital city newspapers later in the year. Ellis said the place was a scandal:

There are no sheets, seemingly few blankets; no pictures on the walls; not enough chairs to seat half a dozen people; no verandahs, so that the heat or the cold or the rain must beat directly on to the walls of the buildings ... There is no water supply at this school: the children themselves carry whatever water is needed over 100 yards from the police bungalow and across the main road. There is one small lavatory; no bathroom except such as is improvised with a tub. There is not enough table accommodation to let these beings ... sit down and have their meals like civilised beings.[4]

The government was stung by the public criticism. Unbeknown to the newspapers' readers, Senator George Pearce from Western Australia was taking steps to improve the situation. He was planning a new home, following calls by humanitarian groups such as the Women's Non-Party Association, of which former Alice Springs resident Ida McKay was an executive committee member.

The Bungalow goes west to Jay Creek

Senator Pearce was elected to the first Commonwealth Parliament in 1901 and forged a reputation as one of the nation's most able Cabinet ministers and administrators. As the Minister for Home and Territories from 1921 until 1926, he was the driving force behind the legislation that split the Northern Territory into two separate regions, in an attempt to improve conditions and productivity.[5]

He ensured £5000 was allocated in the budget for a new Bungalow nearly 50 kilometres west of the town. Jay Creek, the site nominated, would have a school, two dormitories, a dining room and kitchen, bathroom and toilet facilities, staff accommodation, a store and an engine to pump water from a new bore.[6] Negotiations commenced with the Hayes family in February 1925 to excise a suitable block of land from their cattle station lease.[7] Senator Pearce also initiated discussions with the Church of England's Australian Board of Missions about taking over management of the new home once it was built.[8] It wasn't long, however, before the plan ran into a major hurdle: water. A considerable portion of the £5000 was spent on fruitless drilling to procure an adequate and reliable supply of it.[9]

It was clear by June 1927 that the government needed to abandon the Jay Creek site despite the expenditure to date.[10] Attention then turned to alternative locations, including the Alice Springs telegraph station.[11] In November the secretary of the Home and Territories department in Canberra wrote to the PMG asking if it had plans to move into town once the railway was extended from Oodnadatta. Track work had commenced in January of that year. A reply stated such a move would be expensive and of no advantage to the PMG.[12] In December the Department of Works and Railways was asked to test for the availability of water on the south-east side of Temple Bar, between Jay Creek and Alice Springs. Six months later they advised Home and Territories that there was an excellent supply.[13]

There was concern about what might happen to the girls with an influx of construction workers as the railway approached Alice Springs. Pressure mounted to move the children temporarily to Jay Creek, despite the contractor's failure to find sufficient water.[14] The end of the school year seemed the logical time to do this. So, after 14 years in a location no one thought desirable, the sheds behind the pub were dismantled in November 1928 and the Bungalow went west.

Ida Standley, in poor health by this time, wanted to retire on 19 January 1929, her 60th birthday. However, the authorities prevailed on her to go with the children and remain at Jay Creek until a suitable replacement could be found. Her reward for long and faithful service to the government was no Christmas holidays and a long, hot summer living in a tent under a bough shelter.[15] Topsy Smith had also had enough by this time and was equally reluctant to move to the new site. She wanted to go back to her mother's country at Oodnadatta.

The living conditions at Jay Creek turned out to be as bad as they were in town for the 26 boys and 19 girls who made the move.[16] The one positive thing that could be said was that the girls were away from the attention of the young men heading to town with the advancing railway.

The idea of establishing a permanent home on the old telegraph station site was not forgotten and in April 1929 the Honorary Secretary of Adelaide's Aborigines' Friends' Association wrote to Canberra pushing that option.

John Sexton was concerned about the unsatisfactory accommodation at Jay Creek but also wrote of 'the lurking fear in the children's minds of being captured by the old blacks, and taken into the bush for their ceremonies'. He added 'As the half-caste children are going to be trained for citizenship I see every advantage of their being located within easy reach of Alice Springs'. Unbeknown to Mr Sexton, the minister had already written to the Postmaster-General that month raising the idea once more. Again the answer was no, on the grounds that the cost of a move into town, and accommodating the staff, was too high.[17]

In the meantime Ida Standley's health had deteriorated and she was experiencing serious heart problems. Missionaries Erny and Effie Kramer agreed in March to take over from her until the government could find a permanent replacement.[18] The Kramers were associated with the Aborigines' Friends' Association which had taken a keen interest in the plight of the children in recent years. They were also admirers of Mrs Standley who had taught their two oldest children Colin and Mary. Erny Kramer later had the picturesque Gall Springs renamed Standley Chasm in her honour. This followed a suggestion by Australian-born Professor S.D. Porteous, from the University of Hawaii, who visited the place in 1929 with nature writer R.H. Croll.[19]

Ida Standley was made a member of the Order of the British Empire (MBE) in November 1929 for her services to child welfare. She died in Sydney on 29 May 1948. Topsy Smith's dedication and years of hard work were not recognised with any imperial honours. Her daughter Ada took her down to Oodnadatta where her elderly mother Mary was living. She later returned to the Territory and died at the Alice Springs Hospital after a long illness on 6 April 1960.

The Commonwealth Government secured the services of Francis and Jessie Thorne who had spent a couple of years working at Oenpelli Mission in the Top End. They arrived in May 1929 and endured twelve months in very primitive living conditions.[20] South Australian clergyman Rev. W. Morgan Davies spent three days at Jay Creek and described it as 'a standing disgrace to any civilised government' in a letter to the Anglican bishop of Willochra in July 1929. It was forwarded to the government and Rev. Davies made a public statement which was widely reported in newspapers across the country. He said:

> Mr and Mrs Thorne have done wonders and I was much impressed with the excellent discipline and cleanliness of the whole place under such adverse conditions. But the whole place makes one boil that such a thing can be tolerated for one moment in a Christian Country.[21]

The PMG has a change of heart and the town a change of name

It was clear the Minister for Home Affairs had to find a better site for the children. In April 1930 he announced plans to build a new home at Temple Bar, closer to town.[22] Negotiations with the Hayes family had taken place to excise another block of land from their pastoral lease.[23] No sooner was the public announcement made, however, than the PMG finally budged on the old telegraph station site and acknowledged, in June 1930, that building a new post office in town was warranted. They said they would move provided Home Affairs paid the cost of establishing facilities on four blocks of land opposite the new railway station.[24]

It was clear that relocating the children to the existing buildings at the telegraph station would be considerably cheaper than starting from scratch at Temple Bar. The Works Department was instructed not to proceed with the proposal to build a new Bungalow on that site. Cabinet approved the move and plans were drawn up to modify the telegraph buildings to accommodate the children.[25] However, two more years elapsed before they moved there.

Ernie Allchurch, not at all pleased about the prospect of leaving the old telegraph station, avoided relocating. He went south for surgery and died unexpectedly on 15 January 1932, before the new premises on Railway Terrace were finished. Maurie Fuss, acting officer in charge at the time, organised matters and the new post office was officially opened on Monday 25 January 1932.[26] Dudley Adamson was transferred back to Alice Springs to take Ernie Allchurch's place. He had left in 1929. His family moved into the new postmaster's house, next door to the post office, that the Allchurch family was meant to occupy. It was a far cry from the thatched wurley Ernie and Bessie had lived in as newlyweds in 1905.

The town was still officially called Stuart but the new building on Railway Terrace had the words Alice Springs Post Office emblazoned above its entrance. The name Stuart had long been an issue with the local residents. Minister J.A. Perkins visited in June 1933 and resolved to settle the matter. He issued a statement, which was reported in the *Sydney Morning Herald*:

> The Minister for the Interior (Mr Perkins) said today that he had visited many schools in recent months and he said to the pupils: 'Hands up those who know where Stuart is'. Not one hand had been raised except at a little school at Collector, near Goulburn, where one boy had been able to supply the answer. When he had asked to be told where Alice Springs was, however, he had been supplied with the information by whole classes of children. Mr Perkins said he proposed to take steps to have the original name of Alice Springs reverted to. The town had been renamed Stuart ... but it had never been adopted by the postal authorities, and was not favoured by the local residents. When he had visited the place recently, he found the name plate, Stuart, which had formerly been on the railway station at Alice Springs, had been removed and was lying at Port Augusta, 1000 miles away. The name Stuart had led to confusion with another settlement known as Stuart Creek.[27]

At Perkins' direction, the governor-general proclaimed a change from Stuart to Alice Springs on 30 August 1933.

The 'uplift' of the children

Frank Gillen's great friend Professor Baldwin Spencer was the architect of the Commonwealth policy of taking children of mixed descent from their Aboriginal mothers. However, Dr Cecil (Mick) Cook is the figure most closely associated with its administration in the years between the two world wars. He was the Northern Territory's Chief Medical Officer and Chief Protector of Aborigines from February 1927 until 1939. He was proud to report in 1934:

> Practically all half-caste children of both sexes, formerly left to live with aboriginals in compounds and bush camps ... have been removed to half-caste institutions under government control.[28]

He had a low opinion of church missions and believed the Commonwealth Government should take responsibility for the 'uplift' of these children. It wasn't until the Commonwealth terminated Cook's tenure as Chief Protector in 1939 that moves were made to close its two homes, in Darwin and Alice Springs, and transfer the children to church care.

Cook acquired the tag of 'the most hated man in the Northern Territory' and was immortalised as Dr Aintee in Xavier Herbert's bestselling 1937 novel *Capricornia*.[29] He was an albino, a tall, striking figure with snow white hair and pale skin that glowed red after a day in the sun. His one functioning eye was a distinctive blue, the other was glass. Although infamous for his use of the phrase 'breed out the colour', he was essentially a reformer who wanted to raise the standard of living of the Territory's 'half-castes'. He thought it preferable that the women marry whites and would not allow them to marry 'half-caste' men unless they met his standards. He defined the children of 'half-castes' and whites as European.

While most people take a dim view of Cook these days, there was broad support in the 1920s and 1930s for the policy he was implementing. Caring individuals and humanitarian groups may have expressed outrage at the conditions at the original Bungalow and the one at Jay Creek but they accepted what the government was trying to do. Most Australians supported the absorption of the children into Australian society to live as whites and thought little of the detrimental aspects of institutionalisation. The White Australia policy, so dominant at the time of Federation, was still a strong part of the Australian psyche in those interwar years. Attitudes towards Aboriginal people were generally negative; the prevailing view was of the superiority of European culture.

Taking children from their Aboriginal mothers and educating them to live as whites was seen as 'rescue', as providing a better future. Respect for the culture of Australia's first people and the notion of a multicultural nation were barely blips on a far-off horizon when they moved into the old telegraph station. It was a children's home for ten years, until 1942. Their upbringing focused on European values and beliefs: in the schoolroom, at play, at the dinner table and in the dormitory. Their education was directed towards future employment as house servants and stockmen.

Government records refer to the 'Half Caste Institution Alice Springs' but local people continued to call it the Bungalow. The Commonwealth Government ran another home in Darwin and a third one for boys at Pine Creek. Their creation was the result of Commonwealth determination to do something about 'the half-caste problem' that had been an issue in the Northern Territory since relations between black and white moved from avoidance to co-existence. There were a few cases of parents choosing to place their children in these institutions while they worked in the bush. However, the feelings of the Aboriginal mothers were not considered in the overwhelming majority of cases and some never saw their children again.

When you hear or read the stories of the Bungalow children, you learn they experienced both difficult and happy times; that most of their carers were considerate people who did the best they could, though no one talks kindly of one superintendent who ended up in gaol in 1934. They tell you that living conditions were far from ideal and they were often hungry, but they also recognise that life wasn't much different for many white people in Central Australia at that time. The institution at the old telegraph station operated during the Great Depression when many people across the country struggled to put food on the table and keep a roof over their head. The Bungalow children received some schooling and found employment in Alice Springs, other parts of the Northern Territory or interstate. They later expressed pride in their achievements and the fact that they grew into strong and resilient people.

However, none of this outweighs the pain and the loss they felt being separated from their mothers and extended families. That pain was felt too in Aboriginal camps across the Territory. Taking young children from their mothers was cruel, no matter how much people these days may argue it was done with the child's best interests in mind. Equally cruel is the myth, frequently peddled, that Aboriginal mothers did not want their pale-skinned children. It broke the mothers' hearts when the government took their children away. It wasn't just the children who cried at night.

The children were segregated because the government thought that 'older natives' entering the institution precinct would be detrimental to their assimilation into white society. Despite this, some mothers managed to sneak up to the buildings at night and contact their children by tapping on the dormitory windows. Some white fathers took an interest in their children though most had scant regard for them and took no responsibility for their upkeep.[30] The Bungalow children's dormitory companions became their new family and strong bonds developed between them. Despite their good and bad experiences they remained united in their common sorrow, a sorrow shared by their descendants today. Many years have passed since the Bungalow closed but the pain and sadness still remain for the families of the Bungalow children who identify as members of a stolen generation.

21

The 'new' Bungalow Half-caste Institution

The appalling conditions at Jay Creek didn't deter the many applying to replace the Thornes when they did not seek renewal of their 12-month contract. In April 1930, Gordon Keith Freeman and his wife Daisy got the nod as the new superintendent and matron.[1] Two of their three children travelled to Central Australia with them, from Berowra NSW where the family was farming: 12-year-old Judith and 10-year-old Joan.

Freeman was a war veteran who served in France. The couple worked at the Church of England's Forrest River Mission near Wyndham for a time after the war and then in New Guinea from 1922 until 1924. Daisy had some nursing experience but was not qualified. She was also expected to teach the Bungalow children. Her lack of teaching qualifications and a paucity of books and equipment, combined with the large numbers in her care, meant the children received little education at Jay Creek.

The Freemans plugged away at Jay Creek for two-and-a-half years until a hot Thursday afternoon in November 1932 when the children's new home was finally ready. Jay Creek was nearly 50 kilometres from the old telegraph station and some of the older children walked all the way. The place was officially opened by Deputy Administrator Vic Carrington the following day, 18 November. A correspondent from Adelaide's paper the *Chronicle* was on hand and he declared the place 'one of the finest institutions of its kind in Australia'. He wrote that the boys would receive schooling and technical training in saddlery, stockwork, blacksmithing and carpentry. The girls would be skilled in domestic economy.[2] Government officials interstate were no doubt pleased to finally get positive publicity, though it wouldn't be long before the limitations of the place became apparent.

The government had spent £2500 and made substantial alterations to the buildings in the months after the telegraph staff vacated them. A large corrugated-iron dormitory built between the barracks and the store was furnished with rows of double bunks: girls slept in the eastern wing and boys in the western. The store was converted to a laundry and shower block and there was a septic system with flushing toilets. The dividing walls in the southern wing of the barracks were removed to create a long dining room for the children. The building that had housed the batteries became their schoolroom, with an enclosed verandah and extra windows on the eastern side. The post and telegraph office became a clinic and infirmary.

Sixty-one years after Charles Todd's men took over the place, the Commonwealth of Australia made it off limits for white people. On 7 December 1932 an area of approximately 674 acres surrounding the Alice Springs waterhole was proclaimed an Aboriginal Reserve.[3]

Emily Liddle (nee Perkins) was 11 at the time. Years later she remembered the dormitory as a big improvement on conditions at Jay Creek:

> When we come to this home here, Telegraph, we were shocked to see beds and mattresses. Coming into a mansion after sleeping on concrete floors. We were shocked really ... We rushed around and they said, Oh, they even got a shower and bath tubs.[4]

Herbie Laughton had less fond memories: 'It was stinking hot in summer and real cold in winter. There was no heating at all. We used to hang around the coppers on washday to keep warm.'[5] It soon became apparent that the government had not allocated enough money and problems arose as the number of inmates at the home quickly grew. The 73 children in November 1932 rose to 114 when the 33 boys from Pine Creek moved down to Alice Springs after that home closed on 20 May 1933.[6] The Chief Protector Cecil

Cook wrote to the Administrator expressing concern about suggestions of housing up to 144 children in the dormitory.[7] The septic system, built for 60 to 70 people, was unable to cope with the demand, and the old well wasn't able to deliver enough water for the vegetable garden.[8] The *Chronicle*'s declaration on opening day started to look hollow.

Sister Styles

The Bungalow received an additional staff member in January 1934 with the appointment of newly trained nurse Eileen Styles (later Fitzer) to run the clinic. She was also to assist the Freemans with educating the children under the guidance of Nance Taylor, the teacher in charge of the school in town.[9] Eileen's appointment was linked to the government recognising the need for a trained nurse in Alice Springs to handle obstetric cases involving Aboriginal people. Government officials got the message that the town's white population did not want Aboriginal people admitted to Rev. John Flynn's nursing facility, Adelaide House.[10]

The townspeople had access to a doctor by this time, as well as Flynn's nursing sisters. Dr Frank McCann was employed by the Commonwealth Department of Health and based at the government offices in Hartley Street. He arrived in August 1932 to succeed Dr D.R. Brown who in turn had replaced Dr Bruce Kirkland, the first doctor appointed in December 1929.

The government erected a galvanised-iron medical hut that became known as the blacks' hospital, on the east bank of the Todd. There was a gazetted camping ground in that area for Aboriginal people who had permission to be in town. Tom Taylor, a white pensioner, was put in charge of the medical hut when it was completed in February 1934.[11]

Eileen Styles, born in the Top End in 1902, was the granddaughter of Darwin pioneers Ned and Eliza Tuckwell. She trained in Melbourne in general nursing and midwifery and headed to Alice Springs as soon as she had finished her final examinations in early 1933 to stay with her sister Lillian Lovegrove, wife of the Alice Springs police sergeant John. She told author Barbara James in the 1980s:

While I was there I think we made medical history in Alice Springs because a very, very severe trachoma eye epidemic broke out in the Alice and I was in isolation with seventeen patients in the old Police Station through the Gap, while we treated them. With me were a couple of teenage girls, part-Aboriginals, who were helping me. We only saw the doctor, the baker and the butcher all the time we were there. The treatment was drastic and continuous and I think we were there for two months administering the treatment to at least a hundred patients.[12]

She wrote an application for a nursing position at the Darwin Hospital in July 1933. The following month the government decided to base a nurse at the Bungalow's clinic to assist the Freemans and tend Aboriginal people from the bush needing medical attention. Unable to recruit someone with both nursing and teaching qualifications, they approached Eileen who expressed a willingness to give it a go, even though she lacked teaching experience. She was appointed for 12 months from 1 December 1933.

Hetti Perkins

Hetti Perkins was a stable figure in the lives of the Bungalow children through the four difficult years at Jay Creek and a decade at the old telegraph station. She took over from Topsy Smith running the kitchen, managing the food supplies and looking after the smallest children.[13]

Hetti was born at Arltunga around 1895. Her mother was Arrernte woman Nellie Araka (aka Errerreke) and her father a white miner Burke Perkins, known as 'Harry'. He was from Broken Hill and went to Arltunga in 1890 or thereabouts. His son joined him on the mining fields. Nellie and Harry had two more children, Mary and Burke. They squatted on pastoral country near Claraville station when the short-lived Winnecke goldrush declined after 1903. Charlie Perkins's biographer Peter Read wrote of Hetti:

She was raised around the mines. She could ride horse and camel, lay a fuse, skin a bullock, dig and assay the gold-bearing ore. When, stricken with arsenic poisoning, Perkins left his family and returned to Broken Hill to die, Nellie Errerreke took Hetti and the other children back to the bush.[14]

Hetti worked at Arltunga's Glencoe Hotel when she was old enough to get a job. She had her first child Percy while she was working there. The father was storekeeper Harry Lake.[15] She then spent a number of years with the Turner brothers, first Alf and then Jim. Alf made money working as a carter and had a spell carrying the mail between Alice Springs and Powell Creek, though it's unclear exactly when. He wanted to acquire land and become a pastoralist. By 1915 he had approval to use the land on the Waite River north of Arltunga. It became Alcoota station after the war. Alf and Hetti had a child Bill.

Hetti teamed up with Jim Turner after Alf enlisted in 1916 but there was trouble when he came back from the war late in 1919. He was unhappy to find his brother living with her and having fathered a couple of children. He took five-year-old Bill to live with him at Alcoota. Jim ended his long relationship with Hetti in 1927 to marry Gertie Elliot, leaving her and their youngest children to fend for themselves. Against Hetti's wishes, he sent their two older daughters Nita and Margaret to Adelaide to get an education. Hetti and her remaining children went to the original Bungalow behind the Stuart Arms Hotel. It seems she went willingly because it would allow her to work and stay close to her children. She went out to Jay Creek when the institution moved there, describing herself as Ida Standley's chief 'dormitory girl'.

Hetti had another child during the Jay Creek years, May born in 1931. She met Martin Connelly from western Queensland during the telegraph station years and had three more children, Charlie and twins Ernie and Gary. Charlie, born in 1936, made a name for himself as the first Aboriginal man to earn a university degree. He inherited his mother's strength and determination, becoming a legendary figure in Aboriginal politics as well as a Commonwealth Government departmental head.

Hetti is remembered as very strict but a hard worker who did her best to provide the Bungalow children with the best upbringing she could. Her niece Emily Liddle recalled:

Everything had to be done properly. We had to do things spotless ... Yes, she was strict, just like the Turner family, I think. She was brought up by a Turner (laughs) ... we always had plenty of bread ... We had plenty of vegies, but we only used to get that at lunchtimes ... stew and vegetables ... Well, old Auntie Hettie used to cook it up so's everybody'd get a good feed.[16]

Emily was the daughter of Hetti's brother Burke. She was sent to Jay Creek in 1929 when she was 10, along with her younger brother Gordon. Other nieces and nephews were taken to the Bungalow at the end of 1936: George Bray, his brother Harry, and his sisters Elsie and Ollie, all children of Hetti's sister Mary and Billy Bray.[17] George said of his auntie years later 'Yes, she was a great old battler'.[18]

Father Percy Smith

Father Percy Smith was a frequent visitor to the Bungalow throughout the 1930s. He was the first Church of England priest based in town, arriving in November 1933 with 'work among the mixed blood children of Alice Springs' one of his main tasks.[19] The majority of the children at the institution were nominally Church of England at that stage. Both the Thornes and the Freemans were of that denomination and led the children in daily prayers, as well as providing Bible instruction.

The church's interest in the Alice Springs region dated back to July 1901 when Bishop Gilbert White turned up at the telegraph station in an old-fashioned black frock coat and clerical gaiters.[20] He was from the newly established diocese of Carpentaria, which covered Far North Queensland and the Torres Strait Islands, the Gulf of Carpentaria and the Northern Territory. Rev. William Wilkinson followed in 1913, conducting another service at the telegraph station after an epic journey from Laura in Queensland with packhorses.[21] Bishop Richard Thomas, from the South Australian diocese of Willochra, visited Alice Springs in the early months of 1928. He was shocked by conditions at the Bungalow, still behind the pub at that time, and took the matter up with Prime Minister Stanley Bruce. Priests from his diocese visited regularly over the next four years. The first to visit, Brother Louis De Ridder, at the end of 1928, baptised all the children at a marathon ceremony.[22]

Father Smith lived at Mrs Jessie Roper's guesthouse when he first came to town. It was not flash but accommodation was limited in those days. When longtime resident Ben Walkington died in April 1934, his derelict cottage Myrtle Villa, on Wills Terrace, became an option. Policeman Bob Hamilton and his wife Ena were the new owners and planned to demolish it but said Father Smith could live there rent-free until that happened. Ida Standley had lived in it for a number of years. However, the health inspector Dr Frank McCann condemned the place. Father Smith pleaded with the doctor to let him move in and he gave his consent on the proviso it was cleaned up and made habitable.[23] He lived there until he was able to build a church and presbytery in Bath Street in 1936.

He conducted a service at the Bungalow on Sundays and provided religious instruction one day during the week. He would then stay and play games with the children. A favourite game for the boys was bowling old tyres along and having races, usually with smaller boys curled up in the rims. The girls loved hockey, whacking a tennis ball around the place with curved mulga sticks. He had a genuine concern for the children's welfare and was unhappy about the way Freeman treated them and the punishments he dished out. He said:

> There was an air of gloom and repression about the place and the children were silent and sullen. There was no laughter ... The Superintendent, who was also a Protector of Aborigines, was a bully and a drunkard. The children cowered under his rule. They were supposed to have school every day but what a farce! ... There were no trained teachers on the staff and the Superintendent only put the children into the classroom when he got the 'tip off' from his scouts in Alice Springs that an official was coming. However, a great shake up occurred shortly after I arrived.[24]

Superintendent Freeman is gaoled

On 27 February 1934, Deputy Administrator Vic Carrington opened a letter written two days earlier by a 16-year-old girl at the Bungalow. It began with the words 'I am longing to have someone to help me'.[25] It's unclear how the letter made it to his office in Hartley Street but Percy Smith thought it might have been entrusted to the butcher's boy when he went to deliver the meat.[26]

Freeman had gone to the girls' dormitory around 11 pm on Saturday night, taken her away and forced her to have sex with him. It was not the first time this had happened. It later emerged he had been interfering with girls at Jay Creek.

Vic Carrington took immediate action. The next day he and Dr Frank McCann took sworn statements from other girls at the Bungalow and from nursing sister Eileen Styles.[27] Dr McCann was a justice of the peace and Deputy Chief Protector of Aborigines. Eileen Styles was not aware of Freeman engaging in inappropriate activity with the girls but testified to his heavy drinking. He was suspended from duty and charged with a breach of section 53 (1) (c) of the *Aboriginals Ordinance 1918–1933*, which prohibited white men consorting with 'a female aboriginal or half-caste'. The maximum fine that could be imposed for the offence was £100. If Freeman was convicted and failed to pay the fine, he would be imprisoned for three months.

He appeared in the Alice Springs courtroom on 2 March charged with carnal knowledge of a 16-year-old girl. Two local men, who were justices of the peace, presided over the case: the Commonwealth's resident engineer in Central Australia David Smith, and businessman David Neck. Dr McCann prosecuted while the local solicitor Beecher Webb represented Freeman. Vic Carrington wrote to the Secretary of the Department of the Interior:

> whatever the outcome of the Police Court action, I am convinced that Mr Freeman has been guilty of interfering with more than one of the girls and I intend to recommend his dismissal from the Service.[28]

Freeman denied the charge but his victim was resolute and stuck to her story. Five of her fellow Bungalow residents gave damning evidence against him, including Hetti Perkins who later incurred Mrs Freeman's wrath. He was found guilty at the end of a two-day hearing and given a month to pay the fine. It later emerged that both David Smith and David Neck felt the penalty was too light. Police sergeant John Lovegrove had heard rumours for some time about Freeman's activities but had insufficient evidence to take action.[29]

Freeman couldn't pay and was taken to the town gaol on Parsons Street on 4 April 1934. Constable Bill McKinnon handed him over to gaoler Jim

Shannon at 10 am.[30] The old gaoler retired soon afterwards and no doubt had lots of enquiries from the locals, keen to know how his most high profile prisoner was enjoying his new accommodation. Freeman's sentence of three months was light but the shame was great for a man of his status to be incarcerated with Aboriginal prisoners. He was put to work with them, cutting and carting firewood for local people and digging trenches at the sanitary depot. He was due to be discharged on 3 July 1934 but a remission of 30 days for satisfactory work and conduct meant he was in fact discharged on 2 June.

Bob Hamilton moved out from town with his wife Ena and son Robert to take Freeman's place until a new superintendent could be found. A Queenslander, he'd joined the Northern Territory police in 1929, having served as a provost officer in Egypt and France during the war. He was a genial, solidly built man with the habit of pushing his hat forward and scratching the back of his head when thinking about things.[31] He was a sub-protector, in addition to his general police duties, and he regularly interacted with Aboriginal people, distributing rations to the elderly and the families of working men at the old police station at Heavitree Gap. Mrs Daisy Freeman was kept on until the end of the year to ensure the Bungalow children continued to receive some schooling.[32]

Chief Protector Cook wanted to maintain the existing staff mix: a superintendent with practical experience in stock work and station craft, a teacher and a nurse. A number of applications were received for the Freemans' positions and a decision made in April to appoint drover Jack Jones and his wife Elsie, a nurse, from Pine Creek. They took up their new appointment in July 1934 and were popular with the children, treating them with a kindness they'd never experienced under Freeman.[33] Elsie had been matron of the boys' home in Pine Creek for a time.

Recognising that the standard of education needed to be raised, the authorities decided to transfer Eileen Styles to Pine Creek and replace her with a trained teacher from South Australia, rather than have two nurses on the staff. She stayed on at the Bungalow until the Jones arrived. Joyce Jamieson then came out from the town school by horse and buggy each afternoon during the second half of the year to help Daisy Freeman with the children. She was an infant teacher who'd arrived in town in February as assistant to Nance Taylor.

Better days at the Bungalow

The Ghan pulled into the station at Alice Springs, late as usual, on Saturday evening 2 February 1935. On board was the Bungalow's new teacher from Adelaide, a tall, imposing 28-year-old, christened May Venetta Robb but known as 'Maise'.[34] She stayed the night in Mrs Roper's not-so-flash guesthouse but the Hamiltons soon came to the rescue, offering her accommodation in their substantial police house, next door to the Residency. Bob drove her out to the Bungalow for her first day at school and introduced her to Jack and Elsie Jones. Sitting still awaiting her in the schoolroom were 82 children, aged from five to 16: boys in khaki shirts and shorts, girls in blue-striped cotton dresses.

Like the new superintendent and matron, Maise Robb had a positive impact on the children and was remembered fondly. Discipline was never a problem, neither she nor Mr and Mrs Jones resorted to corporal punishment, but she soon found the children needed more individual attention than one teacher could provide and wrote to Deputy Administrator Vic Carrington on 27 February about the need for a second teacher. There were approximately 120 children at the home, 82 of whom were attending school.[35] Grace Randall was appointed in June to work as her assistant. However, friction quickly developed between the two women and it was not to be a happy partnership.[36]

Police sergeant John Lovegrove wrote a letter to the administrator on 20 November 1935 in which he described Miss Randall as 'inclined towards making careless and mischievous remarks'. This followed a letter from Matron Elsie Jones to Vic Carrington in September, objecting to the expectation that she provide both teachers with morning tea and a hot lunch each day. Elsie didn't mind doing this for Daisy Freeman and Maise Robb but Grace Randall rubbed her up the wrong way. The children weren't keen on her either, and she found the need to wave the cane around.[37] Both teachers were meant to be there for three years but Maise Robb got a transfer to the school in town in April 1936, after only 15 months at the Bungalow. To her chagrin, Grace Randall was promoted to head teacher and Mavis Penery arrived in May to be her assistant.[38]

Jock and Elsie Jones left at the end of 1936 and the children were sorry to see them go. Their own two children had contracted trachoma in Alice Springs and they decided to return to the Top End where this was not such a problem. They were appointed to run the leprosy hospital on Channel Island in Darwin Harbour. Mrs Jones only lived a few more years. She was ill in Darwin hospital when the Japanese bombed the place on 19 February 1942 but left her sickbed to arrange the transfer of the leprosy patients to the mainland. She in turn was evacuated to Rockhampton Downs on the Barkly Tableland where her condition worsened in March. She was flown to Brisbane but died in hospital on 17 May 1942, only 54 years of age.[39]

Once again policeman Bob Hamilton and his wife Ena relieved for a few months, from early November 1936 until Billy and Isabella McCoy took over in 1937. The McCoys had applied for the positions of superintendent and matron when they were advertised in 1934. They were rated highly but Jack and Elsie Jones preferred at the time.[40] McCoy was a stricter disciplinarian than Jack Jones and sought permission to use corporal punishment. However, George Bray, a Bungalow inmate at the time, later said 'he was pretty fair, old Bill'.[41]

Bill McCoy was only five foot two inches in the old imperial measurements, but a significant figure in local history. He continued to work with Aboriginal people from 1937 until his retirement in the early 1960s. He was always puffing on a pipe and Aboriginal people called him *o bi eeba*, 'man with pipe'. Harry Giese, Director of Welfare from 1954 until 1970, said after his death in 1986:

> I have the greatest respect for Bill and his work in Central Australia, particularly among the aboriginal people. I greatly regret that Bill's work was never formally recognised.

Bill McCoy was a war veteran who served with the 7th Field Ambulance but didn't go to France until two days before the war ended. His older brother Alexander, known as 'Lal', was in the same unit and the two used their deferred pay from the army to lease land in northern South Australia after the war. They ran sheep but were wiped out by bushfire in the early 1920s.

Bill was a pioneer of road transport later in the 1920s, driving trucks for Wallis Fogarty Ltd for eight years. Drawing on his army ambulance experience, he carried sick and injured people when necessary, providing first aid until he could get them to a doctor or nurse. He met Isabella Pope in the course of this work. Bill called her Pat. She was one of the first two nursing sisters John Flynn appointed to Adelaide House when it opened on 24 June 1926. They married in September 1929.

The McCoys had no children of their own but adopted the baby son of Tilly Tilmouth who grew up at the Bungalow. Ronnie Tilmouth was born at Adelaide House on 21 June 1937, '3 months premature and only 3 lb'. He said he probably would have died if it hadn't been for the nursing of Mrs McCoy. 'I was wrapped in cotton wool and kept in a shoe box beside the fire.'[42]

Wally Boehm and Joe Croft

In March 1937, Grace Randall requested a third teacher for the Bungalow. Deputy Administrator Vic Carrington was supportive and went further, recommending that the government build a new school. It never happened but Ellen Kelly arrived in January 1938 to assist Grace Randall and Mavis Penery, working with the youngest children.[43] She was a capable teacher, with 11 years experience in South Australia, but didn't get off to a good start. Carrington wrote to the government secretary on 15 March 1938:

> Miss Randall is of a very unpleasant disposition and I gathered had taken the early opportunity of being unpleasant to Miss Kelly – so much so that the latter considered applying to be returned to South Australia instead of taking up duty at the Halfcaste Institution School.[44]

Fortunately Grace Randall's term was due to end in June 1938 and the decision was made to appoint a male teacher in her place. She stayed on an extra month until Wally Boehm arrived from South Australia in late July. Recognising the need for the boys to receive adequate technical training, Boehm argued for and got approval to purchase woodworking equipment, which was installed in the blacksmith shop early in 1939.[45] He'd grown up on a farm in South Australia and was a keen gardener, encouraging the children in this regard. He also established a scout group, and a drum and fife band.

Another significant development during Wally Boehm's time was the appointment of a domestic arts teacher, Miss Beatrice (Grac) Moore, to replace Mavis Penery when her term ended in April 1939.[46] The girls received instruction in cooking, sewing, knitting and crochet as well as practical tasks such as setting a table, making a bed and household hygiene.

Nathalie Lacey was the final teacher to join the staff. She was appointed in January 1941 to replace Ellen Kelly when her three-year term was up.[47] She later married John Gorey of Yambah station and was instrumental in the establishment of preschool education in Alice Springs in 1947. The Nathalie Gorey Kindergarten (now Nathalie Gorey Pre School) was named in her honour after her death in November 1951 when a young mother with three small children.

Wally Boehm met Agnes Maud Riley in Alice Springs and they were married by Father Percy Smith in September 1941. Known as Molly, she was an infant teacher at the town school in Hartley Street. Wally and Molly formed a close friendship with the very positive Church of England priest. They shared his concern for the Bungalow children and belief in their potential. Joe Croft provided proof their faith was justified.

Joe was born on Victoria River Downs station but taken from his Gurindji mother Bessy as a four-year-old in 1930. He was put on the back of a truck and taken to the Kahlin Compound in Darwin. One of his few recollections was of his mother's crying. He was later sent to the boys' home in Pine Creek and then to the Bungalow in 1933. Joe was clever and was encouraged and tutored by Wally Boehm and Percy Smith so he could go on to secondary education. At the age of 14, he was awarded a bursary enabling him to attend All Souls Anglican Boarding School for Boys at Charters Towers. Father Smith's brother was an accountant, Honorary Register of the Diocese of North Queensland, and a member of the Board of Governors of the All Souls School. Joe's bright personality, academic ability and athletic skills made him popular with the other boys and he was school captain in his senior year.

In 1943 he became the first Aboriginal person to undertake university studies, enrolling in engineering at the University of Queensland. However, he left the university in 1944 to join the army. His engineering studies enabled him to get work as a surveyor after the war. He later opened a newsagency in northern New South Wales where he encouraged local Aboriginal art, craft and culture. He became a leader in a number of Aboriginal cultural organisations, providing encouragement and assistance to artists and dancers. One of the many beneficiaries was Arnhem Land dancer and actor David Gulpilil, who went on to earn international acclaim under Joe Croft's guidance and management.[48]

Joe Croft died of leukemia in 1996 at the age of 70. He overcame the sorrow of his childhood to prosper in life. He is just one of many Bungalow children whose life stories demonstrate the bankruptcy of the racially prejudiced world into which they were born.

Jessie's story

Opinions vary about the Bungalow itself, and the treatment the children received. It depends on who you talk to. Alec Kruger, like Joe Croft, was one of 33 boys trucked down to Alice Springs from Pine Creek in mid 1933. His mother was Polly Yrambul, a Mutpura woman from Wave Hill station; his father was a white man, Frank Kruger. Alec's story is poignant and the trauma of his removal inescapable. His father was away at the time, working, and could do nothing to stop it happening.

> I was born in Katherine in 1924. I was taken away from my mother when I was three-and-a-half years old. They just come down and say, 'We're taking these kids.' They just take you out of your mother's arms. That's what they done to me.[49]

Alec had the misfortune to live at the Bungalow during the oppressive Freeman era:

> They used to flog us for little things like picking the vegetables in the garden we were growing. We had to take our strides down and bend over a box and the girls would be gathered around to watch.

He worked on a cattle station from the age of 11, unpaid like a slave, before sneaking away to join the army in 1942 and newfound freedom.[50] He overcame his tough start in life to become a respected figure in the Alice Springs community, cheerful and accepting of what life dished up, but determined to fight for justice for his stolen generation.

Alec Ross came along later, when care at the Bungalow had improved, and saw his childhood differently. Born in 1936 at Mosquito Creek, close to Neutral Junction station in the Barrow Creek area, he was placed in the institution when he was three following a spell in hospital:

> I was very sick. That's why I was taken from my mother ... I never had it bad, I can tell you that. I always loved where I lived and what I did. If I hadn't been taken away I'd never have enjoyed the life I live today. It was the best thing that ever happened to me.[51]

Alec Ross spent the last years of his varied and productive working life as the main tour guide at the Alice Springs telegraph station, six decades after living there as a small child. He enriched the experience of countless visitors with his remarkably positive persona and wonderful storytelling.

Jessie White was older. She too achieved a lot in life but, in contrast to Alec Ross, always felt the government's shadow hanging over her. Her daughter Cynthia said in 2013:

> The control over her life was always there, until she was at least 25 years old, first by Native Affairs and then the new body that took over from the other one and just followed on, Welfare. It made life very hard as she was always looking over her shoulders.[52]

Jessie White was born at Mount Riddock in 1922 and lived at all three Bungalows. She was taken to the one behind the Stuart Arms Hotel when she was five or six, not long before the move to Jay Creek. Her mother Carrie was the daughter of Nellie Araka and her Aboriginal husband Doctor Jim. Jessie's father was a policeman, Tom White. The police station at Arltunga was a ration depot and children were registered there. Carrie and other relations would visit Jessie at the Bungalow. She cried at night for her mum but was luckier than other children because Carrie's half-sister Hetti Perkins worked there in the Jay Creek and telegraph station years:

> I was staying at the Bungalow with Aunt Hetti so my family was happier. Mostly all the kids knew each other. It was good for all of them to have Hetti.
>
> Aunt Hetti did all the baking of bread. Native people around the area always dropping kangaroo and rabbits for the children. It was a change of meat as the only meat we ate was goat's meat.
>
> All the girls and boys who turned 14 had to work. Boys were sent to stations; girls to work for government officials and hospitals. 1936 I turned 14. I was then sent to Darwin to work at the hospital, the old one, Kahlin Hospital. In 1937 I went to Pine Creek and worked at the hospital there. As a wards maid helping the sisters. At Pine Creek there was only one sister, and us, and the flying doctor would visit. We could call him in an emergency. There was a landing field beside the hospital. After that I worked in Katherine till 1939. Then the war was on. I was working for Major Russell and his wife at Larrakeyah Barracks in Darwin when Timor and Singapore fell.

She was expecting a baby by this time.

> They wanted me to go to Sydney with them, but I said no. I wanted to see my family. I was 18 or 19 years old then.

So she got a job in another household, with Mr and Mrs Tom Harris who ran the Star Picture Theatre. After a while Mrs Harris went to Adelaide but Jessie had her daughter Annette and kept working for Mr Harris until the baby was old enough to travel. The evacuation of women and children from the north accelerated after the Japanese bombed Darwin in February 1942.

> The evacuation was by army trucks, organised through all the church organisations. I was evacuated back here to Alice Springs to the Bungalow. We came down to Alice Springs with the army and the Methodist Inland Mission sisters ... The Bungalow was for refugees coming in, mostly coloured people. Mostly women and kids came there during the war. Then we were sent down south to Balaklava. Then from there different people went different places: Church of England people to

New South Wales; Catholics to New South Wales and to Adelaide. We were working girls. We went to church homes.

Jessie travelled to Sydney and got a job cleaning at Penrith Hospital.

This is where I first saw a bank book and was paid well.

In Darwin she had been given pocket money and the rest was supposed to be put in her bank account, but she didn't see it. After a while, she got a job in the Blue Mountains working at a guesthouse, which she found pleasant.

1945 when the war finished I was working in the Blue Mountains and there was dancing in the street. Then, after the war I worked in Rurru Private Hospital in Adelaide.

Mr and Mrs Harris found out she was working there. They were in Alice Springs and asked Jessie to work for them again. She accepted the job and travelled up on the train.

Mrs Heather Harris had twin girls, and was still in hospital, and I and grandmother looked after the babies. I went back to Darwin with the Harrises in about 1946.
I had my first two kids in Darwin, Brian born in 1947 and Annette. The other kids were born in Alice Springs. Late 1940s I worked for the Administration, in Government House in Darwin, then back to the hospital. Then I worked for the Hotel Darwin.[53]

In 1950, Jessie decided to go home to look for her mum at Bond Springs. When she arrived there, relatives told her that Carrie was 'on walkabout'. Jessie got a job at the station. Eventually she saw her mother and stayed with her. Later she moved into town and lived at the Gap Cottages in Stella Weetra's house before getting a place of her own on the Eastside in 1963.

Jessie worked hard all her life to support herself and her children. She was a cleaner with the Department of Education for 20 years, first at the school in Hartley Street and then at Ross Park. She also worked in the laundry and the staff kitchen at the hospital, in hotel laundries and at the Central Australian

Aboriginal Congress. She retired at the age of 60 but sadly she died in 1991 from cancer. Her daughter Cynthia said in 2013:

> The domestic scene was all they could employ them as; that's all that they were educated for and nothing else, slave labour. This was the first group of the stolen generation, children. The different families that Mum worked for were kind people but when she asked questions about going home and looking for her mother, there was always work to do somewhere else or for some other family. She had two children in Darwin and yearned to go home, so that she could see her mother again and show her the children.
>
> The feeling of coming home was so triumphant that at least she could look after her mum and be part of the community that she loved so much. Her life had some great rewards to cherish and the stories she told of the different places and experiences with other people were exciting and enjoyable to listen to.
>
> The way things unfolded, which had a big impact on our lives and very much distress, with the Welfare taking our three brothers away, left our mum feeling like she failed again and it was her fault. The feeling of having no rights or control of her life was, once again, a hurdle to jump over. This showed on her face many times when the inspection of our house was due.
>
> She worked very hard for over twenty years with the Department of Education as a school cleaner and always did her work with a professional touch; always had things planned and prepared for the work load, such as having enough cleaning material for little and big jobs. Her work was always perfection and professional.
>
> When grown up as young adults, it was comforting whenever she put her arms around us to give us a big hug. It was a beautiful feeling. She missed that when she was taken away from her mother and family. She used to say 'Make sure that you tell your children that you love them, all the time, as hugs are free and don't cost anything. Teach them to care and share for each other as I have done for you and don't let them waste anything.' This is about unconditional love.[54]

22

Two different worlds
before the war

The traditional life of Aboriginal people in Central Australia was still largely intact before the 1939–1945 war. White and black lived separately for the most part, though a large number of Aboriginal people worked for rations on cattle stations and in mining camps. They were prohibited from entering Territory towns unless they had written approval for a specific purpose. The Aboriginal Ordinance gave the Administrator the power to declare any place a prohibited area and the police the authority to remove Aboriginal people from such areas.[1] The regulations associated with the Ordinance included a penalty of a month's imprisonment for any Aboriginal found in town without permission between the hours of 8 pm and 5 am.[2]

The 1920s drought was a difficult time for Aboriginal people with native game and food plants declining as waterholes dried up and stock denuded the country. They gravitated toward town and grew increasingly reliant on government rations. By the late 1920s there was a sizeable camp on the southern edge of town.[3] It was not the only fringe camp. The Charles Creek, on the north side, was another popular camp site. In the 1930s the Bungalow children would sneak there when they got the chance to be fed bush tucker.

Aboriginal people were allowed in town during daylight hours for medical attention. The only time they were allowed in town at night was to go to the pictures. Leslie 'Snow' Kenna and an offsider arrived in Alice Springs from western Queensland in the second half of 1936 with motion picture equipment. Snow began showing his ancient, scratched movies on alternate Saturday nights in the Welfare Hall, at the northern end of town. He lived at the Underdown family's Alice Springs Hotel, opened in 1933, and it wasn't long before Ly Underdown decided to build a picture theatre. This was an open-air job called the Capitol on Gregory Terrace opposite the pub. It was enclosed by galvanised iron three metres high, with patrons reclining in canvas deckchairs. Blazing wood fires in old oil drums kept people from freezing on cold winter nights.[4]

Father Maloney upsets white sensitivities

Father Paddy Maloney came to town from Palm Island in January 1935. He was a good-humoured man, short and somewhat rotund with greying hair and a face wrinkled by the tropical sun. Lay missionary Frank McGarry joined him at the Catholic presbytery in March and Brother Ed Bennett in December. Father Maloney raised the ire of many local people when he began providing instruction for Aboriginal children at the Catholic Church.[5] Brother Bennett said in his 1989 memoir that these were the children of Aboriginal people employed in Alice Springs:

> These natives worked as gardeners, building labourers, house maids, in the laundery etc. They had to be out of town by sunset! Only one night a week were they allowed to go the pictures. The work with the children began with three hours school conducted by Frank McGarry. The curriculum included Catechism and elementary hygiene ... As the numbers increased, facilities at the Presbytery became inadequate. There was an urgent need for toilets. Father applied to the Government for two. After much haggling the request was granted (along with the remark from one of the officials that it was like giving strawberries to pigs!). This also was the attitude of some of the townspeople towards the natives. In 1937 one of the police at the time had a thing about us (what he called 'harbouring the natives'.) He came in one day and began telling me off about this. I referred him to Father Maloney who promptly ordered him off the premises and told him to come back with a warrant. This, of course, he never did. Racism is not new in the Alice.[6]

Father Maloney railed against the attitudes of the town's people in a letter to the Minister for the Interior:

> Had you seen these poor blacks when we took up the work, you would not have thought it possible for White Australians to have left them in such poverty and misery. We boast of our civilisation, our culture and advancement, our broadmindedness and willingness to give every one a fair deal, yet we have shot, poisoned and starved to almost complete extinction a most noble black race. The soil of this Continent has been steeped in black blood, and anyone who takes up the cause of the few that remain, becomes as bitterly hated even as are the Blacks ... I was a grand old man, most popular, until I began to teach the blacks that they are noble human beings, that they must form sanitary habits such as washing themselves and their clothes. That they must not pollute the town water supply – the Todd River ... Another man said to me when I began to teach the black children in the Presbytery, 'You were the most popular man in the district till you brought those Black children into our Town.' I answered, let us have a monster meeting (I should have said a meeting of monsters) and if at that meeting any of those with this strange black complex or this territory disease – Abbophobia – can prove that these neglected creatures are not human beings, and hence have not an immortal soul, and are not above mere animals, I'll gladly shoo them off into the bush ... Who in the South could even dream there was such a Black Complex in Australia. And these white people are as sane as any in the South on other subjects. I would not wish for finer people to live with socially. We are all like one big happy family, but keep off the blacks, except to denounce them. Not all are suffering from the Abbophobia but at least 80 percent.[7]

While deploring the attitudes of so many of the local people, Father Maloney recognised that the town was a prohibited area and the wisest course of action was to find an alternative location where he could minister to the Aboriginal people. The land he wanted was along the Charles Creek, just outside the town's northern boundary but within easy walking distance of his church and presbytery in Hartley Street. The government concurred and increased the size of the Aboriginal reserve around the telegraph station in December 1936 to enable Father Maloney to continue his work. The enlarged reserve extended south to the junction of the Charles Creek and the Todd River.[8] In the process, they provided more grazing land for the Bungalow's goat herd supplying milk for the children. The Catholic Church wasn't given ownership of this land but allowed to establish its Little Flower Mission there early in 1937.[9] Ed Bennett and Frank McGarry sank a well and built a schoolroom, kitchen and laundry. The Aboriginal people constructed dwellings, of as good a standard as they could, upstream along the eastern bank of the Charles. The mission's official designation was Camp IV.

That same year, the government established a compound for Arrernte people west of town at Jay Creek. It was supervised by Native Affairs Branch's first patrol officer Ted Strehlow and his wife Bertha. He was a fluent speaker of Arrernte having grown up at Hermannsburg when his parents Carl and Frieda were in charge of the mission. The Jay Creek settlement was located on the land the government had purchased from the Hayes family in 1926 for a new Bungalow.

A change in government policy

A significant shift in government policy occurred in 1939. Responding to years of criticism of the Commonwealth's record in Aboriginal Affairs, a new Minister for the Interior released a policy statement in February of that year. Jack McEwen announced a series of changes and promised a new deal for Aboriginal people in the Northern Territory.[10] McEwen was strongly influenced by anthropologist A.P. Elkin of Sydney University and keen to establish himself as a reformer. For the first time, the government specified citizenship as the objective of Aboriginal policy. Assimilation into white society became the longterm aim, rather than isolation and 'protection'.

He was critical of Cecil Cook who had been Chief Protector in the Northern Territory since 1927 and he abolished the position. He established a new Native Affairs Branch in the Northern Territory Administration and, in April 1939, Ernest William Pearson Chinnery arrived in Darwin to become its first director.[11] Chinnery had been the director of the Department of District Services and Native Affairs in New Guinea since 1932. He got to work, setting up a system that drew on his New Guinea experience, with district officers and patrol officers.

The changes to government administration had an impact on the Bungalow. The old telegraph station had never been an ideal home for 130 children and the buildings had steadily deteriorated over time. The septic system couldn't cope, the building used as a school was woefully inadequate for the numbers crammed into it, and the flagstone floors in the kitchen and dining room cracked, making it hard for the staff and children to maintain standards of hygiene. Commonwealth approval was given in October 1938 for a new 50,000-gallon elevated water tank to supply the septic system and fire mains, but money for other improvements wasn't forthcoming.[12]

Administrator Charles (Aubrey) Abbott visited the place in early January 1939 and afterwards wrote a letter to the secretary of the Department of the Interior. He declared:

> the whole place stinks and is in exceedingly bad condition ... This is not in any way to be construed as criticism of the present Superintendent and his wife, Mr and Mrs McCoy. They have done their utmost to keep the institution clean and tidy and are most competent but the shortcomings of the buildings make the task almost impossible.

His visit followed a report by government's resident engineer D.D. Smith in December 1938 saying: 'This building is in a deplorable state.' Abbott recommended a new home be built near the town's new hospital, completed in mid 1938, but he was advised later in the year that the government was deferring any action indefinitely for financial reasons. However, £450 was allocated for urgent repairs.[13]

The government was now of the opinion that the care, education and control of children of mixed race could better be handled by the churches, in locations away from the towns and settlements. So, in 1940, Director Chinnery asked the churches to take the children living in the government institutions in Darwin and Alice Springs.[14] He had a more positive attitude towards church missions than his predecessor Cook and doubled their meagre Commonwealth funding in 1939. The Catholic Church began planning a new children's home at Garden Point on Melville Island and the Methodists a similar facility on Croker Island. An agreement was reached for the Church of England children to go to the Church Missionary Society's Emerald River Mission on Groote Eylandt.

Moving the children to the Top End

Europe plunged into another war in September 1939 and once again Australians rushed to enlist. However, the outbreak of war in the Pacific was still nearly a year off as Australians sang 'Auld Lang Syne' to celebrate the start of 1941. Plans were in place to close the Bungalow in a couple of months and move the children to islands in the north.

With this in mind, a decision was made in March 1941 to transfer domestic arts teacher Grac Moore to the school in town. She had come from South Australia for three years like all government teachers working in the Northern Territory at that time, and still had a year to go. Joyce Jamieson was offered a short-term contract to replace her. She had taught at the town school from 1934 until 1936 and returned to Alice Springs to marry local builder Ron Donnellan in December. She had domestic arts experience from teachers college.[15] The Bungalow's infant teacher Nathalie Lacey was informed she would be transferred to Tennant Creek when the 63 Catholic and Methodist children went north at the end of May.[16]

The Catholic children reached Melville Island in June but the Croker Island mission was not yet ready for the Methodist children. They went to a temporary camp at Delissaville, and in September to Goulburn Island, before finally moving to their new home in November. Wally Boehm's three-year term as head teacher was due to expire in July but he agreed to remain until the end of 1941 when the Church of England children – 21 boys and 9 girls – left. Their departure was delayed because the Church Missionary Society (CMS) needed time to build a new mission at Angurugu on Groote Eylandt. It would house the Aboriginal people vacating the Emerald River Mission to make way for the children. However, the CMS informed the government in November that it would be unable to take the children until the following April. The government asked the Church to find a teacher to replace Wally

Boehm for the first three months of the 1942 school year and said it would reimburse them for the salary.[17]

The plan to send the Church of England children north in April 1942 was quickly overtaken by the outbreak of war in the Pacific. Japan attacked Kota Bahru in northern Malaya at 3.15 am Northern Territory time on 8 December 1941 and Pearl Harbour just over an hour later. On 12 December, Federal Cabinet decided to evacuate all white women and children from Darwin, except women required for essential services. Two thousand left, mostly by ship, in December, January and February.[18] When Darwin was bombed on 19 February 1942, the evacuation order was extended to civilians living as far south as Larrimah, though women on cattle stations were allowed to stay.

The Catholic and Methodist children who had left the Bungalow in May 1941 for Melville and Croker Islands were brought south again, along with some children from the Darwin Half-Caste Institution who had been transferred to Pine Creek in 1940 when the army took over the Bagot Aboriginal Reserve. Most of the Methodists went to a church camp at Otford, between Sydney and Wollongong. The Catholics went to either Carrieton in South Australia or to Melbourne. The Church of England children still at the Bungalow were sent to a church institution in the Sydney suburb of Ashfield in May 1942, and then to Mulgoa, near Penrith.[19] The children remained in the southern states for the duration of the war.

The old telegraph station's decade as a children's home officially ended in July 1942. The government intended transferring the McCoys to the Jay Creek Aboriginal Reserve when it decided to close the Bungalow back in 1940. However, they were sent to South Australia instead, to oversee the welfare of families evacuated from the Top End.[20] Wally Boehm also went south, to Blackwood. Hetti Perkins and her children remained in Alice Springs, moving to Rainbow Town and working at the Underdowns' hotel. Rainbow Town was a collection of very basic huts located on the south-east fringe of the town. It was home to most of the town's people of mixed descent.

23

The Territory transformed by war

The arrival of the railway in 1929 was a turning point in the history of Alice Springs. The outbreak of war 10 years later was an event of even greater significance. It was plucked out of slumber and obscurity to become a major service centre. The physical improvements were dramatic and the alterations to the social environment even more far-reaching.

Northern Australia's strategic significance was recognised as long ago as 1824 when a small British garrison was based at Fort Dundas on Melville Island. The OT line put the place on the map but it did not figure strongly in the Australian consciousness. The neglected north only rose to prominence once the nation's focus shifted from the war in Europe to what might happen in South-East Asia. The Northern Territory then acquired a significant military presence as concern about Japan's intentions grew and there was the prospect of hostilities on our northern shores.

In 1940, the Commonwealth Government began pouring military and civilian manpower into the Alice Springs region. It turned the rough track north of the town into an all-weather road and simultaneously upgraded the old OT line to enable long-distance telephone communication for the first time. It improved living conditions in the town with two basic amenities people now take for granted: electricity and running water. The electrical wiring, which commenced in 1937, extended to all parts of the town by war's end. The Commonwealth also established the infrastructure required to pump water into large storage tanks and pipe it to people's homes. The social life of the town improved with better facilities for music, dancing and concerts. The army introduced a number of new sports to Alice Springs, most notably Australian Rules football, which Aboriginal people later embraced with a passion. The troops realised the region wasn't a desert, writing letters home, spreading word of its scenic wonders and generating a postwar tourism boom. The war made modern Alice Springs.

The army takes over Alice Springs

Until the war, coastal shipping lines transported most things to and from Darwin. The Commonwealth Government recognised the strategic importance of an overland transport route but the roads in the north were poor and there was a large gap in the north–south railway. The cost of laying the missing track was prohibitive. So, early in 1940, the government decided to build an all-weather gravel road from Alice Springs to Birdum where construction work on the northern railway had ceased in 1929. Employees of the Department of the Interior and contractors had been steadily improving the track north of Alice in the 1930s, spurred by the 1933 Tennant Creek goldrush. They'd also worked on troublesome sections between Tennant and Newcastle Waters but the route north was still just a set of wheel ruts in many places. A substantial upgrade was needed to make it suitable for heavily laden trucks, should the sea lanes be threatened.

An agreement was reached in August 1940 to split the roadwork between four government authorities, with the army providing logistical support. The Department of the Interior would continue upgrading the section from Alice Springs to Tennant Creek. The very rough stretch from Tennant to Birdum was split between the South Australian Highways and Local Government Department, the Queensland Main Roads Commission and the New South Wales Department of Main Roads. The civilian road-making teams had to move quickly to complete the work before the start of the northern wet season in December. This meant building 1000 kilometres of road in 120 days. Remarkably they took only 90.[1] It was an extraordinary feat.

The new, lightly gravelled road did not withstand the pressure it was put under in its first 12 months and had to be rebuilt – but this takes nothing away from the men's achievement. It is disappointing that a myth developed, still perpetuated occasionally today, that the Americans built the Stuart Highway. The Yanks had nothing to do with it! Skilled Australian labour shone in one of the country's most remote locations. They actually built a bit more than originally intended because Birdum Creek, north of the township, is subject to flooding in the wet season. So the men extended the road a few kilometres north to a spot called Larrimah. A new railhead and army camp were established there.

The military's supporting role was crucial. An integrated army unit called the Darwin Overland Maintenance Force (DOMF) was formed in South Australia for this purpose, comprising approximately 800 men. Their job was to transport supplies and equipment up and down the track and establish staging camps along the way. They were equipped with 150 new three-ton trucks plus a large number of lighter vehicles. The advance party of troops left South Australia by train for Alice Springs. They arrived on 8 September 1940 and set up a camp in the town's recreation reserve, now Anzac Oval.[2]

Their commander, Lieutenant Colonel Noel Loutit, was a decorated veteran of the Great War.[3] A young lieutenant with the first troops who landed at Gallipoli on 25 April 1915, he was one of the few who reached the third ridge on the peninsula, the Anzacs' objective that first day. He and two others from the 10th Battalion were able to look down on the waters of the Narrows before having to retreat.

The army intended disbanding the DOMF once the roadwork was completed but it stayed together longer than expected, until 1 October 1941. A reorganisation then took effect. The drivers and vehicle maintenance men became part of a new Central Australia Motor Transport Column (CAMTC) while the others were transferred back to their separate, specialist units: supply, field bakery, field butchery, signals, sanitary, medical, etc. A second reorganisation six months later split up the CAMTC and separate Australian General Transport Companies were formed to take its place.[4]

Loutit acquired the title Officer Commanding No. 11 Lines of Communication Sub-Area. This fine example of officialese, bound to confuse anyone outside the military, meant he had jurisdiction over all the troops and staging camps between Alice Springs and Larrimah. He was promoted to Brigadier in August 1942 and remained the senior army officer in Alice Springs until December 1944. For five years his convoys of army trucks ran up and down the new road to Larrimah. They transported thousands of troops and supplies, which were then unloaded onto the narrow-gauge North Australian Railway. The first of these troops was a Western Australian contingent of the ill-fated 8th Division. The 2/4th Machine Gun Battalion passed through Alice Springs in March 1941 and ended up in Singapore before it fell to the Japanese.[5] Nearly 200,000 troops ultimately passed through the town in the course of the war.[6]

The town's civilian population was 600 in mid 1941 but it jumped to nearly 1000 in 1942, following the bombing of Darwin. There were 2500 troops in town by January 1942 but there could be as many as 5000 on any one night during that peak period of the war.[7] The army took over the new 60-bed hospital, renaming it the 109 Australian General Hospital. A large number of extra beds were set up in tents when fear of a Japanese invasion was at its height.

A number of other buildings and houses around town were commandeered by the army. The Australian Inland Mission's nursing home Adelaide House was one of them. It accommodated sisters of the Australian Army Nursing Service. The Johannsen family was forced to live out bush at their mica mine in the Strangways Range when the army took over their spacious house in Todd Street to accommodate more nursing staff. Norman and Constance Cain's house at the top end of Todd Street became Loutit's headquarters. In June 1941 the Methodist Church completed Griffiths House, its new hostel built for bush children attending school in town. The church immediately handed it to the army for use as a servicemen's club.

The Northern Territory's civil administration moved from Darwin to Alice Springs in March 1942.[8] Administrator Abbott was still in charge of civilian matters but Loutit called the shots because the army controlled the movement of goods and people in and out of the Territory. The two did not enjoy a good working relationship. Loutit was authoritarian and rubbed many people up the wrong way, including a lot of his own troops who were frustrated and resentful at being forced to spend the war in the Northern Territory rather than posted overseas. Loutit may have preferred an overseas posting but he tackled his role of army supremo with vigour and determination. The town clearly was to his liking because he returned in 1947 with his wife and established a general store in Todd Street.

The wartime upgrade of the historic OT line

The OT line was no longer carrying international traffic when war broke out in 1939 but it was still a key component of Australia's internal communication network. The cables laid across the Indian Ocean in 1901 and the Pacific in 1902 cut significantly into the flow of traffic on Australia's connection to Singapore. It was no longer needed by 1935 when sleepy Darwin's historic cable office was closed.[9] The 1871 cable and the duplicate laid in 1879 remained intact but copped a hammering as Japanese forces swept through Singapore, Indonesia and Timor early in 1942, pummelling buildings and installations.

The overland telegraph line acquired renewed importance when war broke out and steps were taken to protect and upgrade this vital link between Australia's north and south. The days when messages were repeated by hand at regular intervals along major telegraph lines were long gone. Telegraphists tapped away on keyboards connected to high-speed transmitting apparatus. Called teleprinters, they first appeared in Australia in the 1920s. The messages were automatically decoded at the receiving end of the line and printed onto a paper telegraph form. Teleprinters were installed at Alice Springs and Darwin in 1938, the final advance on the OT line before war broke out in Europe in 1939.[10]

People in the Northern Territory were still unable to make a long-distance phone call at the start of the war. The old British-made phonopores located at various points along the OT line had a very limited range.[11] Alice Springs had a local phone network with 45 subscribers in May 1940 but its residents had to write a letter or go to the expense of a telegram if they wanted to contact someone interstate. This was clearly a concern as fear grew that Japan might enter the war and threaten British, Dutch, American and French colonies lying to Australia's north.

In 1941 the Commonwealth Government took action to rectify the situation by installing a second copper wire on the OT line so it could support a three-channel system between Darwin and the town of Gladstone, north of Adelaide: one channel reserved for telegraph traffic and the other two for long-distance telephone calls.[12] A radio telephone system was quickly set up in Darwin in March–April 1941 as an interim measure until the extra wire could be installed along the full length of the OT line. It provided the first regular speech circuit into Darwin from the southern and eastern states but it lacked the secrecy essential for wartime communication. It continued operating until Japanese bombers destroyed the equipment housed in the Darwin Post Office on 19 February 1942.[13] The PMG and the Australian Army Signals Corps began stringing up the new copper wire on the old telegraph poles in July 1941. They finished in December, two months before the first Japanese hit on Darwin, but it wasn't until March 1942 that all the necessary equipment was installed and the system operating.

The OT line had operated on a simple direct current system with an earth return and multiple repeater stations when it opened in 1872. By 1941, communication had advanced; now Alice Springs was the only relay station needed. Its automatic repeating instruments were reliable and there was no difficulty working duplex at 100–120 words per minute between Darwin and Adelaide with machine telegraphy.[14] However, the new carrier system required more frequent, automatic repeating to ensure intelligible transmission of telephone conversations. So, new repeaters were installed at Pine Creek, Larrimah, Newcastle Waters, Tennant Creek, Barrow Creek, Alice Springs, Finke, Oodnadatta, Marree and Port Augusta, along with the other equipment necessary for the operation of carrier systems. None of the old telegraph stations were used to house this new equipment. Prefabricated steel buildings, manufactured by the Sidney Williams Company, were erected instead, except at the major centres Tennant Creek, Alice Springs, Oodnadatta, Marree and Port Augusta where it was installed in each town's post office. Power came from lead acid batteries, charged by windmill-driven generators, backed up by diesel generators when there was insufficient wind.[15] The repeater stations Charles Todd's men had built at Katherine, Daly Waters, Powell Creek and Barrow Creek were now redundant, like the Alice Springs telegraph station, and put to other uses.

By the start of 1942 the new road from Alice Springs to Larrimah was causing headaches for convoy drivers. The gravel surface had broken up along many sections after 12 months of pounding from the army's trucks, it was corrugated, had deep patches of bulldust, and flooded badly after rain where grading had lowered the road surface below the level of the surrounding land. It clearly needed to be built up, re-gravelled and sealed with bitumen. A start was made on this in April 1942. There were many stretches where the road workers knew they would have trouble finding hard stone to crush into aggregate for the bituminous surface. So, pre-mixed material would have to be used and carted along the road, often long distances. Two heavy-duty Barber Greene bitumen-aggregate mixers, with conveyors, were imported from the USA, the first one being delivered to Alice Springs at the end of July 1942.

The Victorian Country Roads Board took on the job of rebuilding the road, supplemented by men from the recently formed Civil Construction Corps. It was an arm of the Allied Works Council, the Commonwealth body that prioritised strategic works across the country. However, the job proved too big for the Victorians. The South Australian Highways Board, the Commonwealth Department of the Interior and a company of the army's Royal Australian Engineers were co-opted to work on some stretches. The sealing of the road was completed in December 1943.[16]

The steady military build-up warranted more telephone capacity by this time and so army personnel erected additional copper wire between Darwin and Alice Springs. Crossarms had to be added to the old poles and bracing so they wouldn't buckle under the increased weight. The sealed road ran east of the original telegraph route in a number of places between Powell Creek and Larrimah. New iron poles with wooden crossarms were installed adjacent to the bitumen on these sections to make line maintenance easier.[17]

Remembering Mr Stuart

The OT line story starts with John McDouall Stuart's three epic journeys through the centre of Australia in the early 1860s. Its final chapter was written in the early 1940s, as new technology replaced old. The old wires were still singing in 1943 but there were many places where they diverged from the route Charles Todd's surveyors originally pegged. Most of the old iron poles were still standing but crossarms supported tonnes of extra wire. Todd's old repeater stations had been put to other uses.

A small stretch of the old line has been reconstructed north and south of the Alice Springs telegraph station. There's another rebuilt section alongside the old Ghan line south of the airport. Outback travellers venturing off the beaten track in fancy four-wheel-drive vehicles can still find remnants of the old line in a few, out-of-the-way places such as Crown Point, a day's drive south of Alice Springs. The rest has passed into history.

Fortunately the man who paved the way for Todd's great line is not forgotten. Today's busy Stuart Highway honours him, even though it doesn't exactly follow his track to the north coast. A search of government files in the National Archives will unearth oodles of information about the highway's construction but its actual naming was shrouded in mystery until fairly recently.

The issue was addressed by ex-serviceman Alex Tanner in his excellent 1995 book *The Long Road North*. He spent the war years based in Alice Springs with 148 Australian General Transport Company (AIF). Tanner tells the story of the Stuart and Barkly highways, from bulldust to bitumen, and the army convoy system. He wrote: 'In April 1944 the North/South road was named the 'Stuart Highway' recognising the journeys of John McDouall Stuart ...' This elicited a letter on 31 October 1995 from Bruce Strong, the National Trust's research officer in Alice Springs. He respectfully queried the date and Alex Tanner responded promptly. He'd checked through his source material and realised he'd made a mistake. He wrote to Bruce Strong:

> Without a doubt I was quoting my 'April 1944' date from a source which
> I deemed reliable ... Notwithstanding, I have gone through file after file

of my research but cannot locate it ... As a last resort I recalled two files handed me only a few months ago by a near resident, Brian Hastings, now well into his 80s and in frail health. Brian was an Intelligence Captain at the time of these reports, later Major. I was shattered and upset to note that in September 1942 he makes reference to the 'Stuart Highway'. I can only express regret ... I have spoken with Brian this morning. He recalls being requested to produce the strip maps for the specific information of the Governor-General, both the date on his map and the visit of the G.G. were July 1941.

Bruce Strong had discussed the matter with Keith Mooney-Smith, an expert on local history employed by the NT Department of Lands, Planning and Environment. Keith sent him a note on 16 November 1995 saying:

Recently, when searching my records for you in respect of the naming of the Stuart Highway, I came across the reference to the *Military Roads Ordinance No 2 of 1942* and thought that it may be interesting. I have since obtained a copy and it may be of interest since you will notice that the name 'Stuart Highway' appears in the definitions.

Bruce Strong was able to establish that Governor-General Lord Gowrie proposed the name Stuart Highway when he visited the Territory in July 1941. C.W. Williams, Engineer in Charge of the Stuart and Barkly Highways, said so in March 1944:

The Stuart Highway closely follows the route taken by the explorer McDouall Stuart, and the Governor-General Lord Gowrie gave the name Stuart to the Highway on the occasion of a visit to the Territory a few years ago.

The wartime Administrator of the Northern Territory, C.L.A. Abbott, confirmed this in his 1950 book *Australia's Frontier Province*, writing 'in 1941, at the request of the then Governor-General, Lord Gowrie, I named the Stuart Highway'. The first official reference to the name was the *Military Roads Ordinance No 2 of 1942* located by Keith Mooney-Smith.[18]

War and the Aboriginal people

World War II was truly a transformative time for Central Australia, not just spurring significant improvement in facilities but also leading to a major shift in black–white relations.[19] Racist attitudes and practices persisted well after the war and many years passed before Aboriginal people were granted all the rights enjoyed by white Australians. However, the seeds of change were well and truly planted as white and black interacted in ways rarely seen before.

Many local blokes enlisted in the army, including former inmates of the Bungalow. Alec Kruger was one of these. His employers, the Bloomfield family of Loves Creek station, tried to stop him but Alec was determined to escape working conditions that he considered exploitative. The final straw was when he met with Native Affairs Branch patrol officer Gordon Sweeney and learned that the Bloomfields had not been paying money into a trust fund for him, as they were supposed to do.[20] Alec did not serve overseas but worked at a number of places up the track including Darwin Harbour. Other blokes of mixed descent who joined up were Gordon Abbott, Jack Ansell, Harry Bray, Alex and Mort Conway, Mick Costello, Bill Dempsey, Roy Dubois, Henry Ford, Jack Hughes, Herbie and Mick Laughton, Harold and Milton Liddle, Alec McDonald, Jack Neal, Gordon Perkins, Henry Ross, Jimmy Smith, Don Stokes and Alec Turner.

Living under canvas was no paradise but life in an army camp was pretty comfortable compared to what they were used to. They had plenty of food in their bellies and money in their pockets. Their movements were no longer restricted by the provisions of the Aboriginals Ordinance. They could go where they pleased when they were off duty, including the army's wet canteens for a bottle of beer and cheap cigarettes. The average Australian's respect for other races and cultures still left a lot to be desired but they found the camaraderie of the army preferable to the prevailing social culture prewar. They were confronted by the racist attitudes of some soldiers but found many others who treated them like other blokes.

The military build-up generated a significant demand for Aboriginal workers in the Territory. People from the bush joined the workforce and received training like never before. The old telegraph station played a key role in this, becoming a camp for the army's native labour gangs. For the first time in their lives, many Aboriginal people found themselves being treated like equals, or at least better than had previously been the case. They were paid for their labour in cash, not just flour, tea, sugar and tobacco. Their pay was less than that of whites but being able to spend it as they wished was a dramatic change from the past. Living conditions on cattle stations continued to be fairly primitive; the army set a higher standard. This raised self-esteem and expectations, just as it raised the ire of many white Territorians who feared things wouldn't return to the prewar status quo, once hostilities were eventually over. The war cast a shadow over the Territory but it also ushered in a new era.

The army's native labour gangs

As the number of troops built up in Alice Springs in the latter part of 1940, so did pressure to push all the Aboriginal fringe dwellers to localities further afield. Jay Creek was touted as the best place but the Aboriginal people weren't so keen on that idea. Alice Springs was part of the Arrernte people's ancestral lands and they had no desire to move away. Procuring an adequate water supply had long been a problem at Jay Creek. A decent amount of rain fell during the summers of 1938/1939 and 1939/1940 but the centre of Australia was entering another dry period by late 1940. In fact much of the southern half of Australia was drought-affected during the war years.

Early in 1941 the government helped the Hermannsburg Mission set up a ration station for western Arrernte people at Haast Bluff and moved a number of aged and infirm out there. At the same time the Administrator declared an eight-kilometre strip of land either side of the north road a prohibited area.[21] This laid the way open to clearing the town of Aboriginal people, except those who were employed.

The Catholic Church had worked hard to establish its Little Flower Mission on the northern side of town but its days were numbered. Before long it was hemmed in by army trucks and tents. The church was advised it would be a 'working blacks' reserve. No rations would be distributed there in future. Those unable to work were to go to Jay Creek or back to the bush.

The Catholic bishop of the Northern Territory applied for a lease at Arltunga and a reserve of 220 square kilometres was approved. His stalwart missionary Frank McGarry drove out there in July 1942 with a group of Aboriginal people to begin well-sinking. A convoy of army trucks loaded with Aboriginal people, nuns, dogs, cats and everything portable from the Charles Creek arrived from town without warning in mid September. The Little Flower Mission was no more.[22]

There was plenty of work in Alice Springs for those who wanted it and the army looked to Aboriginal labour to meet its needs. On 20 May 1942, Colonel Loutit had advised E.W.P. Chinnery, the Director of Native Affairs:

> that the Army was in urgent need of adult aboriginal labor in Alice Springs to release one hundred or more soldiers whose time was at present was taken up in handling railway freight and in other general labour which could probably be performed adequately by aboriginals.[23]

The number of trains rolling into the town each week had risen to an unprecedented level, 124 a month at the height of the military build up in mid 1943.[24] Chinnery concurred and 93 Aboriginal workers were employed by the army in Alice Springs by the start of November.[25] Apart from loading and unloading trains, their work included digging slit trenches, collecting garbage, manning sanitation trucks, cutting firewood, tending vegetable gardens and managing livestock. The army also employed Aboriginal women as domestics doing washing, ironing and cleaning and assisting orderlies in the hospital. The former residents of the Little Flower Mission were still settling into their new home at Arltunga in late September 1942 when a military vehicle pulled up with an army officer on board seeking workers to go back to town. Twenty-three young Aboriginal men promptly climbed aboard his truck. Workers were also being recruited from the Hermannsburg Mission and the Jay Creek settlement.

Native labour gangs were formed at other places up the track, the major ones being Koolpinyah east of Darwin, Adelaide River, Manbulloo, Mataranka and Larrimah. There were smaller ones at Dunmarra, Elliott, Banka Banka and Barrow Creek.[26] The army had nearly 700 labourers on the payroll by the start of 1943, 155 in Alice Springs.[27] Additional men and women were engaged by civilian employers and there was work for stockmen as the cattle industry boomed with the new-found local market for its beef.

Their army supervisors soon learnt that most were good workers, capable of jobs requiring skill and initiative. As a result they progressed from menial work to tasks such as vehicle maintenance and assisting with major building projects and improvements to the town's infrastructure. This included the construction of a new powerhouse, completed in March 1943, and the development of an effective water supply system. Water tanks were installed on Billy Goat Hill in 1940 to supply the new hospital and nearby government houses but everyone else continued to draw their water from backyard wells and tanks. Virtually the whole town had piped water by 1946 with Aboriginal labour playing a role in this development. It was pumped from the town well east of Billy Goat Hill and two new bores the army sunk in 1942 on the northern side of Speed Street.[28]

At the beginning of the war, members of the army's native labour gangs were paid five shillings per week, plus rations and clothing, and given other items such as a towel, blanket, groundsheet, plate, mug and cutlery. Their dependents didn't get money but got the same issue of rations, clothing and other items.[14] This pay rate was set by Native Affairs Branch and well below the basic wage paid to soldiers and white workers. As time went on, some became disgruntled when they learned that other Aboriginal people were receiving more from some civilian employers.[30] Vince White, Deputy Director of Native Affairs, discussed a pay increase with Brigadier E.M. Dollery in March 1943 and they agreed to double the rate to 10 shillings a week.[31]

Dollery was the officer in charge of army administration in the Territory and the key figure in the deployment of Aboriginal workers and their living arrangements. The army's headquarters was relocated to Larrimah after the bombing of Darwin in February 1942 but later moved up to Adelaide River as the threat from the Japanese eased. Dollery was supportive of the Aboriginal people working for the army and wanted to improve their lot in life. He appointed Lieutenant F.R. Morris as Controller of Native Personnel, answerable directly to him. Morris was responsible for hygiene, sanitation, medical matters, quartering, pay, rations, clothing and equipment. He'd worked for Native Affairs Branch before enlisting. The army issued tents to accommodate people at the various labour camps. These were set up in rows, like any army camp, and inspected regularly. Many of the Aboriginal people enjoyed these arrangements and took pride in maintaining them.

Wartime use of the old telegraph station

The old telegraph station remained an Aboriginal reserve, under the control of the NT Administration's Native Affairs Branch throughout the war. Local people continued to call it the Bungalow even though its days as an institution were over. Native Affairs Branch was determined to hang onto it. Colonel Loutit had also eyed off the buildings – as a useful convalescent home for soldiers, but Director Chinnery opposed this, declaring 'it is the only suitable building for our purposes in Alice Springs'.[32] In July 1942 his deputy Vince White wrote to the Colonel setting out these purposes. The primary one was a camp for Aboriginal people employed by the army, along with their immediate dependents. But it also functioned as: a hostel for women employed in town by civilians but not provided with accommodation; an infirmary for Aboriginal people whose condition did not warrant admission to hospital; a clearing house for Aboriginal people discharged from gaol or hospital, pending their transfer back to the bush; a house of reception for 'incorrigibles' pending their transfer to places of detention; temporary accommodation for any more people of mixed descent being evacuated from the Territory; a distribution centre for rations. It also housed Native Affairs Branch staff and their families.[33]

While Natives Affairs would not countenance the idea of soldiers convalescing at the old telegraph station, the branch was happy for the army's pigs to make themselves at home on part of the reserve. In 1942, the Field Butchery Platoon was allowed to establish its piggery on the east bank of the Todd River at the spot known as Middle Park. The intention, initially, wasn't to supply the troops with breakfast bacon and ham sandwiches. Rather, it was set up as a way of disposing of the hundreds of tonnes of edible waste generated by the army kitchens.[34] The pigs no doubt enjoyed their wartime service but suffered a 100% casualty rate. Sadly, none of them were ever mentioned in dispatches. However, the pork production was so successful that piggeries, on a smaller scale, were established at the Barrow Creek, Banka Banka and Elliott staging camps.

The facilities at the old telegraph station were deteriorating by the 1940s but it remained a valuable asset, with its kitchen, dining room, washing facilities and the dormitory that had housed over 120 children. The Aboriginal people working for the army were under the control of Native Affairs outside of work hours. So the branch retained the positions of superintendent and matron, appointing Mr and Mrs Campbell after the McCoys went to South Australia in April 1942 to run the Balaklava Welfare Institution.

John O'Keefe replaced Campbell as superintendent in December 1943 but the position of matron was left vacant until April 1944 when his wife Olive joined him on the payroll. The couple, called Johnno and Keefie, were popular figures with the Aboriginal people. Johnno, an Irishman who migrated to America and then Australia in the 1920s, was a pastry cook by trade. He settled in Katherine in 1929 where he met nursing sister Olive Harvey in 1936. They ran the hotel at Birdum until the Japanese bombing of Darwin led to the evacuation of the north and moved on as their supply of customers shrank. They worked down the track for a while and then Native Affairs employed them at Balaklava, for three months in mid 1943, so the McCoys could take a break. A spell running the Jay Creek settlement followed. Then they were out of a job until the position of superintendent at the telegraph station became vacant.[35] They remained in Alice Springs for 20 years but the north eventually called them back.

Vince White reported to the Administrator in December 1943 that 'some 186 native employees are camped on the reserve at night'.[36] It wasn't home to every Aboriginal person working in Alice Springs. Private employers, such as Gus Brandt, who had a piggery on the north side of Heavitree Gap, and Jim Lackman who had a dairy on the south side, were expected to provide accommodation for their workers. There was also a camp through Heavitree Gap for the sanitary workers who collected the contents of the town's ubiquitous outdoor dunnies. The living conditions at these places drew the attention of Native Affairs.[37] However, the branch struggled with just a skeleton staff by 1943 to oversee matters across the Territory. Chinnery had gone south by this time as Commonwealth Adviser on Native Affairs. He left his deputy Vince White and a woman clerk/typist to run things, with only two patrol officers, Gordon Sweeney and Bill Harney.[38]

With accommodation in town at a premium, Native Affairs arranged in December 1943 to convert the former stationmaster's residence into two flats for staff and the former post and telegraph office into a third flat. Later the old battery room, a schoolroom during the 1930s, was also converted into accommodation. A stove and kitchen were installed in the southern end and partitions erected to create a bathroom. This became the home of Gordon Sweeney, his wife Olive and their three children. The couple had been Methodist missionaries in the north until 1940 when Gordon started work with Native Affairs. Former Bungalow inmate Alec Kruger remembered him as 'a nice, gentle fellow, well respected by the blokes'.[39] Author Jeremy Long has documented the history of the patrol officer service in the Northern Territory, saying admiringly of Gordon Sweeney:

> right through the war years he makes what reads now as heroic trips. Sweeney had no vehicle, he cadges rides on other peoples trucks, finds himself stranded and tries to arrange a lift by air or on somebody else's truck. Working from base in Alice Springs, he gets up to the Granites, into Western Australia, right across the Kimberleys, and returns to Alice Springs on army convoys which are going steadily up and down the road, but is occasionally stranded for days and weeks waiting for the next form of transport to turn up.[40]

None of the buildings at the old telegraph station had power and so residents like the O'Keefes and the Sweeneys relied on kerosene lamps at night; there were no fans for cooling during the long, hot summers. While the authorities maintained a policy of keeping Aboriginal people out of town unless they were employed, there was always a steady stream drifting into the place. They might need medical treatment or have to appear before the courts. A ragtag collection of humpies popped up alongside the river bed, north of the buildings, where they would camp briefly.[41] Maintaining adequate standards of hygiene was a constant challenge and NT Administration files reveal ongoing problems with the water supply from mid 1944 onwards. The pumping plant installed south of the buildings, in place of the 1914 windmill, was constantly breaking down and the well needed deepening.[42] The old place and its infrastructure were wearing out after more than 70 years solid service.

Tragedy struck one summer's afternoon in January 1945. The waterhole in the Todd River, that surveyor Mills named the Alice spring in 1871, was a popular swimming spot. Boys were cooling off there late that day when one, Valentine McGuinness, got into difficulty. He was a member of a well-known Darwin family of mixed descent, evacuated when war came. Billy Harney, the 15-year-old son of patrol officer Bill Harney, dived in to help him. He was able to support Val McGuinness in the water until others came to the rescue but got pushed under in the process. It took a while to locate his body in the muddy water and drag him out onto the bank. He could not be revived. Young Billy had been spending the school holidays with his father, who later became the first park ranger at Ayers Rock.[43] Bill senior was nearby at the time repairing a motor.

Rainbow Town

Rainbow Town sat by the river in the south-east corner of the town, not far from the hospital. It was home to most of the town's residents of mixed descent. The army wanted their motley collection of shacks wiped off the map but the people proved remarkably resilient, with some support from the patrician Administrator Abbott. Many of them were former inmates of the Bungalow.

Abbott saw the way open to developing an improved living area when the holders of two miscellaneous leases in the Heavitree Gap area gave up their land for blocks south of the range. He wrote to Canberra in August 1943 seeking a budget allocation to build 22 homes for the people, at a cost of approximately £300 each. 'I think the Government should step in and help them,' he told his boss, the head of the Department of the Interior. His adversary Loutit, by now a brigadier, posted off a few choice words of his own the following January:

> There are many cases of deserving white people who should receive consideration prior to squandering of £6,600 on Niggers. Their place is in the Mission Stations or in Native Reserves outside the town boundaries ...[44]

Abbott's view prevailed in this instance, one of few wins in his ongoing battle of wills with Loutit. The money was eventually made available but it was war's end before progress was made. The modest complex became known as the Gap Cottages and a tightly knit community developed there in the 1950s. The bonds formed in the Bungalow ran deep.

24

Preserving the town's heritage

Noel Loutit left Alice Springs in October 1944 as army operations scaled down. Military control of the region continued but it no longer warranted a brigadier in command. Administrator Abbott returned to Darwin in July 1945 to re-establish civilian administration of the Territory.

The rapid change of the 1930s and early 40s accelerated in the postwar years. The old Alice was disappearing. New housing blocks went on sale on the east side of town in 1945. The following year, a kindergarten was added to the burgeoning school in Hartley Street and Mick Heenan opened a milk bar on the eastern corner of Gregory Terrace and Todd Street. It would figure in Nevil Shute's famous book *A Town like Alice.* There were 2000 residents in 1947 when the first edition of the *Centralian Advocate* was printed and a progress association formed; and the Central Australian Football League kicked off with players losing a lot of skin on the grassless recreation reserve previously pegged out with army tents. ABC radio broadcasts began in 1948.

A new Alice was developing, with modern shopfronts and concrete footpaths replacing the corrugated iron and dust of the early days, and tourists replacing stockmen on the streets of town. In 1960 the town's population passed 5000.

The Bungalow Aboriginal Reserve
The Commonwealth Government continued to pursue a policy of separate development after the war, although assimilation of Aboriginal people into white society was the long-term aim. Attaining full citizenship was the new

deal announced by Minister John ('Black Jack') McEwen before hostilities broke out in 1939. Aboriginal people in the postwar Northern Territory would be given the skills and experience necessary for assimilation into white society but it would happen on government settlements and church missions away from the towns.

Most the big Aboriginal communities in Central Australia today were set up postwar. Yuendemu was the first, in 1946, established near Mount Doreen station in the north-west by former Catholic missionary Frank McGarry who joined the Native Affairs Branch in September 1944. Santa Teresa was next, in 1954, south-east of Alice Springs. Water shortages dogged the people at Arltunga from the day the army trucked them out there in 1942. When the Catholic Church began looking for a better location, the Commonwealth 'generously' leased the Eastern Arrernte a chunk of their own ancestral lands a two-hour drive from town. Warrabri and Papunya further afield were developed between 1956 and 1958, and the Petermann Ranges settlement Docker River between 1967 and 1968.

The intention, in each case, was to provide better living conditions, health services, education, vocational training and work. No one sat idle, but the control of people's lives continued with each settlement and mission administered by a white superintendent and supporting staff. There were more than 20 of these communities across the Territory by the late 1960s. Living in a controlled environment, after millennia on the move, created new problems and tensions. This was especially the case where people of different language groups were forced to live together some distance from their traditional homelands. Nonetheless, nostalgia for these postwar years periodically surfaces, from both black and white Territorians.

The old telegraph station took on a new role with the departure of the army. Now called the Bungalow Aboriginal Reserve, its primary function, in the eyes of officials, was a bulk store and ration depot to service government settlements in Central Australia. Sections of the original 1872 building and the 1932 children's dormitory became storerooms and additional sheds were constructed. The reserve also functioned as an Aboriginal camping area, replacing those on the fringes of the town prewar. Aboriginal people required a pass to visit Alice Springs and were supposed to return to the bush afterward.

The government was determined to stop the drift of Aboriginal people into the Territory's towns but that was easier said than done. The people were interested in the benefits the towns had to offer, while maintaining their strong ties with their own country. Many had worked for the army or civilian employers during the war and wanted to continue having the privileges they saw white people enjoying.

In 1951, the *Centralian Advocate* reported the case of Agnes Murphy, apprehended after visiting a sick relative in the hospital without a permit and convicted without penalty but ordered to pay 10 shillings court costs. Aboriginals Barney and Frosty were also caught in town and each fined 10 shillings plus 10 shillings costs. Another case before the police court that week was an unnamed man who walked into town from the Bungalow on Saturday night with insufficient funds to get into the pictures. He was outside trying to borrow cash when he was arrested. This man was convicted without penalty, the court directing Native Affairs to ensure that campers on the reserve have enough money to buy a ticket, as well as having an entry permit.[1]

The popular Johnno and Olive O'Keefe continued as superintendent and matron after the war but had their hands full. Maintaining an adequate water supply was an ongoing issue as the well deteriorated and the pumping equipment struggled to cope. The Aboriginal people hadn't got the message that the Bungalow Reserve was for short-term camping and it soon acquired a lot of semi-permanent residents – a challenge for the O'Keefes because the government made few improvements to the place, other than toilet facilities. The official fear was that if conditions were made too comfortable, then the people would never return to the bush.[2] Four huts were eventually built near the riverbank to provide basic sleeping accommodation but the majority of people lived in humpies made of scrap iron. There was a boiler room providing hot water for a few showers but otherwise no hygiene facilities were provided.[3]

The O'Keefes were committed to improving the lives of Aboriginal people but by 1949 were ready to move on. Olive was enticed to the Alice Springs

Hospital in April that year to set up the Native Ward.[4] She was revered by her patients and ruled the roost there in a loving way until 1962 when she and Johnno packed up and moved back to Katherine where'd they met. By 1949 the government had given in to the inevitable and recognised that the Bungalow Reserve was no longer a transit centre. Increasingly officials used the word settlement in correspondence files. A canteen was set up in September that year selling clothes, soft drinks and confectionery, and the 1930s schoolroom was renovated to once more base a teacher on site to cater for the increasing number of school-age children.[5]

By 1956 there were three teachers and 90 children attending school. Every morning the children were showered, exchanged their camp clothes for a school uniform and were given breakfast. At midday they were served a hot meal. The government built a kindergarten for the little ones, albeit from second-hand materials. Ten metres by five with a concrete floor, it had corrugated-iron sides a metre high and flywire to the roof. It was cold in winter and hot in summer, typical of most Alice Springs buildings in the 1950s.[6]

Public Enemy Number One

The McCoys returned to Alice Springs when the Balaklava Welfare Institution closed in 1946. Bill applied for a patrol officer position with Native Affairs. He lacked the educational qualifications required by the Commonwealth Public Service but was appointed an acting patrol officer anyway, primarily responsible for work in the town and placed in charge of the office. He was finally promoted to a permanent position in December 1952 and later assumed greater responsibility as District Welfare Officer. In this role he had the unenviable task of dealing with the regular complaints of local identity Miss Olive Pink, the town's outspoken, self-appointed champion for Aboriginal rights. It was not a harmonious relationship!

They were an interesting pair. Frank McGarry described the diminutive but capable McCoy as 'a nice chap, about the size of a threepence with a pipe that looks the size of ten shillings'.[7] The imperial and slight Miss Pink walked around the town dressed in a long, straight skirt, long-sleeved white blouse high at the neck and buttoned at the wrists, and white cotton gloves – plus a pith helmet in summer. This formal woman with piercing blue eyes never hesitated about putting people in their place.[8] She rates as one of Alice Springs's most colourful characters, evoking opinions ranging from eccentric to visionary; many found her difficult to get on with while others described her as kindly. It's probably best to describe her as complicated.

Miss Pink first ventured into Central Australia in 1930 on the newly completed railway. The 46-year-old was keen to see the desert in bloom after the long 1920s drought and observe the social conditions of Aboriginal people. She enrolled in a part-time anthropology course at the University of Sydney when she returned to New South Wales. Aiming to spend her days undertaking research in anthropology, she moved to Central Australia in September 1940 and spent the war years in the bush north-west of Alice Springs, regularly plying the rough and isolated Tanami Track in an old Chevrolet she had bought with money from a Quaker benefactor. One wag in town remarked that the only thing between Alice Springs and the Japanese in those days was Miss Pink and her goats. Drought eventually forced a permanent move to Alice Springs in 1946.

She advocated the cause of 'full blood' people believing they should have the right of self-determination and be free to live in their traditional manner. This view was at odds with prevailing attitudes and the government's assimilation policy. She would attend court and interrupt proceedings if she considered that tribal law and custom were not being taken into account. When fined for contempt she refused to pay, demanding to be gaoled instead. The head gaoler Phil Muldoon paid the fine himself rather than have her in his custody. She was a prolific letter writer and government files fattened as she fired off copious – often brutally blunt – correspondence and antagonised officials of the Native Affairs Branch who thought her demands were often unreasonable.

Miss Pink, called Public Enemy Number One by some, took a keen interest in the Bungalow Reserve. In 1951 the newly appointed Minister for Territories Paul Hasluck visited Alice Springs and she managed to get an appointment with him. One of the issues she raised was recreational facilities at the

Bungalow, or the lack thereof. She suggested that two recreation halls, a cricket pitch and tennis courts be built. When asked for a comment, Bill McCoy said he didn't think the Aboriginal campers at the reserve were quite ready for tennis. The acting director of Native Affairs asked him to investigate the feasibility of her suggestions. McCoy concluded that 'the provision of amenities would serve no useful purpose whatsoever until such time as adequate staff is provided to supervise activities of this nature'.[9] However, space was made for a small recreation hall: the western wing of the 1930s dormitory.[10]

In October 1953, Miss Pink received a letter from the acting director on another issue of concern to her. It said: 'You will now be aware that formal adult education classes have commenced at the Bungalow Aboriginal Reserve, and that both men and women are catered for.'[11] Aboriginal culture is ever-evolving and an excerpt from a 1959 quarterly report of the superintendent indicates the increasing sophistication of the Aboriginal people living on the reserve. The place was home to more than 300 Aboriginal people by then and a twice-weekly social evening had been introduced. He wrote that 'a number of wards have purchased records which they bring to the social evenings with them. Top tune to date is *The Pub with No Beer*'.[12]

Miss Pink outlived the Bungalow Reserve, dying in 1975 aged 91. She was buried near the Aboriginal section of the town cemetery on Memorial Drive. Headstones in that cemetery face east; her grave faces west. Her long-suffering but loyal friend Reg Harris said the 'old lady would appreciate the fact she is a rebel even in death'. Her fallings-out with friends and her other supporters, often over seemingly trivial issues or perceived slurs, are legendary. But despite her contentious views and blunt opinions, Miss Pink retained a circle of friends tolerant and faithful to the end. One of them was Paul Hasluck, long-serving Commonwealth minister and later governor-general.

Off to Amoonguna

Elvis Presley turned 19 on 4 January 1954. The unknown Tennessee truck driver walked into a Memphis recording studio, plucked a few dollars from his pocket to pay for studio time, and recorded his first two songs. Across

Australia communities were enthusiastically preparing for the visit of Queen Elizabeth II, the first by a reigning monarch. It was also a significant year for Aboriginal people in the Northern Territory. When the Native Affairs Branch was replaced by Welfare Branch in 1954, it was more than a name change. The reforming Minister for Territories Paul Hasluck was implementing the government's new deal for Aboriginal people, shifting from protection to assimilation. Restrictive policies were no longer to be justified on the grounds of race but rather on the basis of special needs.

In Alice Springs there was increasing concern about drink. In February 1954, Bungalow Superintendent J.C. Webb sent off his annual report. It included:

> Since legislation has been passed permitting halfcastes and other mixed bloods to consume alcoholic beverages, I could not fail to notice the increase in drinking by natives with the resulting fights and disturbances in camp.[13]

In mid year, Acting District Superintendent Ted Evans reported to Darwin that 'geographically, the Bungalow is a Town Reserve Superintendent's nightmare'. He decried 'the opportunities provided the "grog supplier" to peddle his wares', and added:

> it presents no problem to any unauthorised native to be on the Reserve for whatever period he wishes without being detected. Invariably the native who secretly resides on the reserve is an undesirable type insofar as Town areas are concerned. They are the drinkers, the loafers and the ringleaders in lawlessness and are responsible for the bad name often wrongfully applied to all town dwelling natives … A Town Reserve should be so situated as to reduce to the minimum the incentive in native residents to walk into the township at unauthorised times.[14]

Water was the other drinking issue. The files bulge with pages detailing attempts to rectify the problem, back to the mid 1940s: repairs to a pump that was regularly breaking down; clearing the well of debris and silt; installing a bigger engine; deepening the well. Attention then turned to securing funds to sink a 150-foot bore next to the well, but drilling only reached the same depth as the well. Test drills in other spots had the same result. The drillers were beaten by the very feature responsible for the original waterhole: impervious granite approximately 14 feet below the surface.[15]

A move was unavoidable. The existing facilities at the old telegraph station were crumbling and too close to town. Ted Evans drew attention to a site on the Todd River 13 kilometres south-east of Alice Springs. A new settlement there with an adequate water supply would allow vegetable gardening on a large scale, plus pastoral activity, providing work for a significant number of Aboriginal people.

At the end of 1954 the government announced plans to make the move. On 10 August 1955, new Director of Welfare Harry Giese approved the name Amoonguna: an anglicisation of *Imengkwerne*, the Arrernte name for the Emily Plain where the new reserve would be located. Boring was underway to locate a good water supply.[16] Responsibility for the big task of planning the new community largely fell to Bill McCoy, and he was up to the job.[17] The number of Aboriginal people living at the Bungalow was growing steadily and reached 370 by November 1957.

Everyone moved to Amoonguna on 27 June 1960.[18] Approximately 80 dogs were destroyed following the transfer. The Aboriginal people were advised to choose the dogs they wished to keep, within prescribed limits, and told the unwanted ones would be destroyed following their departure.[19] Many of the structures from the 1930s, 40s and 50s were demolished soon afterwards, including the dormitory built in 1932 to accommodate the children. Fittings that could be used elsewhere, such as water tanks, cupboards, sinks, baths and water heaters, were removed to Amoonguna or other settlements. However, the Welfare Branch continued using the place until a new central store could be built in town. It remained an Aboriginal Reserve until October 1962.

Three weeks before the move to Amoonguna, another chapter in the town's history closed. A fire destroyed its oldest building, the Stuart Arms Hotel, built in 1889.

The Alice Springs Telegraph Station National Park

Paul Hasluck officially opened the new Amoonguna settlement on Sunday 2 October 1960. He declared in his speech:

> There is not the least doubt in my mind about the future of the Bungalow site and the old buildings there. This is an historical site which, more than any other, enshrines the history of the town and the district ... The site must be dedicated in perpetuity as a public reserve and as a historical memorial and provision must be made to improve and maintain it ... We must make sure that the historical interest, the quietness and the beauty of this place are never damaged.[20]

A decade earlier the Alice Springs Progress Association had raised the issue of tourist access to the historic buildings and the original Alice Springs.[25] Moves to turn the site into a museum accelerated after a September 1954 visit by Mr W.G. Wright, vice-president of the National Trust of Australia, and prominent member of the Historical Society of Australia. He told the *Centralian Advocate* that he 'found so much local support when he mentioned the subject, it was obvious that many Alice people had felt the same way for a long time'. He said a submission was likely to be made to the government shortly.[22] Mrs Adela Purvis from Woodgreen station was the leading figure in this drive to preserve the town's heritage.

In November, she told the paper there were strong moves to form a division of the National Trust of Australia in the Northern Territory with headquarters in Alice Springs. She said the matter would be raised at the first public meeting for her John Ross Memorial Appeal in December.[23] It took a while but one was eventually formed at a well-attended public meeting in Alice Springs on 3 November 1958. Among its objectives was the establishment of a museum at the old telegraph station. Local solicitor Neil Hargrave, chairman of the Northern Territory Reserves Board since it was established in 1955, prepared a draft constitution and chaired the public meeting. He welcomed the formation of a community body to support and complement the Board's work. In December the newly formed Trust sought permission to go onto the Aboriginal reserve and inspect the buildings it hoped would be given to them to manage.

When Paul Hasluck officially opened Amoonguna, he said he would ask the NT administrator for proposals concerning the development and management of the old telegraph station. John Archer informed him there had been considerable correspondence with Mrs Purvis. He pointed out that the care, control and management of reserves was defined in the National Parks and Gardens Ordinance, under which the Reserves Board was constituted, and he felt the Board was doing a good job and recommended the reserve be placed under its control. The Board could deal with proposals the National Trust may have for museum exhibits.

Mrs Purvis and her fellow National Trust members continued to make their case. A deputation met with Minister Hasluck when he returned to Alice Springs in October 1961 and asked for the old telegraph station to be given to the Trust once the Aboriginal reserve was revoked. Hasluck was an astute politician, saying simply he 'commended the work of the Reserves Board and the National Trust and assured them of his full and enthusiastic support of their plans'.[24]

Mrs Purvis didn't win this one. The old telegraph station stayed firmly under government control. In October 1962, the governor-general proclaimed 'a new Reserve for historical and recreation purposes to be known as the Alice Springs Telegraph Station National Park'.[25] While not the outcome she'd sought, Mrs Purvis could be satisfied that her vision was being realised. The government had in fact done the National Trust a favour. It's doubtful they could have rebuilt and restored the place to the state it is today. They got their museum, in partnership with the Reserves Board, and Mrs Purvis continued to do what she did best: collecting and recording pioneer history with her husband Bob. This influential, well-educated and well-read couple laid the groundwork for the strong interest in history and heritage that is a feature of contemporary Alice Springs.

Adela Zimmermann (1907–1982) studied music at the Adelaide Conservatorium and travelled to Alice Springs to work as a governess at

Undoolya station. In 1934 she began teaching music, singing and drama at the Welfare Hall on stilts at the top end of Todd Street. She met Robert Purvis (c. 1885–1965) at a concert where she was singing and playing the piano. Father Percy Smith married them on 29 April 1936 in Myrtle Villa, the old cottage on Wills Terrace where he was living while awaiting his church to be built in Bath Street. Bob, a former cameleer and teamster with the lease for Woodgreen station, a small property north-east of Alice Springs on the Sandover River, was known as the 'Sandover Alligator' because of his prodigious appetite. However, the legendary stories of his eating habits do not do justice to a learned man with some training in law.

Adela Purvis wrote numerous articles on local history for the *Centralian Advocate*, *North Australian Monthly*, *Inland Review* and *Journal of the Royal Geographical Society of Australasia*. Her work has been criticised for relying on old timers' recollections and the occasional error. Most famous of these was her championing of John Ross as discoverer of the Alice spring in 1871 rather than William Whitfield Mills. Her son Bob said in 2002: 'She is remembered for the things she got wrong rather than the things she got right.'[26] What's easily forgotten is that she did her ground-breaking work in the isolated heart of Australia with no easy access to telephones, archives, libraries or, of course, internet. Her contribution should not be underestimated.

Restoration

The Northern Territory Reserves Board announced in June 1963 that it would restore the crumbling buildings to the period 1895–1905. This time span was well documented in photographs taken by Frank Gillen and Tom Bradshaw.[27]

Dick Drogemuller and his son Robert were busy constructing an archway at the entrance to the park using local stone in November 1963 when news came through that JFK was gunned down in Dallas, Texas. Dick was asked whether he would take on the job of restoring the buildings. He gave it a lot of thought and did some research but eventually declined. Another respected local builder John Taylor took it on, beginning with the post and telegraph office in 1966. The job was made easier with the priceless memories of Tom and Attie Bradshaw's eldest daughter Doris.

Her remarkable memoir *Alice On the Line* was published in 1965, vividly bringing back to life all the characters, black and white, from her family's time. The beautiful young woman who shines from her father's photos was a grandmother and living in Adelaide by the time her book was published. She never lost the spell of the inland. In 1922 she married Alex Blackwell, a veteran of the Great War who served as a stretcher-bearer on the killing fields of Europe with her brother Mort. She readily recalled how things used to be, how the buildings were furnished and the household objects and equipment they used. Doris and her sister Consie donated a number of family items to the Reserves Board, including their father's surviving glass negatives, his photography notebook and many original prints, plus his camera and tripod. Tom Bradshaw's extensive photograph collection and his daughter's book became the blueprints for the restoration work.

The sealing of the south road all the way to Adelaide was finished in 1987 boosting tourism to Alice Springs. That year the annual visitation to the telegraph station hit the magic 200,000 mark and locals embraced the place like no other in town. It was the most popular spot for picnics, birthdays, weddings – even funerals. Local school children might be seen in period costume learning about life in earlier days or exploring the local environment in the rocky hills around the old buildings.

In September 1994 grown-up children of the stolen generation, who lived there in the 1930s, gathered for a weekend, truly a joyous and healing celebration of their survival, achievements and love for one another. The old telegraph station, their Bungalow, stood proudly in the sun that day, silent witness to their stories and those of all the telegraph people. It is today what it has always been, truly the heart and soul of Alice Springs.

Postscript

An iconic town

Icon/ noun. 1. a devotional painting or carving. 2. an object of particular admiration. 3. a person who is seen as being closest to an admired stereotype [Latin from eikon 'image']

English writer Nevil Shute Norway moved to Australia with his family in 1950 and settled on a farm at Langwarrin, south-east of Melbourne. He wrote under the pseudonym Nevil Shute and his bestseller *A Town like Alice* was published that year. He'd visited Alice Springs in January 1949 gathering ideas for the book.

It's a gripping story of Englishwoman Jean Paget and Australian soldier Joe Harman captured by the Japanese in Malaya. Joe tells her about Alice Springs where he lived before the war. Surviving the horrors of captivity, she travels to Australia after the war to find him. In Alice Springs she learns he is managing a station in western Queensland at Willstown, a fictional community based on Burketown and Normanton. They marry and she invests her inheritance in the place, wanting to turn it into 'a town like Alice'. Very little of the book was based in Alice Springs but it evoked a lasting image.

The iconic town in the heart of the continent has changed considerably since 1949. No longer the small outback community romanticised by Nevil Shute it is instead a modern regional centre shaped by its remoteness, the magnificent scenery that envelops it, Aboriginal culture, and tourism. Those who come find a vibrant and intriguing community. The magic remains, beneath the trappings and frenzy of 21st century living.

Queen Elizabeth and her husband Philip on a whirlwind tour of Australia spent two nights in town in March 1963. An intuitive speechwriter penned these memorable words for her to say of the town:

> It has a magnetic effect on those who want more out of life than humdrum security and the tidy rules of a comfortable suburbia. After this visit, no one will be able to suggest to me that Central Australia is a dead heart. From now on I shall always look upon it as a living heart, beating with confident energy ...

Alice Springs has a strong sense of community and solidarity, while simultaneously being a fractured community. People proudly report, interstate and overseas, 'I come from Alice Springs.' There's a strong connection to the landscape: stark mountain ranges cut by scenic gaps and gorges, dry creek beds, daytime skies of vivid blue, and clear night skies with countless stars.

Alice Springs is a place of opportunity; everyone has the chance to excel and be noticed – in work, business, sport, art, music, culture and community life – and its people respect and honour those who have excelled.

The *Aboriginal Land Rights Act (NT)* of 1976 brought long-overdue justice for the Territory's first people and pushed the reset button on the Northern Territory story. They have confounded the experts and the prevailing wisdom of the 19th century that they were a dying race. Baldwin Spencer got it wrong. The Territory's first people continue to make their mark despite decidedly poorer health outcomes and life expectancy than the white population.

Contemporary Alice Springs is now very much the capital of Aboriginal Australia rather than the place described by Nevil Shute. Once denied entry by law, Aboriginal people now have an ever-increasing influence on the town. However, daily life continues to be a struggle for many Aboriginal people. Poor school attendance and limited prospects for employment, welfare dependency, grog and drug use are ripping the guts out of some communities.

Relations between Aboriginal people and white Australians have always been complex in the centre of Australia. The region has a complicated history and its people, black and white alike, are still living 'on the line' to some degree. Alice Springs has a strong sense of its history, of how things used to be. Where the iconic town goes from here depends on what we can learn from the past and our ability to create a new future, one that takes the best of our histories and weaves a new, life-giving culture into which we all can happily assimilate, not the culture-denying assimilation deemed in the best interests of the Bungalow children.

Stuart Traynor

Alice Springs Timeline 1860–1960

1860   Explorers John McDouall Stuart, William Kekwick and Benjamin Head are the first white men to reach the centre of Australia.

1870   Construction of the OT line commences with the first pole planted at Port Darwin on 15 September.

1871   Surveyor William Whitfield Mills follows the Todd River upstream from Heavitree Gap on 11 March to the waterhole Atherreyurre, naming it the Alice spring, after Charles Todd's wife.

Gilbert McMinn's men begin constructing the Alice Springs telegraph station in November.

Benjamin Clarke sends the first message south on 30 December.

1872   The Alice Springs telegraph station is completed in July.

The OT line is completed with the final join in the wires east of Frew's Ironstone Ponds on 22 August.

Charles Todd reaches the Alice Springs telegraph station on 28 August on his way south to Adelaide.

Communication with London finally becomes possible in October when the break in the cable north of Australia is repaired.

Work begins on a large store building at Alice Springs.

Exploring parties, led by William Christie Gosse and Peter Warburton, arrive in December and stay for the summer.

1873   Cattle arrive to stock Undoolya and Owen Springs stations in March and April respectively.

Alf Giles delivers a large flock of sheep to Alice Springs in May.

Telegraph stations begin official meteorological observations.

Gosse reaches Ayers Rock in July, climbing it with cameleer Kamran.

The Alice Springs staff is increased from two operators to three.

In the line's first full year, 9000 international messages are transmitted.

1874   Warburton's expedition reaches the north-west coast in January.

Kaytetye warriors attack the Barrow Creek telegraph station in February. Savage reprisals follow the deaths of James Stapleton and John Frank.

A stock reserve is declared around the Alice Springs telegraph station.

1875   Linemen dig a well on the riverbank at Alice Springs, equipped with a windlass, to provide cleaner water.

1876   Thomas Fergusson dies at the telegraph station on 19 January.

The blacksmith shop is built mid year.

1877	German pastors Hermann Kempe and Wilhelm Schwarz arrive in June to establish Hermannsburg Mission on the Finke River.
	Henry Barclay and Charles Winnecke arrive in November to establish a network of trigonometrical survey points in central Australia and accurately determine the border with Queensland.
1878	Alice Springs telegraph station becomes a post office in January with a mail delivery every six weeks.
	Charles Winnecke names Mount Gillen and Mount Johns in February.
	Pastor Louis Schulze reaches Hermannsburg in April with Dorothee Queckenstedt and Wilhelmine Schulz, the fiancées of pastors Kempe and Schwarz: the first white women to live in central Australia.
	John Mueller leaves the telegraph station late in the year and Ebenezer Flint takes his place as post and stationmaster.
1879	Wilhelmine Schwarz, wife of Pastor Wilhelm, gives birth to a daughter Karoline in March, the first white child born in central Australia.
	Mounted Constable John Shirley is posted to the telegraph station in April and sets up a police post near the waterhole at Middle Park.
	A monthly mail service is operating by the end of the year.
1880	Charles Winnecke completes a survey plan for the telegraph station at the end of the year showing three additional stone buildings: a post and telegraph office, a two-roomed house for the stationmaster, and men's hut (later the battery room).
1882	Ebenezer Flint and John Shirley explore east of Alice Springs in May for traces of Ludwig Leichhardt's lost expedition.
	John Shirley is transferred to Barrow Creek and Mounted Constable William Willshire takes his place at Alice Springs.
1883	Alice Springs records its longest dry spell since the telegraph operators began recording weather observations: 214 days without rain.
1884	There are 3400 sheep grazing at the telegraph station.
	The station gets a fourth operator.
	Mounted Constable Erwein Wurmbrand is posted to Alice Springs when William Willshire takes native police to the Top End for a year.
1885	A government well-sinking party led by Ned Ryan begins improving the water supply north of the Peake.
1886	David Lindsay finds red stones he believes to be rubies in the bed of the Hale River east of Alice Springs in March.
	Mounted constables William Willshire and Erwein Wurmbrand relocate the police camp to Heavitree Gap in April.
	The telegraph station's flock of sheep is reduced to a few hundred.
	Wesley and Effie Turton arrive from Mount Gambier, set up a bush store and begin establishing a garden east of Billy Goat Hill.
	Bushman Frank Hansen is the first person buried in the new cemetery at the telegraph station following his death on 1 November.
1887	Ebenezer Flint marries Florence Madeley in Melbourne in January. She is the first woman to live at the telegraph station.

Bush stores are operating at Horseshoe Bend and Bloods Creek.

Joseph Hele and Isaac Smith find gold at Paddy's Rockhole in April.

Graham Stewart surveys a railway corridor through Heavitree Gap from Strangways Springs to Burt Creek, north of Alice Springs.

Ebenezer Flint dies of rheumatic fever in July.

Joe and Cornelia Skinner move to Alice Springs to replace Flint.

1888   Joseph Stead builds a bigger residence for the stationmaster and the post and telegraph equipment is moved into the old house.

There are 260 miners on the ruby and goldfields by May.

David Lindsay surveys a town south of the telegraph station in October; it is proclaimed Stuart on 28 November.

Government geologist H.Y.L. Brown arrives in November, by which time Joe Harding has set up a store at Paddy's Rockhole.

1889   The first auction of land in Stuart is held in Adelaide on 31 January.

William Tietkens' Central Australian Exploring Expedition arrives at the end of February to prospect for minerals west of Alice Springs and takes the first photographs of central Australia.

Wesley Turton builds a brewery near the Todd River on lot 99.

Bill Benstead builds the Stuart Arms Hotel on lots 78 and 79.

Maud Dorothy Skinner is born at the telegraph station on 12 June, the first white child born there.

A well is dug at Heavitree Gap and a new police station built there.

1890   Frank Wallis opens a general store in town on lot 57.

Henry Swan and Charles Taplin arrive in July to investigate the ill-treatment of Aboriginal people in central Australia.

The Stuart cemetery is gazetted in August.

A fire at the telegraph station on 10 October destroys the barracks roof.

The railhead is extended to Angle Pole, north of the Peake, by the end of the year and a town called Oodnadatta is surveyed.

1891   A post office opens at Paddy's Rockhole on 1 January and the place becomes officially known as Arltunga.

Frank Gillen succeeds Joe Skinner early in the year.

The Pastoral Lands Commission visits Alice Springs in April.

South Australia governor Lord Kintore visits Alice Springs in May.

Frank Gillen JP commits Mounted Constable William Willshire for trial in Port Augusta on a charge of murdering two Aboriginal men at Tempe Downs in February. A jury acquits him in July.

Frank Gillen marries Amelia Besley in Mount Gambier in August.

The telegraph station is proclaimed a local court on 30 August and Frank Gillen is appointed special magistrate.

Frank Gillen is appointed a sub-protector of Aborigines in October.

1892   Bond Springs stockman William Lamb dies at the telegraph station on 18 February 1892 and is buried in the station's cemetery.

A separate flour shed and a cellar are added to the eastern and western ends of the telegraph station's store.

1893   Charlie South takes over the store on lot 57 in September.

1894   Fred Raggatt opens a general store on lot 77.

Fred Stone builds a new store for Frank Wallis on lot 84.

1893   Charles Todd is knighted KCMG in June.

The telegraph staff is increased to five telegraph operators.

1894   Walter Baldwin Spencer visits the telegraph station in July with the Horn Expedition and meets Frank Gillen.

Pastor Carl Strehlow arrives at Hermannsburg Mission in October.

1895   John Besley Gillen is born at the telegraph station on 31 January.

1896   Aboriginal elders gather at the telegraph station in September for a major ceremonial gathering that continues to January 1897. The elders allow Frank Gillen and Baldwin Spencer to observe and photograph it.

1897   Jerome Murif reaches the telegraph station on a bicycle in April, riding from Adelaide to Port Darwin.

Duplex equipment is installed at the Alice Springs telegraph station in November, increasing the capacity of the line.

Henry Luce discovers rich gold reefs at the end of the year at White Range, a little east of Arltunga.

1898   Frank Gillen officiates at the opening of a government battery and cyanide works at Arltunga in February.

In March the government announces a decision to add a better-performing copper wire to the poles of the OT line.

A fortnightly mail service commences between Alice Springs and Oodnadatta in April with two mailmen travelling simultaneously in opposite directions.

1899   The copper wire is strung to Alice Springs by mid April with the poles re-routed through Heavitree Gap.

Tom Bradshaw takes over from Frank Gillen at the end of April.

Attie Bradshaw joins her husband at the telegraph station in June with children Doris, Mort, Consie and Jack, plus governess Bertha Easom.

The rewiring of the OT line north to Darwin is completed by the end of the year and the last wooden poles replaced with iron ones.

1900   Don Bradshaw is born at the telegraph station on 15 November.

1901   Ernie Bradshaw dies of tuberculosis on 28 January and is buried in the telegraph station cemetery.

Posts and telegraphs become a Commonwealth responsibility.

Frank Gillen and Baldwin Spencer arrive in late April for a month of anthropology fieldwork. During that time there is a special voice hook-up to Darwin using an early telephone known as a phonopore.

Bishop of Carpentaria Gilbert White visits in July.

1902   The Federation drought is at its worst resulting in many deaths.

Gold is discovered near Winnecke's Depot in October; 300 people are there within a couple of months.

	Edna Almurta Bradshaw is born at the telegraph station on 27 December.
1903	The telegraph station becomes a money order office.
	Flooding rains in March and April end the Federation drought.
	A typhoid outbreak at Alice Springs and on the goldfields brings Dr Patrick Shanahan from Hawker for a couple of months.
	A post office begins operating at Winnecke in September.
1904	The police lock-up at Heavitree Gap becomes a public gaol in February.
1905	A thatched cottage is built for newlyweds Ernie and Bessie Allchurch before their marriage at Hermannsburg in March.
1906	A tennis court is built at the telegraph station and another town.
1907	A line is erected to the Wallis store in June and a phonopore is installed enabling communication with the telegraph station.
	Stonemason Jack Williams begins work on a new gaol in Stuart.
	Alan Todd Bradshaw is born at the telegraph station on 15 November.
	The first motor car visits Alice Springs in December.
1908	The Bradshaw family leave in August and are replaced at the telegraph station by John and Ida McKay.
1909	Jack Williams completes a new police station in town and the Stuart Town Gaol receives its first prisoners in September.
1910	Government workers complete a public well south of the town in February.
	The town is flooded in March – 147 mm of rain in 24 hours.
1911	South Australia relinquishes control of the Northern Territory and it becomes a Commonwealth responsibility.
	The Commonwealth adopts South Australia's 1910 *Northern Territory Aboriginals Act* and enacts its own Aboriginals Ordinance.
	Robert Stott arrives at the end of the year with his wife and family to take over from John Dow as senior police officer in central Australia.
1912	Baldwin Spencer arrives in Darwin to assume the role of Special Commissioner and Protector of Aborigines for one year.
	Ornithologist Samuel and his wife Ethel White visit the telegraph station in midyear on camels.
	Rev. John Flynn's Australian Inland Mission (AIM) is established in September to improve the lives of those in the outback.
1913	Baldwin Spencer presents his Preliminary Report on the Aboriginals of the Northern Territory in May, establishing the policy of taking children of mixed descent from their Aboriginal mothers.
	NT Administrator Gilruth and his chauffeur drive to Alice Springs.
1914	Ida Standley arrives in May after lobbying by the local people for a school to be opened in town.
	A home for 'half-caste' children is established behind the Stuart Arms Hotel and later becomes known as the Bungalow.
	A new well, windmill and water tank are installed significantly improving the water supply at the telegraph station.
	A six-weekly mail service to Powell Creek begins in December.

1915	Ida Standley assumes the extra responsibility of matron of the Bungalow in February, with Topsy Smith as houseparent.
	AIM nursing sister Jean Finlayson arrives to spend a year ministering to the local people.
1916	Fred Price takes over from John McKay in July as officer in charge.
1917	Mrs Price and her children join Fred at Alice Springs in the middle of a protracted drought.
1919	Flooding rains in December end the drought.
1920	Rev. John Flynn lets a contract to stonemason Jack Williams in April to build Adelaide House, Alice Springs's first medical facility.
1921	The first aeroplane lands at Alice Springs on 5 October with pilot Frank Briggs, Francis Birtles and George Bailey on board.
1922	Widespread bushfires devastate large areas of central Australia following very high rainfall the previous two summers. The region then slips into one of the worst-ever droughts, devastating native wildlife populations.
	Hemannsburg Mission's pastor Carl Strehlow dies at Horseshoe Bend on 22 October.
1923	South Australian Governor Sir Tom Bridges and Premier Sir Henry Barwell drive to Alice Springs from Oodnadatta with the Commonwealth's Commissioner for Railways Norris Bell.
	A through service with a sleeping car commences between Terowie and Oodnadatta in August and the train is labelled the *Afghan Express*.
1924	An exhausted Fred Price leaves the telegraph station with his family in April after eight years without a holiday. He dies on 12 August.
	Ernie Allchurch returns to Alice Springs to take over, accompanied by his wife Bessie and daughters Jessie and Maisie.
	The number of children at the Bungalow in town reaches 50.
1925	Sam Irvine pioneers a motor mail service to Alice.
	The Commonwealth reaches an agreement with South Australia in September to finally extend the railway to Alice Springs.
1926	A bill is presented to Commonwealth Parliament splitting the Northern Territory in two along the 20th parallel of latitude, 50 kilometres south of the Tennant Creek telegraph station.
	The town's first medical facility, Adelaide House, opens in June.
	Annie Meyers opens the Stuart Guest Home.
	In August, Wallis Fogarty Ltd starts a fortnightly transport service between Oodnadatta and Alice Springs using trucks.
	Travelling missionaries Erny and Effie Kramer open the Ebenezer Tabernacle, the town's first church, in time for Christmas.
1927	The first sod is turned on 21 January for the railway from Oodnadatta.
	John Cawood takes up the the new position of government resident from 1 March 1927, administering the Territory of Central Australia, with Vic Carrington as government secretary.
	Organised tourism to Central Australia begins with the Victorian Railways Reso Tour in August involving 80 people.

	The town's white population is approximately 90.
1928	Sergeant Stott retires to Adelaide in April with his wife Agnes.
	The mail service to Arltunga ends and its post office closes.
	The Coniston massacre follows the murder of Fred Brooks on 7 August.
	The Bungalow behind the pub is dismantled and a new children's home established at Jay Creek in November.
	Government offices are completed in November and the Residency is ready for occupation in December.
1929	The official inquiry in February finds the Coniston shootings justified.
	Erny and Effie Kramer relieve Ida Standley and Topsy Smith at the Jay Creek Bungalow in March. Francis and Jessie Thorne become the superintendent and matron in May.
	Pearl Burton replaces Ida Standley as the town's schoolteacher.
	Shell establishes a fuel depot in town.
	Phil Windle buys land in town to open its first garage.
	The last rail is laid at Alice Springs on the afternoon of 29 June with the first passenger train rolling into the town's new station on 5 August.
	A Catholic church is built in Hartley Street in time for Christmas.
1930	Drought-breaking rains fall in January and floodwaters wash away the new railway bridge across the Finke River.
	The town population reaches 560 early in the year.
	Gordon and Daisy Freeman replace the Thornes in April as superintendent and matron of the Jay Creek Bungalow.
	Harold Bell Lasseter and other members of the Central Australian Gold Exploration Company arrive in July to search for a fabulous gold reef he said he found in 1897.
	A purpose-built school building opens in Hartley Street in September.
	The Welfare Hall on stilts is built on Wills Terrace.
1931	The *Northern Australia Act 1926* is repealed on 11 June and Central Australia is no longer a separate entity.
	A bakery opens on Todd Street next to the Wallis Fogarty store and Hazel Golder's guesthouse is built nearby.
1932	Ernie Allchurch dies on 15 January following surgery in Adelaide.
	A new post office is officially opened in town on 25 January and the telegraph station closes after 60 years.
	A large dormitory is built and alterations are made to the existing buildings at the telegraph station so it can become a children's home.
	A gold rush to the Granites follows new discoveries mid year.
	The town's first bank, the ES&A, opens in October.
	The Barrow Creek Hotel opens in November.
	The Bungalow children move from Jay Creek to the old telegraph station and an area of 674 acres is declared an Aboriginal reserve.
1933	A 9-hole golf course is laid out near Spencer Hill.
	A gold rush to Tennant Creek is underway by August.

The town's name is changed from Stuart to Alice Springs on 30 August.

The Underdown family opens the town's second pub, the Alice Springs Hotel, in September.

1934   A galvanised-iron medical hut is completed on the edge of town early in the year and becomes known as the blacks' hospital.

Superintendent Freeman is suspended in February and gaoled in April for having sexual relations with one of the Bungalow girls.

Anzac Hill is named and a war memorial unveiled on Anzac Day.

A Methodist Church opens on Bath Street.

The town of Tennant Creek is surveyed and a pub completed in June.

Jack and Elsie Jones become superintendent and matron of the Bungalow.

1935   Maise Robb arrives in February to teach the Bungalow children and a second teacher, Grace Randall, is appointed in June.

1936   Church of England priest Father Percy Smith holds the first service in his new church on Bath Street in May.

Stott Terrace is added to the town plan.

The Aboriginal reserve surrounding the old telegraph station is enlarged enabling the Catholic Church to set up the Little Flower Mission along the Charles Creek early in 1937.

1937   The Underdown family builds an open-air picture theatre, called the Capitol, on Gregory Terrace opposite their pub.

Bill and Pat McCoy become superintendent and matron of the Bungalow.

A power station is built and electrification of the town commences.

Guinea Airways inaugurates a Darwin–Alice Springs–Adelaide service carrying passengers and airmail.

1938   Wally Boehm is appointed head teacher at the Bungalow and begins a process to provide the children with vocational training.

A government hospital is completed midyear and a new gaol built on Stuart Terrace.

The Hartley Street precinct is subdivided and the first house built at the corner of Hartley Street and Stuart Terrace.

A Lutheran church is built on Gap Road.

A high-speed teleprinter is installed at the Alice Springs Post Office, now the only repeater station between Port Augusta and Darwin.

1939   The Flying Doctor Base is built, along with a new Wallis Fogarty store.

Jim Rice builds a glass-fronted shop in Todd Street that becomes one of the town's iconic buildings until demolished amid controversy in 1988.

1940   An army advance party reaches town in September beginning the wartime military build-up.

Civilian authorities build a gravel road in 90 days to link the railheads at Alice Springs and Larrimah.

1941   The governor-general visits in July and names the Stuart Highway.

The Pioneer Theatre and Griffiths House are built.

A second copper wire is added to the existing poles of the overland telegraph line to enable the first long-distance telephone calls.

1942	The Alice Springs population swells to nearly 1000 civilians and 2500 troops in January. The Bungalow Half-caste Institution closes and the old telegraph station becomes the base for the Native Affairs Branch and accommodation for Aboriginal people employed by the army. A Field Butchery Platoon piggery is constructed at Middle Park, along with a powder magazine and military detention facility at Spencer Hill. The army moves the Little Flower Mission to Arltunga in September.
1943	A new power station is completed east of the Todd River in March. Sealing of the Stuart Highway to Mataranka is completed in December and all the way to Darwin the following year.
1945	The first housing blocks on the Eastside are put up for sale.
1946	Adelaide–Darwin public telephone channels become available. An octagonal kindergarten room is added to the school in Hartley Street. Mick Heenan's milk bar opens.
1947	The town's population reaches 2000. The first edition of the *Centralian Advocate* is published. The RAAF aerodrome south of town is handed over to civil aviation. The Alice Springs Progress Association is formed.
1948	ABC radio broadcasts begin.
1949	The first cottage at the Old Timers Home is opened.
1950	A teacher is appointed to the Bungalow Reserve to cater for the growing number of Aboriginal children. The town's first pharmacy opens. Nevil Shute's novel *A Town like Alice* is published.
1951	The School of the Air starts broadcasting from the Flying Doctor Base. Rev. John Flynn's ashes are interred under a Devils Marble west of town. The Alice Springs Memorial Club opens.
1953	A public library opens in Todd Street. A new housing development is built in the Gap area.
1954	The Alice Springs Higher Primary School's new complex opens at Anzac Hill with high school facilities. Pop Chapman's swimming pool opens in Railway Terrace in March. The Nathalie Gorey Kindergarten opens. The first *Ghan* drawn by a diesel-electric engine arrives in July.
1956	The Pioneer Theatre hosts the world premiere of *A Town like Alice*. The John Flynn Memorial Church is officially opened in May.
1957	A footbridge over the Todd River is completed in March.
1959	The Riverside Hotel, later renamed the Todd Tavern, is completed.
1960	The Aboriginal people at the Bungalow Reserve move to Amonguna. The first Alice Springs Show is held at Anzac Oval as part of the John McDouall Stuart centenary. A fire destroys the old Stuart Arms Hotel in June. The town's population reaches 5000.

Notes

PROLOGUE

1 *South Australian Advertiser* 16 April 1866 p. 3 and *South Australian Weekly Chronicle* 21 April 1866 p. 3

2 Susanna De Vries' 2005 book *Great Pioneer Women of the Outback* has a chapter devoted to Attie Bradshaw. She incorrectly states that Edward Allchurch was captain of the *Atlanta* [*sic*].

3 Bryan Bowman 1992 p. 14

CHAPTER 1 Connecting Australia to the world

1 The *South Australian Register* 29 August 1870 pp. 4–5 & 6 September 1870 p. 6, which list the men. The paper says they left from the 'survey-paddock behind the City Baths'. The baths were on King William Street, near the Torrens River, and demolished in the 1970s so the Adelaide Festival Centre could be constructed on the site.

2 John Hart led ministries in 1865–66, 1868 and 1870–71. See Margaret Dunn's 2004 book *The Captain, the Colonel and the Bishop*.

3 SAPP 29/1861 and SAPP 180/1861

4 Margaret Goyder Kerr p. 174 says a total of 665,886 acres.

5 Margaret Goyder Kerr p. 99

6 Elliott Whitfield Mills p. 15

7 Frank Clune pp. 11–13

8 Edgar Harcourt p. 8

9 Charles Todd 1886 p. 153

10 SAPP 127/1859 p. 2 has a letter dated 2 May 1859 from Lord Carnarvon at Downing Street to Governor MacDonnell saying Gisborne 'is now on his way to New South Wales and contemplates visiting several of the Australian Colonies'.

11 SAPP 127/1859

12 Charles Todd 1886 p. 148–149 says Adelaide and Melbourne were linked by inter-colonial telegraph in July 1858 and Melbourne to Sydney in October that year. SAPP 25/1862 p. 14 says Sydney and Brisbane were linked in November 1861.

13 SAPP 18/1860 p. 2 says the Australian colonial governments were asked to pay an annual subsidy to enable the company to raise the £800,000 needed for the submarine cables from Java to Brisbane. This was to guarantee the annual interest on the capital. Gisborne received an offer of £9625 pa from NSW, £13,000 pa from

Victoria, and the promise of a contribution from Tasmania and New Zealand but this fell short of the £35,000 total he wanted.

14   State Records SA GRG2 6/8 G–CO 276/1858 on 8 December 1858: cable to Sir Edward Bulyer Lytton Bart, MP, the Secretary of State for Colonies, at the Colonial Office in Downing Street.

15   Frank Clune p. 140

16   Frank Clune p. 67

17   Charles Todd's report dated 2 December 1858 is in SAPP 33/1858.

18   Alice Thomson p. 10

CHAPTER 2   Arguably Australia's greatest explorer

1   Jack Cross p. 4

2   *Australian Dictionary of Biography* says he left in 1853 but Mona Webster p. 60 says it was 1854 and he didn't return until 1856.

3   Mona Webster pp. 61–62 and Hans Mincham p. 52 who says John McKinlay sold John Chambers the Oratunga run in 1853. He adds on p. 181: 'Chambers and Finke applied for their first two mineral leases on 8 July 1857; later in the month they lodged claims for five more, and subsequently they applied for further leases.' These were later sold to the Great Northern Mining Company.

4   Mona Webster p. 73

5   Robert Gillen p. 55

6   John Bailey pp. 72–73

7   Mona Webster p. 103 and John Bailey pp. 87, 97

8   Mona Webster pp. 103–105 and SAPP 148/1959

9   Frank Clune p. 73 says 'the Ministry was too mean to sanction the expenditure' and, on p. 76, refers to them as 'penurious and parsimonious'. He also says Police Commissioner Peter Warburton was jealous of Stuart and exerted influence to prevent him being given money.

10   Mona Webster pp. 87–90 and Hans Mincham pp. 181–183

11   Hans Mincham pp. 74–76 says he left in October and got back to Adelaide two days after Christmas. Frank Clune p. 78 says he set off in September.

12   MacDonnell's Despatch 360 to the Duke of Newcastle, Secretary of State for the Colonies, dated 11 January 1860. It is in the appendix to SAPP 83/1860. See also Mona Webster p. 90 & Hans Mincham p. 183

13   SAPP 234/1862

14   Jack Cross p. 7 says MacDonnell was recalled in 1862 because of his connection with the scandal.

15   See Valmai Hankel's introduction to *John McDouall Stuart's Explorations, 1858–1862*, published by the Friends of the State Library of South Australia in 2001. It is a reprint of South Australian Parliamentary Papers 119/1858, 65/1861, 169/1861, 219/1862 and 21/1863–1863. She managed to locate an unpublished epitome of Stuart's expeditions in which he wrote: 'I have named this Grand Centrepoint after my former much esteemed commander Capt. Sturt, but the Governor-in-Chief, on my return to Adelaide, observing it on my map, said, not so, it shall be named Mount Stuart.' It's in the archives of the Royal Geographical Society, London, along with those of the Institute of British Geographers. The

reference is JMS 13/125. Valmai Hankel says this epitome almost certainly formed the basis of a talk Stuart presented to the Royal Geographical Society in London in November 1864.

16 Mona Webster p. 250

17 Alan Powell 2000 pp. 75–76 says a special meeting of the Pastoral Association of South Australia on 19 November 1962, a month before Stuart returned to Adelaide, saw members declare that this land rightly belonged to South Australia because of the efforts of Stuart and other explorers from the colony.

CHAPTER 3   Queenslanders get the rough end of the pineapple

1 SAPP 229/1862

2 Frank Clune p. 113, SAPP 236/1862 and SAPP 191/1884 p. 140

3 SAPP 54/1967 and SAPP 15/1868–69 pp. 10–11

4 Henry Parkes led several New South Wales governments. In those days the position of leader was called prime minister rather than premier.

5 SAPP 18/1867 pp. 5–6 and Edgar Harcourt p. 40

6 SAPP 15/1868–69 pp. 50–53

7 Edgar Harcourt pp. 23, 29–30 and Frank Clune p. 135

8 http://www.atlantic-cable.com

9 SAPP 118/1869–70

10 SAPP 41A/1868–69 p. 2

11 SAPP 118/1869–70 pp. 15–17

12 SAPP 24/1870–71 p. 1

13 SAPP 24/1870–71 p. 1, SAPP 191/1885 p. 141, and Charles Todd 1886 p. 155

14 See letter by J. Boothby, Under Secretary in SAPP 24/1870–71 p. 1

15 SAPP 24/1870–71 p. 2

16 Letter from H.B.T. Strangways to H.W. Varley, Mayor of Glenelg, 7 February 1906, South Australian State Library D8339

17 SAPP 24/1870–71 p. 3

18 Edgar Harcourt pp. 49–50

19 SAPP 63/1870–71 p. 66

20 Anderson was skipper of the ship *Great Eastern* when it successfully laid the Atlantic cable in 1866. He became a director of the BAT Co. and later of John Pender's amalgamated cable empire called the Eastern Extension, Australasia and China Telegraph Co.

21 Charles Todd 1886 pp. 173–174

22 SAPD 1870–1871 pp. 202–210 properly called 'Debates of the Houses of Legislature During the First Session of the Sixth Parliament of South Australia from May 27 1870 to January 13 1871'. The bill is on pp. 55–56 of SAPP 63/1870–71. Mervyn Hartwig p. 144 says 'By 16 June the Bill had passed both Houses and received the Governor's assent'. He quotes Act No. 2 of 1870. Frank Clune p. 163 incorrectly says that on 18 June an Act of Parliament was rushed through.

23 SAPP 131/1870–71 p. 6

CHAPTER 4 A positive and popular man

1   The quote from Sir William Bragg is from George Symes & Brian Ward 1980–1981 p. 72

2   Different sources give different numbers of camels. The entry for 2 February 1871 in the *Diary of Thomas Frederick Smith* mentions 140 camels.

3   Mervyn Hartwig p. 191 and Alfred Giles 1926 p. 38

4   Edgar Harcourt p. 53

5   *Adelaide Observer* 9 July 1870 p. 5 says under the headline 'The Overland Telegraph': 'We understand that, in response to Mr Todd's call for tenders for the construction of the overland telegraph to Port Darwin, six offers have been received to construct various portions of the line. There is one tender at least for the whole distance ...' Under the same headline on 16 July 1870 p. 8 it says: 'We are in a position to state that the Government have resolved on accepting Messrs. Darwent and Dalwood's tender for constructing the northern end of the overland telegraph – about 500 miles, and Mr. J. Rounsevell's for the southern portion – 1200 miles. The whole of the line will, in fact, be carried out by these two tenderers ...'

6   SAPP 60/1871 pp. 1–2 and SA Parliamentary Debates for 26 July 1870 in 'Debates of the Houses of Legislature During the First Session of the Sixth Parliament of South Australia from May 27 1870 to January 13 1871' p. 269

7   SAPP 60/1871 p. 7

8   Peter Donovan 1981 p. 87

9   NT Reserves Board file 40/2 folio 8 in the Parks & Wildlife archive building, Alice Springs

10 SAPP 60/1871 p. 5

11 SAPP 191/1884 p. 142

12 *Adelaide Observer* 27 August 1870 p. 6 covers the departure of the men for Darwin on the SS *Omeo* late on the previous Saturday.

13 SAPP 60/1871 p. 1

14 See the entries for 22 & 23 November 1870 in the *Diary of Thomas Frederick Smith*. Peter Taylor p. 65 says he died shortly after reaching Adelaide but this is incorrect. He lived another 15 months. The *South Australian Advertiser* 4 March 1872 p. 2 carried a notice of his death at his home in Adelaide the previous day.

15 Elliot Mills pp. 24–25 has Charles Todd's letter to Mills, written at the Peake on 25 November 1870, after Beckwith left for Adelaide.

16 *South Australian Register* 29 August 1870 pp. 4–5 & 6 September 1870 p. 6

17 SAPP 191/1885 p. 143

18 Alfred Giles p. 62 and the entry for 25 March 1871 in the *Diary of Thomas Frederick Smith*.

19 Christine Stevens p. 20

20 Christine Stevens p. 18 and Samuel Stuckey's letter in *Adelaide Observer* 2 May 1891 p. 27

21 Entries for 13 August 1871 and 4 September 1871 in the *Diary of Thomas Frederick Smith*.

22 Mervyn Hartwig p. 201, quoting Todd's diaries, says Todd 'consigned to Harley Bacon 1,933 sheep that had been purchased from stations to the south, many

of which were to become the first sheep overlanded into the Northern Territory, decreeing that party A should have 240, B 290, C 370, D 450, E 550 and Bacon and his assistants 33 for the trip'.

23 Ralph Milner gave these numbers in the article 'Intersecting Australia, Adelaide to Port Darwin. New Zealander's Adventure Sixty Years Ago. First Crossing with Stock' on p. 8 of *New Zealand Evening Star* 24 August 1927. However, Arthur Ashwin p. 48 says there were 7000 sheep.

24 Arthur Ashwin p. 48 says 'At the time it was understood the then South Australian Government had offered a reward for the first 1,000 sheep or 100 head of great cattle delivered from South Australia to Port Darwin overland ... All the men engaged with Ralph Milner at 25s. per week each, and were to have had half the reward divided amongst them, but the Government offer was cancelled when the party were half-way over and the reward was never paid'.

25 Charles Todd 1886 p. 155

26 G.W. Symes 1956–1957

27 Charles Todd's instructions to Ross 7 July 1870, Mervyn Hartwig p. 196 and W.L. Manser p. 53

28 *Diary of Mr. John Ross, Leader of the Overland Exploring Party, 1870–1871. Adelaide Observer* 27 August 1870 has a letter from Ross to Todd headed '13 August Humbum Station Mount Margaret' saying he got there on 10 August. The station was often called Humbum or Umbum, because the original homestead was located on Umbum Creek.

29 Alfred Giles 1926 pp. 25–26

30 Diary of Thomas Frederick Smith

31 SAPP 191/1884 p. 144 and John Ross's diary. Both Frank Clune p. 187 and Mervyn Hartwig p. 202 incorrectly say they met at Mount Margaret/Umbum.

32 Charles Todd's second set of instructions to Ross written at the Peake on 15 November 1870.

33 *Diary of Thomas Frederick Smith* says Todd got to the Peake on 7 November and left on 23 November. However, Alfred Giles 1926 p. 38 says Todd arrived on 10 November 1871. Mervyn Hartwig p. 202 says he headed back to Adelaide on 26 November. Frank Clune pp. 185–186 says the first of the work parties arrived on 28 October. Alfred Giles 1926 p. 38 states: 'The first surveyor to arrive with his party was Mr. Gilbert McMinn, and he made his temporary camp on the Blyth Creek, nine miles south of the Peake. This was on the 2nd November.'

34 John Ross's diary says they left on 16 November. See also Alfred Giles 1926 p. 37. However, Charles Todd says 18 November on p. 144 of SAPP 191/1884.

35 John Ross's diary entries for 1–3 December 1870

36 John Ross's diary entry for 21 December 1870

37 Alfred Giles 1926 p. 47

38 John Ross's diary entries for 14–16 January 1871

39 Alfred Giles 1926 p. 54

40 John Ross's diary entry for 15 January 1871

41 Alfred Giles 1926 pp. 56, 57, 61

42 Alfred Wood's diary in State Records SA GRG154/6 Todd Papers Overland Telegraph. G.W. Symes 1960 p. 42 says 'Woods was at odds with Ross because he

considered that the explorations had no positive value to the route of the line and that Ross should have devoted his time to the major task of finding a suitable route through the range instead of adhering to the letter of his instructions'. Later on p. 42 Symes says 'Woods opinion of Ross was far from high and it is likely that at this stage he was disinclined to commit himself completely to a course of action advocated by Ross'.

43   Alfred Woods's journal entry for 30 January 1871 begins: 'Shifted our camp to a better place as we shall be here some time. After shifting had crosscut saws set up (?) as I intend the men to build a temporary store during their stay for the protection of the stores, in case the contractor should wish to change loading from drays to camels'. Alfred Giles 1926 p. 62 says 'At the junction of the Finke and the Hugh Rivers on 31 January Mr Woods' party started to build a depot store'. The 2 February 1871 entry in the *Diary of Thomas Frederick Smith* says 'Commenced splitting slabs for store ...' On 7 February, 'Commenced building store 30 ft. long 12 ft. breadth, walls 7 ft. To be covered with tarpaulin ...'

44   Alfred Giles 1926 p. 63

45   William Whitfield Mills's report to Todd on 12 December 1872 says 'The drays were detained for several weeks in the heart of the sandhills at the junction of the Hugh and the Finke'. Frank Clune, Peter Taylor and Elliott Mills all got the location of the depot wrong. Frank Clune p. 189 refers to 'the new depot at the junction of the Hugh and the Finke (Alice Well)'. Peter Taylor p. 69 writes about 'the new depot at Alice Well'. Elliott Mills p. 25 says 'Todd advised them that the base camp for the central section would be at the junction of the Hugh and Finke Rivers, at the lagoon known as Alice Well'.

CHAPTER 5   The singing wire to Alice

1   Gilbert McMinn's diary entry for 16 February 1871 and Mervyn Hartwig p. 209

2   Gilbert McMinn's diary entry for 23 February 1871 and G.W. Symes 1960 p. 43

3   *NT Places Names Register* refers to London's Temple Bar as 'the historic structure on the boundary of London, UK where British monarchs on state occasions would observe the ancient custom of securing the London Lord Mayor's permission "to pass the Temple Bar" '.

4   *NT Places Names Register* says there's another Temple Bar near Beltana with a very similar appearance and suggests this may have something to do with McMinn's name choice.

5   See the entry for 15 May 1871 in the diary of Dr Frederick Emil Renner who Todd appointed as medical officer for the construction parties on the central section of the line. He left Owen Springs that day and says: 'Bitter cold night. Started at 10 o.cl. am followed the creek for about two miles. After crossing the creek we followed a flat (valley) on both sides rocky hills. Beautiful grassed flat, the timber great deal burnt. The telegraph line follows this flat. By 3 o.cl. we came to a gorge. Looking through the same we had a beautiful mountain view. The hills are high, steep and ruggy. Passing through a gorge a little farther on we came to the creek. This gorge is called the Toll Gate. The line follows through the first gorge. The road took a direction to the east, the gorges on the north side. We found little water a mile from the camp for the horses and dug for it for our own. Came to camp by 4 o. cl. Distance 18 miles.' At the end of the next day's entry he says 'Distance from Tollbar to Temple Bar 6 miles, from there to Alice Springs, 11 miles'.

6   Mervyn Hartwig p. 210 says 'With one man and an Aboriginal, Mills started from the Junction on 7 March; and on the same day Ross and party set out for the Roper'. Frank Clune p. 194 suggests the white man was Adam Burt but Alfred Giles 1926 p. 66 makes it clear this was not the case; Burt was camped with the rest of his men '3 miles below the junction' while Mills was away.

7   Jenny Brands's article 'A Grand Old Lady of the Bush Dies' in the *Centralian Advocate* 28 December 1985 says Unchalka was also known as Erruphana but it's actually Erupmua according to Ted Strehlow's genealogies. Baldwin Spencer's personal copy of the 1927 book *The Arunta* has a handwritten note spelling it Irapma. These days it's spelt Irrapmwe. See Jason Gibson's footnote on p. 40 of *Walter Baldwin Spencer's Diary from the Spencer and Gillen Expedition 1901–1902*. Unchalka/Ntyarlke's skin name was Paltara/Peltharre.

8   G.W. Symes 1960 p. 45

9   Alfred Woods's 30 January 1871 diary entry ends with: 'Mr Harvey desires me to state that he himself positively declines to go out again, unless he knows from his own observation and enquiries that they are equipped for a sufficient length of time: that he will not again trust to Mr Ross's judgement on this point, when so little of that quality has twice been displayed.' Mervyn Hartwig p. 196 describes Harvey as 'a middle-aged surveyor whose gentle disposition and somewhat delicate constitution were not designed for the bush'. On p. 207 he says Harvey had suffered much because of the shortage of rations and refused to serve under Ross again.

10   Alfred Giles 1926 p. 70. Mervyn Hartwig p. 211 says they met 'a mile north of the Alice Spring and 6 miles south of Bond Springs'.

11   Arthur Ashwin pp. 49, 52, 54

12   Frank Clune p. 195

13   See the entry for 13 May 1871 in Dr Frederick Renner's diary.

14   Arthur Ashwin pp. 57 and 66 says they lost 2000 sheep and all of their goats. The *Diary of Thomas Frederick Smith* also says 2000 sheep. However, Frank Clune says their losses totalled 3000 sheep and 100 goats. Milner gave these figures in his account published in 1927. Mervyn Hartwig p. 235 says the bones of 3000 of Milner's sheep and lambs lay on Sutherland Creek.

15   Arthur Ashwin pp. 57–61

16   Arthur Ashwin pp. 61–62.

17   Ralph Milner says they experienced a total eclipse of the sun on the way. Arthur Ashwin p. 68 says it was on 12 December but doesn't say where they were at the time.

18   Todd stipulated that the poles be planted 20 to the mile, or 4 chains apart. A cricket pitch is one chain long. Given that a chain equals 22 yards, the poles were meant to be 88 yards apart (approx. 80 metres).

19   SAPP 29/1873 p. 1

20   SAPP 191/1884 p. 144

21   SAPP 191/1884 p. 144 and SAPP 29/1873 p. 2

22   Mervyn Hartwig p. 213

23   SAPP 29/1873 p. 3

24   Frank Clune pp. 202–203, though Peter Taylor says on p. 89 that they sailed on 6 June.

25   Edgar Harcourt pp. 58–59

26   Frank Clune p. 232

27   Alan Smith 2002 pp. 119–120

28   SAPP 29/1873 p. 7

29   *South Australian Register* 7 September 1872 pp. 2–4 and Frank Clune pp. 230–231, who incorrectly says the final join happened a bit after 3 pm.

30   John Lewis p. 96

31   *South Australia Advertiser* 23 August 1872 p. 2 and *South Australia Register* 23 August 1872 p. 5

32   SAPP 191/1984 p. 149 gives a figure of £338,059 14s 5d but by 31 December 1883 this had grown to £479,174 18s 3d with repoling costs.

33   SAPP 29/1873 p. 6

34   Mervyn Hartwig p. 133 and Ann Moyal p. 38

35   Frank Clune p. 17 and John Bailey p. 180

36   G–CO No. 276 of 1858 and despatches sent from London to MacDonnell on 29 May 1858 and 27 July 1858

37   See SAPP 33/1858, which also includes Todd's report to MacDonnell on 2 December 1858.

38   G–CO 296/59 on 21 January 1859, State Records SA GRG2 6/8. Frank Clune p. 17 states MacDonnell sent a despatch to the Colonial Office in London in January 1859 saying 'I am opposed to any scheme of a line of telegraph to be brought round the continent by the west or by the east coast, until it be first ascertained whether it could not be taken across the continent in a direct line from Adelaide to the Cambridge Gulf'. However, G-CO 296/59 doesn't contain these words. Edgar Harcourt has the same quote on p. 18 but he may have just lifted it from Frank Clune because there's no reference for it in his Sources.

39   G–O 334/59 on 18 July 1859 at State Records SA GRG2 6/9

40   Charles Todd's 18 July 1859 report to the Commissioner of Public Works, SAPP 127/1859 p. 5

41   G–O 338/59 at State Records SA in GRG 2 6/9

42   Both Frank Clune p. 73 and Sarah Murgatroyd say MacDonnell wrote this letter on 19 July 1859 but neither book cites a source. It looks like Sarah Murgatroyd simply took it from Frank Clune because they both have 'It would settle forever the practicality of carrying the wire, as well as sending horses for export to India by that route ... I strongly recommend immediate action'.

43   G–O 358/59 at State Records SA in GRG 2 6/9 and printed in SAPP 47/1861 p. 1

44   'Unofficial letter' from Charles Todd to Governor in Chief Sir James Fergusson dated 30 August 1869, in State Records SA GRG 154/6 Todd Papers Overland Telegraph.

45   SAPP 24/1870–71 p. 2

46   SAPP 44/1878 p. 34

47   Charles Todd 1886 p. 153

48   SAPP 118/1869 p. 5

49   Mervyn Hartwig pp. 134–146

50   *Observer, Adelaide* 4 February 1905 pp. 24, 38, and *Chronicle* 4 February 1905 pp. 26–27

51 Letter from H.B.T. Strangways to Mayor of Glenelg H.W. Varley, 7 February 1906, South Australian State Library D8339

52 SAPP 47/1861 and the despatch G–CO 358/1859

CHAPTER 6 Atherreyurre, the Alice spring

1 Frank Clune p. 219 and Elliott Mills p. 36

2 Gilbert McMinn's diary

3 *Advertiser*, 24 March 1939, p. 27. The spot chosen for the new well was a short distance south of the blacksmith's shop built in 1876. It was equipped with a windlass at first and later a brass hand pump.

4 Dick Kimber 2011 pp. 17, 27, 54 and Dick Kimber 2002 pers. comm.

5 Charles Todd's *Instructions to Overseers in charge of Works*, issued on 30 September 1870. A copy is located in the Arid Zone Research Institute Library at Alice Springs. It was supplied by the old Telecommunications Museum in Adelaide, now located at Whyalla.

6 Gilbert McMinn's diary p. 132

7 SAPP 191/1884 p. 150

8 Benjamin Clarke's diary entries for 2 December & 17 December 1871

9 John Mueller's diary entries for 8–16 December 1871

10 He was five kilometres south-east of Rocky Camp Waterhole. See Benjamin Clarke's diary entry 20 & 25 December 1871 and John Mueller's diary entry for 20 December 1871.

11 Supplement to the *Australian* 18 August 1972 *Overland Telegraph Centenary*

12 Benjamin Clarke's diary entry for 15 December 1871

13 John Mueller's diary entries for 29–31 December 1871 and Gilbert McMinn's diary p. 132

14 Neil Christoph pp. 30–31, 33–40, 65. See also http://lobethal.sa.au/history/european-history

15 John Mueller's diary entries for 27 September–2 October 1871

16 SAPP 191/1884 p. 144

17 Peter Taylor pp. 143–144 and *Chronicle* 14 October 1899 p. 17. *South Australian Register* 21 October 1872 p. 6 says Richard Knuckey, Charles Wells, A. Warren, a man named Harpur and a cook were also with Todd when he arrived at Barrow Creek on 16 August 1872. Charles Wells went north with Todd on the SS *Omeo* in January that year according to the *South Australian Register* 2 January 1872 p. 1S.

18 Frank Clune p. 227

19 SAPP 29/1873 p. 5

20 Charles Todd's notebook for 1872 in State Records SA GRG 154/15

21 *South Australian Register* 6 September 1870 p. 6

22 Benjamin Clarke's diary entry 25 December 1871 and Frank Clune p. 220

23 Doris Blackwell & Douglas Lockwood p. 162 and Bruce Plowman 1957 p. 142

CHAPTER 7 The line in John Mueller's day

1 SAPP 191/1984 p. 145

2 *South Australian Register* 2 January 1872 p. 1S

3   SAPP 191/1885 pp. 145–147

4   *South Australian Register* 20 May 1876 p. 6 refers to work being given to teamster Jack Bond in 1876.

5   SAPP 44/1878 pp. 32–33

6   W.L. Manser p. 122

7   SAPP 191/1884 pp. 161–162

8   H.W. Jenvey p. 10

9   B.E. Woodrow p. 169

10   Benjamin Clarke's diary entries for 1 June, 22 June & 2 July 1872; F.P. O'Grady 1972 p. 23 and B.E. Woodrow p. 169

11   R.C.M. Dale p. 162 says Alice Springs was the only repeater station on the copper wire by 1939, apart from Port Augusta. Marree, Alice Springs and Powell Creek were the only repeaters on the iron line.

12   D.E. Kelsey p. 85

13   Edgar Harcourt pp. 59–60, 71

14   18 July 1893 memorandum from Charles Todd to all repeater stations on the OT line, provided by the old Telecommunications Museum, in Adelaide, now located at Whyalla

15   See p. 59 of the Alice Springs Telegraph Station notes *Historical Use of the Area* produced by the Conservation Commission of the Northern Territory.

16   *South Australian Chronicle and Weekly Mail* 14 June 1879 p. 14

17   Mervyn Hartwig pp. 357–358

18   Peter Taylor p. 166

19   Gilbert McMinn's letter is State Records SA GRG 154/6. Mervyn Hartwig pp. 221–222 says he left Alice Springs on 29 July 1872.

20   Charles Todd's notebook for 1872 in State Records SA GRG 154/15 says he got to Tennant Creek on the afternoon of 24 July.

21   See Edwin Berry's drawing of the telegraph station, showing the unfinished store, in *Australasian Sketcher with Pen and Pencil* of 14 June 1873. This popular monthly magazine published by the proprietors of the Melbourne *Argus* between 1873 and 1889 provided a pictorial account of life in the Australian colonies before the widespread use of photography.

22   It's not clear if the new telegraph office was finished before John Mueller left in 1878.

23   Simpson Newland pp. 19–20

24   *South Australian Register* 5 October 1875 p. 6

25   Article entitled 'Central Australia' and dated 20 January, published on p. 6 of the *South Australian Register* 20 May 1876

26   Charles Todd's report SAPP 191/1984 p. 146 states: 'The supervision of the southern stations, viz., Attack Creek to Beltana, was entrusted to Mr J.F. Mueller, then station-master at Alice Springs. He was succeeded, in 1878, by Mr E.S. Flint, who still holds the appointment.'

27   Frances O'Kane p. 10

28   State Records SA GRS 1 1890/625

29   State Records SA GRS1 1894/284

30 Keith Mooney-Smith 1994 quoting the entry for 5 September 1906 in volume 3 of T.A. Bradshaw's diary and *Port Augusta Dispatch, Newcastle and Flinders Chronicle* 30 November 1906. Kate Holmes 1980 says the offence occurred in the Winnecke goldrush days 1902–1903 but she was unable to discover a reason for the delay in prosecution.

31 Adela Purvis 1971 p. 79 says that 'having been too stout for active labour, he took positions as bookkeeper on several Central Australian stations'.

32 Frances O'Kane p. 26

CHAPTER 8 The dawn of civilisation and Christianity

1 Charles Todd's SAPP 191/1884 p. 152 says 'In 1874 a Government reserve of twenty-five square miles was secured round each of the following stations: Charlotte Waters, Alice Springs, Barrow Creek, Tennant's Creek, Powell's Creek, Daly Waters, and the Katherine'.

2 SAPP 21/1875 p. 1 and Gilbert McMinn's diary entries for 29 June 1872

3 *Advertiser* 11 July 1934 p. 22. Ted Johns says Harley Bacon was camped 400 yards from the spot where McMinn was building the telegraph station. See also the telegram in State Records SA GRG 154/8/2–5 sent by Alice Springs stationmaster John Mueller to Gilbert McMinn c/o Charlotte Waters on 10 August 1872. It concerned the amount of flour McMinn and Bacon had left at Alice Springs.

4 Neville Laybourne-Ward's *Australia's Overland Telegraph Line 1870–1872* shows the line crossing the Finke downstream from its junction with Lilla Creek. This is near Mount Humphries and north-west of Crown Point.

5 Charles Todd says on p. 2 of SAPP 29/1873 that the masts were planted 'at some distance from the bank. On the north side the mast is fifty-two feet long, planted eight feet in the ground, and on the north side, which is higher, thirty-nine feet. Both masts are securely strutted and stayed, and the longer one is built round with several tons of large stones'.

6 SAPP 21/1875 p. 1 and Ernest Giles Vol. 1 p. 85

7 Ernest Giles Vol. 1 p. liv, p. l

8 Ray Ericksen p. 55

9 SAPP 21/1875 p. 28

10 Ernest Giles Vol. 1 pp. 7–9

11 Ernest Giles Vol. 1 pp. 67, 72, 79, 81

12 The source for this is a 1980s information sheet *In Search of the Olgas* produced by the Ayers Rock Resort. It was based on information provided by Derek Roff, former Chief Ranger of Uluru National Park.

13 It said: 'Will you take charge of Exploring party from Central Mount Stuart or near there to the Westward towards Perth – When would you be ready – What remuneration expected – Mr Keckwick will probably act as second. Four Affgahans & any number of camels placed at your service. Reply. Major Warburton will lead an expedition to the eastward. Will communicate with Mr Todd on receipt of your reply. If you accept offer immediately proceed to nearest Telegraph Station.'

14 Gilbert McMinn's diary

15 Frank Clune p. 77

16   *Australian Dictionary of Biography* entry for Peter Egerton Warburton by Denison
     Deasey
17   Mervyn Hartwig p. 223
18   Peter Egerton Warburton pp. 138–139 says he'd been 'assured by those who had
     resided two years in that part of the country that the summer rains would prevent
     my moving till the early part of April ... I had much reason to regret this ...'
     Fayette Gosse pp. 114–117 says it became something of 'a Gilbert and Sullivan
     situation' with a flurry of telegrams between Adelaide and Alice Springs.
19   *South Australian Register* 3 April 1873 p. 5 has a short article entitled 'North to
     South Australia'. It says: 'We are informed by Mr C Todd CMG that there are now
     congregated at Alice Springs the following travelling parties:- Mr Campbell's of
     nine men and 250 horses, going overland; Messrs Gilbert and Bagot's comprising
     6 men, and having in charge 450 cattle, also about 30 horses; Mr Gosse's
     Government Exploring Expedition, including 8 men, besides the leader, 11 camels
     and 27 horses; and Major Warburton's private exploring party, fitted out by the
     Hon. T. Elder, in which there are 7 men, accompanied by 20 camels and 19 horses.
     Major Warburton is waiting the arrival of Mr A.G. Burt who is now somewhere
     near Charlotte Waters with additional stores for the expedition.' Warburton's
     account of his journey says he had 17 camels so there is doubt about the accuracy
     of Todd's other numbers.
20   Mervyn Hartwig p. 301 says there were 3200 cattle in October 1874.
21   James Churchill Smith says in his diary they met at Humbum station. Charles
     Todd's SAPP 1873/29 p. 6 says he 'rode overland, arriving at Beltana on 19th
     October'.
22   James Churchill Smith's diary entry for 2 January 1873 says 'Hassel a Melbourne
     man arrived here today with buggies on his way to the N.T. with horses'. On
     3 January he wrote 'Hamilton arrived with the horses today. He and Hassel
     are partners in the transaction'. He added, on 11 January, 'Campbell arrived
     today with 230 odd head of horses belonging to Mr Elder on his way to the NT',
     followed by an entry on 13 January 1873: 'Campbell's waggon arrived.' See also
     notes on the website http.//ehive.com/account/3492/object/78006/William_
     David_b_Hamilton_12th_May_1857_Invercargill compiled by the Stockman's
     Hall of Fame. John Mulvaney & J. H. Calaby p. 375 also refers to this overlanding
     expedition, citing E.M. Tiegs, nee Ethel Hamilton, from the *Age*, 11 June 1932 p. 8.
     'The Hamilton family stemmed from hardy pioneering stock which registered its
     mark in Australian history. Jean's grandfather was a pastoral pioneer in Victoria's
     Western District. While he was still a schoolboy, her father participated in a
     droving saga initiated by Tom Hamilton, his zestful uncle. In 1872 they mustered
     120 horses at Bringalbert station, near Edenhope, and for months they trekked
     across the continent ... before successfully reaching Darwin with their horses.'
23   James Churchill Smith's diary entries for 24 March & 9 April 1873
24   It's derived from the Arrernte name Antulye, pronounced *un-tool-ya*.
25   Alfred Giles 1929 p. 8
26   James Churchill Smith's diary entry for 23 May 1873 says 'Mail arrived yesterday,
     brought by Giles who has arrived with the Government sheep'.
27   SAPP 48/1874: entry for 2 July on p. 7
28   SAPP 48/1874: entry for 20 July on p. 9

29   Warburton never went there. It's in a range that in November 1873 Ernest Giles generously named the Colonel's Range after his rival. See Ernest Giles Vol. 1 p. 228.

30   Peter Warburton 1875 and SAPP 28/1875

31   Augustus Gregory's party included Ernest Giles's patron Baron Ferdinand von Mueller.

32   John Strehlow p. 362

33   SAPP 209/1878, SAPP 121/1882 and Mervyn Hartwig pp. 295–299

CHAPTER 9   'The Giant of the Interior'

1   *South Australian Register* 12 November 1872 p. 6 'North Australia to South Australia, Notes of an Overland Journey by a Correspondent'

2   *South Australian Register* 3 March 1874 p. 6. 'Stapleton Relief Fund' has details of him and his family.

3   Alfred Giles 1926 p. 86 says the depot was 125 miles from Port Darwin.

4   Alfred Giles 1926 pp. 90–91

5   Howard Pearce 1987 says his appointment followed the spearing of a horse and sheep in 1873. He quotes SAA GRG 5/2 803/73.

6   Charles Todd's diary says John Frank was originally posted to the Tennant Creek telegraph station when the line opened in 1872.

7   See Sam Gason's report to the commissioner of police, written the following day, 23 February 1874, and the article 'Our Undeveloped Territory' part XI on p. 6 of the *South Australian Register* 8 August 1891. The newspaper says the name of the Chinese cook was Si Jin; Gason wrote Saith Jexm in his report.

8   The doctor was the father of William Christie Gosse who had only recently returned from the 1872–1873 South Australian Government exploring expedition in Central Australia.

9   *South Australian Register* 24 February 1874 pp. 5–6 & 27 February 1874 p. 5

10   Doris Blackwell & Douglas Lockwood p. 56 and the *Mail* 30 May 1942 p. 12

11   *South Australian Register* 26 February 1874 p. 5

12   *South Australian Advertiser* 27 February 1874 p. 2; and p. 5 of *South Australian Register* 27 February 1874. Mervyn Hartwig p. 271 says 'That evening unexpected relief arrived in the shape of Cowan and two men who were on their way to the Top End'.

13   This comes from an account of events in the files of the Conservation Commission of the Northern Territory, compiled from a number of telegrams to and from the commissioner of police. The account was found by historian Howard Pearce in the trunk of Tom Roberts, longtime caretaker at Barrow Creek, who died in March 1988. See also *South Australian Register* 27 February 1874 p. 5 and Mervyn Hartwig p. 272.

14   *South Australian Register* 28 February 1874 p. 5

15   Mervyn Hartwig pp. 274–275

16   *South Australian Advertiser* 26 February 1874 p. 2. Mervyn Hartwig p. 278 says 'The Barrow Creek "outrage" heralded the end of the phase of conciliation in Central Australia and the beginning of the phase of pacification'.

17   Robert Gillen pp. 60–61

18   Charles Winnecke's 1881 survey plan of the station shows a post office, stationmaster's house and men's hut in addition to the original barracks, main store, blacksmith shop and line party store. It's unclear exactly when these three additions were built.

19   It seems Mounted Constable John Shirley went to Alice Springs on 28 April 1879 but his appointment wasn't advertised in the *South Australian Government Gazette* until 28 August 1879. See Chris Torlach's notes HGPS-00020 at the Arid Zone Research Institute Library, Alice Springs.

20   Howard Pearce 1987

21   1987 *Heritage Walk* notes compiled by Howard Pearce, Peter King and Chris Torlach, held at the Arid Zone Research Institute Library, Alice Springs AP 148; Alice Springs Telegraph Station Historical Reserve Draft Plan of Management May 1999 Appendix 1

22   *South Australian Advertiser* 29 January 1876 p. 2S says Thomas Fergusson was from The Valleys near Nairne in South Australia, 54 years old with a wife and five children.

23   A cross bearing Frank Hansen's name was placed on his grave but replaced with one saying The Surveyour when the original disappeared some years later. The people who erected the new cross were apparently under the impression it was the grave of Frank Rees George, a geologist and mining engineer who died on 4 April 1906. However, he is actually buried in the Stuart Town Cemetery established in 1890.

24   *South Australian Register* 24 January 1880 p. 5, E. Leske p. 17, and John Strehlow pp. 366–367

25   Peter Donovan p. 69 says: 'The Aranda avoided the mission except for brief visits to satisfy their curiosity. Only after the mission station became a depot for the distribution of rations in 1879 did groups of Aranda camp there. Adult classes were begun in 1880, but it was 30 May 1887 before the first baptisms were performed.' Peter Vallee 2007 p. 33 says 'The years 1877 to 1879 were good years of above average rainfall and the Western Aranda mostly stayed away'.

26   *South Australian Register* 30 March 1866 p. 3

27   *South Australian Register* 19 October 1880 pp. 5–6

28   Letter from Charles Todd on p. 5 of *Sydney Morning Herald* 30 December 1880.

29   SAPP 121/1882 p. 23

30   Darrell Lewis pp. 280, 291–294

31   See *South Australian Register* 24 June p. 5 'Supposed Traces of Leichhardt', reprinted on p. 1 of the supplement to the *South Australian Register* 5 July 1882. Shirley's journal for the expedition was published under the heading 'A Far North Expedition' by several newspapers: the supplement to the *South Australian Register* 1 August 1882; *South Australian Advertiser* 3 August 1882 pp. 9–10; *South Australian Weekly Chronicle* 5 August 1882 p. 6; and *Adelaide Observer* 5 August 1882 pp. 34–35. Darrel Lewis p. 296 says that Charles 'Winnecke produced a map which showed the furthest point reached was about 300 kilometres north-north-east of Alice Springs and roughly 40 kilometres south-east of present-day Jervois Station'. This map G9041.S12svar. is in the National Library of Australia; there's a copy at the NT Archives in Alice Springs.

32   SAPP 54/1886 *Half-yearly Report on Northern Territory to June 30th 1886*

33 Flint's obituary in the *Adelaide Observer* 23 July 1887 p. 29 says he'd only arrived back at the telegraph station with his wife six weeks before his death on 17 July.

34 SAPP 34/1887 and SAPP 34A/1887

35 See the Flinders Ranges History website and John Deckert's Westprint map 'Birdsville and Strzelecki Tracks' which says the post office and railways continued to use the name Hergott Springs rather than the gazetted name Marree. Signs were changed in 1918 amid the anti-German hysteria of the 1914–1918 war.

36 Basil Fuller p. 99

37 Basil Fuller p. 124 says the railhead reached Stuart Creek, near Lake Eyre South, in June 1886. 'Two years to build a trifle more than sixty miles of line in flat country! Scarcely an epic in railway construction!'

38 The commissioners recommended the land-grant option on 26 October 1887, rather than further borrowing, but the government ignored this. Late in 1887 it decided to pay for an extension of the line to Angle Pole, now Oodnadatta. See Basil Fuller pp. 135, 138–139.

39 Basil Fuller p. 130 says 'the plate layers brought the permanent way into Strangways on Tuesday 1 March 1887, a month after Coward Springs was opened to traffic'.

40 Basil Fuller pp. 126–127

41 Basil Fuller pp. 134, 144 and SAPP 204/1890

42 *South Australian Advertiser* 2 July 1887 p. 5 and Simpson Newland pp. 6–7

43 *Register* (Adelaide) 29 August 1925 p. 11 contains an article 'In Central Australia. Mr Joseph Harding Reminiscent'.

44 Simpson Newland pp. 18–20

45 *Adelaide Observer* 23 July 1887 p. 29

46 See the entry for 23 July 1889 in William Tietkens 1891.

47 *South Australian Register* 8 February 1888 p. 6 'The MacDonnell Range Ruby-field'

CHAPTER 10 Trouble brewing on the frontier

1 Alfred Giles 1929 p. 20: 'About the end of 1874 I received a wire from Adelaide from my father, Mr Christopher Giles, saying he had been approached by Mr Todd as to the possibility of my undertaking the droving from Adelaide of another 5,000 sheep and, if so, to return overland at once and, in the meantime, he would engage men and outfit and start the sheep from Beltana and they would proceed on until they met me.' On p. 24 he says he heard of the sinking of the *Gothenburg* when he was at Charlotte Waters.

2 Alfred Giles 1929 p. 25 says he met them 10 miles west of Mount Margaret.

3 Alfred Giles 1929 pp. 30–31

4 Mervyn Hartwig pp. 301–302 says there were 3200 cattle in October 1874 and Undoolya was declared stocked in December 1874. Howard Pearce 1985 says Owen Springs was declared stocked in November 1875.

5 *South Australian Register* 5 October 1875 p. 6, and Alfred Giles 1929 p. 32 who says there were a hundred and they were going to a butcher named Abbott.

6 Alfred Giles 1929 pp. 32–34 says he dried some of the plants and sent them to Baron Von Mueller in Melbourne. The botanist named the species *Bauhinia gileseii* after him, and Giles responded by sending pressed plants.

7   Alfred Giles 1929 pp. 35–43

8   Breaden became a significant figure in the central Australian pastoral industry. Differing spellings of his name appear in documents with Allen the most common.

9   See www.todmorden.com.au/guestbook where Bob Parke responds to what's on www.todmorden.com.au/history.htm. 'Edmund and Walter Parke did not come from Todmorden in Lancashire. They came from Dorset (south England). The family estate there was Henbury, hence the name given to Henbury Station, craters etc. They were the sons of Charles Joseph Parke, son of Charles Parke who first rented then purchased the Henbury Estate in Dorset on his return from Jamaica. Charles Joseph Parke was my Great Grandfather.'

10   Mervyn Hartwig p. 294

11   These numbers come from Alfred Giles 1929 but Mervyn Hartwig p. 308 has different ones.

12   Mervyn Hartwig p. 359

13   Mervyn Hartwig pp. 347–349 and *South Australian Register* 23 November 1886 p. 6

14   Alfred Giles 1929 p. 114

15   Alfred Giles 1929 pp. 106–108

16   *South Australian Chronicle and Weekly Mail* 1 March 1879 p. 7

17   Commonwealth Parliamentary Paper No.76 of 1922 pp. 187–188

18   Charles Chewings wrote 'A Trip to the MacDonnell Ranges' an article published in the *Adelaide Observer* in three parts on 22 July 1882 p. 42, 29 July 1882 pp. 41–42, and 5 August 1882 p. 42.

19   Charles Chewings had an Aboriginal companion Jimmy with him for part of the trip. It seems he joined him at Owen Springs, on the way west to Hermannsburg. Jimmy left him at Charlotte Waters on the way back south.

20   Mervyn Hartwig pp. 335–336 and Howard Pearce 1985. Valmai Hankel says on p. xii of her introduction to the Friends of the State Library of South Australia facsimile reprint *The Sources of the Finke River* that the Tempe enterprise was not profitable and Chewings sold his share to Fred Thornton in 1893 for £2500, a loss of £27,000.

21   Mervyn Hartwig pp. 337–338

22   Mervyn Hartwig pp. 330–331 and Howard Pearce 1985

23   Mervyn Hartwig pp. 379–382 talks of the early pastoralists 'overestimating the country'.

24   John Strehlow p. 377 says stories of shootings started reaching the Hermannsburg missionaries' ears early in 1883 and reached their peak in 1884.

25   Bill Benstead's unpublished memoir

26   Mervyn Hartwig pp. 332–335 and *South Australian Register* 10 February 1883 p. 7, 17 February 1883 p. 1S & 30 April 1883 p. 6. Bill Benstead's unpublished memoir says there were 4000 head of cattle and 600 horses.

27   *Travels by Ridley Williams from Bierbank Station in Queensland to the Overland Telegraph Line in the Northern Territory of South Australia* reproduced in Adela Purvis 1971

28   *Maitland Mercury and Hunter River General Advertiser* 12 August 1884 p. 5

29   *Adelaide Observer* 16 August 1884 p. 29

30 Research notes compiled by Mervyn Hartwig in 1963 say McBeth was a former police trooper stationed at Orroroo and Blinman. It's unclear what he and Summard were doing when Willshire recruited them.

31 *South Australian Register* 17 September 1884 p. 5 and *Adelaide Observer* 20 September 1884 p. 31

32 *South Australian Register* 25 September 1884 p. 3S and *Adelaide Observer* 20 September 1884 p. 31

33 *Adelaide Observer* 4 October 1884 p. 34

34 *South Australian Register* 25 September 1884 pp. 2S, 3S

35 John Strehlow p. 380, Mervyn Hartwig p. 398, Peter Vallee pp. 88–91, and Amanda Nettelbeck & Robert Foster pp. 28–30

36 Bill Benstead's unpublished memoir pp. 10–11

37 Amanda Nettelbeck & Robert Foster p. 22

38 Amanda Nettelbeck & Robert Foster p. 26 citing PCO 920/84, SAPHS papers 004651

39 Peter Vallee pp. 84–85, 151–152

40 Ben Rogers later said that the attack was the result of a dispute over an Aboriginal woman who was living with him. See *South Australian Register* 25 June 1891 p. 3.

41 Bill Benstead's unpublished memoir chapter 5 and Mervyn Hartwig p. 399

CHAPTER 11 The 'rush' to the East MacDonnells

1 David Lindsay married a woman with the same surname, Annie Theresa Stuart Lindsay, on 10 March 1881.

2 David Lindsay 1889 pp. 650–651

3 *South Australian Register* 6 October 1885 p. 6

4 *South Australian Register* 19 October 1880 pp. 5–6

5 David Lindsay 1889 pp. 650–652

6 David Lindsay 1890 p. 5

7 David Lindsay 1890 p. 7

8 Mervyn Hartwig p. 578

9 David Lindsay 1889 pp. 659–660

10 David Lindsay 1889 p. 665

11 Barry Allwright 2009 pp. 46–47

12 *Port Augusta Dispatch, Newcastle and Flinders Chronicle* 30 September 1887 p. 3

13 Frances O'Kane p. 9, Service Enterprises 1983 p. 18 and Kate Holmes 1983 p. 86

14 *South Australian Register* 25 June 1898 p. 5 and *Adelaide Observer* 2 July 1898 p. 13

15 Peter Donovan 1988 pp. 70–71, and Jack Cross p. 328 who says 'The so-called Great Depression of the 1890s hit South Australia in 1884, six or seven years before the rest of Australia ...'

16 Frances O'Kane p. 10 and Mervyn Hartwig p. 552; Barry Allwright 2009 p. 53 says there were 60 white men and a number of natives by early 1888.

17 State Records SA GRS 1 1888/477 has a letter from Wesley Turton dated 21 May 1888 stating that he had 'carried on the business of a storekeeper there for two years'. Mervyn Hartwig p. 579 mentions Wesley Turton selling goods and brewing beer.

18   *South Australian Chronicle* 17 December 1892 p. 6
19   Keith Mooney-Smith 1988 p. 6
20   *South Australian Advertiser* 15 July 1887 p. 5 and Simpson Newland p. 18
21   Adela Purvis 1952 says: 'Frank Speed, an enterprising bullock-teamster, had
      discovered this passage into the ranges by bringing his teams over the Ooraminna
      Range through the narrowest of the three gaps (Jessie Gap) to Undoolya Station.'
      She says teamster Joe Harding also used it. See also Mervyn Hartwig pp. 578–579.
22   *South Australian Advertiser* 2 July 1887 p. 6, 15 July 1887 p. 5, and Simpson
      Newland pp. 11, 15
23   The identity of Blood is unclear. John Deckert's 1993 Westprint map *Alice Springs–
      Oodnadatta* says the creek was named after the first telegraph stationmaster at the
      Peake, J.H.S. Blood. Peter Taylor p. 70 says Alfred Woods named it after William
      Blood, the storeman in charge of the OT depot at the Peake.
24   Mervyn Hartwig p. 581
25   Jack Ryan 1991
26   Barry Allwright 2009 pp. 50–51, 56
27   *Adelaide Observer* 26 May 1888 p. 40 reported that 'By latest accounts there were
      260 men working on the ruby-fields'. The *Port Augusta Dispatch, Newcastle and
      Flinders Chronicle* 29 May 1888 p. 3 says there were about '150 whites and about
      half as many natives' assisting them. It also mentions two small stores selling
      provisions and other goods at enormously high prices and two butchers supplying
      beef and mutton at a reasonable price.
28   Barry Allwright 2009 p. 62 and Rennie's paper in *Transactions and Proceedings and
      Report of the Royal Society of South Australia, Volume XI, 1887–1888*, Adelaide 1889
      pp. 17–18

CHAPTER 12   A town is born

1   Robert Gillen pp. 31, 33, 35 and *South Australian Register* 5 October 1875 p. 6
2   *Adelaide Observer* 23 July 1887 p. 29 says work had started on the new house when
     Ebenezer Flint died but the foundation stone has the date 11 January 1888.
3   Mervyn Hartwig p. 348 says 'And so it was that at race meetings in the
     mid-eighties go-carts or bum boats were numerous and whiskey flowed like
     water at £1 a bottle ...' *South Australian Register* 21 June 1886 p. 3 has comments
     by Charles Chewings about picnic race meetings, sly grog and the activities of
     spielers.
4   Mervyn Hartwig p. 348 quotes State Records SA MCNT Correspondence In 36/88:
     'for instance, one Palmer made an appearance at Alice Springs in December 1887
     with "no less than 14 camels all loaded with intoxicants" and was welcomed by all
     except the police and some station-managers and telegraph officials.'
5   State Records SA GRS 1 1887/670
6   State Records SA GRS 1 1887/821, 1888/91 24 February 1888, 1887/902,
     1887/939 & 1888/91
7   State Records SA GRS 1 1888/363 includes a note from the minister on 21 May
     1888: 'Ask if the writer is practical Gardener and how he proposes to carry on the
     garden.'
8   State Records SA GRS 1 1888/477

9   The entry for 6 May 1888 in the *Police Journal, Alice Springs, 1883–1889*, NT
      Archives Alice Springs F255 A86, says 'MC South left at 1 pm Patroled miners
      hawkers and storekeepers camps and returned at 6 pm. All quiet and orderly'.

10   State Records SA GRG 67/14/4 Register of Northern Licensing Bench Port Augusta
      says Bill Benstead was granted a slaughtering licence at the 13 March 1888
      meeting.

11   Adela Purvis 1945 p. 68 and State Records SA GRS 1 1888/604 which includes
      a minute from Charles Todd dated 9 July 1888 saying 'After conferring with Mr
      Skinner I respectfully recommend that Turton should not be allowed to select a
      site for garden nearer to the Telegraph Station than place known as Murdoch's
      camp – about a mile from the Office ...'

12   The entry for 19 August 1888 in the *Police Journal, Alice Springs, 1883–1889*,
      NT Archives Alice Springs F255 A86, says: 'At 10 pm received a letter by a black
      boy from PJ Fitzgerald dated 18th from Florence Creek reporting that Alexander
      Murdock storekeeper had shot himself dead by blowing his skull nearly away.'
      Northern Territory Times and Gazette 20 October 1888 p. 3 says 'News has been
      received from Central Australia that a man named Alexander Murdoch shot
      himself on the Florence Creek on the 18th August last'.

13   *South Australian Register* 18 May 1888 p. 7

14   Mervyn Hartwig p. 579

15   State Records SA GRS 1 1888/477

16   State Records SA GRS 1 1888/604

17   NAA A421 1950/3576

18   SAPP 204/1890

19   NAA A421 1950/3576

20   Barry Allwright 2009 p. 20

21   NAA A421 1950/3576

22   Mervyn Hartwig p. 578

23   State Records SA GRS 1 1888/1093

24   State Records SA GRG 67/14/4 and *South Australian Weekly Chronicle* 6 October
      1888 p. 1. His application was put on the agenda for 14 December 1888 meeting of
      the Bench but the matter was adjourned.

25   *Northern Territory Times and Gazette* 3 March 1888 p. 1, 17 March 1888 p. 3

26   State Records SA GRG 67/14/4 state that the plans for Bill Benstead's Great
      Northern Hotel were tabled at 19 June 1888 meeting of the Northern Licensing
      Bench and a licence granted at 11 September 1888 meeting. This was reported
      in the *Port Augusta Dispatch, Newcastle and Flinders Chronicle* 11 September 1888
      p. 2. See also 18 December 1888 p. 2 about him being granted a three-month
      extension.

27   Keith Mooney-Smith 1988 pp. 7–8

28   State Records SA GRS 1 1888/1093

29   State Records SA GRS 1 1889/230 has a telegram from Joe Skinner dated 14 June
      1889 saying Wesley Turton had erected the building, plus a stockyard, garden and
      well.

30   State Records SA GRG 67/14/4 and the *South Australian Chronicle* 23 March 1889
      p. 9

31 *Port Augusta Dispatch, Newcastle and Flinders Chronicle* 15 March 1889 p. 4
32 State Records SA GRG 67/14/4 says he was granted the licence at the 12 June 1889 meeting.
33 State Records SA GRG 67/14/4
34 Keith Mooney-Smith 1988 p. 12
35 *South Australian Chronicle* 17 December 1892 p. 6

CHAPTER 13 Rough justice on the frontier

1 SAPP 24/1889
2 Mervyn Hartwig's 1976 entry for W.H. Tietkens in *Australian Dictionary of Biography*
3 rgssa.org.au/Exploration.htm
4 William Tietkens 1891 and SAPP 111/1890: journal entry for 19 June 1889
5 Frances O'Kane pp. 14–16, 19
6 Peter Vallee p. 197
7 Bob Wells was the mail contractor between Alice Springs and Oodnadatta in the 1890s and may well have been employed on the mail run in 1887 when his son was baptised. It was a packhorse service until 1 April 1888 when a wagon was introduced to prevent parcel damage and carry passengers if there was space. The government awarded a contract to Port Augusta businessman Norman Richardson following agitation by politician Simpson Newland for a wagon. See *Port Augusta Dispatch, Newcastle and Flinders Chronicle* 10 February 1888 p. 2.
8 Adelaide's *Advertiser* 2 May 1889 p. 4. Births: 'Benstead. On 8 April, at the town of Stuart, Alice Springs, the wife of William Benstead, of a daughter. Both doing well.'
9 *South Australian Register* 26 September 1889 p. 4. Deaths: 'Benstead. On 25 September of croup and bronchitis, at the Private Hospital, South-Terrace, Triphena Stuart (Queenie), darling baby of W and T Benstead, of Alice Springs, Central Australia, aged 6 months.'
10 John Strehlow p. 382 and SAPP 148/1890
11 *South Australian Register* 10 January 1890 p. 6
12 *South Australian Register* 20 February 1890 p. 7, 1 April 1890 p. 7, & 6 May 1890 pp. 4–5
13 Peter Vallee pp. 189–191
14 *South Australian Register* 30 August 1890 p. 3
15 Peter Vallee pp. 142, 196, 208
16 *South Australian Register* 24 September 1890 pp. 4–6 and SAPP 148/1890
17 There were good falls of rain in the first half of 1889 but then the country dried out. Peter Vallee p. 131 called 1889 'the year of the toxic wind'. He says the 'north-west wind continued to blow through the winter, bringing only heat, an adhesive drought, foul waters and repeated bouts of disease to black and white alike'.
18 Frances O'Kane pp. 18–20
19 Report of H.Y.L. Brown's 1891 trip on p. 6 of *Advertiser* 20 April 1891: 'This place is known as Paddy's Rockhole, but on the establishment of a post office lately, it was renamed Arltunga, which is the native name.'
20 John Deckert's 1991 Westprint map 'Oodnadatta Track'

21 SAPP 128/1896
22 *South Australian Register* 6 August 1888 p. 2
23 Christine Stevens p. 2 asserts that they were Afghans: 'Most of them were in fact Pathans, tribesmen either from within the late nineteenth century boundaries of Afghanistan, or from border tribes that straddled the Durand Line, a somewhat troublesome area that was known to the British as the North-West Frontier Provinces.'
24 Christine Stevens p. 95 says 'about 5½ tons to Charlotte Waters, each loading to be delivered within four weeks of collection from the railhead; 10½ tons to Alice Springs Telegraph Station, within nine weeks; 5½ tons to Barrow Creek Station, within thirteen weeks and 7 tons to Tennant Creek Station, within seventeen weeks of collection ...'
25 Christine Stevens p. 70 and Dick Kimber 1985 p. 33
26 Pearl Powell & Eileen McRae p. 38
27 *Chronicle* 14 October 1899 p. 17
28 Vox on p. 31 of *Chronicle* 3 September 1942
29 *Postmaster* Vol. 7 No. 5
30 Bruce Strong 1998 p. 6 says Thomas and Mary Ann Gunter leased the pub for five years but ended up running it until 1900.
31 *Kalgoorlie Western Argus* 8 December 1898 p. 27
32 *Centralian Advocate* 26 January 1978

CHAPTER 14 'Gillen time'

1 Notes supplied by Clare Gillen Meldrum to the Conservation Commission of the Northern Territory with family photos on 7 August 1980.
2 Shirley Brown 2002 p. 1
3 Clare Gillen Meldrum
4 Dick Kimber 1998 pp. 49, 51
5 Robert Gillen pp. 25, 31, 33, 35, 74
6 *South Australian Register* 5 October 1875 p. 6 and 20 May 1876 p. 6
7 John Mulvaney, Howard Morphy & Alison Petch p. 327 and Frank Gillen, 1968, p. 14
8 Frank Gillen wasn't officially promoted to the position of post and telegraph stationmaster at Alice Springs until 1 December 1892.
9 *Adelaide Observer* 2 May 1891 p. 32
10 Mervyn Hartwig pp. 339–341
11 SAPP 191/1884 p. 152 says there were 538 sheep at Charlotte Waters, 3400 at Alice Springs, 280 at Barrow Creek, 183 at Tennant Creek, and a further 530 up the line at Powell Creek.
12 *Report of the Government Resident* for 1889
13 SAPP 33/1891 pp. xv, xli, 123–127,166–167
14 Amanda Nettelbeck & Robert Foster p. 94
15 *South Australian Register* 12 May 1891 p. 3, 22 May 1891 p. 6, 25 May 1891 p. 6, and 26 May 1891 p. 3; *Advertiser* 24 June 1891 pp. 5–6; and *South Australian Chronicle* 27 June 1891 p. 7

16   John Mulvaney, Howard Morphy & Alison Petch p. 68: Frank Gillen to Baldwin Spencer 2 February 1895

17   *Adelaide Observer* 25 July 1891 pp. 33–34

18   *Adelaide Observer* 25 July 1891 p. 32

19   Peter Vallee pp. 252–253

20   Amanda Nettelbeck & Robert Foster pp. 96–98, citing State Records SA GRS 1/2/1891/253 and GRG 52/92

21   Peter Vallee pp. 261–262 and John Strehlow p. 420

22   *Adelaide Observer* 25 July 1891 p. 32

23   Dick Kimber 1991 p. 15 and 2011 p. 54

24   *Northern Territory Times & Gazette* 14 October 1892 p. 4

25   SAPP 33/1891 pp. xlii, 127

26   Mervyn Hartwig pp. 440–442 says rations were issued regularly from these places by 1894.

27   John Mulvaney, Howard Morphy & Alison Petch pp. 10–11

28   John Mulvaney, Howard Morphy & Alison Petch: Frank Gillen to Baldwin Spencer 13 March 1896

29   Doris Blackwell & Douglas Lockwood p. 54

30   Barbara James p. 80

31   Howard Pearce 1985

32   John Strehlow pp. 454–460

33   Frances O'Kane p. 23

34   John Strehlow pp. 467, 469 says Gillen was 'then a balding man of middle-aged appearance though he was only thirty eight' and Arrernte nicknamed him 'the pot-bellied one'.

35   Robert Gillen p. 14 and Dick Kimber 1988 p. 57; John Mulvaney, Howard Morphy & Alison Petch: Frank Gillen to Baldwin Spencer 2 February 1895, 29 July 1895, 13 August 1895 & 20 December 1895

36   Doris Blackwell & Douglas Lockwood pp. 27–28, 37–38, 62–64 and Adelaide's *Advertiser* 7 April 1924 p. 8

37   John Mulvaney, Howard Morphy & Alison Petch: Frank Gillen to Baldwin Spencer 23 March 1897, 30 July 1897 & 22 October 1897

38   Mervyn Hartwig pp. 572–573

39   E.C. Stirling 1896 p. 5

40   Walter Baldwin Spencer 1896 p. 50 & and John Strehlow pp. 370–371

41   D.J. Mulvaney & J.H. Calaby p. 167

42   John Mulvaney, Howard Morphy & Alison Petch: Frank Gillen to Baldwin Spencer 7 November 1895 and D.J. Mulvaney & J.H. Calaby 1985 pp. 170–171

43   Dick Kimber 1998 p. 57

44   Dick Kimber 1998 pp. 62–63

45   D.J. Mulvaney & J.H. Calaby pp. 173, 175 say Baldwin Spencer left Melbourne on 28 October 1896, arrived at Alice Springs during the second week of November, and departed again on 8 January. He was back in Melbourne at the beginning of February 1897. See also John Mulvaney, Howard Morphy & Alison Petch: Frank Gillen to Baldwin Spencer 9 February 1897.

46   Dick Kimber 2002 pers. comm.

47   D.J. Mulvaney & J.H. Calaby p. 172

48   Jason Gibson 2013 pp. 57–72

49   John Mulvaney, Howard Morphy & Alison Petch: Frank Gillen to Baldwin Spencer 6 May 1897

50   Peter Forrest 1981 p. 26

51   Keith Mooney-Smith 1995 citing State Records SA GRS 1 1893/90

52   D.J. Mulvaney & J.H. Calaby pp. 164–165 and John Mulvaney, Howard Morphy & Alison Petch: Frank Gillen to Baldwin Spencer August 1896, 13 January 1898, 11 March 1898, 13 May 1898, & 10 July 1898

53   Frances O'Kane pp. 29–31

54   Keith Mooney-Smith 1995 and Kate Holmes 1980 pp. 44–45. John Thomas Byrne was subsequently a member of Allan Arthur Davidson's 1900 Central Australian Exploration Syndicate Ltd. He died of cardiac failure at the Heavitree Gap police station on 3 January 1903 aged 45.

55   Peter Vallee p. 160 says 'In the 1890s Frank Gillen blew enough money on speculations on the Arltunga goldfields east of Alice Springs to have kept him and his widow comfortably in a retirement he did not himself live to see'.

56   John Mulvaney, Howard Morphy & Alison Petch p. 16 and D.J. Mulvaney & J.H. Calaby p. 249

57   *South Australian Register* 10 April 1897 p. 6 and *Adelaide Observer* 1 May 1897 p. 21

58   Jerome Murif 1897 pp. 70, 73

59   *South Australian Register* 22 May 1897 p. 6

60   *Advertiser, Adelaide* 24 May 1897 p. 5

61   *Adelaide Observer* 26 June 1897 p. 21

62   *Adelaide Observer* 29 May 1897 p. 22

63   *South Australian Register* 2 June 1897 p. 5 and 22 June 1897 p. 6; *Adelaide Observer* 3 July 1897 p. 20

64   *Border Watch, Mount Gambier* 2 March 1898 p. 2

65   *Adelaide Observer* 23 October 1897 p. 14. See also J. Fitzpatrick 1980 *The Bicycle and the Bush*, Oxford University Press.

66   John Strehlow pp. 703–704, 779 and E. Leske p. 26

67   State Records SA GRS 1 1897/426 contains correspondence about goat problems in town. A letter dated 21 October 1897 from F.B. Wallis and Chas W. Benson says 'Around Alice Springs there are up to 2000 head of goats owned by five inhabitants, ourselves included, and as we have had no rain to speak of since the beginning of the year, feed and water is very scarce, in fact stock is dying everywhere ...' See also a letter on the same file from publican Thomas Gunter and storekeepers Charles South and Fred Raggatt dated 4 December 1897. It finishes with 'PS We may mention the population of Stuart Town consists of about twelve persons, One Hotel, Three Stores, one Gardener, one house unoccupied'.

68   State Records SA GRS 1 1888/1169: letter of 22 November 1888 from Bill South and a note from the Minister on 10 December 1888 authorising him to take the requisite steps to protect the timber.

69   Letters of 3 and 4 December 1897 on State Records SA GRS 1 1897/426

70   *Postmaster* 30 August 1927

71 John Mulvaney, Howard Morphy & Alison Petch: Frank Gillen to Baldwin Spencer 11 March1898

72 *Chronicle* 12 March 1898 p. 27 and 16 April p. 12

73 R.M. Todd p. 175

74 John Mulvaney, Howard Morphy & Alison Petch: Frank Gillen to Baldwin Spencer 3 April 1898

75 John Mulvaney, Howard Morphy & Alison Petch: Frank Gillen to Baldwin Spencer 17 April 1898

76 Bruce Strong 1996 pp. 767–771 and *The Book of Albert MacDonald of Orroroo by One Who Knew Him,* The Austral Cycling Agency Ltd pp. 26–37

77 *South Australian Register* 12 September 1898 p. 7 *Our Coloured Kindred; Advertiser* 24 September 1898 p. 5, and *South Australian Register* 24 September 1898 p. 7

78 John Mulvaney, Howard Morphy & Alison Petch: Frank Gillen to Baldwin Spencer 23 December 1898 & 8 January 1899

79 John Mulvaney, Howard Morphy & Alison Petch 1997: Frank Gillen to Baldwin Spencer 19 March 1899

80 D.J. Mulvaney & J.H. Calaby p. 180

81 Michael Cannon p. 265

82 Dick Kimber 2002 pers. comm. and 1998 pp. 61–62

83 John Mulvaney, Howard Morphy & Alison Petch: Frank Gillen to Baldwin Spencer 15 April 1899

84 *South Australian Register* 1 November 1898 p. 4 and *Advertiser* 20 May 1889 p. 4

85 Dick Kimber 2002 pers. comm.

86 *Advertiser* 10 January 1900 p. 4

87 Walter Baldwin Spencer 1901–1902

88 John Mulvaney, Howard Morphy & Alison Petch: Frank Gillen to Baldwin Spencer 18 January 1902

89 John Mulvaney, Howard Morphy & Alison Petch p. 15

90 Correspondence between Gillen's youngest daughter Clare and Christine Torlach in 1985

91 Robert Gillen p. 20

92 D.J. Mulvaney & J.H. Calaby p. 219

93 John Mulvaney, Howard Morphy & Alison Petch 1997: Frank Gillen to Baldwin Spencer 27 July 1902

94 D.J. Mulvaney & J.H. Calaby 1985 p. 219–220

CHAPTER 15 The Bradshaw era

1 Doris Blackwell & Douglas Lockwood p. 19

2 *South Australian Register* 20 April 1899 p. 8

3 Doris Blackwell & Douglas Lockwood, pp. 21–22. The train to Oodnadatta wasn't called the *Ghan* in those days. There are different versions of the origin of the name but the one most widely accepted is attributed to George Williams who spent much of his long railway career on the Central Australian Railway. He said the first use of the name was in August 1923 when a new through service was introduced from Terowie to Oodnadatta with one sleeper car, but no dining car. A railwayman saw an Afghan passenger quickly alight when the train pulled

into Quorn at dusk and head to a quiet corner of the station yard to face Mecca and recite his evening prayers. He remarked that the train should be called the *Afghan Express*. Railway employees quickly adopted the name. It was shortened to the *Ghan Express* and finally the *Ghan*, in the years before the line was extended to Alice Springs. See p. 27 of John Evans's 'Journeys on the Ghan, 1927 to 1946' in *Australian Railway History* September 2014 Vol. 64 No. 923. See also the August 2001 pamphlet for the *Old Ghan Railway Heritage Trail* produced by the Northern Territory Department of Lands, Planning and Environment and the South Australian Tourism Commission.

4   Doris Blackwell & Douglas Lockwood pp. 38–39

5   *Port Augusta Dispatch, Newcastle and Flinders Chronicle* 17 May 1901 p. 2

6   Doris Blackwell & Douglas Lockwood pp. 19–20, 67

7   John Mulvaney, Howard Morphy & Alison Petch: Frank Gillen to Baldwin Spencer 19 March 1899

8   *Advertiser* 19 March 1940 p. 19

9   Doris Blackwell & Douglas Lockwood p. 134 and *Mount Barker Courier* 19 April 1951 p. 5

10   John Mulvaney, Howard Morphy & Alison Petch: Frank Gillen to Baldwin Spencer 21 May 1902, 3 September 1902, and 26 October 1902

11   John Mulvaney, Howard Morphy & Alison Petch: Frank Gillen to Baldwin Spencer 30 May 1900 and 21 June 1900

12   State Records SA GRS 1 1900/305 8 June 1900

13   John Mulvaney, Howard Morphy & Alison Petch p. 331 citing an entry in Frank Gillen's diary on 22 April 1901 at Alice Springs: 'The effects of the drought are everywhere perceptible ... Many of the pepper and gum trees which I planted around the Station fell victims to the all devouring drought as did several old favourite buggy horses.'

14   *Advertiser* 12 June 1901 p. 4; *Adelaide Observer* 12 April 1902 p. 43; *Advertiser* 16 May 1902 p. 6; Doris Blackwell & Douglas Lockwood p. 134

15   *Register* 2 May 1902 p. 4 and *Adelaide Observer* 14 March 1903 p. 26

16   *Advertiser* 15 August 1929 p. 15

17   *Register* 30 March 1906 p. 6

18   Doris Blackwell & Douglas Lockwood pp. 26–27

19   NT Reserves Board file 5/2 371/02 7 has a copy of this letter.

20   Doris Blackwell & Douglas Lockwood p. 67

21   *Register* 22 September 1903 p. 5 and 2 November 1903 p. 6

22   Record of Prisoners held by the NT Archives in Alice Springs and NT Reserves Board file 5/2 534/05 5 with a copy of a letter by Sub-Inspector Thomas Clode on 28 November 1905

23   *Advertiser* 4 December 1905 p. 7 and State Records SA GRS 1 1905/573

24   NT Reserves Board file 5/2 371/02 7 with letter of 16 September 1902

25   Frances O'Kane p. 36–37, 40 and Dick Kimber 1986 p. 2

26   Frances O'Kane pp. 41–42

27   Doris Blackwell & Douglas Lockwood pp. 165, 167–170

28 Frances O'Kane p. 50 citing *Gee, L.C.E. Diary – Arltunga, 18 March to 9 April, 1903; 5 December to 15 December, 1903*; also *Memoirs of a Rush* by Lionel Gee in the *Register* 27 August 1923 p. 9 & 8 October p. 9

29 Frances O'Kane pp. 46–47

30 *Register* 8 October 1923 p. 9

31 Transcript of a letter of 21 June 1977 from Jessie Allchurch Wolfe to Doreen Braitling, at the National Trust office in Alice Springs

32 *Adelaide Observer* 27 June 1903 p. 1S, *Advertiser* 9 November 1903 p. 3, and *Register* 8 October 1923 p. 9

33 Frances O'Kane pp. 54–58

34 Frank Gillen 1968 pp. 12–13

35 *Register* 10 September 1903 p. 6

36 Doris Blackwell & Douglas Lockwood pp. 173–174

37 Rosemary Kennedy pp. 53, 57

38 Rosemary Kennedy p. 73

39 Doris Blackwell & Douglas Lockwood p. 146

40 Rosemary Kennedy pp. 14–15

41 Rosemary Kennedy p. 55

42 Doris Blackwell & Douglas Lockwood p. 199

43 Simpson Newland p. 20

44 Doris Blackwell & Douglas Lockwood pp. 61–62, 133

45 Rosemary Kennedy pp. 34–35, 38

46 *Advertiser* 25 March 1909 p. 6

47 *Centralian Advocate* 1 June 1951 p. 7 & 6 June 1952 p. 1

48 Rosemary Kennedy p. 22

49 Doris Blackwell & Douglas Lockwood p. 117

50 Kate Holmes 1987 p. 24

51 Doris Blackwell & Douglas Lockwood pp. 57–58

52 *Advertiser* 15 April 1903 p. 6; Doris Blackwell & Douglas Lockwood p. 202

53 Doris Blackwell & Douglas Lockwood pp. 53, 99, 108

54 Doris Blackwell & Douglas Lockwood p. 201

55 *Centralian Advocate* 28 December 1985

56 Doris Blackwell & Douglas Lockwood pp. 77–78

57 *Gillen's Diary* 1968 p. 68

58 NAA D960 B 1932/127

59 Bruce Strong pp. 256–259 citing *Journey by Territory Tramp from Oodnadatta to Alice Springs April 1909* which mentions Harry Kearnan telephoning Bloods Creek from Charlotte Waters in 1909 to see how the mail coach was going. Bruce Plowman 1957 p. 55 mentions Ted Hayes going to Alice Well to telephone the Alice Springs telegraph station when his child was ill in 1914. Kurt Johannsen p. 18 says: 'Also in 1922 our telephone was reconnected. During World War I (1914–1918) it had been removed because Dad was of Danish–German descent. It was a bit ridiculous because the range of the telephone was only about 100 miles at that time and my parents were hardly likely to be spies out in the desert!'

60   *Weekend Australian Magazine* 4, 9–10 April 1988; Bruce Strong pp. 261–266; Doris Blackwell & Douglas Lockwood pp. 150–158

61   Bruce Strong 1996 pp. 778–780

62   Fred Blakeley 1938 pp. 102–221 and Bruce Strong 1996 pp. 771–778

63   *Advertiser* 22 September 1953 p. 4

64   Doris Blackwell & Douglas Lockwood p. 203; *Advertiser* 13 August 1908 p. 6

65   John Blackwell 1985 pers. comm. to Chris Torlach on 2 September

66   *Age* 3 November 1925 p. 13 and *Advertiser* 5 November 1925 p. 10

CHAPTER 16   Thirty-two years on the line

1   *South Australian Register* 8 August 1891 p. 6 noted John McKay's presence at Barrow Creek with Jack Besley and lauded 'the excellent instruction and training the new stationmaster had received before joining the Telegraph Department'.

2   *Centralian Advocate* 24 December 1954 p. 8; electoral rolls for 1884–1990; and *Adelaide Observer* 25 July 1891 pp. 33–34

3   Kate Holmes 1990 notes for lot 100

4   Shirley Brown 2002 p. 30

5   Bruce Strong 1997 p. 5 quoting *Territory Tramp*

6   *Register* 7 July 1903 p. 4

7   *Alice Springs Star* 3 June 1981

8   Typescript of Jessie Allchurch Wolfe's letter to Doreen Braitling 16 August 1977 at the National Trust office in Alice Springs

9   NAA A3 1913/11189

10   *Report on Inspection OT Line Stations* by J. McL. Johnston, December 1909, Telecommunications Museum Cat. No. TMA 254

11   State Records SA GRS 1 1910/192: McKay complaint 15 March 1910

12   *Advertiser* 9 March 1910 p. 10 & 10 March 1910 p. 10

13   State Records SA GRS 1 1910/192: letter from Allchurch to Dow 24 April 1910; letter from McKay to Allchurch 25 April 1910; report from Dow 3 May 1910

14   Bryan Bowman 1992 pp. 11, 17

15   Commonwealth Parliamentary Paper No. 76 of 1922 pp. 42–43

16   Bruce Plowman 1957 pp. 106–108

17   Will Fox's 1961 letter to Bill McKinnon at the National Trust's office in Alice Springs

18   Kate Holmes 1990 notes for lot 64 quoting an article written by Michael Terry in *The Territorian* December 1967

19   Jack Cross pp. 370–371 citing SAPP 27/1901

20   Alan Powell 2000 pp. 137–138

21   Alan Powell 2000 pp. 139–140

22   Baldwin Spencer's *Report of the Preliminary Scientific Expedition to the Northern Territory* presented to the Commonwealth Minister for External Affairs who had responsibility for the Northern Territory at that time

23   Samuel White 1914

CHAPTER 17 The 'half-caste' problem

1   Dick Kimber 2011 p. 54 quoting Baldwin Spencer and Frank Gillen's 1927 book *The Arunta Vols I & II*, McMillan & Co. Ltd, London

2   The term 'half-caste' is now considered offensive but is used here because it was the most-common expression in the Northern Territory for people of mixed descent for much of the 20th century.

3   The NT Reserves Board file 5/2 355/10 3(a) has a copy of this letter in the Parks & Wildlife archive building at the Arid Zone Research Institute, Alice Springs.

4   John Spencer 2012 pers. comm. He is the grandson of Bill Liddle and told the author on 24 July that Mary Earwaker's child to Sonny Kunoth was called Linda. She spent most of her life in Adelaide but used to write to her mother who later married Bill Liddle. Linda married Arthur Holmes.

5   NAA A1 1912/9236

6   A letter of 26 May 1912 on NAA A1 1912/11495 refers to him as Mounted Constable Stott but another of 25 June that same year says Corporal Stott.

7   NT Dictionary of Biography Volume 1

8   Correspondence dated 26 May 1912 and 29 July 1912 on NAA A1 1912/11495

9   Tony Austin p. 37 and note 38 on p. 226. See also Stephen Gray 2012 p. 32 who says 'Undoubtedly the passage of the Northern Territory Aboriginals Act 1910 (SA) marked the end of the worst excesses of the "frontier" period'.

10 Act 1024, *An Act to make provision for the better protection and control of the Aboriginal inhabitants of the Northern Territory and for other purposes.*

11 *Australian Dictionary of Biography Volume 7 1891–1939 A–Ch* p. 202: 'He was averse to being supervised by the Territory's acting administrator [Justice Mitchell] who had found him "tactless and impractical", lacking "balance of mind" and entertaining "unwarranted large ideas of his position".' Stephen Gray 2011 pp. 54–55: 'Basedow was typical of a certain type of person who is attracted to the Territory only to quickly tire of its charms. A swaggering, self-aggrandising, self-confident German nearly two metres tall, Basedow claimed an "impudent parade" of prestigious but questionable European medical qualifications. He spent most of his time in Darwin pushing for better conditions for himself. His most memorable recommendation regarding Aboriginal people was the suggestion that – for identification and administration purposes – they be required to wear a permanent tattoo.'

12 Tony Austin p. 44

13 John Mulvaney & J.H. Calaby p. 278

14 See Section 3(1) of *Aboriginals, No. 16 of 1911, An Ordinance Relating to Aboriginals, Notified in the Gazette, 8 January 1912.* It states: 'Without limiting or affecting any other powers conferred upon him by the Act, the Chief Protector shall be entitled at any time to undertake the care, custody or control of any aboriginal or half-caste, if, in his opinion it is necessary or desirable in the interests of the aboriginal or half-caste for him to do so.'

15 Stephen Gray 2011 p. 50

16 See *Preliminary Report on the Aboriginals of the Northern Territory* by Professor W. Baldwin Spencer MA, CMG, FRS, Professor of Biology in the Melbourne University in the 'Report of the Administrator for the Year 1912', pp. 36–52.

17   Spencer's report pp. 46–47

18   Alan Powell 2000 p. 145 quotes Gilruth once saying to a member of an audience: 'The difference between your opinion and mine is that yours doesn't matter.'

19   John Mulvaney & J.H. Calaby pp. 296–299

20   *Northern Territory of Australia. Report of the Administrator for the Year 1913*, 13 November 1914 p. 8

21   Mary Kemp was born c. 1860. Dick Kimber 1986 p. 23 says her father may well have been one of John McDouall Stuart's men.

22   See the brief biography of Topsy Smith compiled by the National Trust's research officer Bruce Strong on 21 December 1993. He quotes Certificate of Death No.100 Book 4. See also Ada Wade's 1981 oral history NTRS 226 TS 348 at the NT Archives.

23   Dick Kimber 1986 p. 20

24   Dick Kimber 1986 p. iv

25   Kate Holmes 1987 p. 29 says he was there from 1897 until 1914, mostly at White Range. However, he and Topsy must have gone there several years earlier because their oldest son Walter was born at Arltunga on 2 July 1893, according to p. iv of Dick Kimber 1986. Dick says on p. 24 that Mary and Topsy remembered the arrival of the first train at Oodnadatta. The line was opened to Oodnadatta in 7 January 1891.

26   Family members maintain that Bob Stott prevented her from going on to Oodnadatta. See Philip Selth's unpublished 2013 research paper 'Gordon Keith Freeman (16 May 1890–4 October 1966)'. He says: 'At least one of Topsy's children later claimed that Bill Smith had wanted the family to go to Oodnadatta where the children could be properly educated, thinking that with the goats and other possessions she could support herself with a little help from her relations, but that Stott refused to allow them to continue on to Oodnadatta.' He quotes Aborigines' Friends' Association correspondence files, Mortlock Library, Adelaide: CP SRG 139//67.

27   Kate Holmes 1990 quotes a letter from Bob Stott in NAA A518 F241/6/1 in her history of lot 63: 'Have had building erected for accommodation of coloured children … Coloured children now attending school have been removed from Aboriginal camp within immediate vicinity of Alice Springs.'

28   NAA A1 1927/2982 27 November 1914

29   Cecil Madigan p. 70: 'Men came around openly and spoke to the children, and gave them sweets, children bearing well-known names in the district, for old Sergeant Stott, the Protector of Aborigines, enforced the rule that half-castes should be given their father's name, and for this he was dependent on the mother's story.'

30   Tony Austin p. 79: 'Her salary and conditions of service were greatly inferior to those of a beginning teacher in Darwin.'

31   Kate Holmes 1990 notes for lot 63 and Tony Austin pp. 60–61

32   NAA D959 IA1915/2295; Pearl Powell & Eileen McRae p. 41

33   *Register* 15 September 1924 p. 8 & 16 September 1924 p. 9

34   Barbara James p. 125

35   *Adelaide Chronicle* 4 July 1946 p. 17

CHAPTER 18 Worn out by the work

1   Pearl Powell & Eileen McRae pp. 63–64
2   Pearl Powell & Eileen McRae pp. 29–30
3   Faith Kramer Metters & Elva Schroeder pp. 48–54 say that travelling evangelist Erny Kramer and his family left Oodnadatta on 1 August 1919 and got to Alice Springs in middle of December, with the drought breaking shortly after they arrived.
4   Pearl Powell & Eileen McRae p. 52
5   The old iron wire was mostly used for hand transmission of local traffic after 1899.
6   The NT Archives photo ASTS 1310 shows Fred Price sitting at the table on the northern side of the Alice Springs telegraph office, with a Wheatstone receiver next to his sounder.
7   Commonwealth Public Service Permanent Officers Lists 1910–1927
8   Pearl Powell & Eileen McRae p. 44
9   Pearl Powell & Eileen McRae pp. 33, 66, 69–73
10   Pearl Powell & Eileen McRae p. 30
11   Doris Blackwell & Douglas Lockwood p. 197
12   Commonwealth Gazette No. 103, 29 June 1917
13   See the 1954 letter from Bessie Allchurch to Adela Purvis at the National Trust's office in Alice Springs. She wrote of her sister-in-law Attie Bradshaw: 'Mrs Bradshaw was a good living woman, & trained her children well. Every Sunday to mark the day, she would have a little service with the children, tell them a bible story, with an illustrated picture, the eldest girl [Doris] would play the piano and they would sing hymns. The working lubras would always put on their clean clothes & were allowed to sit on the floor & listen to the bible story & they loved looking at the pictures. One Sun Mrs Bradshaw was telling the one of Elijah lost in the wilderness and being fed by the ravens. Some time afterwards, one of the lubras had a baby boy, and brought him to show Mrs Bradshaw, who asked what she called him. The lubra said Elijah & when asked why that name, she said that she remembered the bible story & thought that some day her boy might get lost in the bush & God would send food to him by the ravens. Years after when we were at Marree a smart looking half caste boy called to see us. We recognised him straightaway and said "Hello Elijah." He told us he was taking his own name Harry Hablett & had enlisted for the war that was the 1914. Some white people had taken him from a small boy & educated him. Later he sent a photo of himself in uniform, & then one day we saw his name in the paper in the list of killed. Today his name is on the honour roll in front of the Marree post office, just one amongst many, but that is the true life story of the boy.' Doris Blackwell & Douglas Lockwood pp. 108–109 also has the story of Polly and Elijah. Doris said Elijah 'grew into a fine man' and added 'He was one of the few Central Australian aborigines who enlisted in the army in the first World War'.
14   Letter written by Barrow Creek postmaster Andrew Sands on 10 September 1918 in National Archives of Australia, Service Records, Harry Havelett, Service No. 3498
15   Pearl Powell & Eileen McRae p. 45
16   www.flupandemic.gov.au

17   T.G.H. Strehlow pp. 158–159 relates a conversation between Mrs Strehlow and Mrs Elliott about the Oodnadatta outbreak. Mrs Elliott says: 'Mr Kramer helped the police to bury the dead. So many died that the rest all fled out bush and did not stop even to bury their relatives.' She goes on to say: 'Hundreds of them died within a few weeks at Oodnadatta. It was the same at all stations between there and here; and nobody'll ever know how many died out bush after they'd rushed away from the stations.' See also Faith Kramer Metters & Elva Schroeder pp. 47–48.

18   Pearl Powell & Eileen McRae p. 50

19   Bruce Plowman 1957 pp. 55–58

20   Bruce Plowman 1957 p. 169

21   Pearl Powell & Eileen McRae p. 38

22   Pearl Powell & Eileen McRae p. 20

23   Commonwealth Parliamentary Paper No.65 of 1922: Report by Sectional Committee of Parliamentary Standing Committee on Public Works on Various Matters Appertaining to the Territory, Other than the Proposed North–South Railway

24   NAA ACT A1/1 1926/7609 Memorandum from Secretary Postmaster-General's Department to Secretary Department of External Affairs 11 January 1915

25   Pearl Powell & Eileen McRae p. 42

26   Cecil Madigan p. 77

27   Bruce Strong 1996 pp. 269–273 citing NAA ACT A458/1 item Q120/2

28   Bruce Strong 1996 pp. 266–268 citing *Express and Telegraph* 9 September 1920 p. 4h and T.G.H. Strehlow pp. 80–81

29   Commonwealth Parliamentary Papers No. 65 & No. 76 of 1922 and the photo on p. 524 of Bruce Strong 1996

30   Bruce Strong 1996 p. 274 citing p. 63 of *The Australian Motorist* 1 October 1921

31   F.S. Briggs & S.H. Harris 1938

32   NTAS NTRS 226 TS 259

33   Bob Laver p. 4

34   Bruce Strong 1996 pp. 275–278. One of the sources he cites is S. Nichols' 1978 book *Bullock Tracks and Bitumen*, which claims there were nine people in addition to the Aunger brothers. However, photos taken by Samuel White and published in the 29 July 1922 edition of the *Observer*, indicate this was not so.

35   Peter Donovan 1988 pp. 117–120

36   T.G.H. Strehlow p. 17

37   T.G.H. Strehlow pp. 18–19, 50–51

38   T.G.H. Strehlow pp. 127–128, 181

39   Pearl Powell & Eileen McRae pp. 64, 66–68

CHAPTER 19   'Make it an Allchurch!'

1   Susanna De Vries's 2005 book *Great Pioneer Women of the Outback* says on p. 107 that Tom Bradshaw told his wife in 1899 Ernie could come and live with them at the Alice Springs telegraph station and he would find a job for him there. She wrote: 'That thought cheered Atlanta [sic] up. She loved Ernest, her boisterous handsome young brother, and hoped he would soon settle down to a regular career and get married.' This has no basis in fact. It is quite clear, from the

telegraph department records, that Ernie worked for the department for 15 years before his sister and her family moved to Alice Springs. He was not an unsettled young bloke given a job by his brother-in-law.

2 See the 10 March 1954 letter Bessie Allchurch wrote from Moonta to Adela Purvis in Alice Springs. The original is at the National Trust's office in Alice Springs.

3 Winty Calder p. 84

4 *Advertiser* 16 January 1932 p. 17

5 *Transcontinental* 29 January 1932 p. 4

6 Edgar Harcourt p. 173

7 Barbara James p. 103

8 NT Archives photo ASTS 1432

9 Adela Purvis's letter to Mona Byrnes 22 April 1966 held at the National Trust's office in Alice Springs

10 See a letter written by Bob Stott, cited in Kate Holmes 1990.

11 *1927 Commonwealth of Australia, The Territory of Central Australia, Report of the Government Resident for the period 1st March to 30th June 1927* says there were 411 people in the territory of Central Australia, south of the 20th parallel.

12 10 March 1954 letter from Bessie Allchurch to Adela Purvis at the National Trust's office in Alice Springs

13 Barbara James p. 104

14 Peter Donovan p. 138

15 *1927 Commonwealth of Australia, The Territory of Central Australia, Report of the Government Resident for the period 1st March 1927 to 30th June 1927*

16 L.B. Long

17 R.M. Todd p. 175 refers to phonopores being installed south of Darwin 'in approximately 1925'. The Nicker family got one at their store at Ryans Well and another was installed at Bill Heffernan's Tea Tree Well store.

18 Bruce Strong pp. 335–341 & 347–351. *Report on the Administration of Central Australia for the Year Ended the 30th June 1928* says: 'In August the Reso Party, organised by Victorian Railways, visited Central Australia. This party consisted of 80 persons, and included prominent representatives of the pastoral, financial and manufacturing interests. Although the country was then suffering from the effects of unprecedented drought, the consensus of opinion was that Central Australia was not a "desert land", and that, given normal seasons, the greater part of the Territory as a pastoral proposition was sound.'

19 Bruce Strong pp. 324–326, 344–346 & 353–355

20 See Dick Kimber's story published in *Alice Springs News* in 18 parts: issues 1032–1046 from 10 September 2003 to 17 December 2003; and issues 1101–1103 from 4 February 2004 to 18 February 2004.

21 Bill Wilson & Justin O'Brien p. 73

22 William George Murray was involved in the search for the *Kookaburra* in 1929 but little is known of his other activities in the years between 1928 and World War II. The website of the NT Police Museum and Historical Society Inc. says that documents from his police file 'were mislaid and never refiled in the correct location'.

23 Kurt Johannsen p. 66

24 Kurt Johannsen p. 18, and Peter Latz p. 32 who refers to one big fire, probably in the summer of 1922, reputedly burning for a thousand kilometres from Oodnadatta to Tennant Creek.

25 Margaret Ford p. 84

26 Dick Kimber's Coniston Massacre Part 15, *Alice Springs News*, Issue 1046 17 December 2003

27 Margaret Ford pp. 114–118 & 122

28 Peter Latz p. 32

29 Kurt Johannsen p. 34

30 Basil Fuller pp. 223–224

31 Peter Donovan p. 141

32 *The Commonwealth of Australia, The Territory of Central Australia, Report of the Government Resident for the period 1st March 1927 to 30th June 1927* p. 7

33 *Report on the Administration of Central Australia for the Year Ended the 30th June 1929*

34 *Annual Report by the Government Resident on the Administration of the Territory of Central Australia for the Year 1st July 1929 to 30th June 1930*

35 Bruce Strong 1997 p. 23

36 Cecil Madigan p. 58

37 1977 letters from Jessie Wolfe to Doreen Braitling at the National Trust's office in Alice Springs

38 Cecil Madigan pp. 107–156

39 The Central Australian Gold Exploration Company used the place as a base camp for its expedition to locate Lasseter's Reef. The expedition's leader Fred Blakeley called it Ilbilba but the NT Place Names Committee's website now spells it Ilpili.

40 Michael Cannon pp. 275–277

41 Max Cartwright p. 85

42 Fred Blakeley 1972 pp. 6–7

43 *My Father's Story* by Bob Lasseter on the Westprint map 'Alice Springs to Uluru'. Harry Lasseter said the reef ran for seven miles, was four yards wide and between four and seven feet high.

44 Barry Allwright 2016 pers. comm., though Fred Blakeley 1972 p. 10 says 21 July

45 Fred Blakeley 1972 p. 9 & Errol Coote pp. 39–40

46 It seems Johns's appearance was no coincidence but prearranged by Lasseter. See Dick Kimber 1986 pp. 86–87.

47 Max Cartwright pp. 96–97 quoting the Sydney *Daily Mirror* 29 April 1931

CHAPTER 20 From telegraph station to children's home

1 There were 50 children at the Bungalow in 1924 when the white population of the town was less than 40. See Baldwin Spencer's report written after his 1923 visit to Alice Springs with Keith Ward: NAA A1 1927/2982 f. 312–316. The staff consisted of part-time matron, three other women, two goat shepherds, a gardener and his wife. All except the matron were of Aboriginal descent and received clothes and rations, but no pay.

2 Baldwin Spencer visited the mission in May 1923 and considered this suggestion. See Tony Austin pp. 73–76 and E. Leske pp. 34–35.

3   NAA A1 1927/2982 f.245–247 of 20 January 1923 and correspondence following it on that file.

4   Adelaide's *Advertiser* 9 October 1924 p. 10, and p. 5 of Hobart's *Mercury* 20 December 1924. There are cuttings of the same article from Sydney's *Daily Telegraph* 8 October 1925 and Brisbane's *Daily Mail* 13 November 1924 on NAA A1 1927/2982 f.190 & f.204.

5   See *Parliament of Australia, The Biographical Dictionary of the Australian Senate, Online Edition.* Australia's longest serving prime minister, Robert Menzies, remembered Pearce in 1965 as the ablest man he had encountered among the many ministers with whom he had worked. He attributed him with an unrivalled capacity for analytical thought and for the clear exposition of ideas and policy recommendations. Menzies also noted Pearce was blessed with a 'profound and reflective mind', the prerequisite for drawing profit from one's mistakes.

6   NAA A1 1927/2982 f.293–299 & 322–332 and blueprints dated 16 April 1925

7   An agreement was in place by September 1925 to purchase 25 square miles for £175. See NAA A1 1927/2982 f.388–390 of 3 April 1925, f.394 of 4 April 1925, f.1 of 4 September 1925, f.14 of 2 February 1926 & f.29 of 23 April 1926

8   NAA A1 1927/2982 f.421–422 of 11–12 August 1925 & f.47–50 of 13 July 1926

9   Roughly half of the allocation was spent on drilling. See NAA A659 1939/1/996 f.146–147 of 30 August 1929, f.223 & 224 of 25 February 1930 & f.293 of 17 September 1930. However, NAA A1 1927/2982 f.101 says this was not all on drilling for water. The concrete floor and framework for one dormitory were also completed.

10 NAA A1 1927/2982 f.91 of 11 May 1927, f.105 of 22 June 1927 & f.123 of 4 August 1927

11 NAA A1 1927/2982 f.144–145 of 19 September 1927

12 NAA A1 1927/2982 f.147 of 5 November 1927 and reply f.150 of 17 November 1927

13 NAA A1 1927/2982 f.166–168 of 3 November 1927 & 24 March 1928. See also NAA A659 1939/1/996 f.146–147 of 30 August 1929

14 *Report of the Administration of Central Australia for the Year ended the 30th June, 1929* p. 6 says: 'In view of the approach of the railway construction work to Alice Springs, it was considered desirable that the half-caste home situated in the town should be removed to a temporary site, pending the location of water at alternative sites selected for the erection of permanent buildings. The water supply at a site on Jay Creek was tested and found to be adequate for domestic purposes if care was exercised.'

15 NAA A659 1939/1/996 f.62 telegram from the government resident to the Department of Home & Territories 22 January 1929

16 NAA A659 1939/1/996 f.177–179 report by Cecil Cook to the Department of Home Affairs on 25 October 1929

17 Correspondence of 18 April 1929, 19 April 1929 & 8 May 1929 on NAA D961 C1932/14

18 Faith Kramer Metters & Elva Schroeder p. 98 and NAA A659 1939/1/996 f.80, 82, 90

19 November 1962 edition of *Walkabout* magazine has a letter from Professor Porteous saying he came up with the name Standley Chasm when in Central

Australia in 1929 'at the invitation of the Australian National Research Council to study the mentality of aborigines'.

20 *Annual Report by the Government Resident of the Territory of Central Australia for the year 1st July 1928 to 30th June 1929* says 'Mrs Standley, who had been matron for fourteen years, retired from the service in March 1929. Mr and Mrs Thorne were appointed temporarily as Superintendent and Matron respectively'. See also NAA A659 1939/1/996 f.106, 115.

21 NAA A659 1939/1/996 f.131–133 31 July 1929. See also *Sydney Morning Herald* 7 August 1929 p. 16 & Adelaide's *Chronicle* 8 August 1929 p. 54. There are four photos of the place: NAA A1 1929/5189 PHOTO 11A, 11B, 11C & 11D.

22 NAA A659 1939/1/996 f.237. See also *Sydney Morning Herald* 7 April 1930 p. 6 and Adelaide's *Chronicle* 10 April 1930 p. 31

23 NAA A659 1939/1/996 f.155, 163, 172

24 NAA D961 C1932/14 19 June 1930

25 NAA A659 1939/1/996 f.293 Department of Home Affairs memorandum 17 September 1930 & f.408–410 correspondence to the treasurer 12 April 1932

26 Port Augusta's *Transcontinental* 29 January 1932 p. 4

27 *Sydney Morning Herald* 4 August 1933 p. 8

28 *Australian Dictionary of Biography*, entry for Cecil Cook by Tim Rowse

29 Stephen Gray 2011 p. 82

30 See NAA A1 1929/5189 f.16–17. G.W. Burns visited the Jay Creek Bungalow in June 1929 while acting as accountant for the Home & Territories Department. He reported: 'A list of names of half-caste children was inspected. A number of the surnames were identical with those of settlers in the Territory. Section 44 of the Aboriginal Ordinance provides that the father of a half-caste may be called upon to contribute up to 15/- per week towards the maintenance of the child. Out of 40 or 50 children in the Bungalow, only about 4 are being maintained by their fathers. This seems a very low proportion. It is considered that the Government Resident should be instructed that in future the provisions of Section 44 of the Ordinance should be more strictly enforced.'

CHAPTER 21 The 'new' Bungalow Half-caste Institution

1 *The Annual Report by the Government Resident on the administration of the Territory of Central Australia for the year ended 30th June 1930*

2 *Chronicle* 24 November 1932 p. 20

3 Commonwealth Gazette No. 87 of 8 December 1932 and NAA A1 1936/9423 f.27

4 Northern Territory Archives Service NTRS 226 TS 660. Emily was born on 31 October 1919.

5 Herbie Laughton 2002 pers. comm.

6 *Report on the administration of the Northern Territory for the year ended 30th June 1934* p. 9, and Harry Griffiths p. 113 who says Pine Creek people wanted the boys out of the town.

7 NAA NT F1 1937/30

8 Tony Austin pp. 163–164

9 Letter dated 18 January 1934 on NAA F1 1937/30

10   NAA A1 1935/1375 and a letter from John Flynn on F1 1938/666 dated 10
      November 1933
11   NAA A1 1935/643 f.83–84 and Frank O'Grady p. 14
12   Barbara James p. 172
13   There are three different spellings of her name. Peter Read uses Hetti in his book
      Charles Perkins, A Biography but it's spelt Hetty in Charles Perkins's autobiography
      A Bastard Like Me. Then there's the Hettie Perkins Home in Alice Springs.
14   Peter Read p. 3. He says on p. 19 that Nellie died in 1947.
15   Robert Harold Lake is listed on the 1909 electoral roll as a storekeeper at Arltunga.
      Peter Read p. 4 says 'Harry Lake went to World War I in 1914, leaving Hetti at
      the Crossroads pub with her son Percy'. However, there is no service record in the
      National Archives to confirm that he did enlist.
16   Northern Territory Archives Service NTRS 226 TS 660
17   Bruce Plowman 1957 pp. 57–58 describes the marriage of Billy Bray and Mary
      Perkins at Deep Well.
18   Northern Territory Archives Service, NTRS 226 TS 659. George Bray was born
      on 2 June 1927. See *Centralian Advocate* 2 October 1981 p. 1 and 15 August 2000
      p. 12
19   John Smith 1999 p. 13
20   Doris Blackwell & Douglas Lockwood pp. 137–144
21   John Smith p. 16 though Bruce Strong 1998 p. 26 says it was 1914.
22   John Smith p. 44
23   John Smith p. 17
24   John Smith p. 50
25   NAA A1 1935/1375, letter from Tilly Tilmouth 25 February 1934
26   John Smith p. 50
27   See file NAA F125 2 and the extensive, unpublished research on Gordon Keith
      Freeman compiled by Philip Selth, Executive Officer of the NSW Bar Association
28   NAA A1 1935/643 memorandum of 3 March 1934: Important
      Happenings – February.
29   Letter 5 March 1934 from Erny Kramer to Reverend J.H. Sexton, located by Philip
      Selth: Aborigines' Friends' Association correspondence files, Mortlock Library,
      Adelaide, Dismissal of Superintendent Half Caste Home Alice Springs, CP SRG
      139/1/265
30   Northern Territory Archives Service F110 *Register of Prisoners for Stuart Town Gaol*
      and F109 *Gaol Journal.*
31   Maise Chettle p. 66
32   NAA A1 1935/643
33   NAA F1 1937/30
34   Maise Robb married late in life. She published her memoir *Just Me* in 1997 under
      her married name Maise Chettle.
35   Maise Robb pers. comm. quoted in Tony Austin p. 167
36   Maise Chettle pp. 90–91
37   NAA F1 1937/30 where Grace Randall says the children were hard to discipline
38   NAA F1 1942/91

39   *NT Dictionary of Biography* Volume 1
40   NAA F1 1937/30
41   Northern Territory Archives Service NTRS 226 TS 659
42   Ron Tilmouth 2008 pers. comm.
43   NAA F1 1940/153
44   NAA F1 1942/84
45   NAA F1 1942/70(b)
46   NAA F1 1940/153
47   NAA F1 1940/153
48   *Australian* 23 August 1996 p. 21 and John Smith pp. 43, 55–56
49   Alec Kruger 2002 per. comm.
50   *Sydney Morning Herald* 8 September 1998
51   Shirley Brown 2002 pp. 7–8
52   Cynthia Mallard 2013 pers. comm.
53   This account of Jessie White's life was provided by Cynthia Mallard in 2013, from
      the transcripts of two interviews her mother gave in the 1980s. In 1982 Jessie told
      her story to Christine Palmer of *Alice Springs Star* 4 November 1982 p. 12. On 25
      March 1988 she talked to Frances Coughlan, Community Welfare Officer, Central
      Australian Aboriginal Congress.
54   Cynthia Mallard 2013 pers. comm.

CHAPTER 22   Two different worlds before the war

1   *Aboriginals Ordinance No. 9 of 1918*, section 11 prohibited areas
2   *THE NORTHERN TERRITORY OF AUSTRALIA, Regulations under the Aboriginals
     Ordinance 1918–1933*, Extract from the Commonwealth of Australia Gazette no.
     40, 29 June 1933
3   See p. 7 of John Cawood's 1927 *The Commonwealth of Australia, The Territory of
     Central Australia, Report of the Government Resident for the period 1st March 1927
     to 30th June 1927*. The camp was located near where the hospital now stands and
     spread across to the river. See also NAA A1 1936/10413.
4   Maise Chettle pp. 154–155
5   Frank O'Grady p. 12
6   Edward Bennett pp. 34
7   NAA A1 1935/643 f.104–106 of 3 January 1938
8   NAA A1 1935/643 f.27 of 8 December 1936
9   Frank O'Grady p. 40
10   *The Northern Territory of Australia: Commonwealth Government's policy with respect to
     Aboriginals*, February 1939, National Library of Australia NP 572.99429 MCE. See
     also Andrew Markus p. 106 in which he cites NAA A452 1952/541 part 2.
11   Tony Austin pp. 199–203
12   NAA F1 1940/153
13   NAA F1 1942/70(b) and A659 1942/1/4499
14   NAA F1 1940/478
15   NAA F1 1940/153
16   NAA F1 1942/91

17 NAA F1 1942/70(b), F1 1940/153 and F1 1949/53
18 Alan Powell 1988 p. 56
19 NAA F1 1942/367, F1 1942/406, A885 B400 and A885 B402
20 NAA F1 1943/75

CHAPTER 23 The Territory transformed by war

1 Alex Tanner p. 17
2 Harry Griffith pp. 172–173 and Alex Tanner p. 3 give this date but Alan Smith 2000 p. 67 says it was 9 September 1940.
3 Alex Tanner p. 233 says Lieutenant Colonel Loutit was promoted to colonel in February 1941 and brigadier in August 1942.
4 Alan Smith 2002 pp. 45, 49
5 Alex Tanner p. 23 and Tony Wege 2015 pers. comm. Tony Wege said they were initially posted to Darwin and then landed in Singapore on 24 January 1942.
6 Harry Griffiths p. 173 says 194,852 troops.
7 J. Macdonald Holmes p. 402 and Alan Powell 1988 p. 225 who says there were 956 civilians and 4600 troops in January 1943.
8 Douglas Lockwood p. 163 says Administrator C.L.A. Abbott left Darwin for Alice Springs on 2 March 1942.
9 Ann Moyal p. 154, though a National Trust pamphlet for Lyon's Cottage in Darwin says the cable was officially taken out of service in 1938. NAA F1 1937/61 has correspondence from 1935 to 1937 about the acquisition of Eastern Extension Telegraph Co. property adjoining the post office: mess, tennis court, manager's residence, well and underground tanks.
10 R.M. Todd p. 175
11 Kurt Johannsen p. 18
12 Alan Smith 2002 p. 113
13 R.M. Todd p. 175
14 R.C.M. Dale p. 162
15 R.M. Todd p. 176 and Alan Smith 2002 pp. 108–109, 116
16 Alex Tanner pp. 147–153 and Alan Smith 2002 pp. 69–70. Alan Powell 1988 p. 231 says: 'Work went slowly, at the rate of little more than 2 kilometres a week, until the arrival of two modern Barber-Green plant mix units from the U.S.A. allowed a great increase, to an average of 22–30 kilometres per week. Sealing of the Tennant Creek–Larrimah road was completed in February 1943. By mid December of that year the bitumen joined Alice Springs to Tennant Creek.'
17 R.M. Todd p. 176
18 Bruce Strong 1996 pp. 418–419
19 Peter Donovan p. 214 and p. 266 says 'The war years were watershed ones for the Aborigines about Alice Springs'.
20 Alec Kruger & Gerard Waterford pp. 122–123
21 Alan Powell 1988 p. 248
22 Frank O'Grady pp. 71, 75–76, 78
23 NAA A659 1942/1/4499 21 May 1942
24 Alan Smith 2000 p. 248

25 NAA AA1978/215, 41 6 November 1942
26 Alan Powell 1988 p. 257
27 NAA F1 1942/406 8 January 1943
28 Technical Report 1964/R2 *Pumping for the Alice Springs Water Supply* April 1964 by District Engineer H.F. Eggington
29 NAA AA1978/215, 41 20 June 1943
30 NAA F1 1942/433
31 NAA AA1978/215, 41 10 March 1943
32 NAA A659 1942/1/4499 21 May 1942
33 NAA F1 1942/70 (b) 17 July 1942
34 Alex Tanner p. 217
35 NAA F1 1942/397, F1 1942/406 & F1 1943/75
36 NAA F1 1943/75 13 December 1943
37 NAA F1 1942/433
38 Alan Powell 1988 p. 258 citing NAA A431 1946/915
39 Alec Kruger & Gerard Waterford p. 123
40 Jeremy Long p. 6
41 Gordon Sweeney 2014 pers. comm. Gordon Sweeney's son, also called Gordon, said there were 30–40 Aboriginal people camped there at times during 1943–1945.
42 NAA F1 1943/75
43 Gordon Sweeney 2014 pers. comm. See also Frank O'Grady pp. 93–95
44 NAA AA1978/215,53 26 August 1943 & 16 January 1944

CHAPTER 24 Preserving the town's heritage

1 *Centralian Advocate* 9 February 1951 pp. 6, 9
2 Peter Donovan p. 273
3 NAA F1 1953/515 & F1 1954/952
4 *Centralian Advocate* 8 April 1949 p. 1
5 NAA F1 1951/523, F1 1952/443 & F1 1954/952
6 NAA F1 1952/223, F1 1955/1137, F1 1956/739 & E51 1960/673
7 Frank O'Grady p. 119
8 Shirley Brown 2002 p. 83
9 NAA F1 1951/523
10 NAA F1 1953/515
11 NAA F1 1952/211
12 NAA F1 1955/1137
13 NAA F1 1953/515
14 NAA F1 1954/952
15 NAA F1 1943/75, F1 1948/223 & F1 1951/523
16 *Centralian Advocate* 10 December 1954 p. 2 and NAA F1 1954/952
17 Northern Territory Archives Service NTRS 219 TP 215
18 *Centralian Advocate* 1 July 1960
19 NAA F1 1955/1137

20   NAA F1 1960/921 and *Centralian Advocate* 7 October 1960 p. 1
21   *Centralian Advocate* 13 January 1950 p. 1
22   *Centralian Advocate* 17 September 1954 p. 13
23   *Centralian Advocate* 26 November 1954 p. 16
24   NAA F1 1960/921
25   Commonwealth of Australia Gazette, no. 88, 25 October 1962
26   Bob Purvis 2002 pers. comm.
27   *Centralian Advocate* 21 June 1963

Bibliography

Books

Austin, Tony. 1993, *I Can Picture the Old Home So Clearly*, Aboriginal Studies Press, Canberra

Birtles, Francis. 1909, *Lonely Lands: Through the Heart of Australia*, Bookstall Co. Sydney

Blakeley, Fred. 1938, *Hard Liberty*, George Harrap & Co. London

Blakeley, Fred. 1972, *Dream Millions: New Light on Lasseter's Lost Reef*, Mary Mansfield (ed.), Angus & Robertson, Sydney

Bowman, Bryan. 1992, *A History of Central Australia Vol. III, The Stuart Highway 1921–1991*, self-published

Briggs F.S. & S.H. Harris. 1938, *Joysticks and Fiddlesticks*, Hutchinson & Co. London

Brown, Shirley. 2002, *Legends of the Red Heart*, Central Queensland University Press, Rockhampton

Calder, Winty. 1993, *Telegraph Tourists, Crossing Australia with 'Vauxie' and 'Baby'*, Jimaringle Publications

Cannon, Michael. 2001, *The Exploration of Australia*, Readers Digest, Sydney

Carter, Jeff. 1969, *In the Steps of the Explorers*, Angus & Robertson, Sydney

Cartwright, Max. 1991, *Ayers Rock to the Petermanns, The Legend of Lasseter*, self-published

Chettle, Maise. 1997, *Just Me*, Seaview Press

Chewings, Charles. 1886, *The Sources of the Finke River*, W.K. Thomas & Co., Adelaide

Clune, Frank. 1955, *Overland Telegraph*, Angus & Robertson, Sydney

Christoph, Neil. 1983, *Three Brothers from Birnbaum, The Muller Family History*, Lutheran Publishing House, Adelaide

Colwell, Max & Naylor, Alan. 1974, *Adelaide, An Illustrated History*, Lansdowne Press

Coote, Errol. 1981, *Hell's Airport and Lasseter's Lost Legacy*, Investigator Press, Hawthorndene

Cross, Jack. 2011, *Great Central State, The Foundation of the Northern Territory*, Wakefield Press, Adelaide

Cummings, Barbara. 1990, *Take This Child*, Aboriginal Studies Press, Canberra

Donovan, Peter. 1981, *A Land Full of Possibilities: A History of South Australia's Northern Territory, 1863–1911*, University of Queensland Press, St Lucia

Donovan, Peter. 1988, *Alice Springs, Its History and the People Who Made It*, Alice Springs Town Council

Ericksen, Ray. 1978, *Ernest Giles Explorer and Traveller 1835–1997*, Heinemann

Feeken, Erwin & Gerda. 1970, *The Discovery and Exploration of Australia*, introduction by Professor O.H.K. Spate of ANU, Thomas Nelson, Australia

Ford, Margaret. 1978, *Beyond the Furthest Fences*, Rigby Seal Books

Fuller, Basil. 1975, *The Ghan, The Story of the Alice Springs Railway*, Rigby

Giles, Alfred. 1926, *Exploring in the Seventies and the Construction of the Overland Telegraph Line*, W.K. Thomas & Co., Adelaide

Giles, Ernest. 1889, *Australia Twice Traversed: The Romance of Exploration*, Double Day Australia

Gosse, Fayette.1981, *The Gosses, An Anglo-Australian Family*, Brian Clouston, Canberra

Gray, Stephen. 2011, *The Protectors, a journey through whitefella past*, Allen & Unwin, Sydney

Gray, Stephen. 2012, *Brass Discs, Dog Tags & Finger Scanners, The Apology and Aboriginal Protection in the Northern Territory 1863–1972*, CDU Press, Darwin

Griffiths Harry. 1975, *An Australian Adventure*, Rigby, Adelaide

Harcourt, Edgar. 1987, *Taming the Tyrant*, Allen & Unwin, Sydney

Hall, Robert. 1997, *The Black Diggers*, Aboriginal Studies Press, Canberra

Hardman, William (ed.). *Explorations in Australia, The Journals of John McDouall Stuart*, Saunders, Otley & Co., London (Facsimile edition, 1984, Hesperian Press)

Holmes, J. Macdonald. 1963, *Australia's Open North*, Angus & Robertson, Sydney

James, Barbara. 1989, *No Man's Land, Women of the Northern Territory*, Collins

Jenvey, H.W. 1898, *Practical Telegraphy: a Guide for the Use of Officers of the Victorian Post and Telegraph Department Vol.1*, Government Printer, Melbourne

Kelsey, D.E. 1975, *The Shackle*, Ira Nesdale (ed.), Lynton Publications, Blackwood

Kennedy, Rosemary. 2011, *Mabel Taylor's Diary & Letters from Alice Springs 1905 to 1907*, Historical Society of the Northern Territory, Darwin

Kruger, Alec & Waterford, Gerard. 2007, *Alone on the Soaks, The life and times of Alec Kruger*, IAD Press, Alice Springs

Latz, Peter. 1995, *Bushfires and Bushtucker, Aboriginal Plant Use in Central Australia*, IAD Press, Alice Springs

Leske, E. 1977, *Hermannsburg: A Vision and a Mission*, Lutheran Publishing House, Adelaide

Lewis, John. 1922, *Fought and Won*, W.K. Thomas & Co., Adelaide

Lockwood, Douglas. 1966, *Australia's Pearl Harbour*, Cassell Australia, Melbourne

MacDonald, Rowena. 1995, *Between Two Worlds*, IAD Press, Alice Springs

Madigan, Cecil. 1944 revised edition, *Central Australia*, Oxford University Press, Melbourne

Metters, Faith Kramer & Schroeder, Elva. 2008, *Outback Evangelist, The Story of Ernest Kramer*, Peacock Publications

Miller, Ann. *I See No End to Travelling*, Bay Books, Sydney

Mills, E.W. 1993, *William Whitfield Mills*, published by Elliott Whitfield Mills, Glenside, and printed by Lutheran Publishing House, Adelaide

Mincham, Hans.1964, *The Story of the Flinders Ranges*, Rigby, Adelaide

Moyal, Ann. 1984, *Clear Across Australia, A History of Communications*, Nelson, Melbourne

Mudie, Ian. 1968, *The Heroic Journey of John McDouall Stuart*, Angus & Robertson, Sydney

Mulvaney, D.J. with J.H. Calaby. 1985, *So Much That Is New, Baldwin Spencer 1860–1929, A Biography*, Melbourne University Press

Murif, Jerome J. 1897, *From Ocean to Ocean, Across a Continent on a Bicycle, An Account of a Solitary Ride from Adelaide to Port Darwin*, George Robertson and Co. Melbourne, Sydney, Adelaide, Brisbane and London

Nettlebeck, Amanda & Foster, Robert. 2007, *In the Name of the Law*, Wakefield Press, Adelaide

O'Grady, Frank. 1977, *Francis of Central Australia*, Wentworth Books, Sydney

Plowman, Bruce. 1957, *The Man from Oodnadatta*, Third Edition, Angus & Robertson

Powell, Alan. 1988, *The Shadow's Edge, Australia's Northern War*, Melbourne University Press

Powell, Alan. 2000, *Far Country*, Centenary of Federation edition, Melbourne University Press

Read, Peter. 1990, *Charles Perkins, A Biography*, Viking Press, Ringwood

Scherer, P.A. 1971, *Venture of Faith, An Epic in Australian Missionary History*, Lutheran Publishing House, Adelaide

Smith, John. 1999, *The Flower in the Desert – A Biography of the Reverend Canon P McD Smith, MBE*, Seaview Press

Smith, Alan. 2000 revised edition, *Convoys Up The Track*, Griffin Press, Adelaide

Smith, Alan. 2002, *Outback Corridor*, Griffin Press, Adelaide

Strehlow, John. 2011, *The Tale of Frieda Keysser Volume 1*, Wildcat Press, London

Strehlow, T.G.H. 1969, *Journey to Horseshoe Bend*, Rigby, Adelaide

Tanner, Alex. 1995, *The Long Road North*, Hyde Park Press, Adelaide

Taylor, Peter. 1980, *An End to Silence*, Methuen, Sydney

Thomson, Alice. 1999, *The Singing Line, Tracking the Australian Adventures of My Intrepid Victorian Ancestors*, Anchor Books, New York

Tietkens, William. 1891, *Journal of the Central Australian Exploring Expedition, 1889, Under Command of W. H. Tietkens*, C.E. Bristow Government Printer, Adelaide

Vallee, Peter. 2007 Readers' Edition, *God, Guns and Government on the Central Australian Frontier*, Restoration, Canberra

Warburton, Peter Egerton. 1875, *Journey Across the Western Interior of Australia*, Sampson Low, Marston, Low & Searle

Webster, Mona Stuart. 1958, *John McDouall Stuart*, Melbourne University Press

White, Samuel. 1914, *Into the Dead Heart*, Australiana Facsimile Editions No. 216, republished by The Friends of the State Library of South Australia in 1998

Diaries

Allchurch, Edward. *The Voyage of the Atalanta, Plymouth to Adelaide 1866*, published by Janet Lumsden and Harold Baker and printed by Metropolitan Printers Pty Ltd Lakemba in 1978

Clarke, Benjamin. *Diary of Benjamin Clarke 27 Sept 1871–5 August 1872*

(Original held by Mitchell Library, State Library of NSW call number ML B1605 CY Reel 3464. A copy, transcribed and annotated by Bruce Strong 19 July 1996, is held at the National Trust office in Alice Springs 384.1 CLA)

Gillen, Robert. S. 1995, *F.J. Gillen's First Diary 1875*, Wakefield Press, Adelaide

Gillen, Frank. 1968, *Gillen's Diary, The Camp Jottings of F.J. Gillen on the Spencer and Gillen Expedition across Australia 1901–1902*, Library Board of South Australia, Adelaide

McMinn, Gilbert. *Diary of G.R. McMinn*, State Records South Australia GRG 154/8 (Formerly SAA item 565/24A.)

Mueller, J.F. *Diary. Journey from Adelaide to Alice Springs McDonnell* (sic) *Ranges. Commenced September 26th 1871. Finished December 31st 1871*. (A photocopy is held at the National Trust office in Alice Springs with a covering letter to Paul France from William Chappell, great-grandson of Mueller's brother Paul.)

Renner, Frederick. *Diary of Dr Frederick Emil Renner Apr. 4 to June 6, 1871*, State Library South Australia D7919/2(L)

Ross, John. *Diary of Mr John Ross, Leader of the Overland Exploring Expedition, 1870–1871* (A photocopy of a transcript is held at the National Trust office in Alice Springs.)

Smith, James Churchill. *Diary for 1872, MacDonnell Ranges* (Original is held by the State Library of South Australia. Photocopy is in the reading room of the NT Archives, Alice Springs.)

Spencer, Walter Baldwin. *Walter Baldwin Spencer's Diary from the Spencer and Gillen Expedition 1901–1902* (Available on line.)

Articles and Papers

Allwright, Barry. 2009, *Rivers of Rubies, The History of the Ruby Rush in Central Australia*, Barry M. Allwright, Alice Springs (Second Edition)

Ashwin, Arthur. *From South Australia to Port Darwin with Sheep and Horses in 1870–71*, Proceedings of the Royal Geographical Society of Australasia, SA Branch Vol. XXXII, 47–93

Bennett, Edward. 2007, *Memoirs of Brother Edward Bennett O.A.M. M.S.C.*, first printed by In Fine Print 1989, reprinted in 2007 by Recycled Printing, Alice Springs

Benstead, Bill. *Short Stories of My Life and Travels* (A copy of the unpublished manuscript is held at the National Trust office in Alice Springs, courtesy of Stuart Benstead.)

Bucknall, Graeme. 1984, *Flynn's Mantle of Safety, The Story of Adelaide House*, published by the John Flynn Memorial Book House, Alice Springs

Dale, R.C.M. 1939, *Alice Springs and the Overland Telegraph Line* in *Telecommunications Journal of Australia*, Vol. 2, No. 3 February 1939

Forrest, Peter. 1981, *Arltunga Reserve Historic Goldfield Volume 1 of 3: A report prepared by Mr P. Forrest on a study of historic sites and materials undertaken by the National Trust of Australia (NT) with funds provided from the National Estate Program 1979/80.*

Gibson, Jason. 2013, *Addressing the Arrernte: FJ Gillen's 1896 Engwura Speech*, Australian Aboriginal Studies 2013/1 pp. 57–72

Giles, Alfred. c. 1929, *The First Pastoral Settlement* (The unpublished original, handwritten manuscript is held at the State Library of South Australia PRG 1389/2. It was formerly SA Archives 1082. A photocopy is held at the National Trust office in Alice Springs.)

Hartwig, Mervyn. 1965, *The Progress of White Settlement in the Alice Springs District and its Effects upon the Aboriginal Inhabitants*, Thesis submitted for the degree of Doctor of Philosophy in History in the University of Adelaide

Holmes, Kate. 1980, *The White Range settlement area, Arltunga Goldfield, N.T., A look at the lifestyle of an isolated mining area using the written and archaeological record*, M.A. Thesis, University of Sydney, March 1980

Holmes, Kate. 1983, *Excavations at Arltunga, Northern Territory*, in *Australian Historical Archeology*, 1, 1983

Holmes, Kate. 1987, *Arltunga, Northern Territory: The use of Artefacts to Augment the Documented History, Results of a survey covering occupation from the 1890s to the 1950s*. Thesis submitted in fulfilment of the requirements for the degree of Doctor of Philosophy, Historical Archaeology in the Faculty of Arts, University of Sydney, December 1987

Holmes, Kate. 1990, *Arltunga, A Remote Mining Settlement, An Archaeological Investigation of an Historic Site*. Thesis submitted in fulfilment of the requirements for the degree of Doctor of Philosophy, Historical Archaeology in the Faculty of Arts, University of Sydney, July 1990

Holmes, Kate. 1990, *Alice Springs, The First 104 Lots*, report of a project to document the ownership and building history of the original township of Stuart, now Alice Springs, from 1888 to the present, for the National Trust of Australia (NT)

Kimber, R.G. 1991, *The End of the Bad Old Days: European Settlement in Central Australia, 1871–1894*, State Library of the Northern Territory, Darwin

Kimber, R.G. 1992 report for the National Trust *Finke River Survey Parts II & III*

Kimber, R.G. 1990, *Flint, Ernest Ebenezer Samuel* in *Northern Territory Dictionary of Biography Volume 1* pp. 101–103, David Carment, Robyn Maynard & Alan Powell (eds), NTU Press, Darwin

Kimber, R.G. 1998, *Gillen Time: The Creation of an Era* in *Connection and Disconnection, Encounters between settlers and indigenous people in the Northern Territory*, NTU Press

Kimber, R.G. 2003/2004 *The Coniston Massacre*, published in *Alice Springs News* in 18 parts, Issues 1032–1046 from 10 September 2003 to 17 December 2003 & Issues 1101–1103 from 4 February 2004 to 18 February 2004

Kimber, R.G. 2011, *Cultural Values Associated with Alice Springs Water*, commissioned by the Alice Springs Water Management Branch of the Department of Natural Resources, Environment, the Arts and Sport

Laver, Bob. 1978, *Memoirs of Robert Laver, 1921–1925* in the Alice Springs Public Library's Alice Springs Collection

Lindsay, David. 1889, *An Expedition across Australia from South to North, between the Telegraph Line and the Queensland Boundary, in 1885–6*, Proceedings of the Royal Geographical Society and Monthly Record of Geography, Vol. XI November 1889

Lindsay, David. 1890, *Explorations in the Northern Territory of South Australia* read to the Royal Geographical Society of Australasia (SA Branch) on 29 June 1887 and published in their 1890 Proceedings Vol. 2 (3): 1–16

Long, Jeremy. 1992, *The Go-Betweens: The Origins of the Patrol Officer Service in the Northern Territory*, Occasional Paper no. 31, State Library of the Northern Territory, Darwin 1992

Long, L.B. Undated, *Alice Springs – Telecommunications History*, memorandum written by District Telephone Manager, Central Adelaide. (Typescript labelled AP 1625 in ASTS Raw Data files ASTS-20 at the Arid Zone Research Institute Library in Alice Springs.)

Manser, W.L. 1961, *The Overland Telegraph*, thesis presented to the University of Adelaide as part requirement for an Honours Degree in History

Milner, Ralph. 1927, *Intersecting Australia, Adelaide to Port Darwin. New Zealander's Adventure Sixty Years Ago. First Crossing with Stock* in *New Zealand Evening Star*, 24 August 1927

Mooney-Smith, Keith. 1988, *Quaint Spot, Town of Stuart's first decade 1888–1897*, lecture delivered at YMCA Hall Alice Springs, 23 November 1988

Mooney-Smith, Keith. December 1994, *Arltunga Timeline*, unpublished paper at the Arid Zone Research Institute Library, Alice Springs

Mooney-Smith, Keith. 1995, *Arltunga Biofile*, unpublished paper at the Arid Zone Research Institute Library, Alice Springs

Newland, Simpson. 1887, *The Far North Country*, Burden & Bonython, Advertiser Office, Adelaide (Originally appeared in *South Australian Advertiser*, 2 July 1887 pp. 5–6, 15 July 1887 p. 5, 19 July 1887 pp. 5–6, 29 July 1887 p. 5, 9 August 1887 pp. 5–6)

O'Grady, F.P. 1972, *The Overland Telegraph Line Technology of the 1870s*, The Centenary of the Adelaide–Darwin Overland Telegraph Line, Symposium August 1972 Papers pp. 19–29

O'Kane, Frances. 1969, *A History of the Arltunga Goldfields 1887–1916*, thesis submitted as part of the final year of BA (Hons) Melbourne University

Pearce, Howard. July 1985, *Homesteads in Central Australia, Survey and Documentation for a Register* (A report for the National Trust of Australia under a grant from the 1983–1984 Northern Territory Heritage Program.)

Pearce, Howard. 1987, *Chronological History of Barrow Creek Telegraph Station* from *Former Telegraph Station Barrow Creek, A Conservation Plan December 1987*, Allom Lowell Marquis-Kyle Architects

Purvis, Adela. 1945, *This Township Named Stuart, Now Alice Springs* (Extract from the 1945–1946 *Proceedings of the Royal Geographical Society of Australasia*, South Australian Branch)

Purvis, A.V. 1952, *Our Alice Springs, A Brief History from the Earliest Times to the Present*, booklet printed by The Mail Newspapers Ltd

Purvis, Adela. 1971, *Heroes Unsung*, unpublished manuscript in Alice Springs Public Library's Alice Springs Collection

Ryan, Jack. 1991, *Ryan's Camel Party, An account of well-sinking in Far North South Australia and the Northern Territory*, an extract from *The Axemen*, an unpublished family history, Ridgehaven, SA

Ryan, Jack. 1991, *Well-sinking in Far North of South Australia and the Northern Territory, 1885–1890. The Work of Ryan's Camel Party*, Facts & Events, Vol. 6 No. 1. August 1991

(A copy is held at the Arid Zone Research Institute Library Alice Springs catalogued AP1487 & AP1488.)

Service Enterprises. 1983, *Arltunga: a Conservation Study* (4 volumes) held in the Arid Zone Research Institute Library, Alice Springs

Spencer, Walter Baldwin. 1896, *Report on the Work of the Horn Scientific Expedition to Central Australia. Part 1 Introduction, Narrative, Summary of Results, Supplement to Zoological Report, Map*

Stirling, E.C. 1896, *Report on the Work of the Horn Scientific Expedition to Central Australia, Part IV Anthropology*

Strangways, H.B.T. 1906, Letter to H.W. Varley, Mayor of Glenelg, on 7 Feb 1906, South Australian State Library D8339

Strong, Bruce. 1996, *Documentation of the History of Transport Routes in Central Australia for the National Trust of Australia (Northern Territory)*, Alice Springs Public Library's Alice Springs Collection

Strong, Bruce. 1998, *Alice Well: Wayside Stop*, self-published booklet

Strong, Bruce. 1997, *The History of Wallis Fogarty Ltd in Alice Springs*, self-published booklet ISBN 0 646 31311 8

Strong, Bruce. 1998, *The Stuart Arms Hotel*, self-published booklet

Symes, G.W. 1956–1957, *The Exploration and Development of the Northern Part of South Australia between 1850 and 1869, and the Early Life of John Ross*, Royal Geographical Society of Australasia, South Australian Branch, Proceedings for the Season 1956–1957, Vol. 58, December 1957, pp. 1–22

Symes, G.W. 1957, *The Penetration of the MacDonnell Ranges with respect to the Discovery and Naming of Alice Springs* (Copy of a paper prepared for the Royal Geographical Society of Australasia, South Australian Branch, April 1957.)

Symes, G.W. 1959, *The Discovery and Naming of Simpson's Gap*, The Historical Memorials Committee of the Royal Geographical Society of Australasia, South Australian Branch, December 1959 (Copy in the Arid Zone Research Institute Library Alice Springs catalogued ASTS-00174)

Symes, G.W. 1960, *Exploring in the MacDonnell Ranges 1870–1872*, Royal Geographical Society of Australasia (South Australian Branch) Proceedings for the Season 1959–60, Vol. 61, December 1960, pp. 37–53

Symes, G.W. 1968, *James Churchill Smith's Diary for 1872* in *South Australiana, Vol. 7 (1) 1968* pp. 39–46

Symes, G.W. 1971, *The Discovery of the Alice Spring – March 1871* in *Overland Telegraph Line, 1870–1872* (Copy in the Arid Zone Research Institute Library Alice Springs catalogued 384.10994 SYM)

Symes, George W. & Ward, Brian J. 1980–1981, *Charles Todd and the Overland Telegraph*, Proceedings, Royal Geographical Society of Australasia, South Australian Branch, Vol. 81 1980–1981 pp. 59–73

Todd, Charles. 1870, *Instructions to Overseers in charge of Works 30 September 1870* (Photocopy held in the Arid Zone Research Institute Library Alice Springs)

Todd, Charles. 1872, Notebook March–April in State Records SA GRG 154/15

Todd, Charles. 1886, *Telegraphic Enterprise in Australasia: Address to the* 4th Ordinary General Meeting of the Royal Colonial Institute (Great Britain) *9 February 1886,* Proceedings Vol. 17 1885–1886 pp. 144–179

Todd, R.M. 1972, *A Century of Telecommunications in the Northern Territory Part 2: The Subsequent Development of the Route* in *Telecommunications Journal of Australia,* October 1972

Wilson, A.N. 1986, *Relics of the Overland Telegraph Line, Alice Springs to Port Augusta*

Wilson, Bill & O'Brien, Justin. 2003, *'To infuse a universal terror': A reappraisal of the Coniston killings,* Aboriginal History 2003 Vol. 27 pp. 59–78

Woodrow, B.E. 1972, *A Century of Telecommunications in the Northern Territory Part 1: The Overland Telegraph,* in *Telecommunications Journal of Australia,* October 1972

South Australian Parliamentary Papers

SAPP 127/1859	European & Australian Telegraph
SAPP 83/1860	Report of the Select Committee of the House of Assembly Appointed to Report on Prospectus of the Great Northern Copper Mining Co.
SAPP 29/1861	Annexation of Additional Territory to South Australia
SAPP 47/1861	Telegraphic Communication Between Australia and Europe via India
SAPP 180/1861	Annexation of Additional Territory to South Australia
SAPP 25/1862	Report on Public Works, 1861
SAPP 229/1862	Anglo–Australian and China Telegraph
SAPP 236/1862	Report on Ocean Telegraph Scheme
SAPP 234/1862	Report of the Select Committee of the House of Assembly on Chambers's Mineral Leases Question
SAPP 54/1867	Extension of Telegraphs Between England and Colonial Possessions
SAPP 18/1867	Intercolonial Postal Conference
SAPP 15/1868–69	Public Works Report, 1867
SAPP 41A /1869–70	Report on Anglo–Australian Telegraph
SAPP 118/1869–70	Report on Anglo–Australian Telegraph Schemes
SAPP 24/1870–71	British–Australian Telegraph
SAPP 24A/1870–71	Anglo–Australian Telegraph
SAPP 131/1870–71	Correspondence on Anglo–Australian Telegraph
SAPP 60/1871	Construction of Overland Telegraph
SAPP 29/1873	Adelaide and Port Darwin Telegraph
SAPP 48/1874	W.C. Gosse's Explorations, 1873
SAPP 215/1874	Mr. E. Giles's Explorations, 1873–4
SAPP 21/1875	Mr Ernest Giles's Explorations, 1872
SAPP 28/1875	Colonel Warburton's Explorations, 1872–73

SAPP 44/1878	Report of the Proceedings of the Conference Respecting the Duplication of the Telegraph Lines between Australasia and Europe Held in Melbourne in May 1878
SAPP 209/1878	Journal of Mr. Barclay's Expedition, 1878
SAPP 121/1882	Herbert River And North-Eastern Exploring Expedition
SAPP 191/1884	Report on the Post Office, Telegraph and Observatory Departments
SAPP 54/1886	Half-Yearly Report on Northern Territory to June 30th 1886
SAPP 34/1887	Report of Commission on Transcontinental Railway
SAPP 34A/1887	Final Report of Commission on Transcontinental Railway
SAPP 24/1889	Government Geologist's Report on a Journey from Adelaide to the Hale River
SAPP 204/1890	Plan and Report of Preliminary Examination of Route for Proposed Extension of Transcontinental Railway from Angle Pole to Alice Springs
SAPP 111/1890	Journal Of Mr W.H. Tietkens' Central Australian Exploring Expedition
SAPP 148/1890	Report Of Messrs. Swan and Taplin on their Visit to Finke, &c., Mission Stations
SAPP 204/1890	Extension of Transcontinental Railway from Angle Pole to Alice Springs
SAPP 33/1891	Report of the Pastoral Lands Commission

National Archives of Australia Files

A1 1927/2982	Alice Springs Bungalow Central Australia
A1 1929/5189	G.W. Burns – Visit to Central Australia, June 1929
A1 1935/643	Mr & Mrs G.K. Freeman, Superintendent & Matron, Half-Caste Home, Alice Springs
A1 1936/10413	Native Camps, Alice Springs
A1 1938/403	Sacred Heart Mission School Alice Springs
A431 1950/3576	Proclamation of Reserves – Alice Springs
A518 F214/6/11	School Facilities – Alice Springs, NT
A659 1939/1/996	Half Caste Home Alice Springs
A659 1942/1/4499	Half Caste Home Alice Springs Northern Territory
A659 1944/1/168	Transfer of half-castes from the Northern Territory to the racecourse at Balaklava, South Australia
A885 B400	'Milleewa' half caste home Ashfield Mulgoa
A885 B402	Church Missionary Society half caste Home–Mulgoa
AA1978/215, 21	Native Personnel
AA1978/215, 41	Native Compounds
AA1978/215, 53	NT Half-caste Housing Alice Springs

D960 B1932/127	Stuart–Alice Springs – telegraph & telephone facilities 21.7.1907 closed 16.1.1932–change of name –postal and local history –Telegraph Reserve
D961 C1932/14	Alice Springs NT transfer of office from Old Telegraph Reserve
D959 1A1915/2295	Alice Springs – water supply – windmill and tank – erection of 1915
F1 1937/30	Half-caste Home Alice Springs
F1 1940/153	Half-caste Institution School Alice Springs
F1 1940/478	Aboriginal & Half-caste Matters
F1 1940/807	Northern Standard Press Attacks on Native Affairs Branch & Reports in Southern Papers
F1 1941/549	Enquiries in Aboriginal Affairs by Missionary Societies, etc
F1 1942/70(a)	Half-caste Institution to November 1938
F1 1942/70(b)	Alice Springs Half-caste Institution from December 1938 to December 1942
F1 1942/84	Education General Correspondence
F1 1942/91	Half-caste Institution School Alice Springs
F1 1942/367	Evacuation of Missions & Isolated Stations
F1 1942/397	Opening of Institution at Balaklava
F1 1942/406	Native Affairs Branch Staff & Policy Matters
F1 1942/433	Native Population Alice Springs Control & Employment
F1 1943/75	Half-caste Institution Alice Springs General
F1 1948/223	Bungalow Reserve Alice Springs
F1 1949/35	Methodist Overseas Mission Croker Island – Part Aboriginal
F1 1949/355	Transfer of Half-castes from Mulgoa
F1 1949/420	Education – Aboriginals General Correspondence
F1 1951/523	Aboriginal Reserve, Bungalow Alice Springs
F1 1952/211	Aboriginal Welfare Education Policy
F1 1952/212	Aboriginal Education General Correspondence
F1 1952/433	Bungalow Aboriginal Reserve, Daily Journals
F1 1953/515	Bungalow Aboriginal Reserve, General
F1 1954/952	Proposed New Site for Aboriginal Reserve, Alice Springs
F1 1955/1076	Welfare Branch Employment of Aborigines General
F1 1955/1137	Welfare Branch Bungalow Aboriginal Reserve, Monthly Returns
F1 1956/466	(Name illegible) but deals with Teacher Transfers
F1 1956/472	(Name illegible)
F1 1956/739	Welfare Branch Bungalow School Operational Matters
F1 1959/2463	This is the replacement file for F1 1956/739.
F125 2	Enquiry – Freeman Case (1934)

Acknowledgements

Thank you to all those who have generously shared their knowledge and helped in other ways: Barry Allwright, Phil Asmussen, Kathryn Bailey, Jane Bathgate, Stuart Benstead, John Blakeman, Wally Braitling, Stewart Brash, Gavan Breen, Andrew Bridges, Shirley and George Brown, Maise Robb Chettle, Rod Cramer, Prue Crouch, Jo Daniel, Stephen Davis, Chris Day, Robert Drogemuller, Margaret Ellis, Emily Findlay, Paul Fitzsimons, Harold Furber, Wayne Gaskon, Robin Gregory, Reg Harris, Bill Hayes, David Hewitt, Joan Higgins, John Houlder, Maurie Johns, Megg Kelham, Bob Kessing, Bern Kilgariff, Dick Kimber, Peter King, Alec Kruger, Bob Lasseter, Herbie Laughton, Carmel and David Leonard, Emily Liddle, Elizabeth McLean, Eileen and Geoffrey McRae, Lis Marnie, John Meyers, Nora Meyers, Jill Meldrum, Barb Michel, Chippy Miller, Keith Mooney-Smith, Rick Moore, Murray Neck, Carolyn Newman, Alex Nelson, Max O'Callaghan, Mandy Paull, Rachel Perkins, Jose Petrick, Pearl Powell, Andrew Pridham, Bob Purvis, Olga Radke, Jenny Richter, Bid Rose, Alec Ross, Anne Scherer, Philip Selth, John Spencer, John Strehlow, Bruce Strong, Doris Stuart, Neil Sutton, Gordon Sweeney, Keith Thomas, Ron Tilmouth, Christine Torlach, Neil Tranthem, Ian Trapnell, Olive Veverbrandts, Cynthia White and Bob Whiteford.

I appreciate the support of the NT Archives Service, Alice Springs, who provided a base for my research between 2008 and 2013, gave me easy access to their records and provided the historic photos used in this book.

My thanks also to editor and 'wordsmith' Julia Beaven, whose assistance and encouragement I appreciate very much.

Index